THE
PENTATEUCH

THE SERIES

INTERPRETER'S CONCISE COMMENTARY

THE PENTATEUCH

A COMMENTARY ON GENESIS, EXODUS, LEVITICUS, NUMBERS, DEUTERONOMY

By
John H. Marks
John Gray
Jacob Milgrom
Harvey H. Guthrie, Jr.
Norman K. Gottwald

Edited by Charles M. Laymon

Abingdon Press
Nashville

Interpreter's Concise Commentary
Volume I: THE PENTATEUCH

Revised and Concise Edition

Copyright © 1971 and 1983 by Abingdon Press

Third Printing 1984

All rights reserved.

Library of Congress Cataloging in Publication Data

Main entry under title:
The Pentateuch: a commentary on Genesis, Leviticus,
   Numbers, Deuteronomy.
   (Interpreter's concise commentary; v. 1)
   "Previously published . . . as part of the Interpreter's
one-volume commentary on the Bible"—Verso t.p.
   Includes bibliographies.
   1. Bible. O.T. Pentateuch—Commentaries.   I. Marks,
John H. (John Henry) II. Laymon, Charles M.   III. Series.
BS491.2.I57   1983 vol. 1   220.7s [222'.107]   83-2507
[BS1225.3]

ISBN 0-687-19232-3 (pbk.)

(Previously published by Abingdon Press in cloth as part of
The Interpreter's One-Volume Commentary on the Bible, regular ed.
ISBN 0-687-19299-4, thumb-indexed ed. ISBN 0-687-19300-1.)

Scripture quotations unless otherwise noted are from the Revised
Standard Common Bible, copyright © 1973 by the Division of Christian
Education, National Council of Churches, and are used by permission.

MANUFACTURED BY THE PARTHENON PRESS AT
NASHVILLE, TENNESSEE, UNITED STATES OF AMERICA

EDITOR'S PREFACE

to the original edition

A significant commentary on the Bible is both timely and timeless. It is timely in that it takes into consideration newly discovered data from many sources that are pertinent in interpreting the Scriptures, new approaches and perspectives in discerning the meaning of biblical passages, and new insights into the relevancy of the Bible for the times in which we live. It is timeless since it deals with the eternal truths of God's revelation, truths of yesterday, today, and of all the tomorrows that shall be.

This commentary has been written within this perspective. Its authors were selected because of their scholarship, their religious insight, and their ability to communicate with others. Technical discussions do not protrude, yet the most valid and sensitive use of contemporary knowledge underlies the interpretations of the several writings. It has been written for ministers, lay and nonprofessional persons engaged in studying or teaching in the church school, college students and those who are unequipped to follow the more specialized discussions of biblical matters, but who desire a thoroughly valid and perceptive guide in interpreting the Bible.

The authorship of this volume is varied in that scholars were chosen from many groups to contribute to the task. In this sense it is an ecumenical writing. Protestants from numerous denominations, Jews, and also Roman Catholics are represented in the book. Truth cannot be categorized according to its ecclesiastical sources. It is above and beyond such distinctions.

It will be noted that the books of the Apocrypha have been included and interpreted in the same manner as the canonical writings. The value of a knowledge of this body of literature for understanding the historical background and character of the Judaic-Christian tradition has been widely recognized in our time, but commentary treatments of it have not been readily accessible. In addition, the existence of the Revised Standard Version and the New English Bible translations of these documents makes such a commentary upon them as is included here both necessary and significant.

The commentary as a whole avoids taking dogmatic positions or representing any one particular point of view. Its authors were chosen throughout the English-speaking field of informed and recognized biblical scholars. Each author was urged to present freely his own interpretation and, on questions where there was sometimes a diversity of conclusions, each was also asked to define objectively the viewpoints of others while he was offering and defending his own.

Many persons have contributed to the writing and production of this volume. One of the most rewarding of my personal experiences as editor was corresponding with the authors. On every hand there was enthusiasm for the project and warmth of spirit. The authors' commitment to the task and their scholarly sensitivity were evident in all of my relationships with them. The considerate judgments of the manuscript consultants, Morton S. Enslin, Dwight M. Beck, W. F. Stinespring, Virgil M. Rogers, and William L. Reed, were invaluable in the making of the character of the commentary. The copy editors who have worked under the careful and responsible guidance of Mr. Gordon Duncan of Abingdon Press have contributed greatly to the accuracy and readability of the commentary.

—Charles M. Laymon, Editor

PUBLISHER'S PREFACE

The intent of the *Interpreter's Concise Commentary* is to make available to a wider audience the commentary section of *The Interpreter's One-Volume Commentary on the Bible*. In order to do this, the Publisher is presenting the commentary section of the original hardback in this eight-volume paperback set. At the same time, and in conjunction with our wish to make *The Interpreter's One-Volume Commentary* more useful, we have edited the hardback text for the general reader: we have defined most of the technical terms used in the original hardback text; we have tried to divide some of the longer sentences and paragraphs into shorter ones; we have tried to make the sexually stereotyped language used in the original commentary inclusive where it referred to God or to both sexes; and we have explained abbreviations, all in an attempt to make the text more easily read.

The intention behind this paperback arrangement is to provide a handy and compact commentary on those individual sections of the Bible that are of interest to readers. In this paperback format we have not altered the substance of any of the text of the original hardback, which is still available. Rather, our intention is to smooth out some of the scholarly language in order to make the text easier to read. We hope this arrangement will make this widely accepted commentary on the Bible even more profitable for all students of God's Word.

WRITERS

John H. Marks
Associate Professor of Oriental Studies, Princeton University, Princeton, New Jersey

John Gray
Professor of Hebrew and Semitic Languages, University of Aberdeen, Aberdeen, Scotland

Jacob Milgrom
Associate Professor, Department of Near Eastern Languages, University of California, Berkeley, California

Harvey H. Guthrie, Jr.
Dean, Episcopal Theological School, Cambridge, Massachusetts

Norman K. Gottwald
Professor of Old Testament and of Biblical Theology and Ethics, American Baptist Seminary of the West and Graduate Theological Union, Berkeley, California

CONTENTS

THE BOOK OF GENESIS

John H. Marks

INTRODUCTION

Genesis is the first of the five Old Testament books known as the books of the Law or the Pentateuch. Exodus, Leviticus, Numbers, and Deuteronomy complete this body of material. These books are often referred to also as the five books of Moses, but scholars disagree as to whether Moses was the author.

In the Hebrew the books of the Law had no individual titles. The name Genesis, meaning "beginning," was given to the first of them in the earliest Greek translation.

This book may be described as the story of Hebrew origins. It is the introduction to the collection of historical, cultural, and legal traditions which circulated among the tribes of Israel. These traditions were concerned with the time before the Hebrews were established in Palestine. Genesis cannot be studied by itself, therefore, as though it were a special unit of divine revelation. Genesis can be properly understood only when one knows the larger framework of which it is an essential part. Likewise, the exodus from Egypt and the conquest of Canaan are best understood when one knows the traditions contained in Genesis.

The Traditions of Israel

Israel had traditions about its past which were crucial to an understanding of its life in Palestine. The motive for collecting these traditions was not idle curiosity. It was rather the attempt to come to terms with its own existence as a divinely chosen people who formed a small state clinging precariously to political independence on the arid land lying between the great fertile river valleys of Egypt and Mesopotamia. Genesis contains some of the oldest of those traditions.

The mass of diverse material in Genesis is arranged according to a simple chronological scheme. First the traditions about the origins of the world and humanity (chapters 1-11) are presented according to time-honored chronological sequence: the Creation and the mythology about the first people, then the Flood, and finally the establishment of civilization in the East.

In each of these cycles of tradition the compiler adheres to his final purpose, the telling of Israel's story. The main thread of the "sacred history" is carefully followed. Thus when the reader comes to the second section of the book—the stories of the patriarchs and the descent into Egypt—the transition from the primeval to the patriarchal history is natural and logical.

Genesis concentrates attention on the direct line of Israel's forebears from Adam to Jacob and his family. From this genealogical line hangs the mass of varied traditions about Israel's own past and that of its contemporaries.

The Compiling of the Traditions

Where did these traditions originate and how were they finally compiled?

A serious reading of Genesis reveals that the book is not the work of a single author. No writer would be guilty of discrepancies like those between the accounts of Creation (cf. 1:26 with 2:7, 18, 19, 22) or of the Flood (cf. 7:1-3 with 6:18-21). The book is rather a compilation in which we recognize at least three strands of tradition. Though these strands can no longer be isolated precisely in their original form, it is possible to assign most of the content of Genesis to one or another of them (see the following table). The traditions have a long history of formulation, elaboration, revision, and combination until they received their final form in Genesis.

These sources of tradition are known as "J" (Yahwist), "E" (Elohist), and "P" (Priestly). In addition there are traditions like those of chapter 14 which do not seem to belong to any of these sources. The symbols J, E, and P do not signify individual authors, but rather clusters of traditional material. These clusters are distinguished from one another by their use of differing names for God (Yahweh, translated as "the LORD"; Elohim, translated as "God") and by other preferences for favorite words, phrases, and facts.

For example, the Priestly tradition was much concerned with genealogies and precise dates. The Elohist was interested in dreams and divine revelations through intermediaries. The traditional accounts of J were in many instances early combined with those of E so that the original accounts have become almost inextricably entwined.

The exact process by which this mass of traditional material assumed its final form is unknown. Clearly the compilers were unwilling to remove the obvious discrepancies between the various accounts. It seems likely that they worked with existing documents which were themselves final formulations of earlier oral traditions. These earlier traditions had circulated among "schools" in Judah (J) and Ephraim (E) or were taught by the priests (P).

When these documents were combined, the Priestly chronology became the final framework for the traditions about Israel's early history. The scope and form of the story, however, had been laid down by the literary and religious genius whose work is conspicuous in the J source. Customary dates for the documents are around 950 for J, 750 for E, and after 539 for P. However, these dates do not indicate the age of individual traditions, which are often much older.

The literary forms represented in Genesis indicate the

diverse and independent origins of the material. Folklore (for example, the story of the Flood, chapters 6–9), local traditions (for example, about Bethel, 28:19), tribal traditions (for example, about Simeon and Levi, chapter 34), traditions about Israel's neighbors, songs, and lists—all are incorporated into the book. All doubtless owe their origin as well as their inclusion to political and religious events and concerns which we can no longer determine.

The long and complicated history which lies behind Genesis as we have it cannot be encompassed by neat phrases or simple theories. An explanation of the history of this book would also mean the unfolding of Israel's history. That is what makes the literary problem of Genesis so fascinating.

Sources of Genesis

Most of the content of Genesis has been attributed by scholars to one or another of the three strands of tradition listed in the tables on pages 6 and 7. Certain passages which cannot be assigned to one strand only are listed in both columns followed by the letters indicating their composite structure. Passages especially difficult to assign are indicated by question marks. Chapter 14 appears to come from an independent source. Longer editorial additions and glosses are recognized in 15:19-21; 16:9-10; 18:17-19; 19:17-22; 30a; 20:18; 22:15-19; 31:47; 48:7.

Religious Values

The values we gain from reading Genesis are not scientific or primarily historical; they are religious. The stories of creation do not contain scientific materials of use to geology, biology, or zoology. The primeval history as a whole (chapters 1–11) contains no historical records of primitive peoples. Rather this primeval history poses the perennial riddles of human life: dominion over animals, the nature and cause of evil, the reason for death, the meaning of life, the values of civilization. These riddles are posed in the language and form of mythology and are answered from the faith by which Israel learned to live.

The patriarchal stories undoubtedly contain historical material and are meant to convey historical fact. But the interest in "proving the Bible true" reveals their dearth of historical information apart from the mass of knowledge made available through archaeology. Archaeology does not simply confirm biblical statements—it clarifies them first and foremost.

The patriarchal stories combine historical fact, tradition, poetry, and symbolism. Today this is recognized as unscientific historical method. Their value lies not so much in the bits of historical information they provide as in the religious insights they disclose. These insights are the more convincing for being clothed in credible historical garb. Whether the Abraham of Genesis actually lived or not is an idle question for which an answer is unavailable. What this Abraham is reported to have done and believed, however, receives added significance from the probability that the traditions about him were not invented. The environment in which he is said to have lived is established for the second millennium by historical research. Abraham's story thus becomes exemplary for a life of faith.

The main theme of Genesis is the remarkable story of Israel's ancestors, who were chosen mysteriously by God, the Creator of the universe and Lord of history, to be the "founders of a holy nation." The fact of this choice in the tangled web of Palestine's history in the second millennium B.C. became clear to the prophetic writers who assembled these traditions. Israel, they believed, existed for a purpose, and they were interested in tracing Israel's ancestry. But more decisively than that they wanted to confess their faith in Yahweh as unique among the gods of the nations. The Lord of their history must indeed be the Creator of the universe and the Lord of all history, revealing himself to the people he had made and establishing justice and mercy in the world. What they emphasize is a conception of God which remains worthy of our noblest thought and profoundest reverence wherever the mysteries of life are soberly and steadfastly accepted.

5

J (Yahwist)	E (Elohist)	P (Priestly)
		1:1-31
2:4b-25		2:1-4a
3:1-24		
4:1-26		
		5:1-32
6:1-8		6:9-22
7:1-5, 7, 8-9JP, 10, 12, 16b, 17b, 22-23		7:6, 8-9JP, 11, 13-16a, 17a, 18-21, 24
8:2b-3a, 6-12, 13b, 20-22		8:1-2a,3b-5, 13a, 14-19
9:18-27		9:1-17, 28-29
10:1b, 8-19, 21, 24-30		10:1a, 2-7, 20, 22-23, 31-32
11:1-9, 28-30		11:10-27, 31-32
12:1-4a, 6-20		12:4b-5
13:1-5, 7-11a, 12b-18		13:6, 11b-12a
15:1(?), 3-4(?), 7-12, 17-18	15:2(?), 5, 6(?), 13-16(?)	16:1a, 3, 15-16
16:1b-2, 4-8, 11-14		17:1-27
18:1-16, 20-23		19:29
19:1-16, 23-28, 30b-38	20:1-17	
	21:6a, 8-24, 27, 31, 34	21:1b, 2b-5
21:1a, 2a, 6b-7, 25-26, 28-30, 32-33		
22:20-24	22:1-14	23:1-20
24:1-67		25:7-11a, 12-17, 19-20, 26d
25:1-6, 11b, 18, 21-26c, 27-34		26:34-35
26:1-33		

27:1-45JE	27:1-45E	27:46
28:10, 13-16, 19	28:11-12, 17-18, 20-22	28:1-9
29:2-14, 31-35	29:1, 15-23, 25-28, 30	29:24, 29
30:1-43JE	30:1-43JE	
31:1, 3, 17-18a, 43-44, 46, 48, 50	31:2, 4-16, 19-42, 45, 49, 51-55	31:18b-d
32:3-13a, 24-32	32:1-2, 13b-23	
33:1-17	33:18a, 18c-20	33:18b
34:1-31JE(?)	34:1-31JE(?)	
35:21-22a	35:1-8, 14-20	35:9-13, 22b-26, 27-29
36:20-30(?), 31-39(?)		36:1-19, 40-43
37:3-4JE, 12-20JE, 21, 25b-27, 28c, 31-35JE	37:3-4JE, 5-11, 12-20E, 22-25a, 28ab, 28d-30, 31-35JE, 36	37:1-2(?)
38:1-30(?)		
39:1-23	40:1-23	
41:29-44JE, 45, 46b-57JE	41:1-28, 29-44JE, 46b-57JE	41:46a
42:2-7JE, 27-28a, 38	42:1, 2-7E, 8-26, 28b-37	
43:1-13, 15-34	43:14	
44:1-34		
45:1a, 4-5a, 9-14, 28	45:1b-3, 5b-8, 15-27	
46:1a, 28-34	46:1b-5	46:6-27
47:1-5a, 6cd, 12, 13-26(?), 27a, 29-31		47:5b-6b, 7-11, 27b-28
48:9b-10a, 13-14, 17-19	48:1-2, 8-9a, 10b-12, 15-16,	48:3-6
		49:1a, 28b-33
50:1-11, 14	50:15-26	50:12-13

I. THE PRIMEVAL HISTORY (1:1–11:32)

A. CREATION OF THE WORLD (1:1–2:4a)

1:1-5. *The Beginning.* Creation begins when God imposes order on primeval, nonpersonal chaos by calling **light** into existence. This is a P account. It has obvious parallels in the Babylonian creation and flood epics. It seems to picture a chaotic storm churning over the primordial dark and mysterious abyss of infinite and formless waters. Out from this God summons order, thus creating the universe. Time begins with that creation.

Nothing is said of the origin of the chaos or of God's activity prior to creation. The question about whether creation is out of nothing *(creatio ex nihilo)* is also irrelevant to the story. God's creation **in the beginning** is unique and inexplicable. Appropriately, the Hebrew word *bara,* here translated "create," is applied in the Old Testament only to God's activity. An ordered universe is conceivable only as a divine act of creation.

1:4-5. The most obvious sign of order is the gift of **light** and its daily separation from the **darkness.** God's lordship is expressed further in the naming of God's works. The **one day** seems to be reckoned from morning to morning. That is, God works all day till **evening** and begins his work again the next **morning.**

1:6-8. *The Firmament.* A translucent dome, like an inverted basin, placed **in the midst of the waters** defines the spatial boundaries of God's further work. This God-given vault sets limits to the universe and provides focus for the story of humanity which follows. The author is interested ultimately in the phenomenon of man, not that of nature. The solid, "hammered-out" firmament restrains **the waters** of chaos from above and receives its blue color from them. **Heaven** is therefore the upper protective limit of created order.

The contradictions in terminology between creation by word (verses 6, 14, 20, 24, 26) and creation by act (verses 7, 16, 21, 25, 27) may reveal parallel original accounts of creation. Significantly both ideas have been preserved.

1:9-13. *Earth and Vegetation.* God further restrains the waters of chaos and there appears the earth, which is thought to be a disk resting on waters. Order has by now so replaced chaos that the earth can produce vegetation and achieve part of its God-ordained function (cf. verse 24) as "mother earth." One observes that the author does not consider the vegetation to be "life."

1:14-19. *Celestial Lights.* Time too is ordered. Light is assigned to luminaries in the firmament, which are to preside over day and night and to provide convenient guideposts for marking time and regulating activity. The stars and planets are denied any divine character or power. Their primary function is to give light at their appointed times, thus restraining the darkness in an ordered fashion.

1:20-23. *Sea Creatures and Birds.* The waters likewise are freed to their destined purpose, and they bring forth swarms of living creatures. Also birds can exist where chaos is restrained. But all these are conceivable only as the creation of God, since the watery remnants of chaos are incapable of producing life. To insure continuation of this life God blesses the creatures with reproductive functions.

1:24-30. *Land Creatures and Human Beings.* Everything is thus ready for the appearance of land creatures and human beings. The creatures are the offspring, as it were, of the earth, and their reproductive functions derive from the earth; nevertheless God makes them. Humans, however, have a different position in the world. They are unique among the creatures of the universe, resembling but not to be equated with members of the heavenly court (cf. I Kings 22:19-22; Psalm 82:1). They are to rule living things on earth as they in turn are ruled by God. But such creatures must be created by God. Order, birds and fish, and human beings are thus considered unique—unthinkable apart from God's special creative activity, expressed in the Hebrew word *bara*.

1:27-28. God creates male and female. This act of God's creation embraces humanity as a whole. God also blesses humans with reproductive capacity, thus removing sexuality

9

from being either divine spark in man or a terror. Procreation is both God's gift and his command. Humanity's task from creation is to **fill the earth and subdue it,** to join in God's will for order.

1:29-30. For **food** people are given every grain and pulse and every fruit; to animals are assigned as food **every green plant.** The eating of meat is passed over in silence and therefore presumed to be absent at creation.

1:31–2:1. *Creation Finished.* God now surveys the work and is well pleased. It has come from God's hand precisely as God intended it and is therefore **very good.** The chaos has been effectively restrained, and order prevails. The world is furnished and populated. Humans have been brought into being to maintain God's created order.

2:2-4a. *The Day of Rest.* One work remains to fill out the week of creation (the measurement of time by weeks is taken for granted); it is called God's rest. God takes delight in creation. In sanctifying **the seventh day** God wills that human beings shall take similar delight. This rest is thus considered to be God's climactic work and humanity's highest good.

The text says nothing explicit about the cultic institution of the sabbath, the origins of which are unknown. Implicitly, however, the institution of the sabbath is traced to God's creative act. Significantly, the formula **there was evening and there was morning** is omitted. The work of creation has ended; there is to be no new seven-day cycle.

Various interpretations of the significance of sabbath observance are given in the Old Testament. It is a sign that one keeps God's covenant (Isaiah 56:2-8), a memorial of Israel's deliverance from Egypt (Deuteronomy 5:12-15), a memorial of God's rest after creation (Exodus 20:8-11). Here, however, the author is content to record the fact of God's rest as the climax to the work of creation and God's blessing and hallowing of the day of rest. Apparently the seventh day of God's rest is to be fruitful in a fashion analogous to that stated in the blessing of sea creatures, birds, and human beings. So ends the P account of the creation **of the heavens and the earth.**

This account of creation is best described in both narrative and doctrinal terms. The sequence of days provides the narrative framework for recounting God's creative activity at the beginning of time. The author, claiming the freedom to tell his story in a form most appropriate to his purpose, probably meant for the days to be understood literally as twenty-four-hour periods. But he desired also to transmit doctrine. He used terms which reflect the "scientific" understanding of his time, and he incorporated the religious truths which in P circles had become accepted as dogma: "God created"; "God said, . . . and it was so"; "God saw that it was good"; "God blessed them"; "God created man in his own image . . . to have dominion . . . over all the earth, and over every creeping thing that creeps upon the earth"; "God rested on the seventh day [and] blessed the seventh day and hallowed it."

Here is a view of humanity and the universe which sees life in religious, theological perspective. The reader is given a theological view of primeval history, not a scientific account of nature. The setting is provided for the drama of humanity. The account thus presents with soberness and exaltation something of the grandeur of a human being, the beauty of creation, and joy in the gift of life.

B. THE STORY OF PARADISE (2:4b–3:24)

2:4b-9. *Creation of Human Beings.* The J story which follows differs from the preceding account in both form and content. The form is no longer pedagogical, strictly chronological, or liturgical. Stylized expression and doctrinal repetition yield place to charmingly simple narration.

In the first story the reader saw the world of nature created day by day, in increasing complexity, with humanity as the result. Now the reader is again taken to the beginning of time to see God form the first man from the damp soil of a barren plain, prepare a garden to place him in, and then find a companion for him. The setting for this second story has been said to be Palestinian, in contrast to the Mesopotamian background of the previous account. The mythical nature of this story is very different from the formal, doctrinal account which precedes. But the view of man's relationship to God presented by each is essentially the same.

2:4b-7. When God made the world, this J story begins, the **earth** was barren. There was no **rain** and no cultivation. The narrator, taking for granted other features of the universe, focuses attention at once on man's immediate physical environment, the fields from which he lives. The barren land is moistened by some underground source of water. Nothing is said about the chaos of chapter 1, and water appears to be not a part of chaos but a necessity for vegetation.

To end the unproductiveness of the earth, God molds a man from clay of the plain and **breathed into his nostrils the breath of life.** This animated **dust**, man, therefore bears a unique relationship to God. All creation is for his enjoyment and well-being.

2:8-9. God prepares a park, a paradise, **in the east** to be man's home. God places him there **to till it and keep it** (verse 15). The location of **Eden** is unknown (cf. II Kings 19:12), if indeed the author considered it a geographically identifiable place. The name may be derived from Babylonian *edinu*, "plain" or "steppe." If so, the meaning might be that God miraculously created an oasis in the desert plain.

The park contains all trees of aesthetic charm and practical value, and in their midst **the tree of life.** Also present is **the tree of the knowledge of good and evil**—that is, knowing, by personal experience, everything. Two traditions have been combined here. It is the tree of knowledge about which the story centers. The tree of life is not mentioned again till 3:22, 24.

2:10-14. *A Geographical Note.* This digression interrupts the story and appears also to place the garden outside Eden. It indicates that the world is watered by **four rivers** which are branches of the one great **river** originating in Eden. Only the third and fourth of the branch rivers, **Tigris** and **Euphrates**, can be identified. Their known sources in the mountains of Armenia make it appear that the author located Eden in the north rather than in the east. Proposed identifications of **Pishon** as the Indus or a river in Arabia and of **Gihon** as the Nile or "Nubian Nile" lack support.

Cush here probably refers, not to Ethiopia, but to the land of the Kassites in the mountains east of Mesopotamia (see below on 10:8-12). On this basis it has been suggested that originally the rivers flowed into rather than out of Eden and that the garden was therefore located at the head of the Persian Gulf. The paragraph reveals the vague knowledge about rivers and oceans which was common in the ancient world and persisted at least to the time of Alexander the Great.

2:15-25. *Creation of Woman.* The garden provided for man's enjoyment is also the setting for his responsible obedience. The author here suggests that the problem of human freedom is the proper relationship between obligation and unrestricted enjoyment. Man's destiny is conceived soberly in terms of his pleasure in creation, his work in the garden and his obedience to God. The question about obedience to God is the larger context within which the problem of human knowledge must be considered. The author concludes that knowledge without obedience is perverse, and such perversion means death (not mortality; see below on 3:4-5). The bliss of ignorance is implied. There is no mention of the tree of life.

The symbolic nature of the story must be taken earnestly. Questions, therefore, about God's purpose in making this prohibition must be treated as unanswerable.

2:18-20. Having created man's physical world and established the limits of his destiny, God decrees an end to man's solitude. Thus he provides opportunity for the widest range of human fulfillment. God determines to provide man with **a helper fit for him**—a being corresponding to him as his opposite. None of the animals, though obviously kin to man, fulfill this function, for man cannot find fellowship with them. By giving the animals their names the man exerts his rule over them (cf. 1:26-28).

2:21-23. Man's relationship with his woman involves not only authority (in naming her) but also irrepressible joy (in at last finding her) and dependence and companionship (she was made from his rib). The statement about the creation of woman from man's **rib** may derive from a Sumerian pun. The goddess created to heal Enki's rib is called Nin-ti, "the lady of the rib" and/or "the lady who makes live."

2:24-25. Man's sexual drive results from God's creative activity. A man and woman belong to each other because originally they were **one flesh.** The man and the woman were **naked** before each other, un-self-conscious and unashamed. Nudity is here the symbol for mutually frank and honest self-giving.

3:1-24. *Temptation and Fall.* Temptation through the **serpent** next enters the story. The question of time is here irrelevant. It does not become relevant to human beings until the Fall conditions their future life. In Christian symbolism the serpent usually stands for evil. Here, however, the serpent represents cleverness and magical power. It is not the devil, a god, or the dragon of chaos.

3:1b-3. With an innocent question the serpent awakens the woman's desire for the forbidden tree and arouses in her a feeling of rebellion at being denied its **fruit.** God's prohibition has been a trial to her. Her exaggerated answer to the serpent is a step toward her further temptation.

3:4-5. The serpent uses the occasion to deny that death is the penalty for disobedience. It implies that God has ulterior, selfish motives. It insinuates that God has deceived the woman about the tree. Eating the fruit will bring not death but knowledge.

In the light of the final expulsion from the garden, the precise meaning both of that knowledge and of the threatened death penalty seems relatively clear. The idea that humans here lost immortality is not in accord with biblical ideas. The Old Testament does not think in terms of immortality, but of life as fulfillment rather than mere existence. The serpent speaks of death as the end to mortal existence and therefore in a sense speaks truly. The man does not die. But the author obviously means to express by "life" more than existence. The death threatened by God thus can be understood as separation from the possibility of free and perfect enjoyment of life, expulsion from the garden where fulfillment was granted. Death is separation from God, the giver of "life."

3:6-7. Thus man and woman exchanged "life" for knowledge, and the first pair **knew** at once with shame **that they were naked;** they experienced their nudity as embarrassing. The suggested interpretation of the passage to mean that man received sexual knowledge from eating the forbidden fruit is improbable—in spite of the usage in Deuteronomy 1:39; II Samuel 19:35; and Isaiah 7:15. This interpretation is too restrictive of the knowledge acquired. It also degrades human sexual experience by viewing it as unplanned by God and acquired only at the price of man's disobedience. A more satisfactory interpretation would be the knowledge about the increase and mastery of life which was reserved for God, the Creator.

3:8-19. The instinctive reaction to guilt is to hide, to cover one's nakedness, to excuse oneself. But the gulf of separation cannot be concealed, and the consequences of this alienation are inescapable. Suffering and misery enter the world. Motherhood and **childbearing** become painful, fatherhood and labor become wearisome, and futility hangs like a pall over life. The serpent becomes a symbol of evil, and hostility between man and beast begins.

3:20-24. Nevertheless, paradoxically, the man affirms life in the naming of his wife. He has indeed become like a god, refusing to think of himself as a creature. The author thinks of God's gift of clothing as a special act of grace. Paradise and perfect fulfillment are, however, irretrievably lost. **Cherubim** are known from ancient Near Eastern lore as mythological winged animals, usually with human faces.

C. THE SPREAD OF POPULATION (4:1–6:4)

4:1-16. *Cain and Abel.* The penalty for rebellion against God is separation from God. As the narrative will show, it also means separation from other humans. The story of Cain and Abel, which illustrates further the consequences of the Fall, does not agree in detail with the narrative of chapter 3. It probably derives, therefore, from a different source of tradition which the J author incorporated into his material.

The account assumes the existence on earth of other people who are presumably unrelated to Cain, of an accepted practice of sacrifice, and therefore of settled community life. In addition, two pictures of Cain are preserved side by side, one of Cain the agriculturalist turned nomad (verses 1-16) and one of Cain the city builder (verses 17-24). Both narratives are contained within the genealogical statements of verses 1 and 25.

4:1-2a. The man **knew . . . his wife**—that is, had sexual intercourse with her. This euphemism reveals both the Hebrew attitude toward knowledge and the Old Testament ideal of marriage. Knowledge and sexual union are elevated above the plane of mechanical and academic detachment to the realm of spiritual commitment and fulfillment. The first son of this union is named **Cain**, which may mean "spear" or possibly "smith." The circumstances are obscure; verse 1*b* can scarcely be translated, still less understood. His younger brother is named **Abel**, which suggests the Hebrew word for "breath."

4:2*b*-7. The boys represent two ways of life, the agricultural and the pastoral. Both seek divine favor by means of sacrifice, but only Abel receives a favorable omen. Does the author intend to suggest that seminomadic pastoral life is superior to settled agricultural community? (For a New Testament interpretation cf. Hebrews 11:4.)

Cain, angry and sullen, apparently asks the reason for the failure of his sacrifice. In verse 7 he receives a reply which can no longer be understood. In its present form it stresses Cain's responsibility with regard to his sin and guilt. The interesting suggestion has been made that originally this verse referred to a specific demon, "the croucher," who lay in wait secretly for his victim.

4:8-16. Cain's action in killing Abel seems to be premeditated, but his motivation cannot be unmistakably learned from the text. The usual interpretation that it was jealousy and chagrin fits the present context. But the hypothesis that the text is the remnant of an original cult-ritual story of human sacrifice, performed to secure fertility of the soil, cannot be easily dismissed.

4:9-16. A man is responsible, however, for his brother's life. Cain, the first to rob another of life, becomes as a consequence **a fugitive** both from the soil which has drunk his **brother's blood** and from the family which he has also deprived of a life. But God protects the accursed man with a **mark** (tattoo?), a kind of sign often used to distinguish members of a class, for example prophets (cf. Zechariah 13:6). Cain, who is usually recognized as the name ancestor of the Kenites (cf. Numbers 24:21-22), goes to dwell in the land of **Nod,** which may mean "wandering" and which is geographically unknown. Thus the theme of alienation unfolds.

4:17-26. *Genealogy of the Kenites.* In the genealogical account which follows, **Cain, not a nomad but a settler (in the land of Nod?), is considered to be the father of civilization. But culture, with all** the benefits it brings, does not close the spiritual rift which has opened between human beings and God. The consequences of alienation can be frightful, as the account of Lamech shows.

4:17-22. A comparison of the seven-generation genealogical list in verses 17-18 with the parallel P ten-generation list in 5:3-27 reveals the range of Hebrew traditions about the descendants of the first man.

4:23-24. The song of **Lamech** may originally have explained the origin of tribal blood revenge. **Seventy-sevenfold** vengeance is required to satisfy justice because of harm done to one mighty man.

4:25-26. The final genealogical notice is fragmentary and suggests the beginnings of what might be called "true religion"—**to call upon the name of the LORD** (Yahweh). The notice may have been included here to show that as the beginning of civilization led to further alienation among people, so the beginning of Yahweh worship opened an avenue of reconciliation. Here the worship of Yahweh is considered to have begun before the great Flood. This is in contrast to the traditions in Exodus 3:14 (E) and 6:3 (P), which consider Moses to be the first to learn this revealed personal name of God.

5:1-32. *Adam's Descendants Until the Flood.* This enumeration of the ten human generations between the Creation and the Flood is the continuation of the P account of creation in chapters 1–2:4*a*. According to the Hebrew text the account covers a period of 1656 years, during which the human span of life is about 900 years. Thereafter it is reduced to 200-600 years for the period from Noah to Abraham, to 100-200 years for the patriarchal period, and finally to 70-80 years as the normal limit (cf. Isaiah 65:20 for a statement about longevity in the messianic age). The significance of the numerical systems is unknown.

This is the book of the generations of . . . was doubtless originally the title of an actual book, from which the genealogical formula repeated at 6:9; 10:1; 11:10, 27; 25:12, 19; 36:1, 9; 37:2 may derive. The formula in 2:4*a* was artificially fitted into the system. Together the genealogies provide a structural pattern for arranging the material in Genesis.

The genealogical list resembles the Sumerian king lists of the period before the Flood. Ten names are given; both lists conclude with the hero of the flood story; and in each text a new era begins after the Flood. Both this P list and the parallel J list (4:17-22) reflect indirectly, therefore, Mesopotamian prototypes.

Curiosities regarding the longevity figures here and in 11:10-26 have often been noted. Adam lived to see the birth of Lamech. Seth died shortly before the birth of Noah. Enoch lived 365 years, which may somehow be related intentionally to the number of days in a sun year. Noah died in Abraham's sixtieth year. Shem outlived Abraham to see the birth of Esau and Jacob. According to one Greek manuscript Methuselah died fourteen years after the Flood. The consequences, if any, to be drawn from these facts are not intimated in the text.

5:21-24. Enoch (the same person as in 4:17?) receives special notice as one who **walked with God**, that is, one who led an exemplary life. As a result of his exemplary life, apparently, he

18

did "not see death," **for God took him**. Only a fragment of the original Enoch tradition is preserved here.

5:28-31. The etymology of the name **Noah** (a form of Hebrew *naham,* "he comforted") is an allusion to 3:17, 19 and is therefore from the J source of tradition. The reference is to Noah's discovery of the cultivation of the vine (9:20) and the cheer which wine gives. The suggested derivation, however, leads obviously to the name Naham, not Noah. It is not clear whether **Lamech** is to be identified with the Lamech of 4:23-24.

6:1-4. *The Birth of Demigods.* The J source now emphasizes the cosmic nature of man's fall. The heavenly beings wantonly marry mortal women. The text of verse 4, the interpretation of which is not entirely clear, seems to imply that the gods married gigantic earthly women and these marriages produced the **mighty men** (heroes) of saga and legend, the demigods of gigantic size and superhuman strength.

Verse 4 has also been interpreted to mean that the **Nephilim** (giants) on the earth were the offspring of the divine-human marriages, but this interpretation seems less reasonable in the light of other Old Testament references to giants (cf. Numbers 13:33 and Ezekiel 32:27).

The passage suggests the early existence of a race of supermen on earth. It also suggests the destruction at that time of the boundaries between heavenly beings and humans, the explanation for the popular hero tales about an age long past, and the further weakening of primeval man's original stature and strength. The difficult verse 3 seems to mean that humans did not achieve immortality through union with the heavenly beings. Rather as a consequence their life span was reduced to a **hundred and twenty years.**

D. THE FLOOD (6:5–9:29)

The account of the Flood is an interweaving of the J and P versions, both of which in turn derive from Mesopotamian originals. The fullest Babylonian account is preserved on the eleventh tablet of the Gilgamesh epic, where the context is the search for immortality. But the proper context of the Babylonian flood story is probably to be found in the epic of Atrahasis, in which the flood is the climax of a series of punishments inflicted on humans. The biblical story reveals the use which the Hebrews made of traditional mythological material to illustrate and reinforce their conceptions both of God's judgment and mercy and of human dignity and recalcitrance. The popularity of the story among the Hebrews is suggested by allusions like that in Isaiah 54:9.

The composite character of the story is apparent from its repetitions and discrepancies. Repetitions include the following:

God sees the corruption on earth (6:5, 11-12)

God announces the imminent destruction (6:17; 7:4)

Noah enters the ark (7:7, 13)

The Flood comes (7:10, 11)

The waters increase (7:17, 18)

All flesh dies (7:21, 22-23)

The Flood ceases (8:2*a*, 2*b*)

There will never be another flood (8:21-22; 9:9-17)

Startling inconsistencies are not removed. The animals entering the ark are one pair of every species in P (6:19-20; 7:15-16), seven pairs of clean animals and one pair of unclean in J (7:2-3). In J the Flood is caused by heavy rain; in P by the release of the waters above the sky and beneath the earth. Yet the composite account is remarkably unified and loses little of its force as a result of its uneven composition.

6:5-13. *Human Corruption.* In verses 5-8 J summarizes the condition of people as the pre-Flood age ends: complete and continued corruption of will and thought, which apparently has also corrupted the animal world. And God is heartsick; he is sorry that he has made them. His solution is to begin again (in contrast to his solution in verse 3?), but not in such a way as to obliterate the past. Nevertheless the emphasis falls, not on continuity with the past, but on a new beginning and on God's grace in allowing it at all.

6:9-13. This P passage is parallel to the J summation in verses 5-8, yet the difference is clear. As in the paradise story J has emphasized the human aspects of the situation, but P states facts without comment or explanation. God has decided to put an end to **all flesh** (a favorite expression in this account) because of corruption and **violence** on earth. Rebellion against God has brought a return to chaos. Only Noah is **righteous** and **blameless,** the last of those about whom it is reported that he **walked with God.**

6:14-22. *The Building of the Ark.* The P narrative continues. Noah is commanded by God to construct a large, watertight, three-storied boat **of gopher wood.** It is to be about 450 by 75 by 45 feet. Gopher wood may be cypress. The reason for building the ark is then explained to Noah.

The word **flood** in this story is not that used elsewhere of overflowing rivers but refers to the **waters** of the heavenly ocean (Psalm 29:10; cf. 1:6-7). These waters are to drown the earth in a catastrophe of cosmic proportion. But in the ark Noah and his immediate family, together with one pair of every kind of living creature, will be spared. God will establish his **covenant** with Noah, who will become thereby the new father of humankind, virtually replacing Adam. He will be bound by the covenant to recognize in gratitude and obedience God's sovereignty and grace.

7:1-16. *The Entrance into the Ark.* The J story takes up again here. After the decision to destroy life on earth Yahweh commands Noah to **go into the ark.** Noah has no doubt built it according to a divine command once related in the J story but now omitted in favor of the P version (6:13-22). J clearly suggests that Noah learns only after he has finished building the boat the purpose it is to serve. The distinction, which is religious rather than hygienic, between **clean** and unclean animals is doubtless primeval; for biblical legislation cf. Leviticus 11 and Deuteronomy 14.

The Flood is to result from **forty days** of **rain,** which will begin to fall **seven days** after the command to enter the ark and will destroy **every living thing.** Noah and his family go aboard as commanded, and after seven days the Flood begins. Verse 6 is from P, and verses 8-9 are mixed.

7:11-16. P dates the catastrophe with apparent precision. No doubt this is a mark of the importance he attaches to its occurrence at the end of an era. The destructive waters are released on the **seventeenth day** of the **second month** of Noah's **six hundredth year** (see below on 8:1-19). The waters come, not from rain as in the J account, but from the **fountains of the great deep** (the great underworld ocean) and the **windows of the heavens** (the ocean above the firmament). **On the very same day** the waters are released Noah and his family and the animals enter the ark. In verse 12 the **rain** falling for **forty days** and in verse 16*b* the use of the LORD (Yahweh) identify interspersed bits of the J story.

7:17-24. *The Ark on the Waters.* J tells briefly that the ark rises **high above the earth** on the swelling waters and that **every living thing** except those in the ark is destroyed. With characteristic statistical interest P reports in repetitious detail how the waters reach a depth of **fifteen cubits** (about 22½ feet) above the highest mountains. Thus if the ark can be assumed to draw fifteen cubits of water it just floats above the mountain peaks and is ready to ground as soon as the waters slightly abate. P's period for the Flood's duration is **a hundred and fifty days.**

8:1-19. *The Subsiding of the Waters.* The P account of the Flood's end (verses 1-2*a*) is reminiscent in some respects of the P account of creation (cf. 1:2, 7, 9). God's remembrance of Noah carries the theological force of his creative will for order over chaos, and his remembering is thus synonymous with his faithfulness (cf. 19:29; 30:22). By God's action the Flood ends as abruptly as it began. Immediately the waters recede so that the ark grounds the same day **upon the mountains of Ararat**— probably somewhere in northeast Armenia. The date is the **seventeenth day** of the **seventh month,** precisely five solar months of thirty days each after the Flood's beginning (see above on 7:11-16). On the **first day** of the **tenth month**—about two and a half months later, dry land is visible. Verses 2*b*-3*a*, telling how the **rain** stopped and **the waters receded** . . . **continually** is a part of the J account.

8:6-12. Noah, J continues, opens a **window,** which evidently is so placed that he cannot look out of it on the world. Hence he releases first a **raven** and then a **dove** in order to discover whether the earth is habitable. The **olive leaf** perhaps has some mythological or symbolic value, but it is unknown.

8:13-19. P gives further dates for the end of the Flood. It is not clear how verses 13*a* and 14 are to be harmonized, but according to the latter the cataclysm has required one year and ten days to run its course. Thereupon Noah, his family, and the animals disembark. Verse 13*b* is from J.

8:20–9:17. *God's Covenant with Noah.* J concludes the story (verses 20-22) with a report of God's resolve never again to **curse the ground** and **destroy every living creature** by a flood. The reason for this resolve is the same as that for sending the Flood. A similar paradoxical statement about God's resolves is made by the prophets (cf. Hosea 11:8-9 and Isaiah 54:9-10). Noah's gratitude for his life, as expressed in his sacrifice, may summarize J's view of a person's proper relationship with God.

9:1-7. P considers the age after the Flood to be guided by divine commands which have been modified from their original form at creation (verses 2-3; cf. 1:28-30). God now permits the eating of **flesh** from which the **blood,** the symbol of **life,** has been drained and specifically orders blood vengeance. No distinction is drawn between clean and unclean animals.

In contrast, J has recognized blood vengeance as existing before (4:11, 23). He therefore does not regard the Flood as having significantly altered either God's purpose or created order. God's original purpose expressed in the command to be **fruitful,** is here repeated immediately after Noah's deliverance and forms a framework within which the new divine enactments are contained. **Man,** not God, is made legal guardian and avenger of the sanctity of human life.

9:8-17. The P account closes with God's covenanted assurance that **never again** will a **flood** . . . **destroy the earth** and **all flesh** (cf. 8:21-22, J). The composite nature of the P account here is

23

revealed by the doublets, verses 9 and 11*a*, 12 and 17, 14 and 16.

The use of the term **covenant** seems out of place, unless the author intends verses 1-7 to be included in it, as appears unlikely. A covenant is made to clarify the relationship between two parties and puts an obligation on each. Since no living creature is here called on to affirm God's ordinance, the "covenant" cannot be broken except by God. The **sign** serves to remind all participants in the covenant relation of its existence. The rainbow (here seen for the first time?) is the sign of God's everlasting mercy toward his creation. He has laid aside his **bow** of war.

E. The Discovery of Wine (9:18-29)

The Noah who discovers wine and its properties in this J story is distinct from the Noah of the Flood. Here he has **three** apparently unmarried **sons** (cf. 7:7) living with him **in his tent.** Possibly he is a nomad. The passage reveals a combining of two genealogies. In one, Noah's youngest son is **Canaan** (verses 24-25), whose brothers are **Shem and Japheth** (verses 26-27). According to the other (verse 18*a*) the brothers are **Shem, Ham, and Japheth.** Verse 18*b* and the words **Ham, the father of** in verse 22 are apparently meant to harmonize the two.

9:20-21. Noah is here apparently considered to be **the first tiller of the soil** (cf. 4:2). The text of verse 20 is difficult to understand, however. "Tiller of the soil" is literally "man of the ground." Does this mean the first farmer or the first man (cf. 2:7)? The Jewish Publication Society translation reads: "Noah, the tiller of the soil, was the first to plant a vineyard." The fruit of the vine was greatly esteemed in Israel.

9:22-27. Canaan's wrongdoing probably consists in ridiculing his father in what he reports to his brothers, though more may be implied in verse 24. Noah's curse and blessings are doubtless meant to describe the conditions prevailing in Palestine at the time the poetic lines originated (cf. chapter 49). Canaan becomes the slave of Shem and Japheth, Shem's God is Yahweh, and Japheth occupies **the tents of Shem**. The references may be to the Canaanites, Israelites, and Philistines; but historical precision is impossible.

9:28-29. The P account of Noah's death is the conclusion of the genealogical statements of 6:9-10 and 7:6.

F. THE TABLE OF NATIONS (10:1-32)

The composite genealogical table of nations suggests two questions:

(1) According to what principle are the peoples arranged?

(2) Why is the table included here at all?

In regard to the first, the chapter is an obvious attempt to classify geographically the peoples of the world into three groups who are unified as families because of their descent from Noah's three sons. The list is not organized racially or linguistically but rather territorially and politically. It is not always certain whether the names refer to land (e.g. verse 4) or people (e.g. verse 7). The geographical extent of the P table (for list of verses see table pp. 6-7) is that of the seventh century B.C. in the Near East. Japheth represents the peoples of the west and north, Shem the peoples of the east, and Ham those of the south.

In regard to the second question, the account is transitional. It sketches the political background from which the holy people of God is to emerge. Israel is not mentioned in the table, though its existence must be presupposed as part of the geographical picture of the seventh century. The anachronism of a world inhabited by Medes (**Madai**), Ionians (**Javan**), Etruscans (**Tiras**), and Arameans where the nation is Israel is presumed to be as yet nonexistent cannot be overlooked.

The transition from mythical tradition to history cannot be made with precision. On the other hand Israel had no illusions about its origins in the world family of nations. Kingship did not come down from heaven to Jerusalem as the Sumerian king list declared it had first come to Eridu.

25

The parts of the table assigned to J are more narrowly oriented geographically and are also at some variance—cf. for example verses 7 (P) and 28-29 (J); also **Cush** in verses 6-7 (Ethiopia, P) and **Cush** in verse 8 (the Kassites, J). The idea, therefore, of a "much older Yahwistic table of nations" more or less parallel with and basic to that of P as assumed by some scholars is questionable. The P interest in genealogy (see above on 5:1-32) would account for the collecting of various genealogical bits whose original significance was either unknown or disregarded. The so-called J sections enumerate sons of Shem (verses 21, 24-30), presumably Ham (verses 13-19) and perhaps Japheth (verses 8-12). But the evidence for an original complete genealogy in J descending from Shem, Ham, and Japheth, is inconclusive.

10:2-7. These verses and verse 20 give the **Japheth** and **Ham** sections of the P table.

10:8-12. The J passage about **Nimrod** refers to the Assyrian Empire and its Kassite (**Cush**) founder who **built Nineveh** and three other cities. The editor evidently inserted the passage here because he thought it dealt with the **Cush** (Ethiopia) of verses 6-7.

The Kassites from the East ruled Mesopotamia for several centuries, ending around 1150. The relationship between Nimrod's fame as **the first on earth to be a mighty man** and the mighty men of 6:4 is not clear. Nimrod's Mesopotamian prototype may perhaps be found in the Babylonian god Ninurta or the Assyrian king Tukulti-Ninurta I (about 1246-1206). **Shinar** is probably the Hebrew form of Sumer, or southern Mesopotamia, and **Accad** is Agade, capital of the first Akkadian dynasty. On **Babel** see below on 11:1-9.

10:13-20. That **Egypt** and **Canaan** are "sons" of Ham according to J can be assumed only in the light of the P table (verses 6, 20). The J conception of the extent of Canaanite territory is obscure (cf. verse 19 with verses 15-18a).

10:20-32. Hebrews (**Eber**) and Semites (**Shem**) are according to J two names for the same people. They are represented by sons of **Peleg** and **Joktan,** the father apparently of the peoples of southern Arabia whom P thinks of as stemming from Ham. Verses 22-23 and 31 present the **Shem** section, followed by verse 32 as the conclusion, of the P table.

G. THE TOWER OF BABEL (11:1-9)

This J story is independent of the preceding table of nations—not merely of the P table, in which diversity of **language** is specifically stated (10:5, 20, 31), but even of the J table, in which **Babel** already exists (10:10) and the various descendants are assumed to **spread abroad** gradually (10:18, 30; but cf. 10:25). Here the confusion of tongues and the consequent dispersal of men and women over the earth are an immediate result of divine judgment.

Two stories appear to have been combined to form the present account: (1) the building of a **tower** to gain fame, and (2) the building of a **city** to preserve unity (cf. the doublets in verses 3*a*, 3*b*; 5, 7, 8*a*, 9*b*).

On **Shinar** see above on 10:8-12. The **tower** is obviously a ziggurat, a Mesopotamian type of temple consisting of a number of stories forming a stepped pyramid. **Babel** was the Hebrew name for Babylon. According to the erroneous popular etymology in verse 9, it derives its name from the Hebrew root *balal*, "confusion," referring to the confusion of tongues which occurred there.

The narrative in its present form suggests that civilization, which seeks to bring order out of cultural, economic, and political chaos, can become an end in itself, thus amounting to rebellion against God and resulting in self-defeat. In Genesis the human will to be like God has ended in separation from God, a return to chaos in the Flood, and an alienation which makes communication and cooperation between peoples extremely difficult if not impossible. Having treated the problem of human origins, the authors now offer an interpretation of history which speaks to one who knows oneself as "a possibility entrapped in failure but yearning toward the long light." (John Ciardi).

H. GENEALOGIES OF SHEM AND TERAH (11:10-32)

The authors abruptly narrow their field of vision from **the face of all the earth** to the world of **the descendants of Shem**. They concentrate their attention on Abraham (**Abram;** see below on verses 20-27), by whom according to J **all the families of the earth will bless themselves** (12:3). The account as we have it obviously is meant to have significance beyond the confines of Israel, and in some sense Israel's experience is considered a model for the nations of the world.

11:10-19. According to the P figures in 5:32 (where "after" should read "when") and 7:11 Shem was **a hundred years old** when the Flood began. The discrepancy cannot be removed without deleting the phrase **two years after the flood.** P sees **Eber** as the name ancestor of the Hebrews (see below on 14:13). According to J (10:21, 25-30) he is the father of all Semites.

11:20-27. In spite of the P view that Abraham was born in Ur on the lower Euphrates (see below on verses 31-32) the setting of this genealogy is around Haran in northwest Mesopotamia. **Serug . . ., Nahor . . ., Terah** are all known from nonbiblical tablets as place names in this region (Sarug, Nahur, Turahi). It was the focal point of the Aramean migrations in the first half of the second millennium.

That **Nahor** appears as both father and son of **Terah** indicates that more than one tradition of this genealogy came down to P. **Abram,** originally Abi-ram, means "the (my) father is exalted." In 17:5 this name is changed to Abraham. **Haran** the man is in Hebrew spelled differently from the city of Haran.

11:28-30. This is all that remains of the J genealogy which presumably once connected Peleg (10:25) with Abraham. Two traditions about Abraham's original home were known in Israel (cf. Joshua 24:2 and Nehemiah 9:7). In the view of J it is clearly Haran (24:2-7, 10, 15, 29; 27:43). For this reason, and because apparently the Chaldeans were not in possession of Ur till the eighth century, **in Ur of the Chaldeans** in verse 28 (cf. 15:7) is probably a harmonizing insertion of the editor or a later gloss. **Sarai,** meaning "princess" (perhaps the title of a moon goddess in Haran), is changed to Sarah in 17:15. The information that she is **barren** is given to heighten the effect of the promise in 12:2-3.

11:31-32. P follows the tradition that Abraham originally came from **Ur of the Chaldeans.** He harmonizes with the rival tradition (see above on verses 28-30) by reporting that Abraham and his family **settled** for a time in Haran on their way to Canaan. Archaeology has revealed that Ur was a center of probably the first great civilization on earth, the Sumerian, and in Abraham's time was still a city of notable wealth and culture. The implication here is that **Terah** was prevented by death from going on to Canaan. But from the figures in verse 26 and in 12:4*b* he survives sixty years after Abraham's departure.

II. Patriarchal History (12:1–50:26)

The preceding stories of human origins are symbolic, mythical accounts of the human position in a universe believed to be created and ordered by God. They are not historical; they do not record events which can be validated by contemporary evidence. Rather they record truth in a way more akin to poetry. They provide the background which the Hebrews created as the setting for their conceptions of themselves as human beings and of the history of God's relationship to them. These writings are considered divinely inspired because the truths they proclaim have been experienced as true wherever the tales have been heard.

In the stories which follow the symbols in which the understanding of human life is expressed are more historical. They are drawn from history—which in some respects can be and in fact has been verified by archaeology—rather than from poetry. They come from events rather than from accepted religious concepts.

We therefore distinguish between myth and saga, neither of which can be described in strictly historical categories, but both of which nevertheless have credible historical aspects. Myth describes in historical language the cosmic design overarching and determining history. Saga recounts in historical detail traditionally accepted events which may be used to illustrate accepted myth. Saga often accurately reflects customs and historical events as the environment in which its story unfolds.

Various interpretations of the patriarchal stories have dominated eras of Old Testament study. Julius Wellhausen, whose work in tracing and dating the sources J, E, and P has become classic, declared in 1886 that the patriarchal legends reflected only the beliefs and customs of the period in which they were written, which was after Solomon. Therefore, they are historically useless for the period they seemed to describe.

Others have treated the patriarchs as figures from Palestinian or Mesopotamian myths, as legendary founders of Canaanite sanctuaries, as personifications of tribes, as folk heroes about whom cycles of legends tended to circulate at specific locations, or as combinations of these. On the whole, however, contemporary scholars, recognizing the contributions made by archaeology to our knowledge of the second millennium, tend to find historical elements in these traditions and to forsake purely mythical and legendary interpretations.

A. THE STORY OF ABRAHAM (12:1–25:18)

One can glimpse perhaps in the story of Abraham the purpose for which Genesis was written. The compiler of these traditions desired to present an account of the Hebrews which would give his conception of God's unfolding purpose for his people. In order to do "righteousness and justice" (18:19) Israel must become a nation (12:2). Yet they were not to be reckoned among the community of nations (Numbers 23:9). To this end, and within God's purpose, a land set apart for such a nation was needed.

Two traditions about God's call to nationhood existed:

(1) the account in Genesis, according to which God's call to Israel began with Abraham;

(2) the account in Exodus, according to which God's call to Israel came through Moses in Egypt.

These two traditions were united in literary form through the Joseph story and theologically through the "God of the Fathers" who continually revealed himself. Abraham, therefore, who set out for the Promised Land, became the ideal man of faith and obedience, the type of the "righteous man."

12:1-9. *Abraham's Migration to Canaan.* Abraham responds to the summons to make a complete break with his past so that he might become the founder of a nation in a land as yet unknown to him. This story suggests certain of the J author's religious conceptions:

(1) Abraham is the representative figure who truly apprehends the demand of the God of Truth for absolute commitment, in the interest of future generations. All who respond to the "divine imperative" as Abraham did **will bless themselves** by him—that is, they will account Abraham as their spiritual father. Those who refuse the divine command will suffer the consequences.

(2) The community of those who have accepted the divine summons must possess its own land and become a nation, in order both to preserve its identity and to give light to the nations of the world (contrast the expectation of the tower builders in 11:1-9). Abraham is therefore the type of the true Israelite, and Israel is to be the type of the true nation of God.

(3) God's blessing is his promise of fruitfulness (cf. 1:22), which for Abraham is impossible so long as Sarah remains barren. The facts of God's promise and Abraham's patient and apparently futile waiting (cf. chapter 22) give dramatic content to the entire Abraham saga.

12:4b-5. According to this bit from the P account, Abraham leaves his home for the Promised Land at **seventy-five years** of age. Thus he roams through the land for a hundred years until he dies at the ripe old age of 175 (25:7). In his hundredth year he begets a son, Isaac (21:5). The figures suggest perfection—one hundred years to claim the promise both of a son and of the land.

12:6-7. Abraham's nomadic wandering south from Syria

follows the routes used by migrating peoples in the second millennium. Indeed the stories of the movements of the patriarchs agree substantially with what is known of the nomadic migrations of that period. Abraham's first recorded stopping place in Palestine is **the place at Shechem**—that is, a sacred place (cf. 22:3). Shechem was a Canaanite city located about forty miles north of Jerusalem and one mile east of the pass between the mountains Ebal and Gerizim. It was a mile and a half east of modern Nablus. Excavation of the site has revealed that the city flourished during the Hyksos period, perhaps the time of Abraham's visit (see below on 14:1). It owed its importance to its location at the crossroads of the main north-south and east-west routes of travel in Palestine, its good water supply, and the fertile fields to the east. Rehoboam's journey to Shechem to be crowned king (I Kings 12:1) attests its religious and political importance in Israel. The Sychar of John 4:5 may be Shechem. The **oak of Moreh** was apparently a Canaanite holy place, certainly religiously important to Israel (cf. 35:4; Deuteronomy 11:29-30; Judges 9:37).

12:8. Abraham's next stop is **the mountain on the east of Bethel**—modern Beitin, located about ten miles north of Jerusalem. Bethel was earlier named Luz (28:19). It doubtless owed its importance to an excellent water supply—cisterns were not required for the city until the increase in population during Roman times. It was an ancient Canaanite sanctuary of the god El and was associated wih the traditions of Jacob (28:10-22; 35:1-15) before it became an Israelite cultic center. The oldest excavated stratum is dated 2000-1600. Jeroboam I found it important enough to set up as the rival of the Jerusalem temple in his establishing of the northern kingdom of Israel (I Kings 12:26-33). It served as a royal sanctuary and continued as a shrine until destroyed by Josiah (II Kings 23:15). The site of **Ai on the east** is uncertain.

12:9. The **Negeb** is the southern dry highland of Palestine. It can be marked out roughly by a triangle drawn with its points at Gaza, the northern tip of the Gulf of Aqaba, and the southern tip of the Dead Sea. By careful and ingenious systems of water conservation and irrigation its ancient inhabitants were able to cultivate the land fairly extensively.

12:10–13:1. *Abraham's Visit to Egypt.* The story of a patriarch's sacrificing his wife's honor to save his own life occurs three times in Genesis (20:1-18; 26:6-16). Its occurrence here in the J narrative breaks the connection between 12:8 and 13:2, 5, 7-18 and raises several related questions.

Where did Lot go when Abraham entered Egypt?

Was Sarah really so beautiful as this incident implies (cf. the P idea of her age in 17:17)?

Did Abraham wander so aimlessly between Bethel and Hebron (13:18)?

In spite of its incongruities, however, the incident does reinforce the reader's awareness of Abraham's growing despair regarding God's promise. The promise of 12:7 is jeopardized by the Canaanites (12:6*b*). That of 12:1-3 is delayed by the measures Abraham adopts to save himself first from starvation and then from death (12:10-20).

12:13. The wife-sister motif of this story and its parallel versions has been shown to be based on Hurrian laws whereby sistership was a transferable relationship. Accordingly a woman given in marriage by her brother became legally her husband's sister and insured prestige for herself as well as purity for her children.

The notice about **camels** (cf. 24:10; 30:43; 31:34; 32:16) is believed by many scholars to be an anachronism. Archaeological evidence points to around the twelfth century for the domestication of the camel.

12:17. But what of God's righteousness? Why does God afflict with plagues the **Pharaoh** rather than the cowardly Abraham? The plagues in this instance appear not to have been considered punishment. Rather, they warned of impending evil to Egypt unless Sarah is returned immediately to her husband.

13:2-18. *Abraham's Separation from Lot.* The J story continues. After his unfortunate Egyptian trip, Abraham returns **to the place where his tent had been at the beginning, . . . to the place where he had made an altar.** The words seem to contain a judgment on Abraham's Egyptian excursion, which is now illuminated and emphasized by Lot's decision to settle in the Jordan Valley.

To Israel both Babylon and Egypt represented bondage, and Lot's settlement in **Sodom** would illustrate the nature of that bondage. From **the mountain on the east of Bethel** (12:8) one can survey the lush green of the Jordan rift. The contrast of this sight with the memory of the arid hills over which Abraham and Lot wandered is not lost on either man. In selecting the land which is **like the land of Egypt** Lot chooses what Abraham rejected when he set out from Haran and what his stay in Egypt has seemed to offer him: the enticements, complexities, and compromises of civilization. Abraham here remains faithful to his original call and in dealing with his nephew becomes an exemplary, magnanimous figure. The contrast with his behavior in Egypt is noteworthy. Also significant is the virtual elimination of Lot from the divine promise.

13:14-18. Since the view from Bethel does not provide a panoramic prospect of Palestine, verses 14-17 may be a later insertion into the story. Verse 18 follows most naturally after verse 12.

14:1-24. *Abraham's Victory over the Eastern Kings.* This difficult chapter, which is completely independent from all other biblical sources, is apparently inserted here to establish (1) Abraham's place in the history of the second millennium and (2) his relationship to Jerusalem.

14:1. With regard to the first of these goals we must admit that none of the invading kings can be identified for certain with rulers known to us from contemporary sources. **Amraphel** is a Babylonian name (on **Shinar** see above on 10:8-12), but it cannot be equated, as was once thought possible, with Hammurabi. **Arioch** can perhaps be identified with an Amorite-Hurrian name, Arriwuku, known as king of the city of Mari on the middle Euphrates. The once-accepted identification of **Ellasar** with Larsa in lower Mesopotamia then becomes impossible, however. A well-known but still undiscovered Hurrian city, Alziya, has been proposed for Ellasar. **Chedorlaomer** could be the Hebrew form of an otherwise unattested Elamite name Kudur-Lagamar. **Tidal** has been identified with the Hittite king, Tudhalias.

These suggested identifications place the kings in the late eighteenth or early seventeenth century, a time of unrest in the Near East caused by invading Hurrians, Kassites, and Elamites. It is known, for example, that Transjordan experienced cultural and political upheaval during the first half of the second millennium. The Hyksos, who invaded Egypt during the first half of the eighteenth century, are also part of this picture, and one suggestion is that this account describes a phase of their campaign. On the other hand recent archaeological study of the Negeb has convinced some scholars that Abraham could not have lived in this region later than the nineteenth century.

14:2-4. Thre is no way as yet of identifying the Canaanite kings, but the report of a coalition of Palestinian city-states in revolt against their overlords during this period is credible enough, though unsupported by nonbiblical evidence.

14:5-12. The battle takes place in the vicinity of the Dead Sea. The invading kings follow a surprisingly circuitous route. Coming from the north they move through places along the eastern side of the Jordan-Dead Sea rift (**Ashteroth-karnaim, . . . Ham, . . . Shaveh-kiriathaim**). They then proceed south through Edom (**Mount Seir**) to the Gulf of Aqaba (**El-paran**), then northwest to **Kadesh** in the Negeb. Finally they move northeast to **Hazazon-tamar** and on to meet their rebellious vassals in the **Valley of Siddim**. The purpose of this excursion, it has been suggested, is to keep the route open for travel and trade. The invaders defeat the Canaanite coalition, sack **Sodom and Gomorrah,** and capture Lot.

The repetition of verse 11 in verse 12 suggests that the chapter is not a literary unit. Cf. also the break between verses 17 and 21.

14:13. Abraham is here **the Hebrew** and one of his allies is an **Amorite.** Neither J nor P used the place name **Mamre** as a personal name. J used it to mean a sacred grove and P used it for Hebron.

Hebrew, which occurs here for the first time in the Old Testament, normally was used either by non-Israelites or by Israelites to distinguish themselves from Egyptians. It should probably be connected with the term "Habiru," which has been widely attested in ancient Near Eastern documents, and which designated a wanderer. The use of the name here may identify Abraham as a leader of the Habiru in Palestine. According to some ancient documents, however, the Habiru were disrupting Palestine in the fifteenth and fourteenth centuries—two or three hundred years after the presumed date of the events in 1-12. The telescoping of events in this account thus prevents assigning a more certain date for Abraham than sometime between the nineteenth and fourteenth centuries and reduces the possibility of precise historical interpretation of the chapter.

Clearly aspects of the political turmoil of the second millennium in Palestine are here sketched in vague fashion. But the claim that Abraham is thus removed from the realm of saga to that of history is unwarranted. The account may with reason be considered either a postexilic literary product or an ancient document of uncorroborated historical value. Evidence for either view is inconclusive. Explanatory glosses in verses 2, 3, 7, 17 seem to suggest an early date for the chapter, but then one would also expect to find the older name Laish instead of **Dan** in verse 14.

14:14-16. Abraham and his **trained men** pursue the retreating, victorious kings to the vicinity of **Dan.** They rout them in a **night** attack, follow them on beyond **Damascus,** and rescue goods and captives, including **Lot.** This portrayal of Abraham as a military leader is in striking contrast to all other traditions recorded about him.

14:17-24. Regarding Abraham's relationship to Jerusalem we have only the **Melchizedek** story as evidence. The account is puzzling. Verses 18-20 interrupt the connection between verses 17 and 21-24 and stand in some contradiction to them. One wonders how Abraham can give a **tenth** of the spoil to Melchizedek and still claim not to be taking anything belonging

to the king of Sodom. One is also surprised to find the king of
Sodom still alive after verse 10.

Salem (cf. Psalm 76:2) is considered to be an ancient name for
Jerusalem. **Shaveh, . . . the King's Valley** was apparently close
to Jerusalem (cf. II Samuel 18:18).

The name **Melchizedek** may mean either "king of righteousness" or "my king is Zedek." The recurrence of **Melchizedek** in
Psalm 110, which is evidently based on this passage, suggests
that Melchizedek as both priest and king of Jerusalem was to be
the true prototype of the ideal Davidic ruler.

The story may originally have told the role which the king of
Jerusalem played in the defeat of the eastern kings, possibly as
leader of the Palestinian coalition. As it stands, however, the
episode may be regarded as etiological, that is, as an explanation
for the Jerusalem tithes and position of the Zadokite priesthood.

It may also be symbolic. Abraham, the "friend" of God (Isaiah
41:8), accepts the blessing of a Canaanite priest and accepts the
priest's God as his own (verse 22). That is, Yahweh, God of
revelation, the God of Abraham, is also to be recognized as **God
Most High** (El Elyon), God of the universe, the God of
Melchizedek (verse 18).

15:1-21. *God's Covenant with Abraham.* After describing
Abraham's initial relationship to the land of promise, the
narrative turns to a second of its themes. (cf. 12:1-3), the
promised heir, who is necessary to Abraham's becoming the
father of a great nation. Abraham has begun to possess the land
but still he has no son. Some hint of his anxiety may be implied
in the vague reference **after these things.**

Literary analysis of the chapter is difficult because of a
number of peculiarities:

(1) Verses 2 and 3 are doublets.
(2) The prophetic phrase **the word of the LORD came** (verses
1 and 4) occurs only here in the Pentateuch.
(3) Verse 7 seems a new introduction to the story.
(4) Verse 5 (night) contradicts verses 12 and 17 (**as the sun was
going down**).

We seem to have at least two originally distinct accounts

37

interwoven in this chapter. The first is a promise to Abraham of numerous descendants (verses 1-6), with a possibly related prediction of their future bondage and release (verses 13-16). The second is a description of God's covenant with Abraham regarding the Promised Land (verses 7-12, 17-21).

A fragment of the beginning of the E source is probably to be found in the first of these. But editors have interwoven it so thoroughly with other material, perhaps substituting Yahweh for E's characteristic name Elohim, that it is impossible to make a clear separation (the analysis in the table, pp. 6-7, is only one of the many that have been suggested).

The portion most likely to represent E is verse 5, in which Abraham is promised **descendants** as numerous as **the stars.** The occasion for this promise is no doubt to be found in verse 2 or verse 3, or parts of them. The word translated **continue** is literally "go" and has been generally taken to mean either "die" or "live." A recent suggestion is that here it means "set out." That is, the E story is that while still in his original home Abraham on receiving God's call protests, "I am setting out childless," and is reassured by the promise of verse 5. Some scholars think the E account is continued in the prediction of verses 13-16, or parts of it.

15:1-5. Abraham's **fear** may be caused by his apprehension of Yahweh's presence or by some earlier experience like that of chapter 14. Or, if the connection with elements in the following verse is original, his growing despair at having no son causes fear. The prospect in verse 3, and presumably in verse 2 is that a **slave** in his household will be his **heir** (the name **Eliezer** is textually uncertain, and **of Damascus** is impossible).

Contracts of adoption dating from the fifteenth century found at Nuzi in Mesopotamia show that a slave was often adopted by a childless master to inherit his property. These suggest that we here have to do with an accepted legal safeguard to a man's dying intestate.

15:6. The conclusion is a comment on Abraham's faith, which Yahweh **reckoned . . . to him as righteousness.** Abraham is judged righteous when he accepts and affirms the divine promise. The emphasis rests on the state of mind which makes acts of justice and mercy possible.

15:7-11. If the account of the covenant ritual is from J, as most scholars believe, **Ur of the Chaldeans** must be an editorial revision (see above on 11:28-30).

The incident begins with Abraham's doubts about possessing the Promised Land. These doubts conflict with the preceding statement about his faith and indicate either a different source from verse 6 or an editorial rearrangement of material from the same source. The doubts are apparently to be stilled by the vision of the completed covenant ceremony.

Abraham prepares the elements. **A heifer . . ., a she-goat . . ., and a ram,** each **three years old,** are **cut in two** and the halves placed on the ground opposite one another in two rows. An undivided **turtledove** in the one row and **a young pigeon,** also undivided, on the opposite side, complete the rows. The **birds of prey** which swoop **down upon the carcasses** were probably interpreted as evil omens of Israel's Egyptian bondage, though the text allows no precise interpretation of details.

15:12. God causes to fall on Abraham **a deep sleep.** The same word is used in 2:21; I Samuel 26:12; Job 4:13; 33:15; and Isaiah 29:10. It seems to mean a God-given trance which opens the mind to revelation and ecstasy.

15:13-16. God's extensive speech here may be an E expansion on the idea of verse 5. More generally it is viewed as a later insertion to explain Israel's long bondage in Egypt. As it now stands, the passage appears to interpret the evil omen of verse 11. The Palestinians, as the **Amorites** of verse 16 must be understood, still have not filled to overflowing their cup of iniquity. Abraham's descendants must therefore wait in Egypt until judgment for Palestine is ripe. Nevertheless the stay in Egypt will not be without its benefit (verse 14), and Abraham will himself die at a ripe **old age** in peace.

The time **four hundred years** (verse 13) does not agree with Exodus 12:40 (430 years) or with verse 16 (**they shall come back here in the fourth generation,** i.e. 120 years). It has been suggested that verse 13 be read "they will be oppressed four generations" and Exodus 12:40 "The time . . . in Egypt was three generations, yea four generations." This would mean a date of around 1510-1470 for Abraham's generation.

The passage is remarkable for its view of history. God rules the world according to his plan, which he reveals to Abraham and Israel. The chosen people inherit the land because of the evildoing of its former inhabitants.

15:17-18a. In his trance Abraham sees **a smoking fire pot and a flaming torch** pass down the aisle formed by the divided carcasses. The account ends with the affirmation that **on that day the LORD made** (literally "cut") **a covenant with Abram** to give his descendants the land.

This ceremony can be interpreted as being both retributive (the man who breaks the covenant will perish like the slaughtered animal) and sacramental (walking between the halves of the carcasses results in identification of the persons with the victim, endowing them with certain qualities which the victim is regarded as possessing). There are two difficulties with such an explanation, however. It is not applicable to Yahweh and Abraham does not participate in the ritual.

The purpose of the vision is to reassure the doubting Abraham. Abraham's role in the ceremony consists only in preparing the elements while Yahweh's role is not explicitly mentioned at all (only a fire passes between the pieces). Therefore the incident may have something in common with Yahweh's self-vindication in Elijah's contest with the prophets of Baal: "Then the fire of the LORD fell, . . . and . . . all the people . . . said, 'The LORD, he is God; the LORD, he is God'" (I Kings 18:20-39). It seems fairly clear that the primary significance both of the ritual and of the covenant itself is here strained. But the account suggests many questions to which at present no answers can be given. The sense is that Yahweh obligates himself to keep his promise of land to Abraham in a way which Abraham can accept with renewed confidence.

15:18b-21. The extent of the Promised Land is idealized. These boundaries were approximated only in the reigns of

David and Solomon. **River of Egypt** (the Nile) is probably a scribal error for "brook of Egypt," a wadi about fifty miles southwest of Gaza. Verses 19-21 are thought by many to be an editor's addition (cf. Exodus 3:8).

16:1-16. *The Flight of Hagar.* The Israelites acknowledged their kinship with the Ishmaelites—a name the late Jews gave to all Arabs. Ishmaelite presence in Palestine antedated their own, but they looked down on them as descendants of an Egyptian mother (cf. 21:21, where Ishmael marries an Egyptian wife). This people may have been part of the larger group of Hagrites (Psalm 83:6) or perhaps identical with them since two of Ishmael's sons (25:15) are identical with two of the Hagrites (I Chronicles 5:19). The name **Hagar** is perhaps related to an Arabic word meaning "flee."

This J story, of which the E version is found in 21:8-21, records Abraham's attempt to solve the problem of his childlessness. On another level, however, it explains both Israel's relationship to her neighbors in the south, the Ishmaelites, and the sacredness of a famous well near **Kadesh** in the Negeb.

16:1-6. Sarah, despairing of having a child, gives Abraham her personal maid in the hope that through her slave she herself may become "mother" (cf. 30:3, 6). This procedure, as is known from both Hurrian and Babylonian law, was both legally and morally acceptable.

When Hagar becomes pregnant she turns haughtily against her mistress. In following his wife's suggestion Abraham has apparently gained ownership of Hagar. Sarah's complaint, therefore, is that Abraham alone can deal with Hagar since she is his and justice is his responsibility. The unhappy man's reply is simply to restore to his wife her arrogant slave. Sarah thereupon makes life so miserable for the pregnant girl that she flees toward Egypt, and the question of an heir for Abraham again confronts the reader.

16:7-16. Hagar has almost reached the Egyptian frontier (**Shur**), when at an oasis she is confronted by the **angel** (i.e. messenger) of Yahweh—clearly a circumlocution for Yahweh

41

himself (cf. verse 13). The triple repetition of **the angel of the LORD** probably indicates editorial insertions in verses 9-10. Only gradually does Hagar recognize her visitor as he reveals her condition and foretells her future. She will **bear a son,** to be called **Ishmael** ("God hears") because Yahweh has paid heed to his mother's distress. The description **a wild ass of a man** was no doubt meant to characterize Israel's seminomadic neighbors, who were a constant source of irritation.

16:13-14. The well where the encounter takes place was probably associated with a sanctuary whose name **Beer-lahai-roi** could no longer be explained. The translation of verse 13 is uncertain (see the footnote in the Revised Standard Version).

16:15-16. The original J story of Ishmael's birth, probably at the oasis, has been suppressed in favor of these brief statements which complete the P account of verses 1*a* and 3. In its present context the Hagar story emphasizes Abraham's apparently vain expectation of the fulfillment of God's promise. It casts some light on the way Israel viewed the history of her neighboring kinsmen, the Ishmaelites (Arabs), who also worshiped Yahweh and were blessed by him.

17:1-27. *The Covenant of Circumcision.* This new account of God's covenant with Abraham belongs to P, from which we have thus far had only two extended accounts, the Creation and the Flood. Here the interest centers in circumcision as the sign of a new covenant between God and Abraham. The purpose is to distinguish a new era in God's self-revealing witness to his people, an era which is signified by certain changes in name as well as by giving new significance to an old rite.

17:1-8. The passage begins with a call to Abraham in which the covenant promises are stated (cf. 12:1-3). God reveals himself as El Shaddai. The name, which is either new (so Exodus 6:3) or a familiar name which now receives special meaning for Abraham, has been variously interpreted. The Septuagint reads **God Almighty,** but recently it has been interpreted as "God all-knowing." Either meaning would be appropriate to the context of Abraham's despair of having the promised son at his age.

The command to **walk before me, and be blameless** requires that Abraham conduct himself before God in complete obedience. This is to be his response to God's covenant. Implied specific convenantal requirements may be sabbath observance (2:1-3), abstinence from eating blood (9:4), and circumcision (verse 10).

The promises are (1) numerous descendants, (2) a permanent relationship of his descendants to God as God's own people, and (3) **all the land of Canaan, for an everlasting possession.** The change of the name **Abram** (see above on 11:20-27) to **Abraham** is probably the result of combining two originally independent traditions, one about Abram, the other about Abraham. The etymology in verse 5 would produce, not the name Abraham, but rather Abhamon. The covenant clearly extends to the **nations** of Palestine and is not meant specifically for Israel alone (but cf. verses 20-21).

17:9-14. The sign of the covenant is to be circumcision. Perhaps this passage is intended as an interpretation of verse 1—that is, as man's part in the covenant. Observe the antithesis between verse 4, which begins "As for me" (omitted in the Revised Standard Version), and verse 9, **as for you.**

Circumcision is extremely old; it is known to have been practiced in Egypt in 3000 B.C. The tradition that it was to be performed with stone knives (Exodus 4:25; Joshua 5:3) may attest its extreme antiquity. It was practiced by a number of Israel's neighbors, but not in Mesopotamia or among the Philistines.

Probably the rite began as an initiation ceremony at puberty. Its significance to the P authors as a sign of Abraham's acceptance of God's promise, and at the time of the Exile (Jeremiah 9:25-26) as a sign of allegiance to Yahweh, is quite different from its original cultic significance (cf. **he that is eight days old**). The authors may intend to suggest that only after Abraham accepts God's covenant, signified by his own circumcision, is he eligible to receive the promised heir.

17:15-21. Inserted between the accounts of the covenant and of Abraham's obedience to it is the renaming of **Sarah (Sarai** is simply an older form; see above on 11:28-30) and the promise that she will bear a son. This is in general parallel to the J account in 18:1-15. The name Isaac is associated with laughter (verse 17; cf. 18:12; 21:6), and the name Ishmael is again connected with God's hearing (verse 20; cf. 16:11). The covenant is not to be with Ishmael, however, but with Isaac.

17:22-27. The P account concludes with detailed assurance that Abraham and all males associated with him are circumcised in accordance with the covenant. Perhaps the fact that Ishmael was thirteen years old reflects the customary time for circumcision among Israel's nomadic neighbors. This age would be more consonant with the original significance of the rite.

18:1-33. *God's Visit to Abraham at Mamre.* This resumption of the J story has properly been regarded as the immediate sequel to chapter 13. It belongs in the cluster of legends which places Abraham's dwelling in Hebron. The P narrative of chapter 17 is continued at chapter 21. Nevertheless the unity imposed on the mass of material is seen partly in the sevenfold repetition of the promise to Abraham (12:2; 13:16; 15:5, 18; 17:5, 15; 18:10) and the fulfillment at last in 21:1.

18:1-15. Yahweh appears at midday by the oaks of Mamre (the men are suddenly there). Abraham apparently does not recognize him. Not until the promise of a son is made and affirmed can Abraham suspect who his visitors are.

The relationship of the three visitors to Yahweh is difficult. Yahweh appears; but Abraham, who sees three men, addresses only one in verse 3 (the leader?) and several in verse 4. The men accept Abraham's hospitality and apparently ask together for Sarah, but only Yahweh speaks in verses 10 and 13. The visitors go to Sodom (all three?) but Abraham talks with Yahweh (who remains behind?).

A later interpretation considers Yahweh to be one of the three (19:1), but clearly the tradition is confused on the point. The object of the visit is to predict the birth of a son to Sarah in nine months, a promise that evokes in Sarah a laugh (cf. Abraham's laugh in 17:17) which she then fears to confess. The incident contains a remarkable affirmation of Yahweh's omnipotence (verse 14).

18:16-21. Abraham accompanies the men a short way on their journey and is told that their destination is **Sodom**, to determine its fate. Since in verse 17 the destruction of Sodom appears certain, while in verse 20 it will be decided after Yahweh's personal inspection, verses 17-19 are generally considered to be an insertion. Here Yahweh proposes to tell Abraham what is about to happen in Sodom. He has two reasons for this. (1) In the future Abraham may use the judgment on Sodom in instructing his children. (2) Nothing will hinder fulfillment of Yahweh's promise to Abraham. Abraham is thus considered a prophet, and Yahweh the Lord of history.

18:22-23. The chapter ends with Abraham's intercession for Sodom. He stands with Yahweh looking toward the city from the hills east of Hebron. His problem is not primarily the fate of the city. What troubles Abraham (i.e. the author) is the ambiguity of history. Does the fate of Sodom depend on the righteousness of the majority only? To what limits can God's mercy be pushed? What is justice? **Shall not the Judge of all the earth do right?** The problem cannot be solved. But the author is satisfied to conclude that for the sake of a handful of righteous people God would spare a wicked city.

19:1-38. *The Destruction of Sodom.* The wickedness of the inhabitants of Sodom (cf. 18:20) is immediately revealed in their depraved treatment of the divine messengers. Lot, who knows the customs of these city dwellers, cannot permit the strangers to pass the night unprotected from his neighbors. He is even willing to sacrifice his **daughters** for the sake of the well-being of the travelers, whom he treats as his own guests. He is finally rescued from his plight only by the superhuman intervention of the strangers themselves.

The evil of Sodom was not considered by all the Old Testament writers to have been sodomy. Ezekiel defines it: "She . . . had pride, surfeit of food, and prosperous ease, but . . . did not aid the poor and needy" (Ezekiel 16:48-50). This fact and the similarity of the attempted assault at Gibeah (Judges

19:22-26) suggest that this episode may originally have been an independent tradition. Compare the visitors' reception by Abraham (18:2-8) and by Lot (verses 1-3), also the effect of their message on Sarah (18:12) and on Lot's sons-in-law (verse 14). The judgment apparently is to be accomplished at sunrise, and Lot therefore has to hasten the escape of his family.

19:15-29. The city of **Zoar** is traditionally located southeast of the Dead Sea. The episode in verses 17-22 is usually considered a later addition to the original story. Verse 30*a*, which seems slightly to contradict verse 21, is a transitional, harmonizing gloss.

The statement about Lot's wife is clearly etiological—an explanation for a strange geographical feature. It was suggested by the pillars found everywhere in the vicinity of the Dead Sea and explains in all probability one pillar which remarkably resembled a human female figure.

The story of destruction of the **cities, and all the valley,** which perhaps was considered to have resulted in the formation of the Dead Sea (cf. 13:10; 14:3, 10), may contain a recollection of some natural catastrophe. But the occurrence in folklore of the motif of angel visitation prior to catastrophic destruction suggests a mythological rather than a historical origin of the story. Abraham, forty miles away near Hebron, could see the signs of the disaster.

19:30-38. One further incident in Lot's story (chapters 13; 18-19) remains to be told. Alone with his two unmarried and childless daughters in a cave in the hills east of Zoar, Lot is victimized by them and becomes the father of their sons, **Moab** and **Ammon.**

The etymologies (*ab*, "father"; *am*, "people") are linguistically false. The story may have been told originally to show Israelite contempt for their eastern neighbors. It has also been suggested in the light of verse 31, **there is not a man on earth to come in to us,** that in the original account a universal catastrophe had occurred. All mankind except Lot and his daughters had perished, and the women resorted to this expedient to repopulate the earth. In its present context, however, the account summarizes Lot's bankruptcy.

20:1-18. *Abraham and Sarah at Gerar.* This E narrative—the first material of any length from this source—clearly resembles the J account of Abraham and Sarah in Egypt (12:10-20). Certain ambiguities of the earlier story have here been removed (cf. verses 4, 12, 16) and the moral offensiveness is thereby softened.

The E author is concerned with the problem of guilt—both Abraham's and Abimelech's. No doubt the editor included the story at this point as an appropriate sequel to the determination of Sodom's guilt and the question of God's righteousness. Abimelech's question, LORD, wilt thou slay an innocent people? is reminiscent of Abraham's dialogue with God in 18:22-32. Certainly Abraham's honor is tarnished, in spite of the author's attempts at extenuation.

The story may reveal Israel's early awareness that its life in the world was not one of exemplary piety, in spite of its conviction of being God's chosen people. Some of the "heathen" neighbors were also God-fearing, to Israel's shame and humiliation. Abraham, the **prophet**, appears morally inferior to the God-fearing non-Israelite king; and God mercifully preserves both Sarah's honor and Abimelech's innocence. Technically a compromising incident is whitewashed, but the moral problems of the dilemma are emphasized with uncompromising exposure.

It seems fairly obvious that a familiar story was variously used in the religious and literary circles of Israel to emphasize aspects of Israel's history. In 12:10-20 it emphasizes Yahweh's omnipotent purpose in spite of Abraham's departure from the Promised Land. In this chapter the account struggles with the problem of guilt and righteousness. The final occurrence of the story (26:6-11), perhaps its oldest version, indicates some of the difficulties Isaac found in settling in Palestine.

21:1-7. *The Birth of Isaac.* The story of Isaac's birth combines the three sources J, E, P (only verse 6a comes from E) and brings together the narrative threads of chapters 17–18. The motif of **laughter** which has dominated the story is here finely developed as a sign of unexpected joy (verse 6*a*) finally replacing skeptical incredulity (17:17; 18:12). The neighbors' laughter (verse 6*b*) need not be considered the result of jesting; they too will rejoice with the happy parents.

21:8-21. *The Expulsion of Ishmael.* The story of Ishmael's expulsion from Abraham's household is the E version of the J account in chapter 16. Whereas J placed the event before Ishmael's birth, E has it at the time Isaac is **weaned**—when he is about three years old. Here Hagar's son, who has not yet been named, is described as only sightly older, in contrast with P's statistics (cf. 16:16; 17:25), which make Ishmael fourteen years older than Isaac.

Sarah discovers the two children playing together, and the sight of this equality of status angers the jealous mother. There is no need to suspect the slave's son of any unchaste or arrogant behavior. In Sarah's eyes he threatens her son's position and therefore must go. Abraham's indignation at his wife's demand is removed by God's approval of Sarah and promise of the future of **the son of the slave woman.**

21:15-21. The skillful account of the child's desert plight and rescue originally also included his naming (verse 17; cf. 16:11). He becomes the ancestor of the Ishmaelites, here represented as living south of the Negeb. Thus the narrative has disposed of another of Israel's related neighbors, and the central concern with Abraham's own freeborn son can be developed further.

The responsibility which rests on those who receive the promise (12:1-3) to be the agents of divine blessing is steadily emphasized, as all human claims to be deserving are stripped one by one from Abraham, Sarah, Isaac, Jacob, and even Joseph. God's inexplicable and vaguely apprehended purpose in history becomes an object in turn of incredulity, despair, outrage, joy and hope as human values seem overturned. The bearers of promise are more and more enjoined to follow Abraham, who believed God in spite of everything.

21:22-34. *The Covenant with Abimelech.* The section concerning Abraham and Abimelech can be separated into two distinct narratives. The first (verses 22-24, 27, 31, 34) concerns

Abimelech's anxiety to make an agreement with Abraham to insure his continued loyalty. It is the sequel to the E story of chapter 20 and concludes with an explanation of the place name **Beer-sheba** as the well (**beer**) where the oath (**sheba**) was made.

The other (verses 25-26, 28-30, 32-33), apparently from J, concerns the settlement of a dispute **about a well.** It concludes by identifying Beer-sheba as the well where Abimelech received **seven** (another meaning of *sheba*) **ewe lambs** guaranteeing Abraham access to the water forever.

Beer-sheba, located in the Negeb about fifty miles southwest of Jerusalem, was a famous sacred place, devoted to the **Everlasting God** (cf. 26:25; Amos 5:5; 8:14). **Philistines** is an anachronism, as this people did not enter Palestine till the time of Joshua or later.

22:1-19. *Abraham's Temptation to Sacrifice Isaac.* The story of what we must call the brutal trial of Abraham's faith is a literary masterpiece. In this simple, moving account Abraham appears indeed as the father of the faithful. The trial of his faith involved in God's command that he sacrifice **your son, your only son Isaac, whom you love,** marks the climax of the Abraham cycle of stories.

With fine perception it has been said that Abraham had to cut himself off from his entire past when he left his homeland and now is summoned to give up his entire future. The testing goes to the heart of his life, his hope for meaning, and his trust in Yahweh. He is asked to give up the child of his old age, on whose life the fulfillment of God's promise depends.

God's incredible command and Abraham's unwavering obedience are bearable only because the reader knows the situation is a trial: **God tested Abraham** (verse 1); **now I know that you fear God** (verse 12). An inescapable conclusion is that Abraham's fear of God is revealed in his steadfast obedience, whether or not it results in his son's death. Isaac's deliverance neither invalidates Abraham's act nor serves as his reward for risking everything (as suggested in the later addition, verses 15-19). The thought is close to Paul's on justification by faith in Romans 4.

22:1-14. The original story, which belongs to E, consists of these verses. It may have been told to explain the substitution of animal for human sacrifice at some cultic center, the name of which is now lost. The words of verse 14 are explanatory, but they do not yield the original place name. The Hebrew has been reconstructed and rendered "Abraham called the name of that place Jeruel [cf. II Chronicles 20:16], for he said, 'Today, in this mountain, God provides.'" This suggestion is the best we have, but the name of the cultic center cannot be satisfactorily determined.

References to human sacrifice in the Old Testament indicate that the Hebrews knew and practiced it (see comment on Deuteronomy 18:9-14). Mesha of Moab caused the Israelite armies to withdraw by sacrificing his son in their presence (II Kings 3:27). Ahaz sacrificed his son (II Kings 16:3). And all Israel is accused of practicing this barbarity in II Kings 17:17. The sacrifice of Jephthah's daughter (Judges 11:29-40) and Hiel's sons (I Kings 16:34) are additional instances. The prophetic reflection on proper worship of God is perhaps best summarized in Micah 6:6-8; but the narrative in its present context is best interpreted, not as illustrating general truths about child sacrifice or surrender of the will, but rather as describing the supreme test of Abraham's life.

22:2. The **land of Moriah** cannot be identified. On the basis of II Chronicles 3:1 the place where Isaac was spared is often said to be the hill in Jerusalem on which the temple was later built. This, however, does not accord with the specification here of a **land** containing several **mountains,** or with the fact that Jerusalem was already settled in Abraham's time (cf. 14:18). Perhaps the text has been corrupted from an original "land of the Amorites" (cf. 10:16, where Canaan is father of the Amorites).

22:20-24. *The Genealogy of Nahor.* This J genealogy has probably been included here to prepare for the story in chapter 24. The names of Nahor's twelve sons—like those of Ishmael's twelve sons (25:13-16), Esau's (36:15-19), and Jacob's—represent tribes or tribal territories. They are located in Aram, northeast of Palestine—that is, in either northern Syria or the Syro-Arabian desert.

Bethuel, Rebekah's father (cf. 24:15, 24, 47), is Nahor's son; but Laban, Rebekah's brother (24:29; 25:20; 28:2), is also Nahor's son (29:5; but cf. 28:5, where Laban and Rebekah are both children of Bethuel). At least two traditions appear to have been confused, one about Bethuel's children from Haran and the other about Nahor's from northwest Arabia.

23:1-20. *Abraham's Purchase of a Grave for Sarah.* The account of Abraham's purchase from the Hittites of a grave for his family is generally credited to the P tradition. It is the fourth extensive narrative in Genesis from this source.

23:2. The burial site was near **Kiriath-arba,** later known as **Hebron.** The name may mean "city of four [quarters]" or, as legend suggests, the city of the person Arba (Joshua 15:13).

23:3. The mention of **Hittites** has usually been considered an anachronism, but continued research indicates that isolated Hittite settlements may have been made in southern Palestine early in the second millennium. Nevertheless references in Genesis to pre-Israelite inhabitants of Palestine suggest that the term "Hittite" is often a vague designation for "Palestinian" in P—as are the terms "Canaanite" in J and "Amorite" in E.

23:4-11. The negotiations for the sale of the property are illuminated by a passage from a Hittite legal code found in Turkey. According to this the possession of property carried definite feudal obligations unless only a part of it was transferred. This may explain Abraham's original request for only the **cave** and Ephron's insistence that Abraham purchase the entire **field.**

23:12-16. The **silver** is **weighed out** on a balance, with shekel weights of stone or metal in the other pan. Archaeologists have discovered many such weights. Perhaps **current among the merchants** refers to some sort of weight standard. The price is no doubt meant to be understood as exorbitant.

23:17-18. The final transaction is precisely recorded and the property is described. The witnesses are attested in contractual, legal terms. **Machpelah,** derived perhaps from a word meaning "double," seems to refer to the district rather than to the cave only (cf. verse 9).

23:19-20. The interest of the P authors in this transaction is difficult to determine. Nothing indicates either that the place was considered sacred, unless it be connected with **Mamre** (cf. 13:18), or that the story was told to settle a dispute about who owned the cave. The theory that Abraham's purchase of this piece of "promised land" was a pledge of the future possession of the entire land by Abraham's descendants is scarcely satisfactory. The story reemphasizes Abraham's faith in God's promise, which goes unrewarded. At the end he possesses a grave.

24:1-67. *Isaac's Marriage to Rebekah.* The charming story about the arrangement for Rebekah's marriage to Isaac is usually attributed to J. However, several discrepancies in the account suggest a mixing of variant traditions. Twice **Laban** goes out to meet **Abraham's servant** (verses 29*b*, 30*b*). The relatives agree to the servant's request (verse 51), but later Rebekah is given freedom of choice (verses 57-58). In verse 59 Rebekah is accompanied by her **nurse,** in verse 61*a* by **her maidens.** These and other inconsistencies do not seriously mar the story. Neither do they prove the existence of original parallel accounts.

24:1-9. Abraham's concern that his son not marry a Canaanite woman but obtain a wife from his father's family is not simply an example of normal oriental custom. Rather it must be understood as the aged Abraham's final act of faith in God's promise. His demand for an oath indicates that he expects to die before his steward returns. It is not unlikely that an account of his death was originally a part of this story but was removed by an editor in favor of the P account in 25:7-11.

The practice of swearing by the genital organ (verse 2) was doubtless an ancient custom. The significance of this may have been forgotten at the time the story was incorporated into Genesis—or else was so well known that no interpretation was considered needed.

Abraham's will is that (1) Isaac shall marry only a girl from his relatives in the land from which he came, and (2) Isaac shall not

go to that land. He is convinced that God himself will choose
Isaac's wife and prosper his servant's journey.

24:10-27. On **camels** see above on 12:16. **Mesopotamia** is a
translation of the Hebrew *Aram-naharaim*, "Aram of the two
rivers," meaning the Aramean or northwest part of Mesopotamia. This is called Paddan-aram in the P source (e.g. 25:20). **The
city of Nahor** is presumably Haran.

With the meeting at the well compare the stories of Jacob and
Rachel (29:2-12) and Moses and Zipporah (Exodus 2:15c-17).
Abraham's trust in Yahweh is echoed and confirmed by the faith
of his steward.

24:28-51. The reference to **her mother's household** and the
fact that **Laban** takes the lead in hospitality, as well as later in the
negotiations for Rebekah's departure (verses 55-59), suggest
that her father is no longer living, and that **and Bethuel** in verse
50 is a later insertion.

The narrative may preserve a tradition about a later wave of
settlement in Canaan. This Aramean wave is represented in the
Jacob stories, which supplemented the first migration described
in the Abraham saga. Laban figures prominently here and in
Jacob's attempts to find a wife. It therefore seems likely that the
story is intended to provide the link between the Abraham cycle
of stories and the Jacob, or Aramean, cycle. The steward's
statement that Abraham **has given all that he has to Isaac**
confirms the implication that Abraham is to die before his
return.

24:52-61. Oriental custom would call for a period of
celebration of the betrothal before Rebekah's departure. The
steward's insistence on returning at once points up his fear that
Abraham may not survive his journey. The bridal blessing (verse
60) corresponds to oriental custom (cf. Ruth 4:11-12). It is
reflected in the late addition of 22:17.

24:62-67. The details of the conclusion to the story are
obscured by several problems in the text. Isaac has apparently
moved (from Hebron?) to **Beer-lahai-roi** (cf. 25:11*b*). There,
while out for an evening stroll, he meets the returning caravan

and his bride. The steward's identification of him as **my master** again indicates that Abraham's expected death has occurred. It also suggests that originally the marriage with Rebekah **comforted** Isaac, not for **his mother's death,** but for his father's. Because of the uncertain text, however, this suggested reconstruction is only a conjecture.

25:1-6. *Abraham's Descendants by Keturah.* This passage, a distinct element in the traditions about Abraham, is a footnote to the main narrative. It is probably from J. However, Abraham's marriage to another wife and the naming of his descendants born of her does not follow easily after chapter 24. An earlier position for it would not fit with the uniqueness of Isaac's birth (cf. 15:3-4; 18:10-12).

The passage preserves a tradition about Israel's relationship to her neighbors on the southeast, on the borders of the north Arabian desert. Perhaps the name **Keturah,** almost identical with the Hebrew word for "incense," contains an allusion to the trade in frankincense carried on among Arabia, Palestine, and Egypt. Verses 5 and 11*b* may be fragments from a J account of Abraham's death originally part of chapter 24 (cf. 24:36, 62; see above on 24:1-9).

25:7-11. *The Death of Abraham.* According to the P source Abraham dies one hundred years after his entrance into the Promised Land (cf. 12:4*b*). He is buried in the family grave by **Isaac and Ishmael.** The sons of Keturah are not present, and Ishmael's presence does not accord with the E story of his expulsion (chapter 21). God's blessing is reserved for Isaac. On verse 11*b* see above on verses 1-6.

25:12-18. *Ishmael's Genealogy.* The P genealogy of Ishmael, like those of Nahor, Esau, and Jacob, consists of twelve members. The known tribes and places in verses 13-15 indicate a territory covering most of northern Arabia. But possibly the Hebrews used the name "Ishmaelites," not of a specific tribal group, but of bedouin in general. Verse 18 may be the conclusion to the suppressed J story of Ishmael's birth (see above on 16:15-16).

B. THE STORY OF JACOB (25:19–36:43)

The Jacob stories—that is, the story of **the descendants of Isaac** (25:19; cf. "the history of the family of Jacob," 37:2*a*)—form the next large body of material in Genesis. Aside from chapter 26, which may be called the Isaac story, and chapter 36, which contains Edomite genealogies, the saga of Jacob is related in 25:19–36:43.

The material may be divided conveniently though inaccurately into three cycles: (1) Jacob and Esau, (2) Jacob and Laban, and (3) Jacob's return to Canaan. Several cult legends scattered throughout the material cannot easily be integrated into this scheme.

The saga is unified by a strong biographical interest which is not so evident in the Abraham stories. Whereas Abraham emerges as an ideal figure rather than a historical person, Jacob is clearly an individual. The stories may reflect historical traditions about Israel's relations with her neighbors, the Edomites on the south and the Arameans on the north.

25:19-28. *The Birth of Esau and Jacob.* Except verses 19-20 and the notice in verse 26*d* about Isaac's age, which are from P, the account of the twins' birth comes from J.

25:20. The divergence between P and J can be seen in the genealogy of **Bethuel.** P considers him an **Aramean,** a descendant of Aram, the brother of Arpachshad (10:22), who is the ancestor of Abraham (11:10-27). J considers Bethuel to be Abraham's nephew (22:20-23), his brother Nahor's son (but see above on 22:20-24). On **Paddan-aram** see above on 24:10-27.

25:21-24. Rebekah, like Sarah and Rachel, is **barren.** It is only in answer to Isaac's pleading that Yahweh grants her children. The activity in her womb during pregnancy leads Rebekah, fearing perhaps an evil omen, to consult Yahweh at a sacred shrine. There she receives an oracle proclaiming that she will bear twins who will become **two** rival **nations,** the **younger** of which will dominate the elder.

25:25-28. The nations are characterized in their ancestors. Esau is **red** (a play on "Edom") and **hairy** (a play on "Seir," the mountain range southeast of the Dead Sea where the Edomites lived) and a clever **hunter**. Jacob (here connected with the noun **heel** and the related verb "overreach"), grasping for first place, is a civilized herdsman. Actually the name "Jacob" is extremely old, meaning probably "God protects."

25:29-34. *Jacob Acquires Esau's Birthright.* The story of the birthright, which continues the J account, doubtless delighted the descendants of Jacob with pride in the way their ancestor outwitted the Edomite ancestor, Esau. It has been suggested that Esau may have thought he was bargaining for some kind of magical stew and learned of his brother's treachery only when he discovered the prized dish to be nothing but lentil soup.

The precise significance of the birthright is not clear from this passage. The presupposition is that it gave the firstborn claim to a double share of his father's property, as is known from Assyrian law, as well as the leadership of the tribe. Clearly, however, Jacob becomes the bearer of God's promise to Abraham.

26:1-35. *Traditions About Isaac.* The Isaac traditions contained in this chapter are attributed to J, except for the account of Esau's Hittite wives (verses 34-35), which is from P. Most of the episodes are closely parallel to stories already related of Abraham. The story of Isaac and Rebekah in **Gerar** (verses 1, 6-16) duplicates 12:10-16 and 20:1-18. The renewal of God's promise (verses 2-5) is similar to 12:2-3, 7; 15:7 and 22:17. The incident about the **wells** (verses 17-33) is like 21:22-34. Why these duplicates exist cannot be explained. If there once was an extensive cycle of Isaac legends, it has been largely lost in favor of the Abraham cycle.

Yahweh blesses Isaac **for Abraham's sake** (verses 3, 5, 24). Nevertheless the revelation at **Beer-sheba** (verses 23-25) is recorded as though Isaac were the discoverer of the sacred place (cf. 21:33) And in verse 33 its name receives yet another etymology (cf. 21:25-32).

26:34-35. This P notice about Esau's wives is out of accord with the narrative in chapter 27, where he is still an unmarried member of Isaac's household. It does not even agree with

36:1-3, which also comes from the P tradition. It leads into the P account of Jacob's leaving home (27:46—28:9).

27:1-45. *Jacob's Theft of Isaac's Blessing.* The story of the deception perpetrated by Rebekah and Jacob on the blind and aged Isaac appears to combine parallel narratives from J and E. The most striking evidence of at least two original accounts is the doublet in verses 44*b* and 45*a*.

There have been many proposed analyses of these sources, with fair agreement on certain elements—for example, that the smell of Esau's garments is from J while the hairy kidskins are from E—but the strands are too closely interwoven for precise separation. This narrative is the continuation from either 25:28 or 25:34.

There appear to be two traditions about Esau's home territory. One (J, P) considers him the ancestor of the Edomites (25:29-34; 36:9). The other (E) apparently places him in Transjordan (verses 39-40; chapters 32–33). Therefore the precise relationship between the traditions of this story and 25:21-34 cannot be determined.

Five superbly drawn scenes reveal the depths of hostility and bitterness in Isaac's family (verses 1-5*a*, 5*b*-17, 18-29, 30-40, 41-45). His determination to bless his favorite son is foiled by Rebekah's skillful courage and Jacob's blasphemous audacity. In the end he finds himself in effect cursing Esau. The blessing, once given, is irrevocable—an objective, independent reality. Isaac is incapable of providing a remedy for his unwitting role in the monstrous crime.

The animosity between Edom and Israel is unmistakably attested in the Old Testament. David conquered Edom and made it a vassal state, but Edom won its independence from Israel in the mid-ninth century.

Moral judgments are absent from the story. The drama is enacted in its tragic dimensions, with no suggestion that any member of the family is mindful of or unduly concerned with God's promise to Abraham. Humor and pathos are skillfully blended in the stark revelation of Jacob's character, Rebekah's reckless cunning, Esau's joy in the chase, and the manipulation of Isaac over which he is helpless. The compiler almost seems to suggest that the righteous Abraham never found a worthy successor, that Israel's history moved between faithful obedience and the crassest self-seeking and irresponsibility. No one in the story can escape condemnation. But also in God's providence the more reprehensible brother becomes the bearer of promise, while the victimized, legitimate heir is passed over without recognition or recourse. The story can be interpreted as an illustration of God's providence which overarches and comprehends in its purpose both the best and worst that people can do.

27:46–28:9. *Jacob's Departure.* This section from the P material continues the notice at 26:34-35 about Esau's marriage to **Hittite women** which distresses Isaac and Rebekah. Jacob is sent away, therefore, not to escape Esau's anger as in verses 41-45, but rather to find a suitable wife among his mother's relatives (cf. the note about **Bethuel,** 25:19-20). Esau's hostility to Jacob is ignored in this account. On **Paddan-aram** see above on 24:10-27. Isaac invokes on Jacob God's blessing of Abraham. Esau, in an attempt to please his father too, marries another wife (cf. 36:3) from his father's family. The reference to **Ishmael** may recall tribal kinship between Edomites and Ishmaelites.

28:10-22. *Jacob's Dream at Bethel.* The Bethel story continues the narrative of 27:45. It appears to combine J (verses 10, 13-16, 19) and E (verses 11-12, 17-18, 20-22, with a later insertion in verse 21*b*) traditions.

28:11-12. The vision of the **ladder** (more accurately "stairway" or "ramp") **to heaven** suggests a Mesopotamian temple tower (ziggurat) at whose summit, which was accessible by a ramp, the god was supposed to dwell. The story, therefore, tells how Jacob accidentally (verse 11*a*) discovers the place where God's **angels** (i.e. messengers) set out upon earth on their divinely appointed missions.

28:13-16. God renews his promise to Jacob as previously he has given it to Abraham and Isaac.

28:17-22. Originally the narrative explained the sanctity of a **pillar** at Bethel—it marked the place where Jacob saw in a dream **the gate of heaven** and received a manifestation of God (cf. 35:1-15). Jacob's great strength, shown in his single-handed erection of this monolith, must have been legendary (cf. 29:10; 32:25-26). On **Bethel** see above on 12:8.

29:1-14. *Jacob's Arrival at Laban's House.* The cycle of stories about Jacob and Laban (chapters 29–31) preserves traditions about Israel's relationship with its northeastern kinsmen. Its context is Jacob's search for a wife among his mother's Aramean kinfolk, and the cycle concludes with Jacob's return to the Land of Promise (31:13).

29:1. The goal of Jacob's journey according to J was Haran (28:10) and according to P was Paddan-aram (28:7). But in this verse, which probably continues the E account of 28:20-22, it is **the land of the people of the east.** This designation and the speed with which Jacob later arrives with his flocks in Gilead (Transjordan) after leaving Laban (31:22-23) suggest that the setting for this cycle of stories in the E traditions is not northwestern Mesopotamia but Aramean territory somewhere in the Syrian desert. The stories reflect the movement of the Arameans over northwest Mesopotamia in northwest Arabia in the fourteenth century.

29:2-14. This story of Jacob's arrival at his uncle's house is usually attributed to J. The **well in the field** is quite different from the well "outside the city" of chapter 24. Evidently a cistern, it is covered by a large **stone,** which is to be removed only when all who are entitled to draw water are present. This both helped to lift the stone and avoided any unfair access to the limited supply of water. Jacob is able to lift the stone by himself (cf. 28:18; 32:25-26).

29:15-30. *Jacob's Marriages.* Some consider these verses a continuation of the preceding J account. But the implication in verse 15 that Jacob has already started serving Laban, and especially the new introduction of Rachel in verse 16, suggest that the editor has here shifted to the E account. This coarse story about how the cunning Jacob is outwitted by his scheming uncle is a fitting sequel to the account of Jacob's own trickery.

Jacob is unable to pay the bride price and offers to work for

Rachel **seven years.** Laban's reply to Jacob's proposal is noncommittal (verse 19). Seven years later on the wedding night the heavily veiled bride, **Leah** (meaning "cow") instead of **Rachel** (meaning "ewe"), is escorted to Jacob, who discovers the deception only in the morning. He is then obliged to conclude the week of festivity before he can marry Rachel, for whose hand he obligates himself to another seven years' service. Laban's reason is that **the younger** Rachel cannot be given in marriage **before the first-born,** Leah.

The parentheses in verses 24 and 29 are generally considered insertions from P. However, a similar statement about assignment of a slave girl to a bride, found in a tablet from Nuzi in Mesopotamia, has been cited as evidence that these notices may have been part of the original tradition.

29:31–30:24. *The Birth of Jacob's Children.* That this narrative combines the J and E sources is evident from the varying divine names and the duplicate explanations of the names of Issachar, Zebulun, and Joseph. The account undoubtedly preserves traditions about Israel's tribal history. It has been suggested that this bit of family history symbolizes a new Aramean migration into Canaan, there to be united with the earlier migration symbolized by Abraham. Eleven sons return with Jacob from Aramean territory; only Benjamin is born in Canaan (35:16-21). The order in which the sons are listed may be traditional: first four sons of Leah, then four sons of Jacob's concubines, two more sons of Leah, a daughter, and finally Joseph of Rachel. Whether this arrangement indicates superior and inferior tribes or has some other significance is unknown. The explanations attached to the names are not and probably were not meant to be strictly etymological. The series is rather a sort of game with words which derives its point from the rivalry between Leah and Rachel, Jacob's neglected and cherished wives.

30:1-13. Rachel's demand for children leads her to a solution similar to Sarah's (cf. 16:2), but Jacob is not as understanding as Abraham. Leah also follows the same custom.

30:14-24. In spite of Rachel's preferential status before Jacob she does not bear children, even with the aid of **mandrakes,** thought to be a stimulant to conception. Perhaps Joseph's birth was originally related to her eating of the mandrakes (cf. verse 22, **then God remembered Rachel**).

Jacob's sons, who are to become the fathers of the chosen people, are conceived in passionate rivalry and bitterness, born of preferred and despised wives and concubines—in startling fulfillment of God's promise to make of Abraham a great nation. The sons and daughter are said to be born within the brief span of only seven years (cf. 29:20; 30:25; 31:41).

30:25-43. *Jacob's Wealth.* After fourteen years of service for his wives Jacob is ready to go home. Laban, however, wants him to stay. The two clever and mistrusting men therefore strike a bargain. The doublets such as verses 25 and 26, the discrepancy between verses 33 and 35, and the difficulty of verse 40 reveal the composite nature of this narrative (J and E). For this reason the precise terms of the bargain are not clear.

30:31-36. According to verses 32-34 Jacob is to receive at once his wage for a further term of service. He is to have all the speckled sheep and goats and all the black lambs from Laban's flocks, presumably a small number among the generally white sheep and black goats. According to verses 35-36, however, Laban does not give these animals to Jacob. Instead, he entrusts them to his own sons, whom he sends away a distance of three days' travel, and he places Jacob in charge of the normally colored animals. The agreement therefore turns out to be that all the abnormally colored offspring born to the normally colored animals in Jacob's care will belong to Jacob.

30:37-43. What appears as a bargain favorable to Laban is turned by Jacob to his own advantage through skillful breeding technique. Laban's distance from Jacob keeps him ignorant of Jacob's scheme and eventual flight (31:22). Thus Jacob becomes wealthy.

31:1-42. *Jacob's Flight from Laban.* The story of Jacob's departure from Laban is mainly from E. The fact that it is a composite is revealed by the doublets (verses 1 and 3 from J and verses 2 and 13 from E) and the P name **Paddan-aram.** Both human and divine causes motivate his return to Canaan, indications of the narrator's interpretation of history.

31:4-16. The pious, honest Jacob of this chapter is very different from the scheming, wily man of chapters 29-30. Clearly another conception of the man is here presupposed.

Jacob's trickery is bypassed in this narrative in favor of an assertion of God's activity on Jacob's behalf. In verse 16 the wives speak as though they were Laban's sole heirs. His wives are still considered members of the household of Laban, who must be induced to give them up. Therefore Jacob needs their consent to accompany him to Canaan to avoid legal difficulties. The daughters' complaint that Laban has spent the bride price seems to imply that Laban owes them the equivalent of Jacob's fourteen years of service. For Jacob's vow at **Bethel** cf. 28:18-22.

31:17-20. Jacob chooses the busy shearing season, which normally ended in a feast, as the opportune time for his flight. The significance of Rachel's theft of her father's **household gods** (teraphim; cf. I Samuel 19:13-17 and Ezekiel 21:21) is not unmistakably clear. A Mesopotamian document of adoption from Nuzi suggests that the possessor of these images was the legitimate heir to the family property. This explanation would account for both Laban's agitation at losing the images and Jacob's decree of death for the offender (verses 30-35).

31:21-25. The distance of the **hill country of Gilead** on the east of the Jordan from the closest point beyond the **Euphrates** is some three hundred miles, and from Haran nearly a hundred miles farther. Since Jacob could not drive his flocks this distance in ten days, the phrase about crossing the Euphrates is probably a bit from the J account inserted in the E narrative. E's short time for the journey fits with the evidence of 29:1 that this tradition located Laban's home in northwest Arabia.

31:26-42. Laban overtakes Jacob and accuses him both of wrongfully taking away his daughters and grandchildren and of stealing his household gods. Rachel saves herself from being discovered with the latter and in the process renders the idols temporarily unclean. Thus Laban is tricked. Jacob in his long speech in verses 36-42 emerges as a faithful and generous servant unjustly treated.

31:43-55. *Jacob's Covenant with Laban.* Laban gives up his claims, and the two men agree on a formal compact, which they confirm by setting up a monument. This formality seems unrelated to the situation in the narrative (note the abrupt transition from verse 43 to verse 44). The doublets, which are obvious despite considerable editorial harmonizing, indicate the incorporations of two independent traditions about a landmark in the hill country between the Yarmuk and Jabbok rivers east of the Jordan.

One tradition concerns a **heap** of **stones,** which according to J is named **Galeed** (probably meant to be the source of the name Gilead in verse 48). It is the **witness** to Laban's permitting his daughters to leave his household in return for Jacob's promise to treat them well and marry no rival wives.

Since the two men have been speaking the same language all along, verse 47 is probably a later insertion (see the footnotes in the Revised Standard Version). Verse 50*b* probably should read: "When no man of our (father's) kin is watching, God will be witness."

The other tradition concerns a treaty setting a territorial boundary, which according to E is marked by a **pillar** located at **Mizpah**—probably a play on the Hebrew word for "pillar," *mazzebah.* The men seal their compact by a sacred meal, each invoking his own god (verse 53) to witness the agreement and punish any violation of the boundary by the other. Thus a definite break is made between Jacob (the Israelites) and Laban (the Arameans).

32:1-23. *Jacob's Preparation to Meet Esau.* Having concluded the Jacob-Laban cycle of stories, the compiler returns to the Jacob-Esau cycle. Jacob's preparations for meeting his brother reveal his wealth, his uneasy conscience, and his awareness of the need for reconciliation before his own future in Canaan can be secure. The story may reflect some of the tensions with bordering nomadic people during the Aramean migratory moves into Palestine. But the compiler's main interest lies in

Jacob's awakening consciousness of his relationhip to the God of his fathers.

32:1-2. According to E, Jacob's return to his own territory is marked by an encounter with God's **angels** (i.e. messengers), the meaning of which seems to be that Jacob is now again in God's realm. It is uncertain whether the explanation of the name **Mahanaim** (the dual form of the word for "camp," "company," or "army") is based on the two groups—God's and Jacob's attendants—or simply on the divine **army.** The site of this city, so important in Israel's history, has not yet been identified by archaeologists.

32:3-13*a*. In the J narrative Jacob invites Esau to meet him by sending **messengers** to **Seir,** some hundred miles to the south. This account may think of Jacob as headed toward his old home in Beer-sheba (cf. 28:10) by a route to the east and south of the Dead Sea which would come near Esau's home in Edom (cf. 33:12-14). When the messengers return with news of Esau's approach with **four hundred men** Jacob becomes frightened. As a precaution he divides his companions and property into **two companies.** This may have been the basis for a J explanation of the name Mahanaim that was suppressed by an editor in favor of the E explanation in verse 2.

32:13*b*-23. In the E account Esau's home territory seems to lie, not in Edom, but east of the Jordan (see above on 27:1-45) directly across Jacob's route toward central Palestine. Fearing an immediate encounter, Jacob sends ahead a series of gifts to **appease** his brother while he and his wives and children linger behind.

32:24-32. *Jacob's Wrestling.* The experience at **Penuel** is Jacob's second critical encounter with God (cf. 28:10-22). It seems clear that these two incidents are the poles around which the material of the Jacob cycle is meant to revolve. The God who promised to bring Jacob back to the land of Canaan (28:15) encounters him in deathly struggle on his return and changes his name and cripples him before blessing him. One might indeed find struggle to be the dominant theme of the Jacob cycle.

The story as told by J has lost its original significance in favor of explanations for the place name **Peniel** (i.e. "face of God"), the name **Israel** (which has been derived from roots meaning "God struggles," or "rules," or "heals"), and the law against eating the sciatic muscle (verse 32). Perhaps in its original form the tale was an account of how Jacob (?) in a gigantic struggle was able at night to gain permission from the Canaanite god El to cross the Jabbok into his territory. (For another account of physical struggle between God and man cf. Exodus 4:24-26.)

The site of **Penuel** (of which **Peniel** is a variant used only in verse 30) is said to be the eastern one of two mounds where the Jabbok River enters the Jordan Valley.

33:1-17. *Jacob's Meeting with Esau.* Esau's attitude on meeting Jacob is surprisingly magnanimous, in contrast with his previous murderous intent (cf. 27:41). Jacob remains suspicious and wary. The presence of Esau's **four hundred men** was no doubt reason for pause. The story (from J) follows the previous narrative almost inevitably, and Jacob's remark that seeing Esau's face was **like seeing the face of God** is probably meant to bind the two incidents together.

After the meeting, the only purpose of which is apparently the reconciliation of the two brothers, Esau proceeds alone to Edomite territory, while Jacob moves on only a few miles. **Succoth** has been identified with a mound in Jabbok and Jordan, but recent excavation there has brought the identification into question.

33:18-20. *Jacob's Arrival at Shechem.* According to E and P (verse 18*b*) Jacob on his return re-enters the central part of **the land of Canaan** and stops first at Shechem (see above on 12:6-7). His purchase of land near the city is the second recorded patriarchal land acquisition in Canaan (cf. chapter 23). **Pieces of money** probably designates a weighed amount of precious metal (see above on 23:12-16), but archaeologists have not yet discovered an example of this weight.

34:1-31. *The Rape of Dinah.* This narrative presents many problems. It does not fit the chronology of Jacob's career, since at his return to Canaan Dinah would be a child of six or seven, with her oldest brothers in their early teens (cf. 30:21; 31:41).

Jacob is portrayed in a passive role, with his sons taking the lead in both negotiations and actions. This and the fact that the story concerns the capture and despoiling of a major city (see above on 12:6-7) suggest that it was originally a tradition of the Israelite tribal confederacy, not of Jacob and his family.

The inconsistencies in the story perhaps reveal the existence of two parallel accounts. In one, attributed to J, Shechem violates Dinah and then offers to marry her, but Simeon and Levi take vengeance by killing him and his family. In the other, assigned to E or by some to P, Hamor seeks a treaty with the clan of Jacob, including intermarriage in general and the marriage of his son with Dinah in particular. All the sons of Jacob employ the circumcision ruse to disable the Shechemites so that they may sack the entire city.

On the other hand a number of scholars explain the inconsistencies as the result of successive expansions of an original tale and assign the entire story to J. Some views have attributed this chapter and chapter 38, with various other passages, from a written source independent of J, E, and P.

The historical basis of the events described is anything but clear. The story preserves a tradition of tribal history which is perhaps alluded to in 49:5-7. This no doubt explained both the independence of Shechem and the virtual disappearance at an early time of the tribes of Simeon and Levi from Israel's military history.

Perhaps the Shechemites offered Israelite tribes the opportunity of settling in their territory on conditions involving **trade** and intermarriage. The Israelites added the requirement of circumcision—which here appears as an obligatory tribal custom, a prerequisite to marriage, unrelated to faith in Yahweh (see above on 17:9-14). It is not clear whether the Israelites involved in the treaty negotiated it **deceitfully** or whether the tribes of Simeon and Levi violated an agreement entered on in good faith by other tribes.

The story scarcely fits into the patriarchal age but suggests rather the period of the judges. Jacob's reproach in verse 30 is based on considerations of prudence rather than morality.

Perhaps it reflects the animosities between Canaanites and invading Habiru (see above on 14:13) which arose when Canaanite conciliatory conditions for settlement were flouted by the invaders.

One notes the emphasis on the great value of female chastity as well as on the danger to Israel of adopting Canaanite ways of life—a process which could be followed only by compromising Israel's moral principles.

35:1-15. *Jacob's Return to Bethel.* E describes Jacob's journey **to Bethel** in order to fulfill his vow (28:20-22) as a pilgrimage. It requires renunciation of everything unholy (earrings were used as magical amulets) and ritual purification by washing and changing clothes. Such pilgrimages were probably common in the period of the judges, after the sanctuary was transferred from Shechem (Joshua 24:1, 25) to Bethel (Judges 20:26-28). Jacob's pilgrimage may reflect a tradition of the original transfer of the central shrine, perhaps as a result of the events recorded in chapter 34. **Terror from God** prevents the Canaanites at that time from molesting the Israelites.

35:9-15. The notice about God's appearance to Jacob is from the P tradition (cf. the J tradition in 32:28). The section simply records the change of Jacob's name—without giving an etymology of the new name, **Israel**—and the renewal of the promise made to Abraham and Isaac. The command to **be fruitful and multiply** (cf. 1:28) is scarcely appropriate at this stage in Jacob's life after he has already begotten eleven of his traditional twelve sons. For this reason it has been suggested that verses 11-13 may have been transposed from a location following 28:1-9.

Verses 14-15 probably continue the E account of verses 1-8, though verse 15 has often been assigned to P. Since Jacob has already set up a **pillar** at Bethel (28:18), verse 14 may be an editorial corruption of the marking of the grave of **Deborah** (verse 8; cf. verse 20).

35:16-20. *The Birth of Benjamin.* In this continuation of the E account Jacob moves south from Bethel toward **Ephrath**—erroneously identified by an editorial insertion with **Bethlehem**.

Actually it was a town near Ramah in Benjaminite territory, possibly the same as Ophrah (Joshua 18:23). In this vicinity **Rachel** dies in childbirth, fulfilling her hope for **another son** (cf. 30:24). Jacob changes the ill-omened name "Son of My Sorrow" to "Son of the South" (or "Right").

A marauding tribe of "Southerners," perhaps meaning Benjaminites, is known to have molested the area around Haran in the eighteenth century, and it may be that part of that tribe migrated into Palestine (note that the P tradition places the birth of Benjamin in **Paddan-aram**, verse 26). The story in Judges 19–21 may preserve an explanation of how the once powerful tribe of Benjamin became the smallest of the Israelite tribes.

35:21-22b. The Sin of Reuben. From this point on, the J source regularly uses the name **Israel** for Jacob. The phrase translated in Micah 4:8, but such reference here seems improbable. Reuben's offense may have been an attempt to usurp his father's authority, but the passage is incomplete. The reference is included here no doubt to explain the primacy of Judah after Simeon, Levi (cf. chapter 34), and Reuben disqualified themselves for leadership (cf. 49:3-7; I Chronicles 5:1).

35:22c-29. The Death of Isaac. Verses 22c-26 give the P record of Jacob's sons. That all twelve were **born . . . in Paddan-aram** contradicts verses 16-18. According to the P chronology **Isaac** was one hundred years old when Jacob left home for Paddan-aram (25:26; 26:34; 27:46–28:5). That he should have survived eighty more years is in surprising contrast to the JE view in chapter 27 (cf. 27:41). Esau and Jacob bury their father just as Isaac and Ishmael bury Abraham (25:9).

36:1-43. Edomite Genealogies. The collection of Edomite genealogies (cf. I Chronicles 1:35-54) contains six lists which are surprising both for their similarities and for their discrepancies. The most obvious difficulty concerns their relation to the lists of Esau's wives in 26:34 and 28:9. The names in the two lists of verses 1-8, 15-19 closely parallel those of verses 9-14 with the supplement in verses 40-43. The words **these are the**

descendants of Esau indicate that the original lists were collected to form a part of the P traditions.

The lists of **Horites** (verses 20-30) and Edomite **kings** (verses 31-39) may derive from the J tradition, though this is far from demonstrable. The collection finishes the Jacob cycle of stories in similar fashion to the completion of the Abraham stories by the addition of the Ishmaelite genealogy in 25:12-18.

The historical value of these lists must be determined in the light of future archaeological investigation. They attest the early presence in southern Palestine and Edom of the Hurrians (**Horites**), who entered Mesopotamia in the second millennium, and suggest they were overthrown by Edomite nomads (cf. Deuteronomy 2:12, 22). The lists further indicate the formation in Edom of a monarchy in which kingship was not dynastic but elective, perhaps two centuries or more before its development in Israel. The kinship of the Edomites with the tribe of Judah is shown by some of the names—for example, **Zerah** (cf. 38:30) and **Shammah** (cf. I Samuel 16:9). Numerous references in the Old Testament indicate the relations between Edomites and Israelites.

C. The Story of Joseph (37:1–50:26)

The final section of Genesis—except chapters 38 and 49—is devoted to the story of Joseph. This narrative is distinguished from those of Abraham, Isaac, and Jacob both by its length and by its unified construction. The scenes together form a dramatic unity, in contrast with the disparate and often conflicting traditions about the other patriarchs. Cult legends, revelations of deity, and tribal history, which are prominent elsewhere in Genesis, are here secondary. Joseph emerges as an ideal figure of a wise man, whom the pharaoh finds fitted "to instruct his princes at his pleasure, and to teach his elders wisdom" (Psalm 105:22).

The narrative shows discrepancies and duplications and is generally considered a combination of J and E. Only a few

69

fragments from P are to be found. Use of the name Israel and emphasis on Judah among the brothers identify J material, while use of Jacob and the leadership of Reuben characterize E. These and other clues make it possible to identify the strands in many passages. At other points all attempts to isolate the two sources have proved unsatisfactory. So skillfully has the editor combined the parallel narratives that the successive scenes build up to a moving climax to which both accounts contribute.

The historical period in which the Joseph story is set is difficult to determine. Details about Egypt are accurate but give no indication of a probable date. The pharaoh is not identified, and the only personal names mentioned (37:36 and 41:45) are characteristic of the tenth century. Geographical references (45:10 and 47:11) point at the earliest to the thirteenth century, the probable time of Moses. Of other suggested clues the most significant is mention of a chariot (41:43). This, however, could be expected at any time after the latter half of the eighteenth century.

In sum, the picture of Egypt which emerges from the Joseph story seems to be contemporary with the J and E authors. There is no internal evidence for determining when the original events occurred.

37:1-11. *Joseph Arouses His Brothers' Jealousy.* The beginning of the narrative presents three reasons for the brothers' dislike of Joseph. In verse 2 it is his bearing **an ill report** of some of them to his father. If this verse is all from P—the evidence is contradictory—it suggests that this source contained some account of the brothers' crime against Joseph which the final editor omitted in favor of the much fuller JE narrative.

The other two reasons are his preferential treatment by his father and his dreams of preeminence. It is uncertain whether these represent different sources—in which case the statements that they **hated him the more** in verses 5 and 8 would be harmonizing additions of the editor.

37:3-4. Joseph is here apparently considered to be much younger than his brothers, though according to 30:22-24 he was scarcely the child of Jacob's **old age**. The exact meaning of the words translated **long robe with sleeves** (cf. II Samuel 13:18-19) is uncertain. The familiar King James translation "coat of many colours," which comes from the Septuagint, seems unlikely. The gift is a symbol of Joseph's privileged status and probably indicates that he stands above the necessity of manual labor. Laborers wore shorter garments to free their arms and legs.

37:5-11. This paragraph is attributed predominately to E (but contrast **mother,** with 35:19). **Dreams** play an important role in the story of Joseph. But these dreams are distinguished from those recorded earlier (e.g. 20:3-7; 31:11, 24) in that neither God nor an angel appears or speaks in them. No one in the story takes Joseph's dreams to be divine revelations, and the realization that they convey more than Joseph's youthful vanity is confirmed only in 42:6 and 50:18. The story proceeds without the aid of special divine intervention. God's providence, which is a basic premise to the entire story (cf. 50:20), is made known in human terms which must be interpreted and can be misunderstood.

37:12-36. *Joseph's Transfer to Egypt.* Surprisingly Jacob seems unaware of his sons' hostility toward Joseph and naïvely delivers him into their power. The site of **Dothan** lies about fifteen miles north of **Shechem,** well over sixty miles from **Hebron.** The incongruity of wearing the princely robe of verse 3 on a long foot journey may indicate differing sources, but attempts to identify the two strands in verses 12-20 are mostly unsatisfactory. It is evident, however, that in both the brothers plot to kill Joseph.

37:21-30. In these verses the account is clearly composite. According to J—verses 21, 25*b*-27, and 28*c*—**Judah** persuades the other brothers not to kill Joseph but instead to **sell him** to passing **Ishmaelites**—his second cousins! According to E—verses 22-25*a*, 28*ab*, and 28*d*-30—**Reuben** prevails on the others to throw Joseph alive into a **pit** (an empty cistern), from which **Midianites** kidnap him while the brothers are eating lunch.

37:31-35. Analysis of the sources in these verses has led to little agreement. The brothers' report to their father has been anticipated in verse 20, and the **long robe with sleeves** has been mentioned in verses 3 and 23. Jacob's reaction on hearing of Joseph's supposed death is to embark on life-long **mourning.** He finds no comfort in the thought of a reunion with his son in **Sheol,** the underworld.

37:36. The **Midianites** who, according to the E account have kidnapped Joseph and taken him to Egypt, sell him to **Potiphar,** a high official of **Pharaoh.**

38:1-30. *Judah and Tamar.* This story interrupts the Joseph story, with which it has no connection. It is perhaps from J.

Judah is here separated from his brothers and living in southern Palestine with the Canaanites. He has found a Canaanite wife and had sons, who have now reached the age of marriage. The chief interest of the narrative lies in Tamar's relationship to Judah. This story about two persons is apparently intended to indicate the way in which the tribe of Judah established itself in southern Palestine and produced the important families of Perez and Zerah, mentioned in Matthew 1:3 (cf. Ruth 4:18-22).

38:6-10. Judah arranges the marriage of his oldest son, **Er,** to Tamar, who is evidently also a Canaanite. When Er dies his brother **Onan** is required to beget by Tamar a son to become the heir of Er. This is levirate marriage—marriage to a brother-in-law—a widespread ancient custom (cf. Deuteronomy 25:5-10). Onan refuses to do this. It is not clear whether it is this refusal to perform the duty of a brother-in-law or the sexual act by which he evades the responsibility that is **displeasing in the sight of the LORD.**

It has been suggested that in the original tradition Onan's act may have been a practice associated with the Canaanite fertility cult (cf. the reference to Tamar as a cult prostitute, verses 21-22). After Onan's death Judah is required by the levirate to give his third son, **Shelah,** to Tamar. He fears for his son's life, however, assuming that Tamar has been responsible for the deaths of the other two. Therefore he tries to keep Shelah from her by indefinitely postponing the marriage.

38:12-23. Tamar, becoming aware of Judah's dishonesty, and determined to continue the name of her dead husband, takes matters into her own hands. She abandons her **widow's garments** and disguises herself as a **harlot**.

The Hebrew word used in verses 15 and 24 is the general term for a prostitute, whereas the word used in verses 21 and 22 denotes a cult prostitute. Though some have tried to differentiate the terms in this story, the latter meaning probably should be understood in verse 15. The precise significance of the **veil** and wrapped figure has not been discovered, but they evidently are the marks of a woman offering herself as a religious rite. For Tamar they are also a means to avoid recognition by Judah. The practice of cult prostitution was later forbidden in Israel but obviously sanctioned at the time described in this story (cf. verse 26), though Judah later takes pains to avoid any publicity.

His **signet** is a cylinder of wood, ivory, stone, or metal carved so that when rolled on moist clay it impresses a distinctive design identifying the owner. Near one end is a hole for a **cord** so that it may be hung around the neck. Archaeologists have found examples throughout the Near East.

38:24-30. When discovered to be pregnant, Tamar is deemed worthy of death, apparently because she is considered Shelah's betrothed and therefore guilty of adultery. She is vindicated by the exposure that because of Judah's refusal to give her Shelah she has tricked him into fulfilling the levirate obligation himself. The account of the birth of her twin sons is reminiscent of 25:24-26.

39:1-23. *Joseph and His Master's Wife.* The account of Joseph's unjust imprisonment comes entirely from J except the words **Potiphar, an officer of Pharaoh, the captain of the guard**, which are no doubt a repetition from 37:36 to harmonize this story with that of E.

Joseph is sold by the **Ishmaelites** to a man identified by J simply as **an Egyptian**. Joseph becomes his personal attendant, as well as **overseer of his house**. Because **the LORD was with him** Joseph gains the complete confidence of his master, and the Egyptian needs to care only about his own food (cf. 43:32).

39:6c-10. The harmonious state of affairs is disturbed when the mistress of the house solicits Joseph's affection. Joseph's refusal of her advances is based on honest regard for his master and a morality which Joseph considers God-given. His respect for his master and mistress as well as his fear of God determines his resistance to temptation. Joseph is portrayed in this story as the ideal wise man (cf. Proverbs 7). The use of **God** rather than Yahweh in verse 9 is not a sign of another source but a normal usage when an Israelite is speaking to a foreigner.

39:11-18. The woman finds opportunity for revenge. She produces damaging evidence against Joseph by forcing him to flee from her and leave his robe in her possession.

On **Hebrew** see above on 14:13. The term, which occurs three more times in the Joseph story (40:15; 41:12; 43:32), denotes here not an ethnic group but a social group of low status. Only gradually did it come to designate the people of Israel as a national entity (40:15 may contain something of this later meaning).

39:19-23. The punishment meted out to Joseph, a slave, for his presumed adultery is surprisingly mild. In Israel death was the usual penalty for adultery among free men.

A story similar to Joseph's experience with his master's wife is the Egyptian "Story of Two Brothers," which can be dated to the thirteenth century B.C. In it the older brother's wife tries unsuccessfully to seduce the unmarried younger brother and then accuses him. The woman's husband is finally persuaded of her guilt and kills her.

40:1-25. *Joseph the Interpreter of Dreams.* Joseph's gift for interpreting dreams is told by E (cf. 37:5-11). The situation differs from that in the preceding J account, where Joseph is in prison but has become supervisor of his fellow prisoners. Here he is a slave assigned to wait on two prominent officials who are **in custody of his master's house**.

Joseph's statement in verse 15*a* that he was **stolen out of the land of the Hebrews** agrees with 37:28*ab*. This leads to the assumption that the E narrative went directly from his purchase from the Midianites by Pharaoh's **captain of the guard** (37:36) to the events of this chapter. The J incident of the false accusation of Joseph by his master's wife was apparently not known to E. The references here to **prison** and **dungeon** were inserted by the editor in an attempt to smooth the connection between the two accounts.

40:5-19. In ancient times dreams were thought to be divine communications, and their interpretation was considered a science. Joseph is not trained in its techniques. Rather he believes that God-given dreams must be interpreted through God-given-inspiration. For the two similar dreams he presents opposing interpretations and thus demonstrates his gift. His requested payment for his service is only that he be remembered to **Pharaoh.** He is confident the king will rescue from slavery a freeborn man who has been kidnapped.

40:20-23. The confirmation of Joseph's interpretation is stated in the same words Joseph has used (verse 20; cf. verses 13, 19). Events occur precisely as he has said they would. But his chance for freedom is delayed two years (41:1) because of the happy butler's short memory.

41:1-57. *Joseph Becomes Vizier of Egypt.* The account of Pharaoh's dreams and Joseph's interpretation of them is a continuation of the narrative begun in chapter 40. It is therefore from E. Discrepancies and doublets in the second half of the chapter, however, reveal the existence of originally parallel narratives:

Pharaoh is to **select a man** in verse 33, but in verse 34 **overseers;** a **fifth** of the produce is to be gathered in verse 34, but in verse 35 **all the food;** verse 45*b* is parallel to verse 46*b*.

That **Potiphera** (verse 45; cf. 46:20) and Potiphar (37:36) bear practically the same name may be the result of independent traditions of Joseph's experience in Egypt. Since 37:36 is from E, verse 45 may be from J.

The notice about Joseph's age (verse 46*a*) is from P. This source apparently allowed thirteen years to elapse between Joseph's descent into Egypt (37:2) and his appointment as administrator (see below on 43:3-10).

41:33-36. Public storing of grain was common practice in

Egypt from early times. The narrative seems to represent Joseph as the originator of this policy.

41:37-41. Joseph's sudden elevation from slave to virtual ruler of Egypt is essentially a success story, showing that true wisdom comes from God (verse 38; contrast the **wise men** who could not interpret the dreams, verse 8). Such wisdom is self-authenticating, and its possessor is ultimately rewarded. It carries its own responsibility, which Joseph also recognizes and assumes. Pharaoh needs no other interpretation of his dreams, nor does he seek further advice for official policy. He respects Joseph's charismatic gift and entrusts to him responsibility for providing grain for the country.

41:42-44. Pharaoh's **signet ring** is similar to Judah's signet (see above on 38:12-23) but shaped to be worn on a finger. Its possession is a "blank check" to issue orders in the king's name. The other signs of Joseph's official position are authentically Egyptian: the splendid **garments of fine linen,** the **gold chain** of honor, the **chariot,** and the criers who precede Joseph when he goes out.

The horse and **chariot** were introduced into Egypt by the Hyksos invaders in the eighteenth century. Before this dignitaries were carried in sedan chairs. The precise meaning of the Hebrew word translated **Bow the knee!** is unknown. It may mean simply "make way."

41:45-57. Though the meaning of Joseph's new **name** is uncertain, it probably refers to an Egyptian god. **On** (Greek Heliopolis, "City of the Sun") was a cult center of the sun god Re located a few miles northeast of modern Cairo. The new name and marriage into the ranking priestly family in Egypt are reported simply. There is no hint either of a change of religion or of faithfulness to his father's faith. The impression is that Joseph becomes completely "at home" in Egypt, as the naming of his two sons suggests. Strange that he makes no effort to communicate with his father!

42:1-38. *Joseph's Brothers Visit Egypt.* The way is now prepared for Joseph's reunion with his father's family, the theme of chapters 42-45. Most of this chapter is generally credited to E.

However, the presence of several doublets (verses 1*a* and 2*a*, 5*a* and 6*b*, 7*a* and 8) reveals again the existence of originally parallel accounts.

42:1-25. Since Benjamin is not permitted to go with his brothers to Egypt, one of Joseph's intentions is a reunion with his younger brother. His treatment of his brothers cannot be rationally accounted for. They are now in his power, not he in theirs. Revenge is clearly a motive, but scarcely dominant, especially in the light of 50:20.

Joseph has to satisfy himself about the attitudes and motives of his brothers, and the methods he employs are psychologically credible. He accuses them of being **spies** and intimidates them with a three-day **prison** sentence. Then, overhearing how Reuben meant to rescue him, he keeps the second oldest brother **Simeon,** as hostage for the return of the others with Benjamin.

42:26-35. Finding the money in the grain sacks is an enigmatic and ominous sign to the troubled family. Joseph has meant it to be a gift.

Verses 27-28*a*, which relate how one of the brothers discovers his money **at the lodging place,** contradict both verse 25, in which Joseph supplies provisions that make using the grain along the way unnecessary, and verse 35, in which the brothers are dismayed to find the money after arriving home. That verses 27-28*a* are an insertion from the J account can be seen by the reference to them in 43:21 and the use in them of an unusual Hebrew word for "sack" which is used also in the J narrative of chapters 43-44. Probably verse 28*b* originally followed the discovery of the money in verse 35.

42:36-38. On hearing of the vizier's demand to see **Benjamin,** Jacob accuses his sons of sacrificing his children one by one. **Reuben** offers to sacrifice his own **two sons** if Benjamin does not return in safety from Egypt.

The narrative in this chapter looks forward to an immediate second trip to release Simeon. Therefore it is likely that in the original E account Jacob acceded to Reuben's offer (his response is no doubt to be found in 43:14). To harmonize with the J idea of a delayed second trip (cf. 43:2) the editor rearranged Jacob's replies and placed here verse 38 from J. The result is to make Jacob appear unconcerned about what happens to his son Simeon so long as Benjamin is safe.

43:1-34. ***The Brothers' Return to Egypt.*** The story of the brothers' second trip to Egypt comes from J, as shown by the name **Israel** rather than Jacob. The journey occurs only after the grain secured the first time has been **eaten,** and the reason for it is the severity of the **famine,** not the freeing of Simeon. It is clear that in this account the only pressure exerted by Joseph was a refusal to sell more grain unless Benjamin should come on the next trip. The release of Simeon in verse 23 is an editorial harmonization.

43:3-10. It is **Judah** rather than Reuben (cf. 42:37) who according to J speaks for the brothers and offers himself as surety for Benjamin's safe return. Later in this account Judah takes the lead in all negotiations with Joseph. The conversation seems to call for a reply by the father after verse 7. Perhaps 42:38 originally appeared at this point (see above on 42:36-38).

Benjamin is here called a **lad** (verse 8; cf. **my son,** verse 29). Evidently his age is reckoned on a different basis from the P chronology, according to which Joseph has been in Egypt over twenty years (cf. 37:2; 41:46*a*, 53-54). Some have conjectured that in the original J story Benjamin was born only after Joseph was in Egypt (cf. verse 7; 37:3).

43:11-15. Having yielded to Judah's plea, the anxious father spares no pains in seeking to assure the favor of the Egyptian vizier. He sends some of the precious products of Palestine and **double the money** for grain—that is, the money Joseph returned and an equal amount for the impending purchase.

43:16-25. The brothers present themselves to Joseph at his office, where he sees Benjamin and directs that they be received at his **house.** The frightened brothers speak anxiously with the **steward** and offer to return all the money they found in their sacks (on **in full weight** see above on 23:12-16). The steward apparently knows Joseph's purpose. He congratulates them on their good fortune and informs them of Joseph's invitation to dine **at noon.**

43:26-34. Joseph's emotion on seeing Benjamin is effectively described. At the meal the guests are seated **by themselves,** apart from Joseph and separated from the other Egyptians (on **Hebrews** see above on 14:13; 39:6*b*-18). Much to their astonishment the brothers are placed according to their age. They are honored by **portions** of food served **from Joseph's table,** but Benjamin receives **five times** the honor. The number five is prominent in this story (cf. 41:34; 45:22; 47:2, 24); its significance is not understood. In pleasant conviviality the brothers forget their anxiety and enjoy their feast.

44:1-34. *Joseph Sets the Climactic Trial.* Joseph has one more test for his unsuspecting brothers, and the J narrator records it with dramatic skill. In the evening (cf. verse 3) Joseph instructs the steward to place his **silver cup** in Benjamin's sack of grain. Then, after the brothers have departed, he is to overtake them and accuse them, specifically Benjamin, of stealing it. The note about placing the money in the sacks is apparently a gloss, since there is no mention in verses 11-12 of finding it.

The precise way in which a cup was used to **divine** is not known. In general it appears that water or oil was poured into it and conclusions were drawn from the figures suggested by the motion of the liquid when small objects were dropped into it. The theft of such an object was a serious crime.

44:17. When the brothers are brought before him, Joseph insists that only the guilty man suffer for the crime. This is designed to make the brothers reveal decisively their solicitude for their father. Will they again confront him coldly with the death of his favorite son?

44:18-34. Judah's speech is a good example of Hebrew eloquence. He recounts the events which have led up to the present dilemma—naturally omitting the circumstances surrounding the death of Benjamin's brother. He describes his father's fear of losing Benjamin and what confirmation of that premonition would do to him. Finally he offers to take Benjamin's place **as a slave** in Joseph's household if only his brother may be redeemed. The effect of this speech on Joseph is overpowering, and the narrator moves swiftly to his conclusion.

45:1-27. *Joseph's Self-Disclosure.* The climactic chapter of the Joseph story is a scene of great dramatic impact. Only on second reading does one notice the signs that the J and E narratives have again come together. Though precise separation is not possible at every point, the major blocks can be readily recognized.

45:3-5a. Joseph twice announces his identity, and in each case his following words reveal the source. Since in J Joseph has already asked about his **father** and been reassured (43:27-28), verse 3 must be from E. In Verses 4-5a his reference to being **sold** to the Ishmaelites (37:28c) shows the source is J.

45:5b-8. The name **God** identifies these verses as from E. In them Joseph reinforces his forgiveness of his brothers. He generously insists that God has providentially ordered his fate for the sake of Jacob's family. It was not the brothers' evil intent that was responsible for Joseph's transference to Egypt, but God's will **to preserve life.** This interpretation of their experience will deliver the brothers both from fear of revenge and from mutual recrimination of the kind illustrated in 42:22. They are not absolved of their guilt, but it now can be accepted in the light of God's overarching, all-inclusive providence. This is the recurring theological theme of the Joseph story (cf. 50:20).

45:9-28. In verses 9-11 Joseph on his own authority invites his entire family to move to Egypt and settle **in the land of Goshen.** In verses 16-20 **Pharaoh** hears of the brothers and is delighted at the opportunity to show his gratitude to Joseph by inviting the family to come and enjoy **the best of the land of Egypt.** The two invitations might seem compatible except that later (46:31–47:6) it is told how after the family arrive Joseph carefully coaches his brothers in what to say to Pharaoh in order to secure his permission to settle in Goshen. Thus in one account, which can be identified as J, Joseph informs Pharaoh of his family only after they have arrived in Egypt. In the other, the E account, it is Pharaoh himself who proposes the migration.

Goshen, evidently located in the northeastern part of the Nile delta, is probably the modern Wadi Tumilat, between Port Said and Suez. The Egyptian capital was not **near** this region till the time of Moses.

45:28–46:27. *Israel Goes to Egypt.* The traditions now provide an answer to the question, How did our people ever come to be in Egypt? The J conception of the decision to visit Egypt is presented as an independent choice (45:28–46:1*a*). E represents it as obedience to God's special command, characteristically revealed in a dream, to leave the Promised Land (verses 1*b*-5). The narrator emphasizes the divine purpose which brings the chosen people down into Egypt—from famine and destruction to food and prosperity—and which later will bring them out of slavery into freedom.

46:6-27. These verses bear the unmistakable marks of P. The list of the descendants of Israel entering Egypt appears with some change in Numbers 26:5-50 (cf. I Chronicles 2–8; also Exodus 6:14-16 for Reuben, Simeon, and Levi). Its artificiality is apparent: Jacob's concubines are each credited with half as many male descendants as their mistresses (Leah thirty-three, Zilpah sixteen; Rachel 14, Bilhah 7). Benjamin, the "lad" (see above on 43:3-10), already has a large family.

The author got his total of **seventy** from a tradition in which it was a conventional round number (cf. Numbers 11:16 and Judges 8:30). He stretched the facts a bit to make it exact by counting **Er and Onan,** who **died in the land of Canaan** (cf. 38:7, 10), and Joseph's two sons, who were born **in the land of Egypt** (cf. 41:50-52). The subtotal **sixty-six** may be a gloss pointing out that these four do not fit. **Dinah,** like the **sons' wives,** is apparently not included in the count.

46:28–47:12. *The Arrival in Egypt.* Verse 28 is the continuation of verse 1*a* in the J narrative and therefore **He** means **Israel.** The purpose of sending Judah ahead is obscured by a textual corruption for which the ancient versions offer little help (see footnote in the Revised Standard Version).

This narrative is in contrast with the E story, where it was Pharaoh who suggested the migration to Egypt (see above on 45:9-28). Joseph here has already settled his family in Goshen and must now use his skill as a courtier to inform the king of their presence and get permission for them to stay. He carefully instructs his brothers to stress that they are **shepherds** in order to be assigned to **Goshen**. This was a border territory which otherwise might seem a risky place to settle aliens.

The explanation of an Egyptian prejudice against shepherds cannot be confirmed from Egyptian sources and seems to be an exaggeration. The purpose may be to underscore Egyptian suspicions of immigrants from the north.

47:1-12. The continuation of the preceding J story is found in verses 1-4. A P story of Jacob's interview with Pharaoh appears in verses 7-11. But in verses 5 and 6 the ending of one and the beginning of the other have been confused. The Septuagint apparently preserves the correct order and also some original explanatory material which has dropped out of the Hebrew text. Thus the proper ending of the J story is that Pharaoh tells Joseph that his brothers may settle in Goshen and that some may be appointed as royal herdsmen. Then the P account should begin as given in the Septuagint: "And Jacob and his sons came into Egypt to Joseph. And Pharaoh, king of Egypt, heard of it. And Pharaoh said to Joseph." Verses 5b-6b and 7-11 follow this. Verse 12 returns to the J account.

The land of Rameses is anachronistic. Evidently it means the region around the city of Rameses (or Raamses, Exodus 1:11 and 12:37). This city was built by Ramses II (1290-1224), probably with the help of Hebrew slaves, as described in Exodus 1:8-14.

47:13-26. *Joseph's Agrarian Policy.* This section, which tells how all Egypt except priestly possessions became Pharaoh's property and all Egyptians his slaves, is unconnected with the Joseph story. Is one to imagine that Jacob's sons are exempted from this enslavement? Or is this incident perhaps a parallel to Exodus 1:8 in accounting for Israel's enslavement in Egypt?

Though this material is often attributed entirely to J, its literary analysis and its connection with 41:34-35, 55-57 are quite uncertain. The statements concerning the 20 percent tax follow strangely after verse 23, according to which the land and people belong to Pharaoh.

47:27–48:22. *Jacob's Last Words.* The various accounts of Jacob's deathbed sayings from the three sources bring the Joseph story to its close.

47:27-31. According to P (verses 27*b*-28) Jacob survives his journey to Egypt by **seventeen years.** The other sources imply, however, that his death occurs soon after his arrival.

That verses 27*a* and 29-31 are from J is suggested by the oath by the genital organ (see above on 24:1-9). Jacob desires to be buried **out of Egypt.** Traditions about the place vary, however, so there may be some editorial harmonizing in verse 30 (see below on 49:28*b*–50:14).

Verse 31*b* is obscure. The Hebrew can be read to give the Septuagint translation quoted in Hebrews 11:21, "over the head of his staff." The significance of the gesture is unknown (cf. I Kings 1:47).

48:1-7. The account of Jacob's blessing of Joseph's sons derives from all three sources. That a new source begins in verses 1-2 is obvious: in 47:29-31 Israel, knowing his death is approaching, has called Joseph and given him instructions for his burial. Now Joseph is told of Jacob's illness and goes to him, taking his two sons. Here, then, is the beginning of the E story of Jacob's deathbed blessing of the two boys.

Verses 3-6 present the P account of the blessing, which is strictly tribal rather than personal. Jacob gives to **Ephraim and Manasseh** the status of full tribes and orders that future sons of Joseph are to be counted as clans of those two tribes. The notice about Rachel's death has no connection with what precedes or follows. Since it contains both P and E material, it must be a later insertion.

48:8-12. Despite the use of **Israel** throughout the rest of this chapter, it is obviously derived from both J and E. Though closely interwoven, the strands can for the most part be traced.

The implication of verses 8-9*a* that Jacob is meeting his grandsons for the first time fits the situation of the E narrative, in which he has just arrived in Egypt (46:5). The explanation of his blindness in verse 10*a*, however, contradicts the statement that he **saw** the boys and is therefore from J. The E account continues

83

in verses 10b-12, with Jacob rejoicing to **see** Joseph's sons. The ceremony of placing the children on their grandfather's **knees** is part of the rite of adoption which was apparently so well known as to require no description.

48:13-19. The reason for the J mention of Jacob's dim eyesight is now seen in Joseph's care to guide the sons to him so that his **right hand,** conferring the greater blessing, will be placed on the head of the **first-born.** But Jacob insists on **crossing his hands** in spite of Joseph's efforts to **remove** them. He explains his action by predicting that the **younger brother** will become the **greater**—that is, the tribe of Ephraim will play a superior role in Israel's history (cf. Ephraim as the usual name for the northern kingdom in Hosea).

Since verses 15-16 interrupt this account, they are either out of order or, more probably, from E. In them Jacob's care in identifying the God of blessing as the God of his fathers, who has led and redeemed him, is noteworthy. For Jacob's experiences of the **angel** of God see 28:12; 31:11-13; and 32:1-2.

48:20-22. Though the connection is by no means certain, verse 20 appears to be the conclusion of the blessing of verses 15-16. If so, E joins J and P (verse 5) in attributing Ephraim's preeminence to Jacob's dying words.

Mountain slope (literally "shoulder") evidently refers to Shechem (the same Hebrew word; see above on 12:6-7). But the saying comes from a tradition different both from that in 34:30, where Jacob condemns his sons for their deed at Shechem, and from that in 33:19, where Jacob purchases a piece of ground at Shechem. It seems also to imply that Jacob has already allotted to his other sons their inheritances.

49:1-28a. *The Blessing of Jacob.* This careful compilation of oracles concerning the tribes of Israel contains sayings which differ in significance, type, and age. The oracles taken as a whole refer to no single historical period and seem to be arranged partly by the sons' ages and partly by geography. The statements are unified in a single poem only because of their artificial setting as the words of the aged Jacob to his sons, a picture which is not consistently maintained throughout. Therefore, the final collecting of this ancient material was done probably during the era of David or Solomon.

The implicit situation is the tribal confederacy during the period of the judges rather than the patriarchal family. The collection should be compared with the tribal descriptions in the Song of Deborah (Judges 5:14-18), which are unified and may be older, and the Blessing of Moses (Deuteronomy 33:6-25), which is later.

49:3-4. *Reuben,* Jacob's **first-born,** because of his crime against his father (cf. 35:22) is destined for political obscurity (cf. Judges 5:15-16). This tribe, which once must have been powerful, apparently lost interest in the Israelite confederacy, preferring nomadic life east of the Jordan (cf. Joshua 13:16-23).

49:5-7. *Simeon and Levi* were responsible for the massacre at Shechem (34:25, 30), to which this oracle may refer. They are represented as cruel and dangerous men (tribes) who lost whatever land they originally possessed. Simeon, if it ever existed independently as a tribe, was absorbed by Judah (cf. Joshua 19:1-9 with 15:26-32, 42). The connection between the tribe of Levi and the Levitical priesthood is far from clear.

49:8-12. *Judah,* after the elimination of the three oldest sons, assumes the leading position among the tribes. The oracle extols Judah's prowess in war and the respect which his obedient and grateful brothers give him. The prosperity of his people will be like that of Paradise (verses 11-12).

An unsolved difficulty is the proper understanding of verse 10c. The translations "until Shiloh come" (King James Version) and **until he comes to whom it belongs** illustrate the two possibilities for interpreting the crucial Hebrew word *shiloh*— either as a proper name or as a combination of words. There are objections to both possibilities, and agreement on the interpretation of the passage is therefore impossible. A messianic interpretation, in view of the situation in verses 11-12 and the presumed royal symbols in verse 10ab, is often urged. But against this view one must add that the symbols may be tribal rather than monarchical and that the literary unity of the passage is not entirely certain. The thought seems to be that

Judah will exercise tribal authority (cf. Judges 1:1-2) until the monarchy is established with a Judahite on the throne, at which time peace and prosperity will become proverbial.

49:13. *Zebulon* is simply located on the Phoenician coast, in contrast with its position as stated in Joshua 19:10-16 or presupposed in Judges 12:11-12. The tribe was at one time apparently forced to move.

49:14-15. *Issachar* too gave up its original territory, exchanging freedom for servitude with a promise of ease and comfort (cf. 30:18). The tribe is not mentioned in Judges 1, but its courage in war was well known (Judges 5:18).

49:16-18. *Dan* was apparently one of the weakest of the tribes, but it used its strength as effectively as a snake against a horse and **rider.** The Danites were among the last of the Israelites to secure permanent territory and had to change their area of settlement several times (cf. Judges 1:34 and 18:1-31; also Joshua 19:47-48). Verse 18 bears no relation to the oracles; it marks the middle of the song.

49:19. *Gad,* on the eastern side of the Jordan, could effectively repulse marauding bands of nomads, but eventually succumbed to them (Jeremiah 49:1). A. G. Herbert has reproduced in English the word play of the Hebrew by changing the tribal name to "Rad" and translating: "Raiders shall raid Rad, but he shall raid at their heels."

49:20. *Asher* has a rich land which produces **royal dainties** (cf. Deuteronomy 33:24); therefore he is "happy" (cf. 30:11).

49:21. *Naphtali* was situated on the western shore of Lake Gennesaret in a fertile area (cf. Deuteronomy 33:23). The oracle about the tribe cannot be interpreted.

49:22-26. *Joseph* is treated in a text that is corrupt and difficult to translate. The oracle was apparently composed when it was still a single tribe, before the emergence of Ephraim and Manasseh. The verses stress Joseph's importance (cf. I Chronicles 5:2)—his economic and military prosperity because of God's **help** and the **blessings** invoked on him (cf. Deuteronomy 33:13-16).

49:27-28a. *Benjamin*, whose warriors included seven hundred left-handed sharpshooters (Judges 20:16), was renowned for its predatory abilities. Verse 28a (through **said to them**) is the conclusion to the collection.

49:28b-50:14. *Jacob's Death and Burial.* At least two traditions of the location of Jacob's grave existed:

(1) the cave of **Machpelah**, where the other patriarchs were buried, as reported in P;
(2) a **tomb** prepared by Jacob himself **beyond the Jordan** (50:10), found in material generally attributed to J (but contrast "in their burying place," (47:30).

According to P Jacob's last words (49:29-32) are a request to his sons to bury him in the **cave . . . in the field of Machpelah,** that small parcel of the Promised Land which thus far has been acquired by Israel (chapter 23; cf. the garbled reference in Acts 7:16), along with **Sarah** (23:19), **Abraham** (25:9), and the rest of his family, whose burials are not elsewhere recorded (except Rachel's, 35:19; cf. 48:7). Jacob then dies, and the sons obey his request.

According to J Jacob has given his burial instructions to Joseph alone (47:29-31) before blessing his sons and grandsons. On his death Joseph orders the body **embalmed** according to Egyptian practice. He is mourned **seventy days,** the period reported by the Greek historian Diodorus as normally allotted to a royal funeral in Egypt. Joseph then secures permission from Pharaoh for all the family, as well as Egyptian officials, to journey to Transjordan—to **the threshing floor of Atad,** the location of which is unknown—and return after the burial. In combining the accounts the editor has given the impression that Atad is merely a stopping place for **mourning** on the way from Egypt to Machpelah, whereas Transjordan is actually far beyond **Mamre.**

50:15-21. *Conclusion of the Joseph Story.* After Jacob's death the brothers' anxiety mounts—Joseph may have been waiting for this moment to seek revenge. The E narrator, however, emphasizes again God's providence (cf. 45:5b-8). The matter of the brothers' guilt is included in their deliverance from famine and death. The final verdict has been given. Nothing further need be said: **You meant evil . . . .; God meant . . . good.** How can Joseph add to or detract from what God has done?

The mystery of human freedom and necessity here receives classic statement, and the paradox humbles Joseph and his brothers before one another and before God. Joseph's forgiveness is his acceptance of that divine providential care which includes his brothers' evil deed. There is no possibility of accepting the one without the other, and "brotherly love" thus becomes an expression of humble gratitude for the mystery of divine providence.

50:22-26. Joseph lives to see his great-grandchildren in Egypt and dies after what was considered an ideal life span, **a hundred and ten years** (cf. Joshua 24:29). The E narrative concludes the story of Joseph with the reminder of God's promise of land to the patriarchs and the certainty of the exodus of their descendants from Egypt. Later in this account Joseph's mummy in its sarcophagus is to be carried out of Egypt by Moses (Exodus 13:19) and buried at Shechem (Joshua 24:32).

THE BOOK OF EXODUS

John Gray

INTRODUCTION

Scope and Significance

Exodus is the second of the five books of the Law known as the
Pentateuch. The title, Greek for "going out," comes from the
Septuagint. It indicates that the book tells of the fundamental
experience of God's active power and grace and moral purpose
which formed the factual basis of Israel's faith—namely the
deliverance from Egypt.

The law and the covenant are here placed in the context of
history. Israel continued to experience this history sacramentally
in its drama of salvation at the great central sanctuaries, when the
various tribal groups met to realize their unity in the common
faith. Thus the book presents not only the deliverance itself
(chapters 1-15) and certain traditions of the desert wandering
(chapters 16-18) but the encounter with Yahweh at Mt. Sinai
(chapters 19-40).

After the saving act which was the beginning of Israel, even as
the event of Jesus Christ was the beginning of the Christian
church, God engaged Israel in its divine destiny through the
covenant. God revealed God's nature and will in the law—moral
principles and ritual observances designed to emphasize and
maintain Israel's distinctive status as his "peculiar people."

These principles and rituals comprise:

(1) the categorical imperative of moral law in the nucleus of the Decalogue (20:2-17);

(2) commands to safeguard the worship and ethic of the distinctive people in the Ritual Code (34:14-26);

(3) regulations for a comparatively complex society in the Book of the Covenant (20:23-23:33).

The disproportionately long passage on the sanctuary and its service (chapters 25-31 and 35-40) reflects the interest of late priestly editors in the rehabilitation of people and cult after the Babylonian Exile.

The essence of the book is in the Ten Commandments—the Decalogue—and its historical introduction (20:2), where law and grace are associated in a formula relating directly to the covenant. The recurrence of these themes in the Old Testament indicates the main source of the tradition of the law in the context of covenant—especially in the covenant sacrament.

Sources

Exodus is a composite work assembled during at least half a millennium. There are doublets and discrepancies. There are differences in style—hymn, narrative prose, legal formula, saga, and cult drama—and in theology. These and other clues in the book distinguish the components of three of the main literary sources of the Pentateuch: Yahwist (J), Elohist (E), and Priestly (P).

There are evidences of two stages of P, with a final fusion of the two that supplied the framework of the Pentateuch. The traces of elaboration by the Deuteronomic editor (D) are very slight. The passages attributed to the several sources are shown in the table on pages 92 and 93.

J, E, and P are the literary crystallization of earlier traditions of miscellaneous character and worth. The originally independent bodies of tradition underlying J, E, and P in this book include:

(1) The exodus tradition proper. This was developed with additions from secular saga as the cult legend of the passover when it was a public festival, perhaps at Gilgal (on saga see under Genesis 12:1–50:26).

(2) The tradition of the covenant with the law at Sinai. This developed also with saga accretions as the cult legend of the feast of tabernacles or booths, originally at Shechem.

(3) The tradition of the desert wandering, including a hero saga about Moses at Kadesh and a number of self-contained traditions associated with Kadesh which were not necessarily the record of a sequence of events.

J and E endeavor, not too successfully, to combine these elements into a consecutive narrative. P completes a topographical framework; the late and artificial nature of this, however, rules out our assuming a consistent unity for the whole.

The fact that these traditions developed in cult legends, which were important sources of J and E, does not argue against their genuine historical origin. The frank admission that the Hebrews shared the desert sanctuary of Yahweh with the Midianites—or Kenites (cf. Judges 1:16; 4:11)—is a very strong argument for the historicity and genuine antiquity of the worship of Israel here and indeed of the covenant itself. Israel's continued affinity in historical times with the Kenites seems to support the tradition of their common association with the worship of Yahweh at the holy mountain. Similarly the enmity of Israel toward Amalek, and the memory of the narrative of Saul late in the eleventh century that Amalek waylaid Israel on the way up from Egypt (I Samuel 15:2), supports the historicity of the tradition in 17:8-16.

Sources of Exodus

Most of the content of Exodus appears to come from the three strands of tradition in the columns below. The Decalogue (20:1-17) and Book of the Covenant (20:22–23:33), and perhaps the Ritual Code (34:14-26), seem to have been inserted from other ancient sources. Other probable insertions in the two earlier sources are:1:20*b*-21; 3:19-22; 4:14-16; 9:1-7, 14-16, 31-32; 10:1*b*-2; 11:2-3, 9-10; 12:25-27*a*(D), 35-36; 13:3*b-d*, 5, 8-9(D), 14-16(D); 14:25, 27*b*; 15:19-21*a*, 26(D); 16:8; 18:2-4; 19:3*b*-6(D), 9*b*, 23-24*a*; 24:2, 12*c*, 14-15*a*; 32:8*bc*, 13, 34*b*, 35*b*; 33:2, 5*a*, 18, 19*b*; 34:1*b*, 11*b*-13, 14*b*-16(D).

SOURCES OF EXODUS

J (Yahwist)	E (Elohist)	P (Priestly)
1:6, 8-12	1:15-20a, 22	1:1-5, 7, 13-14
2:11-23a	2:1-10	2:23b-25
3:2-4a, 5, 7-8, 16-18	3:1, 4b, 6, 9-15	
4:1-13, 19-20a, 22-26, 29-31	4:17-18, 20b-21, 27-28	
5:3, 5-23	5:1-2, 4	
6:1		6:2-30
7:14-15a, 16-17a, 18, 20a, 21a, 22, 24-25	7:15b, 17b, 20b	7:1-13, 19, 21b, 23
8:1-4, 8-15a, 20-32		8:5-7, 15b-19
9:13, 17-21, 23b, 24b-30, 33-34	9:22-23a, 24a, 35ab	9:8-12, 35c
10:1a, 3-11, 13b, 14-15a, 15c-19, 24-26, 28-29	10:12-13a, 13c, 15b, 20-23, 27	
11:4-8	11:1	
12:21-24, 27b, 29-34, 38-39		12:1-20, 28, 37, 40-50
13:3a, 4, 6-7, 10-13, 21-22	13:17-19	13:1-2, 20

14:5-7, 9a, 10-14, 19b-20a, 21b, 24, 27cd, 30, 31	14:19a, 20b	14:1-4, 8, 9b, 15-18, 20c-21a, 21c-23, 26-27a, 28-29
15:1-18, 21bc, 22b-25a	15:25b	15:22a, 27
16:4-5, 13b-15a, 27-30		16:1-3, 6-7, 9-13a, 15b-26, 31-36
17:2c-3, 7a, c	17:1b-2b, 4-6, 7b, 8-16	17:1a
	18:1, 5-27	
19:9a, 11b-13a, 15, 18, 20-22, 24b-25	19:2b-3a, 7-8, 10-11a, 13b-14, 16-17, 19	19:1-2a
	20:18-21	
24:1, 9-11	24:3-8, 12ab, 13, 18b	24:15b-18a
		25:1-31; 18a
	31:18b	
32:7-8a, 9-12, 14	32:1-6, 15-34a, c, 35a	
33:1, 3-4, 7-17, 19a, c, 20-23	33:5b-6	
34:1a, 2-11a, 14a, 17-28, 34-35		34:29-33
		35:1—40:38

Historical Background

The history of the Hebrews in Egypt and the date of their departure and settlement in Palestine are problems with no simple solution. The biblical traditions speak only of "Pharaoh." Explicit chronological statements of the latest source are contradicted by evidence implicit in the earlier strands. References in Egyptian records from the twentieth, fourteenth, and thirteenth centuries to the passage of nomads to and from the Delta—"after the manner of their fathers from the beginning," as one inscription states—confirm the historical probability of a Hebrew sojourn in this area. On the other hand, they show that identification of a particular group is hardly to be expected in these sources. Archaeological findings in Palestine are also significant but inconclusive. Basically we must rely on analysis of the biblical traditions.

I Kings 6:1 synchronizes the founding of the temple in Solomon's fourth year (*ca.* 965) with the 480th year after the Exodus, pointing to a fifteenth century date (of around 1445, cf. Judges 11:26). This fits with the theory of some scholars that Joseph rose to power while Egypt was under the Hyksos, "rulers of foreign lands" (about 1750-1570)—kings who came from Asia. Papyrus documents show that they employed some persons with Semitic names as officers. The rise of a "new king . . . who did not know Joseph" (1:8) may refer to the overthrow of the Hyksos by the founder of the native Egyptian eighteenth dynasty. On this assumption the oppression of the Hebrews became especially severe under Thutmose III (1490-1439), who carried on a large building program while extending his empire into northern Syria. Their escape occurred perhaps in the reign of his son Amenhotep II (1439-1406).

The cuneiform tablets discovered at Tell el-Amarna, site of Akhetaton, the capital of Amenhotep IV (Akhenaton, 1369-1353), include letters from vassals in Palestine asking for help in withstanding attacks by Habiru. If the Hebrews led by Moses left Egypt in the fifteenth century, they presumably began their occupation of Palestine early in the fourteenth century. Thus they might be the Habiru of the Amarna tablets. For these and other reasons a number of scholars have favored a fifteenth century date for the Exodus.

There are serious difficulties with this date, however. The pharaohs of the eighteenth dynasty had their capital at Thebes, some 400 miles up the Nile. They apparently did little if any building in the eastern Delta region, where the biblical traditions clearly locate the events leading up to the Exodus.

Thutmose III and most of his successors down to near the end of the thirteenth century were engaged in constant military campaigns in Palestine. On the assumption of a fifteenth century date for the Exodus this activity must have extended well into the age of the Israelite judges, yet there is no reflection of it in the Old Testament.

Archaeological research east and southeast of the Dead Sea has shown no settled occupation there during the nineteenth to fourteenth centuries. But the traditions tell of established nations of Edom and Moab which the Israelites had to skirt around in their trek through this territory.

The terms "Habiru" and "Hebrew" are probably related. However, references to Habiru in documents from widely scattered times and places prevent our identifying all of them with the Hebrews who left Egypt with Moses. The term seems to have denoted, not an ethnic group, but a social class of displaced persons, including political refugees. The Habiru of the Amarna letters may represent peoples later incorporated in Israel—for example, with the references to the Habiru near Shechem cf. Genesis 34. They were not necessarily those involved in the Exodus. Thus the only strong support for a fifteenth century date seems to be I Kings 6:1.

The author of I Kings 6:1 may have calculated his 480 years by multiplying a tradition of twelve generations by the conventional forty years for a generation. If so, recalculation with the more realistic average of twenty-five years per generation gives the date 1265, which is within the period of the nineteenth dynasty now favored by most scholars.

The second king of this dynasty, Seti I (1302-1290), fortified the eastern Delta area as a base for operations through Palestine against the Hittites in Syria. Ramses II (1290-1224) continued and enlarged his father's program in that region. He built Pithom and Raamses (1:11), or Rameses (12:37; Numbers 33:3-5), which he made his chief residence and capital. He was one of several pharaohs whose records mention forced labor by Apiru, probably the Egyptian equivalent of Habiru. His son Merneptah (1224-1214) in an inscription of his fifth year boasts of conquering several cities in Palestine and also the people of Israel.

The biblical traditions speak of two pharaohs oppressing the Hebrews (cf. 1:8; 2:23; 4:19). Moses is described as born and growing up during the reign of the first and leading the deliverance from the second. Since the P source regularly gives exaggerated ages, the statement that Moses was eighty years old when he appeared before the second pharaoh (7:7) is not to be taken seriously, but he was evidently a mature man. Therefore at one time it was widely accepted that Ramses II was the pharaoh who initiated the oppression and that the internal and external troubles which marked the succession of his son Merneptah made possible the escape of the Hebrew serfs around 1220. A few scholars, ignoring the Palestinian context of the reference to the Israelites in Merneptah's inscription, even suggested that it was his effort to claim their escape into the desert as a victory over them.

Archaeological evidence of a major disturbance in Palestine around the time of Merneptah's accession, however, now seems to indicate that the escaping Hebrews were in Palestine by this time. Therefore the Exodus must be dated earlier, during the reign of Ramses II. Some scholars, taking the death of Seti I as the occasion for Moses' return to Egypt (cf. 2:23; 4:19), date the event early in Ramses' reign, around 1290-1280. This view of course requires assuming (1) that the tradition has erred in representing Moses' birth and upbringing in the Egyptian court as occurring during the oppression begun by Seti; or (2) the tradition has telescoped a change in policy toward the Hebrews by one of the kings of the eighteenth dynasty with Seti's inauguration of forced labor on building projects in the eastern Delta.

Though the evidence, both in the tradition and from archaeology, is too complex and contradictory for any certainty, the most probable date for the Exodus now seems to be about the middle of the thirteenth century. On this assumption Seti I, the "new king . . . who did not know Joseph" (1:8), began impressing the Hebrews of the eastern Delta for his building operations at the beginning of the century. After his death, which the tradition has misplaced to a later point in the narrative (2:23), Ramses II stepped up the forced labor for a massive building program in this region, which extended over many years.

Somewhere around 1250 a sizable group of the serfs managed to escape into the desert. There they spent a number of years, which the tradition later magnified to the conventional round number forty. At length they made their way into Palestine. With the help of kindred groups already in the land, they attacked some of the Canaanite city-states which were vassals of Egypt. On one occasion a body of the attackers, which may or may not have represented the group that escaped from Egypt, engaged the army of Merneptah, with results that the pharaoh commemorated in his inscription.

I. The Great Deliverance (1:1–15:21)

A. Beginning of the Oppression (1:1–2:25)

1:1-7. *Transition.* To link the patriarchal history with the originally independent exodus theme the P source (verses 1-5, 7) renames the twelve sons of Jacob who came to Egypt with their families (on **seventy** see Genesis 46:6-27). The large number of their descendants are noted, reflecting the promise to Abraham (cf. Genesis 12:2; 17:6) and anticipating the oppression. The traditions assume that all the tribes sojourned in Egypt and were delivered in the Exodus, but probably only a few of them were involved.

Verse 6 may be the ending of the J story of Joseph. **They**

multiplied and grew exceedingly strong (cf. verse 20*b*) is apparently a fragment from J leading up to the hostility of Pharaoh in verses 9-10. **The land** is actually not the whole land of Egypt but the eastern Delta, including Goshen (cf. Genesis 47:4), which was used by nomads for seasonal grazing.

1:8-14. *Forced Labor.* On the **new king** see the Introduction. During the eighteenth and nineteenth dynasties Egypt's empire in Palestine and Syria required continual military action against invasion from the outside and rebellion within. Remembering the Hyksos (see Introduction) the pharaohs had reason to be sensitive to the danger of potential foreign agents among the aliens settled near their military bases in the eastern Delta. State slavery is well attested throughout the ancient Near East. Especially involved were the displaced persons known as Habiru (Egyptian Apiru), who might be exploited as impressed soldiers or as forced laborers on building projects.

1:9-10. The name **Israel** denotes the community based on a common ancestry and even more on a common religion. It is an anachronism as used here of the scattered groups in Egypt—a "mixed multitude" (12:38)—and anticipates the founding of the community through the experience of the covenant.

Deal shrewdly indicates cunning rather than wisdom. The king visualizes exploitation of the Hebrews which would break their spirit and reduce their numbers through hardship.

1:11. By the time of the Exodus the Egyptian word **Pharaoh**—literally "great house" or palace—had come to mean the king. Not till much later was it used as a title prefixed to his name.

The **store cities** were regional capitals like those of Solomon for storing provisions—no doubt primarily for the military campaigns in Palestine and Syria. **Pithom,** Egyptian for "House of Atum," has been located at a site in the Wadi Tumilat between the eastern arm of the Nile and Lake Timsah where monuments of Ramses II were discovered. **Raamses,** or Rameses (12:37), is an abbreviation of the Egyptian name meaning "The House of Ramses Beloved of Amon." The city was built by Ramses II as his main seat on the site of the former

Hyksos capital, Avaris. Two letters from his reign mention provisions for the Apiru (Habiru) who were hauling stones for the work. The city was later given another name which appears in the Old Testament as Zoan and in Greek writings as Tanis.

These two cities specifically associate the oppression with the reign of Ramses II. Those who favor a different date (see Introduction) must therefore view this reference to them as not an original part of the tradition.

1:13-14. The Hebrews' **hard service** includes not only work with **mortar and brick** (see below on 5:6-21) but also labor **in the field**. No doubt this was mostly raising water from the canals and wells by weighted lever and bucket, treadwheel, or revolving shaft and digging and damming irrigation channels.

1:15-22. *The Order to Kill Infants.* Anticipating the death of the firstborn of Egypt (12:29-30), E introduces a popular Moses saga by setting the stage for the infant Moses' concealment and preservation. **Birthstool** with slightly different vowels may be read as "two stones," which may reflect a custom of sitting or kneeling during labor found today among primitive Arab villagers. **Vigorous** might be better rendered "like wild creatures." The humanity of the **midwives** accentuates the inhumanity of **Pharaoh,** the archenemy in the cult legend.

1:20-22. Verse 20*b* seems to be a repetition of verse 7*b* inserted by an editor, and verse 21 may also be an insertion. Verse 22 is viewed by some scholars as a parallel J account of Pharaoh's attempt to stop the growth of Hebrew population, but more probably it is a further step in the E story. Since his private instruction to the midwives has failed, Pharaoh broadcasts an order for **all his people** to aid in the slaughter.

2:1-10. *Moses' Birth and Adoption.* In contrast to the full P genealogy (6:16-27) the E tradition knows nothing of Moses' parentage beyond the fact that he was of Levitical family. Of his mother the Hebrew reads literally "the daughter of Levi" (cf. 6:20), as if following her name. But the original sense was no doubt simply that she was a Levite woman.

The language of verse 2*a* is that regularly used of a firstborn son but is contradicted by the older sister of verse 4. The fact that nothing is said here of Moses' brother Aaron, whom the P account makes three years older (7:7), suggests that this passage is drawn from a saga of Moses and that the relation with Aaron and with Miriam, the "sister of Aaron" (15:20), is secondary. This relation and even Moses' Levitical connection possibly arose from his role in the revelation of the divine ordinances at Sinai.

2:2b-9. With its directness and naïve detail this story suggests a hero legend. It is much like that of the Akkadian conqueror Sargon (around 2300), said to have been committed by his mother, a temple votaress, to the river in a reed box sealed with bitumen, recovered by a temple gardener, and cherished by the goddess Ishtar, who raised him to the throne. Even so the **daughter of Pharaoh** saves the infant Moses. In God's providence the adversary is thwarted by his own daughter. There is archaeological evidence from Egypt and Palestine of the wide diffusion of Mesopotamian myths and legends, probably by professional storytellers. The **reeds** amid which the baby is hid are papyrus, the Egyptian plant from which writing material was made as early as the fourth millennium.

2:10. The popular etymology of **Moses** here (see the footnotes in the Revised Standard Version) is quite unreliable. If it is Hebrew the name would mean "drawing" rather than "drawn." Instead it is probably Egyptian, meaning "son," and was originally preceded by the name of a diety—for example, Ramses, "son of Ra," Thutmose, "son of Thut." Though adoption as Pharaoh's grandson may be legendary, the Egyptian name and upbringing are elements of the tradition which Israelites would not naturally invent.

2:11-15a. *Stirring of Conscience.* The J writer portrays the sympathy of the quasi-Egyptian Moses awakened by the mistreatment of **one of his people** and contrasts with it the apathy to which slavery has reduced the Hebrews. This incident provides the motive for his flight to the desert with its important consequences.

2:15b-22. *Sojourn in Midian.* Ancient extrabiblical sources locate the **land of Midian** east of the Gulf of Aqaba. Here it may mean simply the place where a group of the nomadic Midianites has settled (see below on 3:1).

In this place Moses comes in contact with the desert sheik-priest whose sacred traditions seem to have played a significant part in the development of Israel's religion (see below on 18:12). He is called Jethro in E narratives (3:1; 4:18; 18:1-12)—though in each case the name seems to have been inserted later. In the J tradition he was apparently known as Hobab (cf. Judges 4:11). Possibly this name was originally included in verse 16. **Reuel** (verse 18) appears to be a later change based on a misunderstanding of Numbers 10:29.

2:16-20. With this story of Moses' meeting with his future wife cf. Genesis 24:11-28 and 29:2-12. The sheik's **seven daughters** indicate the saga. Care of the flocks is still a task of the girls and boys among the bedouin.

2:21-22. In staying with the Midianites, Moses becomes a **sojourner** *(ger)*—that is, a protected alien such as one finds in many bedouin tribes, usually as a refugee in a blood feud. **Zipporah** means "bird" and **Gershom** is taken to mean "sojourner there," but this popular etymology is quite unlikely. The tradition of Gershom as Moses' son is reflected in the claim of the priests at Dan to be descended from Moses through him (Judges 18:30).

2:23-25. *The Cry for Deliverance.* On the **king** who **died** see the Introduction. Verses 23*b*-25 from P reflect the general Pentateuchal theme of promise under **covenant** to the patriarchs **Abraham** (Genesis 15:18 and 17:1-14), **Isaac** (Genesis 26:2-4), and **Jacob** (Genesis 28:13-14).

B. Moses' Call (3:1–4:31)

3:1. *The Mountain of God.* On **Jethro** see above on 2:15*b*-22. The sacred mountain called **Horeb** in E and D is evidently the same as Mt. Sinai in J and P, where the law is given (19:10-23). Traditionally it has been identified since the fourth century A.D. with the peak Jebel Musa near the southern tip of the Sinai

Peninsula. This location is supported by the note in Deuteronomy 1:2 that it was eleven days' journey from Kadesh-barnea. Perhaps it was near the P list of stopping places in Numbers 33, though scarcely any of them can be located. Against it, however, is the tradition that Palestine and Midian lay in different directions from the holy mount (cf. Numbers 10:29-32).

Because the signs of the divine descent on Mt. Sinai in 19:16, 18 suggest a volcano in eruption, some scholars have placed the holy mountain east of the Gulf of Aqaba, in the traditional land of Midian. This is the only area in the entire region where there have been active volcanoes in historical times. But this is too far from Egypt to fit other elements of the tradition. It is more likely, therefore, that the place was somewhere northwest of the Gulf of Aqaba. If the mountain was already sacred to the Midianites (see below on 18:12) they might well transfer to it a tradition of Yahweh's manifestation in smoke and fire and earthquake at a volcanic mountain in their original homeland.

The narrative of the desert wandering breaks off after chapter 17, giving way to the block of material about the stay at Sinai. It then resumes in Numbers 10:11 with incidents which repeat some of the same themes—the manna and quails (chapter 16; Numbers 11) and the springs of Massah and Meribah (17:1-7; Numbers 20:2-13). The setting in Numbers is clearly near Kadesh and suggests that this is where the wandering narrative has brought us in chapter 17.

The tradition of the supporting of Moses' hands at Rephidim (17:11-12), which means "supports," authenticates the association of this place with the battle against the Amalekites, who were nomads of the Kadesh region. Among the mountains near Kadesh the most likely peak seems to be Jebel Helal, around twenty-five miles west of the Kadesh oasis. Moses' taking his flocks to the **west side of the wilderness** fits with this location. The western exposure to the prevailing wind from the Mediterranean would afford better pasture.

3:2-6. *The Burning Bush.* The **angel**, literally "messenger," of God as a manifestation of the divine presence is characteristic of the E source, where usually a visible personal presence is visualized. Here in J, however, **the angel of the LORD** expresses a lively sense of personal confrontation and the urgency of the call.

It is perhaps more than a coincidence that the Hebrew word for **bush**, literally "thornbush," probably comes from the same root as "Sinai." The **burning** may have been due to a natural phenomenon, but in popular religion fire was a sign of a theophany—a deity's manifestation of his presence. The bush is mentioned elsewhere in the Old Testament only in Deuteronomy 33:16. The sanctity of the place is indicated by the divine command for Moses to remove his sandals—a convention still observed by Muslims on entering a mosque.

3:7-10. *Moses' Commission.* The J account (verses 7-8) visualizes not only liberation from Egypt but also the occupation of Canaan, the land of promise which is the subject of the covenant with the patriarchs in J. The emphasis of E (verses 9-10) is rather on Moses' immediate mission, the encounter with Pharaoh and the actual Exodus.

Broad refers, not to the size of Palestine, but to the variety of landscape. It also refers to the scope for settlement, especially for nomads with sheep and goats, in the marginal lands on the thinly populated eastern slopes. **Flowing with milk and honey** is a conventional description of the land in the Pentateuch. This reflects the ideal of the nomad, for whom even the poorest land was a contrast to the desert with its brief spring grazing. **Honey** may refer to the product of wild bees but more probably means a syrup reduced from grape juice, still used by Arab peasants.

3:11-15. *Divine Authentication.* Moses' diffidence emphasizes God's authority behind the human agent—cf. the divine assurance in the call of Gideon, also authenticated by a **sign** (Judges 6:14-18). The sign offered to Moses must have dropped out, for the promise that the **mountain** on which he is standing will become an Israelite sanctuary after the mission is accomplished could scarcely give assurance while it is being carried out.

3:13. Moses is to base his claim to authority on this divine encounter and commission. The meeting reveals the particular purpose, nature, and personality, in God's **name**. One who asked Moses the name of the God whom both he and the Hebrews acknowledge would not merely be testing his claim to a special call. One would seek to know God's immediate purpose in the new revelation, in accordance with which God's presence and aid can be invoked.

3:14-15. In reply we might expect a succinct oracle. Instead we have the well-known word play on the divine name Yahweh. In E this is the first revelation of this name, whereas in J it is represented as known since before the Flood (Genesis 4:26).

The meaning is obscured by the conventional translation **I am who I am**, which implies that God is the ground of his own existence. The Hebrew verb denotes, not abstract being, but manifestation in a definite character, or name. Its form indicates habitual manifestation in past, present, or future. Since English requires a tense, the best rendering is "I will be as I will be." The famous declaration signifies that God is known in the dynamic confrontation of human beings and in their active response to God.

3:16-18. *The Way of Fulfillment.* Having announced the liberation from Egyptian bondage and the fulfillment of the promise to the patriarchs (verses 7-8) the J source turns to the immediate task of Moses in Egypt. He is to assemble the **elders** and with them confront Pharaoh.

Three days' journey is certainly a round number. The destination possibly is the holy place where Moses is now standing, though in this source the locale of the burning bush is not identified with Mt. Sinai. The occasion for **sacrifice** is perhaps a spring festival. The Egyptian frontier police would be quite familiar with pilgrimages for such occasions by the nomads who passed to and from the Delta in their seasonal grazings.

3:19-22. *Predictions of Details.* In verses 19-20 an editor anticipates Pharaoh's opposition and God's convincing **wonders**. The curious tradition of the borrowed ornaments in verses 21-22 (cf. 11:2; 12:35-36) awkwardly interrupts the narrative, and is probably an addition to the original exodus tradition. It may echo the Egyptian poem of Ipuwer describing the social upheaval in Egypt after the invasions at the end of the third millennium, when "gold and lapis-lazuli, silver and turquoise, carnelian and bronze [were] hung about the necks of slave girls" (see below on 7:14–11:10).

4:1-9. *Further Authentication.* The sign of the divine power was often a miracle. In the prophetic experience it is both a token of the will of God proclaimed by the prophet and a confirmation of the prophet's authority as an agent of the will of God—as it is here. In the saga form of the tradition Moses' signs are miracles.

4:2-5. According to J the **rod** is the ordinary shepherd's staff of Moses. According to E it is especially given by God (verse 17), hence E calls it the "rod of God." In P the rod is Aaron's when the miracle, now considerably elaborated, is used to convince Pharaoh (7:9-12). The "rod of God" which became a serpent may reflect the bronze serpent on a pole as the ancient cult symbol of Yahweh (cf. Numbers 21:6-9; II Kings 18:4; see below on 17:9).

4:6-7. The phrase **leprous, as white as snow** is a conventional description for a skin disease, "whiteness," which was not true leprosy.

4:8-9. The last of the three signs—the **water from the Nile** turned to **blood**—is also the first of the plagues (7:17-21). This fact probably indicates a fusion of two literary traditions earlier than J.

4:10-17. *The Association with Aaron.* Moses pleads his lack of eloquence. Yahweh replies that the creator is able to make his creatures effective for his purpose. When Moses still demurs, Yahweh, now exasperated, promises **Aaron** as spokesman.

The reference to Miriam as the "sister of Aaron" (15:20) must cast doubt on the tradition that Aaron was the **brother** of Moses and suggests that verses 14-16 are a later addition to J. **Levite** here probably signifies priestly office rather than tribal affinity.

It has been suggested that the Aaron tradition may have risen from a priestly caste which during the preparation for liberation between the desert shrine and the Hebrews in Egypt in cooperation with Moses; cf. the E tradition of Aaron's meeting with Moses **at the mountain of God** in verse 27. On verse 17 see above on verses 2-5.

4:18-23. ***Departure for Egypt.*** E depicts Moses as taking the initiative to see his **kinsmen** (verse 18), obviously as a pretext for setting out on his mission. J represents Moses as leaving in response to a divine call (verse 19). The fact that Yahweh says nothing of his mission but only that **the men who were seeking your life are dead** seems to reflect a variant tradition that the revelation at the burning bush occurred later, on the way back to Egypt. If so, presumably verses 19-20*a* and 24-26 originally followed 2:23*a* and were transposed here to fit with the order in the E tradition.

The variant traditions are especially obvious regarding Moses' family. In E they are left with Jethro to be reunited with Moses after the deliverance (18:5) whereas in J they accompany him (verse 20*a*). The plural **sons** is used, even though the birth of only one has been mentioned (2:22), and only one is implied in verse 25. This may indicate that J has only partially drawn on the details of a Moses saga. Or it may be due to editorial harmonizing with the E idea of two sons in 18:6.

4:20*b*-21. This may be E's editorial summary of the whole encounter with Pharaoh culminating in the Exodus. It keeps the theme of the passover cult legend in perspective amid the variety of incidents and traditions. The recurring statement that God will **harden** Pharaoh's heart does not imply moral determinism. Instead it emphasizes the fact that willful resistance to God's good intention makes one callous to one's own welfare (cf. Isaiah 6:10).

4:22-23. This passage is probably a misplaced fragment of J. The concept of Israel as the **first-born son** of Yahweh, suggested by the prediction of the death of Pharaoh's firstborn son, is the expression of one of the central J themes, the election of Israel.

4:24-26. ***The Circumcision of Moses.*** This is perhaps the J version of an older Kenite tradition. The repeated phrase **bridegroom of blood** suggests premarital circumcision, probably a Midianite custom. Moses, who would no doubt be already circumcised in infancy either as a Hebrew or as an adoptive

Egyptian, now is said to undergo the rite vicariously at the circumcision of his son. The blood of the severed skin is put on his feet, a euphemism for genitals.

The circumcision occurs at an unknown place in the desert. This plus the hostility of the demonic power, which J identifies with Yahweh, indicate an independent local tradition which does not fit well with the context. The account would perhaps fit better if it is assumed that in the original J narrative the incident preceded Moses' commissioning (see above on verses 18-23).

A flint blade for the operation reflects the primitive inhibition against metal when it was still a novelty; cf. the ban on metal-hewn stones on the altar in Deuteronomy 27:5 and Joshua 8:31.

4:27-31. *Meeting of Moses and Aaron.* On the association of Aaron with the mountain of God see above on verses 10-16. The spokesman to the elders (cf. 3:16-17) is Aaron, who also performs the signs (cf. 4:1-9). The people heard—that is, accepted the fact—that Yahweh had visited them, meaning that he had taken stock of their particular situation.

C. CONFRONTATION WITH PHARAOH (5:1–6:1)

5:1-5. *First Appeal to Pharaoh.* According to E (verses 1-2) Moses and Aaron demand release of the serfs on the pretext of a pilgrimage feast at a desert shrine, presumably the mountain of God (see above on 3:1). According to J (verse 3) they, i.e. Moses and Aaron and the elders, follow the divine instruction to propose a three days' journey into the wilderness for a sacrifice (see above on 3:16-18).

Pestilence and the sword were natural evils in the corridor between Africa and Asia, where caravans or armies might carry plague and bedouin raids were a constant menace. Hebrews here means the social class of Apiru, or Habiru (see Introduction).

5:4-6. Pharaoh does not question the existence of the Hebrews' God; he contemptuously ignores him. The stage is thus set for the conflict between Yahweh and the archenemy—the theme of the cult drama.

It has been suggested that **many** in verse 5 should read "idle" (cf. verses 8, 17). However, **people of the land**—meaning laborers, or the lowest class of the free population—is a usage later than either J or E. The reading of the Samaritan Pentateuch, "they are more numerous than the people of the land," i.e. than the native Egyptians, is to be seriously considered.

5:6–6:1. *The Oppression Intensified.* The black mud of the Delta was puddled and molded into **bricks,** which were dried in the sun. The **straw,** chopped small, preserved the consistency during these operations.

5:16. For **the fault is in your own people** is translated in the Septuagint as "you will wrong your own people," meaning the Hebrews, who were state serfs. A later Greek version reads "and yours is the fault."

5:19-21. The Hebrew foremen realize that their people are **in evil plight;** hence their bitter remonstrance with Moses and Aaron, which is almost as strong as a curse. **Made us offensive,** literally "made our smell to stink," is a common expression in the Old Testament narratives.

5:22–6:1. Moses' confrontation with God introduces a renewed divine assurance of the coming deliverance.

D. THE P ACCOUNT OF MOSES' CALL (6:2–7:7)

6:2-3. *The Divine Name.* In P the name Yahweh is represented as being revealed to Moses for the first time, as it is in E (see above on 3:13). P does not elaborate on its significance. Instead the patriarchs' experience of the same God is emphasized, especially in the covenant and promise of Canaan, which is a prelude to Moses' commission.

For P the specific name of God to the patriarchs was *El Shaddai,* translated **God Almighty** in the Septuagint. El was the ancient Semitic high god, now well known from the myths and legends in the fourteenth century Ugaritic texts found at Ras Shamra in northern Syria. In Genesis the name El appears with several qualifiers according to the content and places of his encounters with the patriarchs. *Shaddai* as a divine title is predominantly late but may reflect earlier usage, possibly coming from an old root meaning "mountain." This patriarchal name may have been selected here because of its use in Genesis 17:1 in the context of God's covenant with Abraham, now to be fulfilled.

6:6-9. *Assurance to the Hebrews.* The repeated declaration of verses 6-8 reflects the revelation of the divine name as a new dynamic self-manifestation of God. Here P foreshadows the drama of salvation in its widest scope, including the Sinai covenant and culminating in the occupation of the promised land. The word **redeem** in verse 6 is also used of the great deliverance in 15:13 and of the exodus from Babylon in Isaiah 40–55. The verb means primarily "play the part of a kinsman," as in reclaiming property (cf. Ruth 4:1-8), revenging a murder, or buying back one who has forfeited his freedom for debt. The Exodus involves both vengeance and rehabilitation from slavery.

Acts of judgment means acts that show kingly power or impose regular government. The word is a leading motif in passages in the Psalms and in the prophetical books which deal with the establishment of order against the menace of chaos. Thus in the cult drama of the Exodus the term means the establishment of God's order against the menace of chaos in history personified in Pharaoh.

6:10-13. *Moses' Commission to Pharaoh.* According to P Moses is instructed to demand complete liberation rather than merely permission to perform religious rites as in J and E (cf. 5:1, 3). **Uncircumcised** is used with **lips** in its secondary sense of "defective"—cf. "uncircumcised heart" (Leviticus 26:41; Jeremiah 9:26; Ezekiel 44:7) and "ears" (Jeremiah 6:10, Revised Standard Version footnote).

6:14-27. *Genealogy of Moses and Aaron.* The recapitulation of verses 10-12 practically verbatim in verses 28-30 indicates that this intervening passage was inserted as a later supplement to P. Loosely incomplete lists are given only of the first three Hebrew tribes—through **Levi,** in which is included the genealogy of Moses and Aaron. The continuation of Aaron's line to **Phinehas** reveals the characteristic interest of the P editor in the family of Aaron as the only legitimate priesthood. This list reflects the relationships among the Levites after the Babylonian exile. However, the Egyptian names **Phinehas,** "Negro," and **Putiel,** "El has given," indicate early historical traditions.

6:28–7:7. *The Mission of Aaron.* P elaborates on the E idea in 4:16 by stating that Aaron shall be Moses' **prophet**—in Hebrew *nabi,* which is related to Akkadian *nabu,* "proclaim." In Mesopotamian mythology Nabu was the messenger of the gods and patron of the arts of speech and letters. The fact that the P source is oblivious of all but the declaratory function of the prophet indicates the decline of prophecy after the Exile. The note on the ages of Moses and Aaron is characteristic of P and obviously artificial. It is to fit the idea that Moses died at the age of 120 after forty years of wandering in the wilderness (Deuteronomy 34:7).

7:8-13. *Victory Over Pharaoh's Magicians.* The wonder wrought here by **Aaron's rod** is obviously prompted by the first of the signs of Moses' rod (4:1-5). The word translated **serpent** usually means "dragon"; probably a young crocodile is meant. The swallowing of the other reptiles may have been suggested by an Egyptian snake charm: "The mottled knife, black, green, and gold, goes forth against it; it has swallowed up for itself that which it tasted."

The word for **magicians** is probably Egyptian. It is always applied to Egyptians in the Old Testament except in Daniel, where it was evidently picked up from the Pentateuch. Later Jewish tradition named the magicians Jannes and Jambres.

E. The Plagues of Egypt (7:14–11:10)

Each of the three sources J, E, and P presents the plagues with its own peculiar emphasis. None by itself describes all ten;

but all three agree on the general theme of a conflict between Yahweh and Pharaoh, a series of natural disasters, and the obtuseness of Pharaoh leading to the last fatal stroke which breaks his will (12:29-32). In J the plagues are sent directly from Yahweh, with Moses merely announcing them. In E Moses is the agent, usually with the rod (cf. 4:17, 20). In P Aaron manipulates the rod and competes with the Egyptian magicians as in 7:8-13.

All of the plagues are natural phenomena, some especially characteristic of Egypt. The Hebrew tradition may have been influenced by Egyptian literature referring to such disasters. In an Old Kingdom papyrus from late in the third millennium Ipuwer laments the eclipse of Egypt by Asian invaders (see above on 3:19-22) and states, obviously figuratively, that the "river was blood." Of the same events Nefer-rohu declares: "The sun is veiled and will not shine so that men may see."

In their sequence, however, the plagues are not naturally explicable. They must be understood in the context of Israel's sacramental experience of the great deliverance as elements in a cult drama.

7:14-25. *Pollution of Water.* The first plague, like the last, is included in all three sources. In J Yahweh kills all the **fish in the Nile** and as a result the water becomes undrinkable. In E and P, by the manipulation of the rod wielded by Moses and Aaron respectively, the water is **turned to blood**. This miracle, on a smaller scale, appears earlier in J as a sign by which Moses convinces the Hebrews (4:9). In J and E only the Nile is affected, but in P the plague extends to all waters in the land.

Egypt, the "gift of the Nile," is cultivable only where the water of the river reaches in its annual summer flood or can be channeled for irrigation. The Nile was also the source of drinking water, as still among the peasantry. During its flood stage the river water regularly has a reddish coloration from mud and algae, but this would not have been regarded as an omen. What is intended is a miracle which demonstrates God's power and purpose expressed in the cult drama.

The word translated **loathe** means rather "weary themselves," i.e. in digging wells (verse 24). **Vessels of** in verse 19 is supplied by the translators. The meaning may be rather "on wood and on stone"—that is, either sap and springs issuing from the rocks or dew on bushes and rocks.

8:1-15. *Frogs.* In J the frogs come from the Nile. In P (verses 5-7) they come from all the waters in the land. The baking **ovens** were open clay cylinders heated from without, the bread being baked within on hot pebbles.

In verses 8-11 J introduces the theme of Pharaoh's bargaining with Moses. This is the beginning of Pharaoh's reluctant but progressive relenting which sustains the dramatic tension—a feature of both cult drama and saga.

8:16-19. *Gnats.* This third plague, from P only, is perhaps a variant of the fourth plague of flies from J (verses 20-32). **Dust** has been thought by some to identify the insects as sand flies, but it may denote the breeding in the drying stagnant waters of mosquitoes, which molest both **man and beast.** Though the tradition is colored by local conditions, again a miracle is intended. The striking of the dust with Aaron's **rod** and the consequent dust cloud suggests imitative magic, like the ashes and boils (9:8-10). This may have been a rite in the Israelite cult drama. The narrative moves nearer a climax with the first failure of the Egyptian **magicians** and their admission that the miracle was by the **finger of God.**

8:20-32. *Flies.* On the relation of this J account to the third plague see above on verses 16-19. Isaiah 7:18 takes flies as a symbol for Egypt, where they are numerous in the congested areas and are potent disease carriers. Some have viewed the flies as a result of the dead frogs (cf. verse 14) but the association is rather in the saga or cult legend. The separation of **Goshen** emphasizes the power of the God of the Hebrews, who are settled there.

8:25-32. Pharaoh now concedes that the Hebrews may **sacrifice.** But in Egypt the cow was sacred to Isis; the Apis bull was sacrificed only when it was ritually clean by Egyptian standards; the ram was sacred to Amon of Thebes. Thus the sacrifice of any of these animals by the Hebrews would be

abominable to the Egyptians. The sudden removal of the flies, so that **not one remained,** is a greater miracle than their appearance and emphasizes the inadequacy of any naturalistic explanation.

9:1-7. *Disease Among the Cattle.* This account appears to be from J. The absence of the characteristic motif of Pharaoh's bargaining for the removal of the plague, however, suggests that it may be a later addition to this source. The statement that **all the cattle of the Egyptians died** is contradicted by later references to such cattle in the J narrative (verses 19-21; 11:5; 12:29).

9:8-12. *Boils.* This P account is possibly a late tradition developed from an earlier variant of either the disease of the cattle or the darkness (10:21-29), in which the tossing up of soot may be a rite of imitative magic. The connection between darkness and the boils may be based on skin irritation caused by the hot sirocco, a wind heavily charged with fine sand particles which obscure the sun—cf. "darkness to be felt" (10:21).

The compiler who inserted this tradition clearly appreciated the dramatic pattern in his note that the **magicians** not only were unable to control this plague (cf. 8:18) but were themselves affected. At this point they disappear from the scene.

9:13-35. *Hail, Thunder, and Lightning.* This narrative is mostly from J but includes a brief E account (verses 22-23*a*, 24*a*, and 35*ab*). The final clause (verse 35*c*) was added by a P editor.

9:14-16. The homiletic and apologetic tone of this part of the address to Pharaoh suggests that it is a later addition. It may have been made by one who was uneasy at Pharaoh's defiance of Yahweh, and felt it necessary to explain it. Pharaoh was allowed to persist only to enhance Yahweh's final victory. **Name** denotes "reputation."

9:17-18. The verb translated **exalting** is the root of the word meaning "siege mound" and therefore has the sense of raising himself in opposition. **People** is used here in its specific sense as a religious community that was like a kin group together with their God. They stand in a moral relationship to God as tribesmen to a sheik or a common ancestor.

9:19-21. The inconsistency in the repeated killing of the Egyptian **cattle** (cf. verse 6 and 12:29) raises the question whether all three passages belonged to the original J narrative. In favor of the originality of this passage is the likelihood that the warning and the presumed obedience of certain of the **servants of Pharaoh** are intended to show that the Egyptian people, in contrast with Pharaoh, are beginning to be impressed. This is an anticipation of the appeal of Pharaoh's servants to release the Hebrews (10:7).

9:22-26. The rarity of **very heavy hail** in Egypt would make its occurrence an omen. In Palestine hail is usually accompanied by **thunder** and **fire**, i.e. lightning. The exemption of the Hebrew settlements in **Goshen** (cf. 8:22) emphasizes the miracle.

9:27-30. Pharaoh's admission **I have sinned** means literally "I have missed the mark"—that is, he was the loser. **The LORD is in the right, and I and my people are in the wrong** is in the technical language of the law court and does not necessarily have a moral connotation. The spreading out of the **hands,** palms up, was the common attitude of prayer in the ancient Near East.

9:31-32. This parenthetical note about the season was probably added by an editor anxious to explain how vegetation completely destroyed by the hail could still be left for the locusts to destroy (cf. 10:5, 12, 15). **In the ear** is a translation of the Hebrew *abib,* the name of the first spring month in the Canaanite calendar. In Egypt the **barley** would have heads a month earlier. **Spelt** is an inferior variety of wheat; it is not certain whether the Hebrew word refers to this grain.

10:1-20. *Locusts.* The J narrative continues, again with intermingling of a brief E account (verses 12-13*a, c,* 15*b,* 20). It describes one of the grimmest of all natural catastrophes in the Near East. It was impossible to cope with the enormous swarms and with the immediate and prolonged effects of their ravages.

10:1-6. Verses 1*b*-2 are generally regarded as a later insertion. Both their style and content are different. Also, the J pattern elsewhere is to give in full Yahweh's instruction of what to say to Pharaoh, as in verses 3*b*-6*b,* which thus may originally have followed immediately after verse 1*a.*

The didactic note in **that you may tell in the hearing of your son** is a new feature. It is characteristic of the D style and viewpoint (cf. Deuteronomy 4:9; 6:7) and thus may come from the editor who added Deuteronomy to JE. More probably it reflects the recital of the cult legend at the sacramental celebration where the experience of the great salvation was communicated to succeeding generations (cf. 12:26-27).

10:7-11. The dramatic tempo now increases as Pharaoh's **servants**—presumably the members of his court—urge him to release the Hebrews. Their attitude emphasizes his own stubbornness. He gives his consent with a qualification—that only the **men,** who alone could participate in the ritual, may go on the pilgrimage. Their wives and **little ones** must remain behind. His curse **the LORD be with you, if ever I let you . . . go!** is really a threat.

10:12-20. Locusts are brought into both Egypt and Palestine by the **east wind.** It is no exaggeration that they **covered the face of the land,** as evidenced from attacks in modern times—for example, a swarm is reported covering an area of ten by twenty miles.

In **I have sinned against the LORD** the sense of guilt is apparently stronger than in 9:27. But **forgive my sin** may mean simply "relieve my disability," without any significant consciousness of guilt, as the sequel indicates. **Not a single locust was left,** as is characteristic in the J narrative, emphasizes the miracle. On **Red Sea** see below on 13:18*a.*

10:21-29. *Darkness.* The ninth plague is described only by E (verses 21-23, 27). On **darkness to be felt,** caused by the sirocco, see above on 9:8-12. But the darkness may also portend the ultimate disaster, the reign of chaos. In Egyptian mythology, the enemy of the sun god Re, of whom Pharaoh was thought to be the incarnation, was Apophis, the serpent of chaotic darkness. Again the tradition may reflect the description of the disasters of the Asian invasions in the papyrus of Nefer-rohu (see above on 7:14–11:10).

10:24-29. In the dramatic J narrative of the negotiations between Moses and Pharaoh this is the final climactic interview.

Pharaoh makes his last offer. The Hebrews may go with their families but must leave their **flocks and . . . herds.** In replying that **we do not know with what we must serve the LORD until we arrive there** Moses is referring to the inspection of the sacrificial victims before and after slaughter.

In saying **I will not see your face again** he may speak ambiguously, for to see the face of a monarch meant to depend on his favor. This statement seems to be contradicted by 11:4-8, but in the original J narrative the passage was the continuation of Moses' speech begun in verse 29, now interrupted by 11:1-3.

11:1-10. *Warning of the Final Plague.* On verses 2-3 see above on 3:19-22. Verses 4-8 continue the J account of Moses' speech to Pharaoh beginning in 10:29 and ending with his departure **in hot anger,** matching that of Pharaoh (10:28). The final stroke **about midnight** relates to the nocturnal rite of passover. The language of verse 5 is repeated with a variant in 12:29. The narrative prose here is influenced by the cadence and style of Hebrew poetry, perhaps reflecting original poetic cult legends.

The slave girl grinding grain into meal represents the lowest status in society. **Behind the mill** suggests a rubbing stone pushed back and forth along a shallow stone mortar. On **cattle** see above on 9:19-21. **Growl** is literally "sharpen his tongue." Verses 9-10 come from a P editor.

F. MEMORIALS OF THE DELIVERANCE (12:1–13:16)

The traditions associate three religious observances of Israel with the Exodus: passover, the feast of unleavened bread, and dedication of the firstborn. It is clear that they were originally separate.

Passover, as bedouin analogies suggest, is most readily understood as a nomad rite on the eve of departure from the desert for summer grazings. But it may also have been associated with the return to the desert by nomads who had seasonal grazings in Egypt. Unleavened bread was an agricultural festival beginning the barley harvest, evidently adopted from the Canaanites after the settlement in Palestine. In the P source, these two observances are associated (cf. Leviticus 23:5-8 and Numbers 28:16-25). But in the ancient festal calendars in 23:15 and 34:18-23 the commands to observe the feast of unleavened bread say nothing about the passover. Hence there is question of how soon the two came to be connected.

The elevation of the passover from a family observance in the home to the status of a pilgrimage feast in the temple is described as an innovation by Josiah late in the seventh century (II Kings 23:21-23). Though this account makes no mention of unleavened bread, it ascribes Josiah's action to a written ordinance, presumably Deuteronomy 16:1-8, which combines the two festivals.

In emphasizing the novelty of Josiah's passover II Kings 23:22 states that it was a reversion to a practice in the time of the judges. This is borne out in the association of the two festivals at Gilgal in Joshua 5:10-12, which appears to be a late passage but may preserve an early tradition.

At any rate it would be natural for the Israelite tribes, in coming together at a common sanctuary to realize their solidarity on the basis of their common experience of the Exodus, sacramentally preserved, to associate with this the feast of unleavened bread, and perhaps also the passover.

This association was designed to preserve Israel from assimilation to Canaanite religion in the settlement in Palestine. The settlers were prone to appropriate with the new techniques of agriculture the rites and ideology of the festivals at the great seasonal crises. Thus also Hebrew groups which had not been in Egypt were associated with the historical experience of the Exodus and the covenant, which were the bases of the Israelite confederacy.

12:1-13. *The P Passover Ordinance.* This passage is an expansion of the older ordinance in J (verses 21-27). The old agricultural and civil year in Israel apparently began in the autumn. It was during, or possibly before, the Exile that the

Mesopotamian calendar with a spring new year was adopted. P, writing after the Exile, here assumes that the calendar used in his day dated back to the Exodus. Sometime before the Exile, perhaps for convenience in international trade, the months came to be known by numbers beginning with a spring new year. Thus in P the passover is regularly dated in the **first month.** This month was earlier known by the Canaanite name Abib and later by the Babylonian name Nisan.

12:3-6. Characteristically P regards the Hebrews as already a **congregation,** a compact religious community. The keeping of the **lamb,** or kid, from the **tenth day** to the **fourteenth**, whatever its origin, is incongruous with a hurried departure and reflects the later rite in a settled community. In the temple festival after the Exile units of ten shared a lamb, but no such strict **count** is visualized here. Rather the number is to be reckoned by what each can eat, taking account of the age, sex, and health of the members of the family.

That the victim must be **without blemish**—that is, ritually perfect—implies inspection both before and after killing. This is again inconsistent with hurried departure. The significance of this domestic ceremony for the whole community is conserved by the simultaneous slaughter. The lambs are to be killed **in the evening,** literally "between the two evenings." The Pharisees interpreted this as meaning between midafternoon, when the sun's heat abated, and sunset, whereas the Sadducees took it to mean between sunset and dark.

12:7-10. The **doorposts** and **lintel** were specifically associated with supernatural influences (cf. 21:6; Deuteronomy 6:9 and 11:20). The sprinkling of **blood** as a prophylactic rite (cf. verses 13 and 23) has analogies in ancient Mesopotamia and among the Arabs, who smear blood on the door of a house during an epidemic. The victim in this rite is called a "redemption." Such a sacrifice is made also before such new enterprises as the completion of a house or the digging of a well, and among the Rashaideh bedouin of the Syrian desert in connection with their early summer migration. **Night** is the transitional period when evil influences are especially active.

The Hebrew word translated **roasted** emphasizes fire, the firepit of primitive desert cooking, as still at the Samaritan passover at Nablus. In Deuteronomy 16:7 the victim may be **boiled.** In addition to the roasting the **unleavened bread** (see below on verses 14-20), the normal bedouin bread, and the **bitter herbs,** the normal bedouin seasoning, are primitive features. Later they were artificially connected with the hasty departure (verse 34) and the bitter treatment in Egypt. The prohibition against eating the meat **raw** grows out of the blood taboo in Israel and may reflect an earlier custom of eating raw meat in the rite. Nothing is to be left over until the next day lest the sacrifice be profaned by persons in an unsanctified state or at an unsanctified time.

12:11-13. The departure of migrant nomads is reflected in **loins girded**—that is, the long robe tucked up in the belt—**sandals on** instead of lying at the entrance to the house, and **staff in . . . hand.** The word translated **in haste** implies anxiety or fear; Isaiah 52:12 promises that the second exodus, from Babylon, will not be "in haste."

The derivation of *pesach,* **passover,** from an assumed Hebrew verb **pass over** (cf. verse 27), i.e. "jump," the houses to be spared is unlikely. The etymology has not yet been determined but the most likely suggestion is that it is related to an Arabic verb meaning "separate." In associating the **first-born** of **man and beast** the P source, following J (cf. 29; 13:11-16), connects the passover with the dedication and redemption of the firstborn.

12:14-20. *The P Unleavened Bread Ordinance.* The leavening of bread was accomplished by mixing with the dough a piece of old dough in which yeast has been allowed to develop. Thus the **leaven** was in a sense a corruption (cf. Matthew 16:6; I Corinthians 5:6-8). The elimination of leaven was designed to preserve the new crop, with its direct association with the supernatural, from contact with the profane until its due desacralizing through the ritual.

Being **cut off from Israel** probably means the equivalent of excommunication, but see comment on Leviticus 20:2-9. **Holy** denotes the condition resulting from ritual contact with what has been consecrated by the divine presence. Hence work was suspended not only as a precaution against the contamination of the holy by the profane but also as a protection of the profane against the dread influence of the holy—cf. Uzzah's touching the ark (II Samuel 6:6-7) The terms **sojourner** (see above on 2:21-22) and **native of the land** clearly refer to the conditions after the settlement in Palestine.

12:21-28. *The J Passover Ordinance.* Since the last sentence of verse 27 is the natural conclusion to verses 21-24, evidently verses 25-27*a* are a later addition, possibly D. In contrast to P (cf. verses 1-14, 43-49) the J author assumes familiarity with the rite requiring no specific description. Therefore there is greater significance to the few details given—the sprinkling with **blood**, the injunction that no one leave the house **until the morning**, and the **destroyer**. This last, obviously some demonic power, is the supernatural agent in J; in verses 26-27*a* the slayer is Yahweh himself. In verse 28 the association of **Aaron** with Moses (contrast verse 21) indicates P.

12:29-36. *The Last Plague.* The dramatic pattern of the J narrative is resumed with the sequel to the warning in 11:4-8. The stroke falls **at midnight** (on the poetic language in verse 29 see above on 11:1-10). Pharaoh now capitulates unconditionally, seeking the favor of Yahweh, whom he has so arrogantly ignored.

This skillfully constructed dramatic narrative, best preserved in J, betrays its origin in saga and in cult legend. The cult legend predominates as the natural association of the ritual of passover and unleavened bread indicates. Some interpreters have suggested that historically only the oldest son of the king himself died, giving the Hebrews an opportunity to escape during the period of mourning. Others theorize about an epidemic of some children's disease. But the suddenness and completeness of the disaster in the traditions admit of no such naturalistic explanation. The incident of the despoiling of the Egyptians is the fulfillment of 3:21-22 (cf. 11:2).

12:37-39. *The Departure.* This passage is generally viewed as a continuation of the J narrative from verse 34. But the fact that hereafter only P gives specific localities in the exodus itinerary, as well as the exaggerated and artificial statistics, suggests the possibility that verse 37 comes from P or has been rewritten by a P editor.

Journeyed, literally "pulled up tent pegs," is reminiscent of Israel's nomadic origins. **Rameses** is the same as Raamses (see above on 1:11). **Succoth,** though spelled like the Hebrew word for "booths," probably represents an Egyptian name for a border town in a district inhabited by foreigners. Its probable site has been located in the eastern part of the Wadi Tumilat, about thirty miles southeast of Rameses.

About six hundred thousand men far exceeds the strength even of imperial armies in the records of the ancient Near East. Even with the crudest weapons such a force could surely have overpowered Ramses II's army of around twenty thousand. With **women and children** the population would have totaled over two million, much more than any oasis in the Sinai region could sustain. The figure may be a round number derived from the census total in 38:26.

12:38-39. The **mixed multitude,** as the use of the same adjective in Nehemiah 13:3 indicates, consisted of non-Israelites. It no doubt included Canaanite deportees in Egypt (see Introduction). With the association of the passover and unleavened bread in mind the J author notices the completion of **unleavened cakes.**

12:40-42. *A P Chronological Note.* The length of the sojourn in Egypt, **four hundred and thirty years** (cf. four hundred in Genesis 15:13 and Acts 7:6), is artificial, like all P statistics. It fits poorly with the P genealogy in 6:16-20, where Moses is Levi's great-grandson. To get around this difficulty the Septuagint includes in the four hundred and thirty years the earlier sojourn of the patriarchs in Canaan. The word translated **watching** has the sense both of guarding (verse 42*a*) and of observing a commemoration (verse 42*b*).

12:43-50. *Further P Passover Regulations.* Unlike a **hired servant,** assumed to be a **foreigner,** a **slave** is a permanent member of the household. Slaves are permitted to participate in the passover if made members of the religious community by being **circumcised.** The word translated **sojourner** in verse 45 means rather "settler," one of a foreign group who may have penetrated the land and taken up residence there—for example, the Edomites who moved into southern Judah after 586. On the other hand **stranger** in verse 48 renders the word usually translated "sojourner" (see above on 2:21-22). In his special relation to the Israelite tribe he is to be admitted to the passover rite if he is circumcised, since he comes under the protection of Yahweh, whose power he thus confesses.

The eating of one lamb in **one house,** nothing being taken **outside,** prevents unlawful participation. The injunction not to **break a bone** probably reflects association of the rite with the health of the flocks. Some interpreters have taken this to be the scripture said in John 19:36 to have been fulfilled when Jesus' legs were not broken after his crucifixion, but the quotation there is from Psalm 34:20.

13:1-2. *The P Ordinance of the Firstborn.* Fuller P regulations for the dedication and redemption of the firstborn appear in Leviticus 27:26-27 and Numbers 3:11-13, 44-51; 8:17-18; 18:15-18. Here P simply endorses the connection with the Exodus already made by J (verses 11-13) and D (verses 14-16). In Deuteronomy 15:19-23, the ordinance is stated as the prelude to the passover ordinance.

Like other peoples of the ancient Near East the ancestors of the Israelites probably at one time actually sacrificed their firstborn children, as Genesis 22:1-14 (cf. Micah 6:7) implies, though perhaps only in critical emergencies. Numbers 3:47 and 18:16 specify five shekels of silver as the redemption price, to be the perquisite of the priests.

13:3-10. *The J Unleavened Bread Ordinance.* No date for the rite is given in J beyond the month of the Exodus, **Abib** (see above on 9:31-32; 12:1-13), but cf. **at its appointed time from year to year.** This passage has been expanded by a D editor in verses 3*b-d,* 5, and 8-9. His redundancy, stereotyped description of the promised land, emphasis on the law in the context of sacramental history, and didactic interest are unmistakable.

13:8-9. Both the corporate consciousness of the ancient Israelite and the continued sacramental experiencing of the Exodus are reflected in **what the LORD did for me when I came out of Egypt.** The language and thought in these verses suggest Deuteronomy 6:4-9. Interpreting the words literally orthodox Jews attach to their foreheads and arms during morning prayer boxes containing miniature scrolls of verses 1-10, 11-16 and Deuteronomy 6:4-9; 11:13-21. These are the phylacteries of Matthew 23:5.

The **law of the LORD . . . in your mouth** indicates the law in the context of the great deliverance, which reflects Israel's sacramental experience of the covenant. Law in Israel implied the gospel of God's grace in the deliverance and his election of Israel sealed by the covenant; it was the expression of Israel's status as the covenanted people.

13:11-16. *The J Ordinance of the Firstborn.* This ordinance is repeated elsewhere in J (34:19-20) and appears also in the Book of the Covenant in E (22:29-30) and in D (Deuteronomy 15:19-23) and P (see above on verses 1-2). Verses 14-16 here are an expansion by a D editor.

The firstborn belongs to Yahweh and is **set apart** as holy (see above on 12:14-20). It must be either sacrificed or desacralized—that is, released for common life and use—by a substitute sacrifice. The word translated **redeem** here is not that used in 6:6 and 15:13, which involves the duty of a kinsman. This verb denotes simply an impersonal transaction of a substitution. An **ass** must be redeemed by sacrifice of a **lamb** because it is ritually unclean; for this reason its **neck** must be broken if it is not redeemed, lest its blood be shed as in a sacrifice. Cuneiform tablets found at Mari on the middle Euphrates mention an Amorite rite involving sacrifice of an ass. Though no traces of this custom are found in Palestine, such a pagan custom may lie behind the ban here.

The association of dedication of the firstborn with the Exodus may have originated with its observance at the pilgrimage feast of unleavened bread (cf. 23:15), when the solidarity of the community was realized by the sacramental expriencing of the deliverance.

G. THE RESCUE AT THE SEA (13:17–15:21)

In the grand climax of the drama of salvation the effect of the J narrative based on the cult legend is again marred by combination with P material and geographical notes. Only a limited amount of E material appears.

Whatever the historical nucleus may have been, the tradition was transmitted as the substance of faith in a highly dramatized cult legend and saga emphasizing the miraculous action of Yahweh. The deliverance at the sea is the supreme divine act of might and mercy and the genesis of the religious community of Israel. It recurs through scripture, especially in Isaiah 40 and 43, and is taken by Paul as the prototype of Christian baptism (I Corinthians 10:1-2).

13:17-18a. *Route of the Departure in E.* Apparently relying on the saga form of the tradition, E notes the avoidance of the **way of the land of the Philistines.** The name is an anachronism, since Egyptian records show that the Philistines did not settle in Palestine till the first half of the twelfth century, but the coastal route had been long the regular military road to the north. The fleeing Hebrews would **see war** if they attempted to pass its fortifications. The mention of it suggests Rameses (cf. 12:37; see above on 1:11) as at least one point of departure.

13:18a. The **way of the wilderness** may have been an alternative inland caravan route. The Hebrew words translated **Red Sea** mean literally "Papyrus Sea" or "Lake." The term is the Hebrew name for the sea on the southern side of the world known to Israel, including the Gulf of Suez and the Gulf of Aqaba. The use of the term is evidently secondary and arose from the tradition that in the Exodus Israel crossed a body of water of this name on the eastern border of Egypt.

There has been much debate about the body of water actually crossed:

(1) Traditionally the nothern end of the Gulf of Suez has been assumed. Such a location, however, would involve too long a journey through desert country. Geological evidence has disproved the theory that in ancient times the sea extended farther north than at present. No papyrus reeds grow along this shore.

(2) The name "Papyrus Lake" indicates fresh water. It therefore suggests the northern or southern end of Lake Timsah, or possibly the northern end of the Great Bitter Lake. Such a location is suggested by the older tradition reflected in the P itinerary (see below on verse 20). This route would lead directly into the wilderness of Shur (15:22).

(3) An arm of Lake Menzaleh may be indicated by an Egyptian text mentioning a Papyrus Lake near Rameses.

(4) East of Lake Menzaleh on the Mediterranean is the salt marsh of Bardawil. This is separated from the sea by a narrow sandspit which is generally a dry salt crust capable of bearing men and light animals but occasionally is flooded. The situation fits with a naturalistic explanation of the sea crossing but is less easy to fit with the traditions about the route of the departure. Whether or not Bardawil was the site of the actual crossing, acquaintance with it by travelers to Egypt may have influenced the later elaboration of the narrative (see below on 14:1-4).

13:18b-19. It is unlikely that the escaping serfs were **equipped for battle.** Probably the word means "by fives" or possibly "by fifties" and thus refers to a regular formation. On the **bones of Joseph** cf. Genesis 50:25.

13:20. *A P Itinerary.* On **Succoth** see above on 12:37-39. **Etham** has not been located but was probably an Egyptian border fortress. Possibly it was the redoubt on the desert edge east of Succoth mentioned in a police report of the late thirteenth century concerning two fugitive slaves. This document is doubly significant for the tradition of the Exodus, indicating the concern of the pharaoh for escaping slaves and the existence in this locale of a route into the wilderness of Shur (cf.

15:22). Here P seems to reflect earlier traditions of a Hebrew departure from Egypt at the eastern end of the Wadi Tumilat (see below on 14:1-4).

13:21-22. *The Pillar of Cloud and Fire.* This feature of the J account has been naturalistically explained as a glowing brazier carried by guides. Fire, however, is a sign of the divine presence, as is a cloud.

14:1-4. *A Change of Itinerary.* The P author presents the divine command to **turn back** as for the purpose of encouraging pursuit so that Yahweh may **get glory over Pharaoh.** This explanation is evidently his attempt to reconcile two different traditions of the itinerary—a southern one starting in the Wadi Tumilat around Succoth (cf. 12:37; 13:20), and a northern one starting in the Delta near Rameses. It is likely that the southern route preserves an older tradition and the northern reflects the memory of Jewish refugees who came that way to Egypt after 586. Each version, however, may reflect the traditions of various groups at the time of the Exodus and at the time of the postexilic settlement in Egypt.

Migdol was probably a fortress on the military road to Palestine. Probably it was located about twelve miles northeast of the modern city of Qantara on the Suez Canal, though an alternative location in the Wadi Tumilat has been suggested.

Baal-zephon evidently took its name from the shrine of a Canaanite god. Inscriptions from the Roman imperial period found a few miles north of the supposed site of Migdol identify a shrine of Zeus Kasios, certainly the Greek adaptation of Baal-Zephon. Some scholars, however, believe that the shrine of Baal-zephon was at Tahpanes.

Pi-hahiroth may come from an Egyptian name meaning "mouth of the canals"; if so, in this context it suggests a site near the easternmost mouth of the Nile. A location in the Wadi Tumilat which is at least etymologically feasible has also been proposed.

The wilderness has shut them in probably means that the desert with its lack of water has confined the Hebrews to established routes, where they are easily followed.

14:5-18. *The Pursuit.* The J narrative now moves forward, with some P material (verses 8, 15-18 and at least the locations in verse 9*b*).

Officers over all of them means rather "charioteers in each of them"; the word originally denoted the third man in a chariot team of three. The dismay of the Hebrews is effectively used by the J author to heighten the approaching climax. Moses' prophetic assurance in response, **Fear not, stand firm, and see the salvation of the LORD,** focuses attention on the coming great act of God. **Salvation** here preserves something of the word's primary physical connotation of width or freedom.

The suspense of the J narrative is ruined by the P synopsis in verses 15-18, which gives away the climax of the story. With theological rather than dramatic interest the P author sees the final event as a convincing demonstration of divine power rather than as the merciful deliverance of the people. P alone particularizes on the actual dividing of the sea (verse 16).

14:19-31. *The Passage of the Sea.* This account is a highly complex interweaving of the three literary sources, though the E contribution is very small.

Having depicted the Hebrews menaced by the Egyptians but reassured of divine aid (verses 10-14), J states that Yahweh's presence symbolized by the **pillar of cloud** shifted position and **stood behind** them—that is, between them and the Egyptians (verse 19*b*). E agrees in the same shift but embodies the divine presence in the **angel of God** (verse 19*a*). Verse 20 probably includes all three sources, but the only clearly identifiable element is the **darkness,** which probably represents the preliterary tradition behind E.

In spite of their variations all the sources agree in emphasizing the element of miracle. This agreement should discourage all attempts at naturalistic interpretation. Even if natural phenomena contributed to the deliverance, their coincidence with Israel's need was in itself a miracle.

14:21-22. In P Moses controls the action by holding out his **hand.** In J, however, the event is entirely the work of Yahweh, who **drove the sea back by a strong east wind all night and made**

the sea dry land. Here it is probably the J author rather than his sources who attempts a naturalistic explanation—the drying up by a sirocco of a moist depression, which is all that the Hebrew word for **sea** need signify (see above on 13:18*a*).

In P the **waters** of the sea are **divided** and form a **wall** on each side of the Hebrews as they walk between. This may be an elaboration of a tradition visualizing passage along the narrow sandspit between the salt marsh of Bardawil and the Mediterranean. More probably it is a prose paraphrase of the poetical representation in the hymnic celebration of the deliverance (cf. 15:8).

14:23-30. In verse 24 J transmits what is probably the original tradition, that **in the morning watch,** i.e. toward morning, **the LORD in the pillar of fire and of cloud looked down upon . . . the Egyptians . . . and discomfited them,** i.e. threw them into a panic. The theme of the sea in verse 27*cd* seems to represent a different tradition, which the J author may have drawn from the hymnic version in the cult—for example, the Song of Miriam (15:21*b*) and its development in the psalm attributed to Moses (15:1*b*-18).

The note that God bound up **their chariot wheels so that they drove heavily** seems secondary, as is suggested by the statement that only thereafter did the Egyptians decide to flee whereas they have apparently already panicked. This detail may indicate the swamping of a depression with ground water by a sudden rainstorm. Yahweh looking forth from the pillar of fire would suggest thunder and lightning with the rain, which was sufficiently rare in the Delta to be considered a miracle, especially when coinciding with the need of the Hebrews. The statement that the sea **returned to its wonted flow,** probably secondary, may be an instance of the saga motif of a striking phenomenon and its reverse—as, for example, the rod and serpent (4:3-4) and Moses' leprosy (4:6-7). **When the morning appeared** possibly relates to the cult legend of the nocturnal passover festival.

14:31. This editorial conclusion clearly indicates the subject of cult legend, a miracle which confirms the faith of Israel in

Yahweh's prophet. Nevertheless the substantial agreement of all sources, in spite of variations, in the deliverance from an Egyptian chariot force at the sea indicates a historical nucleus for the tradition, however this may have been modified in its transmission in saga and cult legend.

15:1-21. *The Song of the Sea.* This poem consists of a hymn on the theme of the deliverance at the sea (verses 1*b*-12) developed from the older "Song of Miriam" (verse 21*bc*), which is apparently contemporary with the event itself. There is a further development on the themes of the occupation of Palestine in verses 13-16 and **thy own mountain** and the **sanctuary** where Yahweh **will reign** as King in verses 17-18. It is clear that verses 13-18 date from after the settlement in Palestine, specifically after the subjection of the Philistines under David and probably after the development of the cult of Yahweh as King in the new year festival in Solomon's temple.

Many scholars have taken verses 1 and 20-21 as parallel J and E versions of the original victory song. They regarded verses 2-18 as a much later composition, late preexilic or even postexilic, inserted by an editor. Recently, however, certain scholars have noted points of prosody which appear to be an early development from Canaanite poetry attested in fourteenth century Ugaritic texts found at Ras Shamra in northern Syria. Certain archaic grammatical forms also give evidence of an early date. Accordingly it may well be that verses 1*b*-12, 21*bc* formed the hymnic culmination of the cult legend of the sacrament of the deliverance at the central shrine of the Israelite tribes before David's occupation of Jerusalem. If so, the addition of verses 13-18 may represent the adaptation of the old hymn to the service of the temple in Jerusalem in the time of Solomon. Thus the whole may have been incorporated intact as the culmination of the J narrative of the deliverance.

The theme of the kingship of Yahweh—symbolized by the establishment of his **abode**, the **sanctuary**, after his triumph in conflict with the forces of chaos represented by the sea—reproduces with historical adaptation the theme of the Canaanite new year festival illustrated in the Ras Shamra texts. This relationship seems to connect the whole psalm to the Israelite festival involving renewal of the covenant with Yahweh and its historical prelude in the exodus theme.

15:1*b*-5. Praise of Yahweh for deliverance at the sea forms the introduction to the ancient psalm in verses 1*b*-12 and the refrain which punctuates it in 5, 10, and 12. Thus introduced and epitomized, the song declares the elation in which the singer praises his **father's God,** who is personally experienced.

Verse 2*a* expresses the consciousness of possession by the divine spirit, which inspires the poet with supernatural insights and powers of expression. **My strength** indicates assurance, urge, and ability to praise Yahweh, whose nature as a **man of war** is revealed by his overthrow of the Egyptians.

The **floods** (verse 5) are the subterranean waters of Semitic cosmology, conceived sometimes naturally (for example, Genesis 7:11; 8:2 and Deuteronomy 8:7), sometimes mythologically (for example, Psalms 46:2-3; 89:8-9; and 93:3-4). The Hebrew word is related to Tiamat, the Mesopotamian mythological monster of chaotic waters overcome by the god Marduk in the liturgy of the Babylonian new year festival.

15:6-10. The second strophe expresses the confidence and eager anticipation of the pursuers by the staccato of verbs in verse 9. The boastful **desire,** i.e. greed, of the **enemy** points up the might of Yahweh. This is elaborated with poetic hyperbole in the piling up of the **waters** by the **blast of thy nostrils**—a phrase that suggests both the hot east wind (cf. 14:21), associated with Yahweh as a desert god, and the figurative sense of the Hebrew word for "nostrils," his anger.

15:11-12. In the Hebrew **holiness** is the proper and exclusive nature of God. The word itself has no moral connotation, though as relating to the God of Israel it has secondarily a moral sense. If textually correct here it emphasizes the exclusiveness of Yahweh's majesty, but the Septuagint reading "among the holy ones" probably preserves the original parallel to **among the gods.** The recognition of the God of Israel as one among other gods indicates an early date. Thus the defiant rhetorical

question **Who is like thee . . . among the gods?** expresses
preeminence over rivals. The basis of it is Yahweh's effective
action, **doing wonders** in nature and history, especially in the
overthrow of the Egyptians.

The earth swallowed them may allude to the bogging down of
Pharaoh's chariots (cf. 14:25a). On the other hand the detail in
the narrative may have been suggested by this passage in the
hymn. If so, the prose author probably misinterpreted it, for by
earth the poet evidently meant Sheol, the underworld abode of
the dead. Verse 12 may have been followed originally by the call
Sing to the LORD and the remainder of verses 21bc, reechoing
the opening couplet of the psalm.

15:13-18. The form of these verses, which are not in strophes
and lack the refrain on the victory at the sea, gives further
evidence that they are a later addition. The opening couplet on
God's guidance of his people introduces and epitomizes the
subject—the desert wandering and occupation of Canaan. The
occupation of Jerusalem is denoted probably in **thy holy abode**
and certainly in verses 17-18.

The Hebrew word translated **steadfast love** always implies
the concept of loyalty to the covenant. On **redeemed** see above
on 6:6-9. The sudden collapse of **Edom and Moab** does not
correspond to Pentateuchal tradition and indicates a date when
the effective resistance of both was long forgotten, i.e. after their
conquest by David. **Purchased** in verse 16 is a possible
translation but the word may also mean "created."

15:19-21. The prosaic summary in verse 19 indicates how a
late P editor, no longer conscious of the original cultic context of
the hymn, interprets its figures literally. Probably verses 20-21a
accurately describe the ritual in which the poem originated,
with prompting by women in a high state of elation to **sing to the
LORD** and response by the worshipers in the remaining words of
21bc.

Miriam, here mentioned for the first time, is identified as the
sister of Aaron (see above on 2:1-10) and said to be a
prophetess—that is, an inspired, ecstatic female like the
prophets of early times. A **timbrel** was a small percussion

instrument made of skin stretched tightly over a frame and used primarily to accompany **dancing.**

II. The Desert Wandering (15:22–18:27)

Three features suggest an originally independent tradition of the desert wandering—or perhaps an independent Moses saga—as a basic source:

(1) The independence and continuity of the traditions of Yahweh's provision of food (chapter 16; cf. Numbers 11:4-35) and water (15:22-27; 17:1b-7; cf. Numbers 20:2-13) in the desert.

(2) The murmuring against Moses.

(3) The vital significance of Moses and his rod before and after the tradition of the giving of the law at Mt. Sinai.

15:22-27. *The Spring at Marah.* This passage is introduced and concluded by geographical details in the style of P. It is basically a J narrative which explains the name of the spring **Marah,** meaning **bitter.** To this has been joined an E fragment (verse 25b) related to a spring named Massah, "proving" (cf. 17:1-7), that has been elaborated by a D editor in verse 26.

The **wilderness of Shur** was apparently the northern Sinai area immediately east of the modern Suez Canal. The name may be a dialectic word, "wall," used by the Semites in Sinai. Possibly it could be a version of the Egyptian name Taru, the key fortress east of the Delta in the chain of fortresses called the "Wall of the Prince."

The period of **three days** without **water** seems saga convention rather than history. Despite reports of Near Eastern shrubs capable of sweetening brackish water no such plant is known for certain.

15:25b-27. The statement that Yahweh **made for them a statute and an ordinance and . . . proved them,** which makes his preservation of Israel conditional on obedience, seems displaced from some point after the giving of the law at the holy mountain.

The preservation from **diseases** is abruptly introduced and associated with the observance of the commandments. It may have been suggested by the concept of Yahweh as **healer**, participle of the verb used of sweetening water at Jericho (II Kings 2:21-22) and the Dead Sea (Ezekiel 47:7-8).

Elim may be the plural of either "terebinth," a species of tree common in Palestine, or "god." If the latter, the name evidently refers to local spirits such as the Arabs often associate with oases, springs, and isolated trees. **Twelve** and **seventy** suggest the stylized manner of saga.

16:1-36. *Manna and Quails*. This chapter is mainly from P but includes a briefer account of the manna only (verses 4-5, 13*b*-15*a*, 27-30) from one of the early sources—probably J. Some scholars, however, connect **that I may prove them** with 15:25*b* and attribute the material to E. That the incident is chronologically out of order (cf. the J quail narrative, Numbers 11:4-35) is shown by the references to Yahweh's **glory** in the **cloud**, which P associates with the tabernacle (cf. 40:34-38), and to the **Testimony**—that is, the tablets of the Decalogue placed in the ark (cf. 25:16).

16:1 Representing the Hebrews as a **congregation** is characteristic of P. Location of the **wilderness of Sin** depends on the location of **Mt. Sinai.** Those who accept the traditional identification with Jebel Musa in the southern part of the Sinai Peninsula assume the wilderness of Sin to lie northwest of that peak. But the probability that the holy mountain should be located in the northern Sinai region near Kadesh (see above on 3:1) points rather to Sin's being a variant form of Zin. The wilderness of Zin is mentioned in connection with Kadesh (Numbers 20:1; 27:14; Deuteronomy 32:51; Joshua 15:3) and is described as west of Edom (Numbers 34:3; Joshua 15:1). In Numbers 13:21 it is the southern limit of the settled land of Palestine.

16:2-12. The murmuring against Moses is one of the themes of the tradition of the desert wandering. **Bread from heaven** is not spiritual food as allegorized by Paul (I Corinthians 10:3) but food in general coming from the sky, as the manna was thought to come. The cessation of manna on the sabbath, anticipated by the double portion on the **sixth day**, may be a secondary elaboration suggested by the special sanctity of the sabbath. Apparently verses 9-12 should precede verses 6-7, and verse 8 is an editorial addition.

16:13*a*. P has inserted the **quails** in this story from the J account in Numbers 11:31-34. Like manna, quails are a natural phenomenon of the northern Sinai region, where they come as autumn migrants from southern Europe. Making their landfall on the coast of Egypt and southern Palestine, they are so exhausted that they are easily netted and sent in large numbers to the cities. The quail tradition shows that the Hebrews came near the Mediterranean coast, perhaps preserving the memory of a seasonal expedition from the inland area generally occupied.

16:13*b*-15*a*. In Sinai and other desert regions manna is a sweet substance found, not **on the ground,** but on the low tamarisk shrubs. It has generally been assumed to be an exudation of the plant, perhaps after perforation by an insect, but according to one study it is an excretion of certain plant lice which solidifies in the dry desert air. The popular etymology which J essays—*man hu,* Aramaic rather than Hebrew for **What is it?**—is obviously unlikely.

16:15*b*-30. In contrast to the general sense of J in verse 4, P uses **bread** in the specific sense—cf. Numbers 11:8, where the manna is said to be actually ground with the millstone. The **omer,** defined as the **tenth part of an ephah,** is around 1.6 dry quarts. It occurs only here. The disappearance of the manna **when the sun grew hot** is due, not to melting, but to its being eaten by ants which come out with the warmth. On the **sabbath** see below on 20:8.

16:31-35. On **honey** see above on 3:7-10. J compares the **taste** to "cakes baked with oil" (Numbers 11:8). In the northern Sinai manna (Arabic *mann*) is still valued for its sugar content, in which the desert diet is deficient. There was a tradition that a pot of manna was preserved **before the Testimony**—that is, with the two tables of the Decalogue. This is specifically denied in a

D statement that the ark contained nothing but these tables (I Kings 8:9).

17:1-7. *Water from the Rock.* The introduction about the itinerary is from P. On **wilderness of Sin** see above on 16:1; on **Rephidim** see below on verses 8-16. The narrative then becomes an interweaving of similar traditions about two different springs from J and E.

In the J account (verses 2c-3, 7a, c) the spring is named **Massah**, "proving" or "ordeal," explained on the basis that there the people tested Yahweh. A fragment of the E tradition of Massah, in which Yahweh tests the people, has been preserved in 15:25b, being confused with the story of the spring of Marah from J. In the E narrative here the spring is called **Meribah**, "contention," reflecting the competition for precious water among desert nomads. The parallel narrative combined from J and P associates Meribah with Kadesh (Numbers 20:2-13; cf. Numbers 27:14 and Deuteronomy 32:51) and suggests that it was one of the minor springs within the Kadesh oasis.

Bring us up is a regular expression for the Exodus—that is, coming up from the Delta to the mountains of northern Sinai and Palestine. As in the plague narrative E is distinguished by the use of the **rod. The rock** probably means "this rock," **at Horeb** (see above on 3:1) being a later addition.

17:8-16. *The Battle with Amalek.* This narrative was possibly incorporated as a unit in the E source from a hero saga about Moses, the leader on whose raised or lowered hands the fortunes of war depend. **Joshua** suddenly appears as a warrior, whereas in 33:11 he is introduced as Moses' **servant** and a **young man.** This indicates that the incident really belongs to a later phase of the desert wandering, probably following the initial defeat by the Amalekites near Hormah southeast of Beer-sheba (Numbers 14:43-45; cf. Numbers 21:1-3). It was perhaps part of a Joshua saga secondarily associated with Moses.

The tradition has become an explanatory legend for the names of **Rephidim,** "supports," and the **altar** called **The LORD is my banner** in the neighborhood of Kadesh.

17:9-10. The **hand** of Moses on the **rod of God** (see above on

4:2-5) is the same motif as Joshua's spear stretched out toward Ai until the enemy was defeated (Joshua 8:18, 26). The rod may actually have been a standard of Yahweh with the serpent symbol—as in the incident of the serpent plague (Numbers 21:6-9), where the Hebrew word for the pole or staff is that translated **banner** in verses 15 and 16. If this was the standard after which the altar was named, and which was the subject of the poetic fragment about Amalek, the fact that it is twice attested in undoubtedly old traditions strongly suggests its originality.

17:11-13. The function of Moses' **hands** is probably a later modification of the primitive concept of the rod or standard as a symbol of the divine presence. The introduction of the hands may be related to the local tradition explaining the name **Rephidim** as "supports" for the arms. Here Moses is the inspired intermediary between Yahweh and the people, his reputation being the source of confidence or dismay. **Steady** is literally "steadiness," an emphatic usage with the meaning "steadiness itself." The noun, used here in its primary physical sense, came also to mean "faith."

17:14-16. The recording of the curse against Amalek **in a book** and its commission to Joshua may have been suggested to the E author by a collection under the name of Joshua extant in his day.

That the word translated **banner** means rather a standard (see above on verses 9-10) is borne out by its use in Isaiah 30:17 in parallelism with "flagstaff," a word that elsewhere is used of the mast of a ship. Such a standard on a hilltop served as a rallying signal. The **altar** was not only a memorial. It was also a place where the people might look for the rallying signal pole, so vital when they were spread out over the Kadesh oasis and constantly menaced by the Amalekites.

The couplet in verse 16 may be a relic of the originally poetic version of the saga source. It might better be translated:

> As [my] hand is on the standard of Yahweh,
> Yahweh will be at war with Amalek for every generation.

18:1-12. *Meeting with Jethro.* This passage is from E, but an editor has added verses 2-4 and perhaps other phrases in an effort to harmonize with the J material about Moses' family (2:21-22; 4:20a, 24-26). Since the name **Jethro** is usually followed both here and elsewhere (3:1; 4:18) by **Moses' father-in-law**—which is the only designation used in verses 13-27—it gives the impression of having been inserted later. Thus the father-in-law may have been nameless in the E tradition. He is called Hobab in at least one J passage (see above on 2:15b-22) but some scholars attribute Jethro to a second J source. Moses' being already **encamped at the mountain of God** indicates that this passage should follow 19:2.

18:6-11. The approach of Jethro is announced as a man of importance, a sheik and a **priest**. Moses goes to **meet** him, bowing to him as his elder, his father-in-law and head of his household, and greeting him in bedouin fashion with a kiss. Then follow the interminable inquiries and reassurances of health so familiar in Arab society. In the tent Moses tells Jethro of the deliverance and the desert wandering, and Jethro acknowledges the power of Yahweh.

18:12. A fellowship meal is characteristic of such encounters in the desert. This, however, is no common meal but a communion meal **before God** in connection with **sacrifices.** Thus the family idyl is quite incidental to this narrative. Rather, Jethro's initiative in the sacrifices and his direction to Moses indicate that it transmits the tradition of the formal adoption of the Hebrews into the cult of Yahweh at the desert sanctuary, probably at Kadesh, where Jethro was priest. This view that the Kenites, or Midianites, were the original Yahweh worshipers is rejected by some scholars, who regard this incident as instead the occasion on which Jethro identified his god with Yahweh. Moses' narration of the deliverance and saving acts of Yahweh, however, and Jethro's acknowledgment of these indicate a decisive development of the cult at the Midianite sanctuary, which was transformed after its adoption by the Hebrews. The omission of Moses in the notice of the ritual may be due to his being already a member of Jethro's family and of the Midianite religious community, whereas **Aaron** and **all the elders of Israel,** representing the people as a whole, are being brought into the community for the first time.

18:13-27. *Administration of Justice.* Though this passage is now linked by **On the morrow** to verse 12 it relates a separate tradition of a later event which occurred after the giving of the law (see below on verses 15-16). Jethro's question about Moses' judicial activity and Moses' explanation follow a common saga convention for introducing a new subject. Here they serve to emphasize Moses' conscientious fulfillment of the ideal of the tribal sheik and ruler in the ancient Near East. In the Ras Shamra legends two kings hear cases and dispense justice as described here.

18:15-16. The phrase **inquire of God** seems to anticipate the institution of the priestly oracle—the use of the sacred lots Urim and Thummim to determine the divine will (I Samuel 14:36-46)—as the final resource in deciding cases (cf. Deuteronomy 17:8-9). No doubt the purpose of this passage is to introduce this practice.

Statutes refers to decrees which have acquired the permanency of statutory law. **Decisions** are directives applied to specific cases. These terms imply the law only later communicated at Mt. Sinai and show that this passage belongs later in the narrative (see above on verses 13-27). Moses' role here may reflect the office of expounder of the law in the tribal assembly, the judge of Israel in the narrower judicial sense during the settlement in Palestine in the period of the judges.

18:17-26. In the original tradition verses 19-20 may have described Jethro's ordination of Moses as an oracle priest. The distinction between this office and that of secular arbitrators, who handled cases that could be decided mechanically by the application of customary law, is significant. **At all times** refers to everyday cases. It suggests by contrast those solemn occasions when the parties came either before an oracle priest or before the judge at the tribal assembly at statutory times and after due ritual preparation. This distinction underlies the difference between the categorical imperatives of the absolute laws and the conditional laws with their many qualifications in the Book of the Covenant (20:22–23:33).

The divisions in verses 21 and 25 reflect the administrative organization for the military levy projected back into the period of the militant tribal confederacy, which is now assumed to be brought into being.

18:27. Jethro's **own country** may mean the Midianite homeland east of the Gulf of Aqaba (see above on 2:15*b*-22 and 3:1). But more probably it was nearer Kadesh. If he was of the smith caste known as Kenites, his clan during the cooler season may have worked the copper ores of the Arabah, the rift valley extending from the Dead Sea to Aqaba, and during the summer taken their flocks to the Kadesh oasis. In the J tradition Moses' father-in-law and some of his clan seem to have stayed with the Hebrews and settled with them in Palestine (see comment on Numbers 10:29-36).

III. THE LAW AND COVENANT AT MT. SINAI
(19:1–24:18)

The theme of the first half of Exodus is the creative divine act of deliverance. That of the second half is the formation of a distinctive community, Israel, on the basis of a divine covenant. This covenant made explicit provisions, both ritual and moral, for Israel's expression of her distinctive status as the people of Yahweh. These provisions make up the law, which is thus primarily the consequence rather than the condition of the covenant and is also a revelation of the nature of the God of Israel.

This account of the awakening of Israel's consciousness as a people of divine destiny is therefore central in scripture. The prospect of the great J work that after the fall all families of the earth should be blessed in the seed of Abraham (Genesis 12:3) now comes near its realization in the adoption of Israel as God's covenanted people, **a kingdom of priests and a holy nation.**

In its present form the material begins with the theophany—that is, the physical manifestation of the divine presence—on the holy mountain (chapter 19). This is followed by the giving of the law (chapters 20-23) and in turn by the making of the covenant (chapter 24, continued in chapters 32-34). This is the order of E, which predominates in this section.

In the J tradition the making of the covenant may have preceded the giving of the law. In J it involves a communion meal on the mountain in which elders of the people participate.

In the later E account Moses is the sole mediator and other details enhance his authority. The theophany is exceedingly complicated. It reflects not only the liturgical variations at the various sanctuaries which preceded Jerusalem as central shrines of Israel—Shechem, Bethel, Gilgal, Shiloh, and perhaps Hebron—but also the development of the theme in psalms of praise. The law, consisting of the Decalogue (20:2-17) and the Book of the Covenant (20:22–23:33), is set loosely in this narrative in such a way as to suggest that these traditions are independent of the narrative.

The general pattern is so well attested in various parts of the Old Testament as to indicate that it derives from an established covenant sacrament. The pattern includes:

(1) admonition before the approach to God (19:4-6; cf. Joshua 24:14-15),
(2) response of the people (19:8; cf. Joshua 24:16, 24),
(3) proclamation of the law (20:23-26; cf. Joshua 24:25; Deuteronomy 27:15-26),
(4) the formality of the covenant (24:4-8; cf. Joshua 24:27),
(5) and blessings and curses as a sanction of the law (34:6-7; cf. Joshua 8:34; Deuteronomy 28:3-6, 16-19).

If the relevant passages in the Old Testament reflect the covenant tradition as it developed in Palestine, that tradition was itself probably determined by an older experience at the desert sanctuary. This experience, however, may be recovered in chapters 19-24 and 33-34 only in general outline.

A. THE MANIFESTATION OF YAHWEH'S PRESENCE
(19:1-25)

19:1-21a. *The Journey to Mt. Sinai.* The P itinerary is here resumed from 17:1. Perhaps verse 2a should precede verse 1.

On the third new moon is reckoned inclusively and thus denotes an interval of two months. Probably this was calculated to agree with the late tradition of the giving of the law at the feast of weeks (Pentecost), fifty days after the passover. On the location of **Sinai** see above on 3:1.

19:2b-8. *Admonition and Response.* Into this section of the E narrative a D editor has inserted the words of admonition in verses 3b-6. God's sure, swift succor of his people **on eagles'** wings probably reflects the hymnic language of the liturgy of the covenant sacrament. On Israel as God's **own possession** cf. Deuteronomy 7:6; 14:2; and 26:18. On the monotheistic concept **all the earth is mine** cf. Deuteronomy 10:14.

A kingdom of priests indicates that the government of Israel is to be theocratic. The executives are to be dedicated intermediaries between God and the community as befits **a holy nation,** i.e. a dedicated people. As a commonwealth of priests belonging to Yahweh, Israel is a community where all have insight into the divine will through immediate fellowship with him. **Holy** is properly a sacramental and physical term relating to health and wholeness. Here it gains moral content in the context of the law and the covenant.

19:9-15. *Ritual Precautions.* In preparation for the theophany E emphasizes the need for ritual purity by the washing of clothes (cf. Genesis 35:2, which also reflects the covenant sacrament at Shechem). Special clothes worn in worship are familiar in Semitic antiquity and are represented today in the simple shift of Muslim pilgrims entering the sacred territory about Mecca. Another tradition, probably J, calls for abstention from sexual intercourse (cf. I Samuel 21:4, indicating this practice by warriors in the holy war).

Clearly from J is the marking of the holy area around **Mount Sinai** by **bounds.** The sacred boundary is a well-known concept.

The idea of contact with the holy as fatal is primitive; cf. the death of Uzzah for touching the ark in II Samuel 6:6-7. The ram's-horn **trumpet** (*shophar*) was used to convoke a solemn assembly and to punctuate ritual.

19:16-25. *Yahweh's Descent on Mt. Sinai.* The J description of the theophany (verse 18) strongly suggests a volcano in eruption. Accordingly some scholars have tried to identify Mt. Sinai with one of the volcanic peaks east of the Gulf of Aqaba in the Midianite homeland (see above on 2:15*b*-22 and 3:1). It is more probable, however, that a Midianite tradition of a volcanic theophany originating in this region was transferred to a sacred mountain near Kadesh.

On the other hand the theophany in the E tradition (verse 16) is evidently a thunderstorm, developed from the cult legend of the Canaanite Baal as adapted by Israel in Palestine in the autumnal new year festival. In the Ras Shamra texts thunder and lightning accompany the manifestation of Baal as king.

Instead of **the whole mountain** certain Hebrew manuscripts and the Septuagint have "all the people." This is supported by the fact that the word translated **quaked,** the same verb as **trembled,** is ordinarily used of the emotional reactions of persons. However, the figure of the earth's trembling at the presence of Yahweh, expressed with other verbs, is common in poetic descriptions of theophanies.

In verse 19 the word translated **thunder** possibly is intended in its literal sense of "a voice" but more probably refers to thunder, as it obviously does in verse 16. Moses' impertinence in verse 23 is evidently an editor's attempt to reconcile the conflicting instructions of J and E.

B. The 10 Commandments (20:1-21)

The Decalogue is an insertion into the E narrative between 19:19 and 20:18, both of which describe the theophany at the holy mountain. The relation of the sabbath to the ordinance in the P account of Creation (Genesis 2:1-3) indicates that, whatever the antiquity of the Decalogue, in its present form it is the product of P editing.

It relates to the sacrament of the renewal of the covenant. In fact it is a concise summary of absolute laws relating to purity of worship and social morality. These absolute laws are stated as declarations and are called "apodictic" laws. Other laws relating to daily practices are stated conditionally—"when a man strikes his slave," etc.—and are known as "casuistic" laws. The characteristically terse nature of these laws indicates that the Decalogue has been expanded by comment and explanation, reflecting a harangue after the declaration of the law in the absolute form at the tribal assembly.

In the past many scholars believed that the high morality of the Decalogue must stem from a later time, under the influence of the great prophets of the eighth century. Now, however, there is a growing tendency to relate to Moses the primitive ten words, apart from the secondary additions, or at least to admit that his authorship can be neither denied nor proved by scientific methods.

In its form the Decalogue resembles treaties imposed by Hittite kings on their vassals in the fourteenth and thirteenth centuries. In these the king declares his name and status (cf. verse 2*a*). He enumerates his benefits to his vassal (cf. verse 2*b*) as a claim to absolute and exclusive obedience (cf. verse 3), introducing the detailed obligations (cf. verses 4-17). Heaven and earth and various natural features are called to witness in the Hittite treaties and oaths are added as sanctions (cf. Deuteronomy 27:15-26).

The covenant formula of the Decalogue seems to reflect this convention of international treaty law at the central shrines of Israel in Palestine. But the laws themselves, which have no parallel in the Hittite covenants, quite conceivably relate to the early religious community at Kadesh.

The numbering of the commandments in most Protestant and Eastern Orthodox churches, followed here, derives from Jewish tradition known to Philo and Josephus in the first century A.D. Modern Jewish usage, following another tradition, counts verse

2 as the first commandment and verses 3-6 as the second. In the Roman Catholic tradition, derived from Augustine and followed by some Lutherans, verses 3-6 comprise the first commandment. Based on the order in the Septuagint (cf. Deuteronomy 5:21), the prohibition against coveting one's neighbor's wife is the ninth and the rest of verse 17 is the tenth.

20:1-2. *Preamble.* In the context of the laws which distinguished the religious community of Israel **I am the LORD your God** indicates a regular sacramental occasion. The historical declaration of God's grace and power in the drama of salvation is a prelude to the moral demands of the prophets. God's grace to Israel in the Exodus is the basis of his claim to exclusive worship and unconditional obedience. The former slaves have a new status—a religious community whose distinctive character is expressed by their keeping of the principles declared in the following commandments, the ethical elements of which reveal also the nature of their God.

20:3. *The First Word.* The meaning of **before me** is "above [or "beside"] my presence," or possibly "against my presence." While not excluding the recognition, as distinct from the worship, of other gods (cf. 15:11) the Decalogue is for all practical purposes monotheistic.

20:4-6. *The Second Word.* The original short commandment was no doubt simply the opening clause, the rest being later expansion. **Graven image** probably means a material representation of Yahweh as well as such conventional figures of other deities in human or animal form as are known from excavations in the whole Near East. The later explanation of this prohibition in Deuteronomy 4:15 probably expresses the idea implied in the revelation of the name Yahweh (see above on 3:14-15). God is known through his action; thus what expresses his whole and indivisible character defies material representation. The suggestion that this second commandment, like the third, was designed to prevent any attempt to control God by magical means is also feasible.

Insofar as representations of other supernatural powers may be implied, the reference may be to such images as the figurines of the fertility goddesses of Canaan and the Egyptian amulets which archaeologists have discovered even in Israelite houses. Even if such cult objects as the ephod (Judges 8:27) and Jeroboam's golden calves (I Kings 12:26-33) are regarded as images of Yahweh, their existence does not militate against the antiquity of the second commandment any more than David's adultery with Bathsheba does against the antiquity of the seventh. More problematic is the tradition attributing the bronze serpent to Moses himself (Numbers 21:8-9; II Kings 18:4). Though the early use of this image is well attested (see above on 17:9-10) Moses' connection with it is less certain. It may have been a Kenite element adopted by certain of the southern Hebrews as an expression of their solidarity with the Kenites.

20:5. Yahweh's being a **jealous God,** demanding exclusive worship and resenting all that impairs his sole dignity, reflects the whole motive of the Decalogue to preserve the integrity of Israel as exclusively the people of God. This point belongs with the first commandment—as in the Ritual Code (cf. 34:14)—rather than with the second.

The punishment of descendants **to the third and the fourth generation,** repeated in 34:7, probably reflects the formula of the ban, under which certain delinquents were put to death with their families. Thus a person's communal responsibility is emphasized.

20:6. The concept of God's **love** as the obverse of his effective wrath (cf. 34:6-7) probably reflects a genuine early practice. The blessing and curse were amplified in public harangue after the adjurations which concluded the presentation of the law in the covenant sacrament (cf. Deuteronomy 28-30 after Deuteronomy 27:15-26).

20:7. *The Third Word.* Verse 7*b* is a homiletic expansion. On the significance of the **name** see above on 3:13. The divine name must not be "lifted for vanity," i.e. for any frivolous or malicious purpose, as in magic. God must be obeyed, not controlled. While primarily relating to magic, the commandment also probably visualizes perjury. Since perhaps as early as the Exile

Judaism has revered the name of God to the extent of refraining from pronouncing Yahweh and using circumlocutions instead—for example, "the LORD," "the Name," "the Place," "the Holy One."

20:8-11. *The Fourth Word.* The original short commandment (verse 8) is to note the special significance of the **sabbath** as a day dedicated to God. Its elaboration in verses 9-10, probably D, and in 23:12 and Deuteronomy 5:13-14 emphasizes the weekly rest day for the whole community, with a humanitarian motive for slaves and cattle. The P expansion in verse 11 connects it with the P scheme of creation (Genesis 1:1–2:4*a*).

The original commandment does not specify how often the sabbath is to be kept, but the seventh day is stated in the commandment in 23:12 and 34:21. The root of the word denotes "abeyance," i.e. suspension of normal activities. This was felt to be necessary at the transitional lunar phases, when the powers of the supernatural were especially dreaded. In Mesopotamia the king on behalf of the community suspended his normal activities on the seventh, fourteenth, nineteenth, twenty-first, and twenty-eighth days of the month.

It is not stated how the sabbath is to be observed apart from the suspension of work to delimit between the sacred and the profane. It may have been designed to facilitate visits to the sanctuary or business with holy persons (cf. II Kings 4:23) and to afford a means for the religious community to realize its solidarity at the local shrine.

The exclusive worship of the God of Israel being defined, the distinctive character and integrity of God's people are now safeguarded by laws affecting their freedom.

20:12. *The Fifth Word.* This commandment is directed to adults as members of the religious community. Possibly it reflects life at the subsistence level, where older persons might be neglected as economically useless. The injunction to **honor your . . . mother** was the more natural in a polygamous society, where an aging wife might well depend on her son rather than on her husband. In the broader sense discipline in the family, where the mature wisdom of parents overrules the impulse and prejudice of youth, is the basis of an ordered society. The D expansion in verse 12*b* connects the covenant and law with the fulfillment of the promise of the **land** (cf. Deuteronomy 28:63-68).

20:13. *The Sixth Word.* Here and generally the verb translated **kill** denotes premeditated homicide. In view of the admission of the vendetta (Deuteronomy 19:11-13; Numbers 35:6-21) the prohibition refers primarily to murder as a breach in the sacral community. It might also refer to the mitigation of the blood feud in the case of accidental death, for which sanctuaries were provided pending decision by the community. The commandment does not prohibit killing in war or capital punishment.

20:14. *The Seventh Word.* As addressed to a man this commandment visualizes **adultery** primarily as sexual relations with a woman married or betrothed to another—a capital offense (cf. Deuteronomy 22:22-27). But extramarital sex with others is not condoned (see below on 22:16-17). The law conserved, not the dignity of the woman, but the right of her husband or father.

20:15. *The Eighth Word.* Joseph's use of the verb translated **steal** (Genesis 40:15) indicates that it refers specifically to kidnapping and selling into slavey. This was a capital offense in 21:16 and Deuteronomy 24:7 and an offense against the community as the people of God.

20:16. *The Ninth Word.* This commandment prohibits false evidence, implying perjury, which might damage the status and even the life of a person. In Deuteronomy 19:16-19 the convicted perjurer incurs the penalty of the crime he has alleged.

20:17. *The Tenth Word.* The original short commandment is the opening clause. By Arabic analogy **house** includes all the possessions mentioned in the amplification. Generally the verb translated **covet** denotes inordinate desire, but in view of the nature of the social offenses in the rest of the Decalogue it more likely refers here to practical measures taken to secure the desired object. Cf. Micah 2:2, where the context indicates violent seizure.

20:18-21. ***Reaction to Yahweh's Manifestation.*** This is a continuation of the E narrative from 19:19, except for the J phrase **and the mountain smoking.** The account of the theophany immediately before and after the Decalogue enhances the solemnity of the law. The request of the people that Moses rather than God should speak to them clearly demarcates the categorical imperatives of the Decalogue from the detailed laws of the Book of the Covenant, which to a large extent is the development of the social law of Canaan in the general legal tradition of the ancient Near East.

C. THE BOOK OF THE COVENANT (20:22–23:33)

The title "Book of the Covenant" for this collection of laws, also called the Covenant Code, was suggested by the allusion in 24:7, which evidently refers instead to the Decalogue. That the collection is not complete is indicated by comparison with Deuteronomy 12–26. That it is not a unity is shown by doublets, by the address in second person plural (e.g. 20:22-23) and singular (e.g. 20:24), and generally by the different superscriptions (20:22*a;* 21:1) and the different forms in which the laws are communicated, namely apodictic and casuistic (see above on 18:17-26). A ritual code, more completely represented in 34:17-26, may be another independent element. The concluding appendix (23:20-33) is not the conclusion of a self-contained body of laws—cf. the solemn adjurations with blessings and curses in Deuteronomy 27-30 and Leviticus 26—but is really an adaptation of the conclusion to the whole Sinai episode.

The Book of the Covenant, then, is a compilation made over a considerable period which was inserted somewhat awkwardly into the E Sinai narrative. It may go back to the first centuries after the settlement in Palestine, for the fact that there is not mention of political institutions points to a time before the monarchy.

In the subject matter there is nothing to suggest Sinai or desert society but much to indicate settlement. The highly detailed laws reflect in form and content the common law of the Near East in the second millennium—cf. e.g. the Code of Hammurabi. On the other hand, in view of the years when the Israelites lived a seminomadic life around Kadesh, where agriculture on a very limited scale was possible, certain laws, especially the ethical commandments, may have been associated with Moses.

20:22-26. *Ritual Ordinances.* The prohibition against the representation of strange **gods** and the provisions for an **altar** safeguard the purity of the worship of Yahweh. They belong with the absolute laws, though in what precise context cannot now be determined. Altars are to be built **in every place** where a theophany occurs (cf. 17:15), as in patriarchal times—contrast the later D restriction to a single altar (Deuteronomy 12:5-14). God's presence is to be invoked in the confidence inspired by the revelation of God's nature and will in the event the altar commemorates. The altar rather than an image symbolizes the presence of God and reminds people that God is known by divine interventions in history.

The **altar of earth** was probably made of compacted clay or crude brick, which would have the added advantage of absorbing the blood of the sacrifices. The motives for prohibiting **stone** dressed with an edged **tool** (cf. Deuteronomy 27:5 and Joshua 8:31, which say "iron tool") probably combine the desire to avoid materials contaminated by man and the early superstitious fear of iron as a trade secret of an alien smith caste. The **steps** now familiar to archaeologists from Canaanite altars of the Bronze Age are prohibited on the basis of modesty, which determined the introduction of breeches for the priests at a later period (28:42-43) and the use of a ramp instead of steps in Herod's temple.

The two main sacrifices made with the effusion of blood are mentioned. In the **burnt offerings,** the whole animal was burned as a sacrifice to God. In the **peace offerings**—better "communion offerings"—the blood, fat, and vital organs were burned on the altar to God and the rest was eaten by the worshipers, who thus effected solidarity with one another and with God.

21:1. *Introduction to the Casuistic Law*. Following the declarative ritual ordinances (20:23-26) this introduction sets out a solid block of civil law (21:2–22:17). This is communicated in casuistic form except for certain insertions of more primitive laws (21:12, 15-17). The material is logically arranged and gives the impression of an extract from a civil code.

21:2-11. *Slavery*. The laws regarding slaves indicate a comparatively developed society with fixed property rights. It is doubtful whether **Hebrew** in verse 2 has an ethnic significance. It may rather refer to the Habiru (see Introduction), an alien and underprivileged class who might in fact sell themselves into temporary or permanent slavery. Except for this possible reference there is no evidence of such a class in Israel after the settlement in Palestine. There was the practice of enslavement for debt, and Israelite slave debtors were apparently regarded as the Habiru had been. The release in the **seventh year** is related to the septennial cancellation of debts. Deuteronomy 15:12-18 also orders release in the seventh year on grounds of humanity, the status of the Hebrews in Egypt corresponding to that of the Habiru.

21:3-6. If the master provides a **wife** for the slave, she and their children are the property of the master. They need not be released when the six-year term ends. For this reason, or because of poverty or insecurity as a freeman, a man may choose to become a permanent slave. If so, the master brings him **to God,** i.e. probably to the sanctuary, to ratify his declaration by oath.

Alternative suggestions are that "God" should be rendered "gods," signifying the household gods, or that it is a corruption of "judges." Probably the **doorpost** to which the slave's ear is to be fixed is that of the master's dwelling—cf. the association with supernatural influences in the family (12:23; Isaiah 57:8). Thus two distinct transactions are visualized.

21:7-11. Verse 7 explicitly discriminates between slaves of this class and a female sold into slavery by her father—probably in discharge of debt. The master may take her himself as wife or concubine or allow his son to do so. In either case her marital status must be recognized and she cannot be reduced to the position of a slave. If he does not wish to keep her she may be **redeemed** by her father. If the master remarries he may not deprive her of her maintenance or her conjugal rights. Otherwise she may claim her freedom without a redemption price. The institution of slavery within the Hebrew community, like that of concubinage, reminds us that we must study the Old Testament against its own background as the records of a community developing over a millennium.

21:12-17. *Capital Offenses Against Persons.* The general principle of capital punishment for manslaughter (verse 12) is stated in only five Hebrew words. This and the similarly terse statements in verses 15-17 are probably part of a brief apodictic code like the nucleus of the Ten Commandments or the Twelve Curses of Deuteronomy 27:15-26. They were probably taken from such a summary as headings for the casuistic modifications which follow.

21:13-14. In blood revenge nomad society does not discriminate between murder and accidental homicide. Thus the principle in verse 12 may indicate an early stage in Israelite society. But in the congestion and complexity of urban and agricultural life unlimited vengeance became intolerable and discrimination must be made.

According to the solution which was developed the death penalty for murder was not waived. However, sanctuary was provided for the killer at the altar of a shrine until it could be determined whether **God let him fall into his hand**—that is whether the death was an "act of God" or the willful act of a murderer. In Israel this sanctuary was eventually limited to six cities of refuge (Numbers 35:6-11; Deuteronomy 4:41-43; 19:1-13; Joshua 20)—possibly when the local cult centers were suppressed under Josiah.

21:15-17. Among the capital crimes is disrespect for parents, here specified as striking or cursing, which for the ancient

Semite had as much force as a physical act. Kidnapping is also a capital crime (see above on 20:15). In Deuteronomy 24:7 an Israelite victim is specified and such is probably to be assumed here. Selling a man to such ready merchants as the seafaring Phoenicians and the Edomite caravaneers would impair the religious community by removing one of its members.

21:18-32. *Compensation for Injuries.* Here is a series of casuistic qualifications on the damages to be assessed in cases of bodily injury.

21:18-19. That a quarrel is unpremeditated is proved by the use of makeshift weapons. **Fist** translates a rare word which possibly means some sort of implement. If one injured in such a situation recovers, the other is punished only by having to compensate **loss of his time,** a single Hebrew word from the root of "sabbath" and which therefore refers to the interruption of his work. **Have him thoroughly healed** probably refers to the expense of a physician and other medical care.

21:20-21. The life of a **slave** also is protected in Israelite law. Though it is not explicitly stated how the master who beats his slave to death is to be **punished,** the verb implies blood revenge, probably executed by the community. On the other hand the survival of the slave even **a day or two** is taken as evidence that the master did not intend to kill him. The loss of valuable personal property is treated as sufficient penalty.

21:22. Even unborn life is protected. In case of a **miscarriage** suffered by a woman who intervenes in a fight, presumably on behalf of her husband, the right of the family to compensation is recognized. **As the judges determine** is a rather free translation of a word that probably should read "for the miscarriage."

21:23-25. The law of retaliation *(lex talionis),* well known from its rejection by Jesus (Matthew 5:38), is here applied to injury suffered by a pregnant woman. But the abrupt change from the general hypothesis to the direct categorical command in the second person singular is noticeable. Thus the passage may be displaced, as some believe, and should follow verse 19. On the other hand the similar formula in Deuteronomy 19:21 suggests that this may be the quotation of a principle which applies to any case of injury caused to a free person.

21:26-27. The master who injures his **slave** is exempt from the principle of retaliation. He is held to be sufficiently punished by the compulsory release of the slave, who is also his capital. Here Israel endorses the general principle of common Near Eastern law that a slave has not the same legal worth as a free person.

21:28-32. A similar distinction is made in the provisions for cases of fatal goring by an **ox**. In any case the ox is to be publicly stoned to death and its flesh may not be eaten, being taboo by blood guilt. If an ox has been notoriously vicious the owner who neglects to confine it is responsible when it kills someone. In such case a free person's death demands the death of the owner—though he may ransom himself, apparently at the discretion of the community. A slave's life demands only the payment to his master of **thirty shekels of silver**, apparently the usual price of a slave.

21:33–22:17. *Compensation for Property Loss.* Underlying the laws of this section is the general principle of requiring equivalent restitution for accidental injury to livestock or other property. Multiple restitution is required where a theft is involved. Thus the man responsible for loss of an animal in an uncovered pit must simply exchange a live animal for the dead one. If one ox kills another unexpectedly the two owners divide the loss, but the owner of an ox known to be vicious who fails to confine it must bear the full loss.

22:1-4. The distinction here between **ox** and **sheep** reflects the added value of the ox for labor as well as meat. The thief who kills or sells stolen beasts is penalized much more heavily than one who keeps them so that they may be recovered. If a thief has neither the money nor the beast to pay his fine—probably the more common situation—he is to be **sold** as a slave.

22:2-3a. This law belongs in a different context (see the footnote in the Revised Standard Version), since it concerns homicide rather than restitution for theft. If the thief is killed in **breaking in**—literally "digging through"—presumably at night, when he himself might have killed the occupants of the house and remained undetected, **no bloodguilt** ensues. But killing the thief in daylight is regarded as a vindictive act and demands blood revenge. Some interpreters take **if the sun has risen upon him** to mean simply "at a later time"; that is, a burglar caught in the act at any time may be killed, but one apprehended afterward may not.

22:5-6. If crops are destroyed, either by animals or by fire, the man responsible must make the equivalent compensation to the owner. Apparently no distinction is made between accidental and malicious damage.

22:7-9. Lacking banks, ancient people had frequent need of pledges for loan or safe deposit. Here it is provided that one alleging theft of a deposit must **come near to God**—that is, at the local shrine, probably to take an oath (see below on verses 10-13. If **breach of trust,** or deliberate infringement of the law of the community, is alleged and a man claims that any of his property is in another's possession, the **case of both parties shall come before God** at the local shrine. The one there declared guilty shall make **double** restitution. Possibly some ordeal is understood, as when a wife is accused of adultery (Numbers 5:11-28).

22:10-13. One who alleges the legitimate loss of a beast in his care must take an **oath by the LORD**—that is, a declaration attested by a ritual invoking severe punishment by Yahweh if it is not true (cf. I Kings 8:31-32). If he satisfies the priests and witnesses of his oath no compensation is to be demanded.

Verse 12 seems inconsistent with verses 10-11 and may be from a different source. Perhaps the distinction is that **driven away** refers to a raid which would be common knowledge even though the taking of the particular animal was not seen, whereas **stolen** refers to alleged theft by an individual. In the latter case the likelihood of negligence if not collusion was considered such as to require restitution as a safeguard. Another suggestion is that **is driven away** may be an erroneous duplication of **is hurt,** which differs by only one letter in the Hebrew, so that verses 10-11 apply only to death or injury of the animal. If so, **accept the oath,** literally "accept it," may mean "accept the dead or

injured animal." If the ravaging of wild **beasts** can be proved by
the evidence of mangled remains, compensation is waived.

22:14-15. Restitution is demanded for the death or injury of a
borrowed beast unless the owner was present and thus could
have prevented abuse. For casualties from natural causes no one
is liable. The final clause of verse 15 is ambiguous. Possibly it
means that if the animal is **hired,** no compensation is due
because the owner has allowed for such risks in setting his fee.
Another possibility is that if the beast is in the charge of a hired
man, the compensation must come out of his wages.

22:16-17. The seduction of an unbetrothed **virgin,** who is
expected to bring a **marriage present** or bride-price to her
father, is treated in the context of damaged property rather than
of family law. This is the only sexual case in the Book of the
Covenant, surely evidence of its fragmentary nature.

Seduction or rape of a betrothed virgin ranks as adultery and
is a capital offense. Seduction of an unbetrothed virgin is a lesser
offense for which the penalty is simply payment of the
bride-price and regular marriage to her. If the father refuses
such marriage the bride-price must be paid nevertheless, since
the loss of virginity, which must be publicly attested if
challenged by the bridegroom, would prejudice the eventual
marriage of the girl. The bride-price was paid to the parents but
might in part or whole be remitted to the bride as a dowry.

22:18-31. *Miscellaneous Ordinances.* This section consists
generally of laws in apodictic form, some of them expanded with
admonitions. Except for the three capital offenses at the
beginning and a threat of death in verse 24 it differs from the
preceding material in that, as in the Decalogue, no penalties are
stated.

22:18 Deuteronomy 18:10*b*-11 includes the masculine form of
sorceress in a list of terms for practitioners of various forms of
sorcery—attempts to secure information from the beyond or to
bring supernatural influence to bear on situations or persons by
other than the regular means of religion. All such practices are
punishable by death (cf. Leviticus 20:6, 27).

22:19. Bestiality (cf. Leviticus 20:15-16 and Deuteronomy

27:21) is covered also in the ancient Hittite laws, where it was a capital offense, though subject to royal pardon. It was punishable with most domestic animals but not with a horse or mule.

22:20. The utter destruction demanded for one who sacrifices to gods other than Yahweh possibly included his family and possessions, as in the case of Achan (Joshua 7:15, 24-25; cf. I Samuel 15:3).

22:21-24. The word here translated **stranger** is *ger* (see above on 2:21-22), which the Revised Standard Version more often renders as "sojourner," i.e. a protected alien. Humanitarian concern for the sojourner, the **widow,** and the **orphan** as persons in need of special consideration is repeatedly enjoined in the legal codes. It is cited as a prime example of righteousness by the prophets.

22:25-27. Further humanitarian ordinances deal with lending **money** to the **poor.** Money is literally "silver," which until postexilic times was reckoned by weight. The prohibition against **interest** refers to exploitation of a poor man's need. It does not refer to a commercial investment, where the interest is simply a share of the borrower's profit. In no way might the religious community of Israel be impaired. One might lend with interest to a resident foreigner, who would own no land but live by trade and might use the loan to his personal advantage.

Garment refers to the long loose robe which served as both overcoat and blanket and therefore was needed at nightfall. In view of the ancient conception of the garment as peculiarly representative of the person, the pledging of it may have signified that in the event of the debtor's selling himself into slavery the holder should have the first option.

22:28. To **revile**—literally "lighten," i.e. divest of weight or honor—the deity or **curse** the civil authority menaced the community at its source. Though it is not explicitly stated here, this was a capital offense (cf. Leviticus 24:15-16; I Kings 21:9-10). **Ruler** is literally "one raised up," probably denoted originally the tribal representative to the common assembly—cf., for example, Numbers 1:16, 44; 7:2, where "leaders" renders the same Hebrew word. It later was understood to mean the king.

22:29-31 *Ritual Ordinances.* These apodictic commandments and their continuation in 23:10-19 are probably fragments of a ritual code parallel to 34:14-26 (see comments). Though apparently incongruous with the moral and civil ordinances of the context, the ritual ordinances actually provided for the visible expression of the solidarity of the people of God and afforded occasions for the public declaration and application of the law.

Verse 29a refers to the offering of first fruits. On the **first-born** see above on 13:1-2, 11-16. The prohibition in verse 31 probably grew out of the taboo against eating blood.

23:1-9. *Ordinances About Justice.* The series of apodictic injunctions in verses 1-3 amplifies the commandment against false witness in 20:16. It names particulars: creating prejudice by rumors, being suborned to perjury, deferring to the majority despite one's true conviction, and partiality.

The prohibition against favoring a **poor man**, if correct, presumably forbids letting pity for him subvert the justice due a richer opponent. "Poor," however, may be a corruption of "great," which differs by only one consonant. Or possibly both words were originally included, as in Leviticus 19:15.

23:4-5. These are casuistic injunctions to neighborliness. They involve cases of an enemy's straying animals or ass foundered under an awkward burden. **Help him lift it up** is an emendation of the Hebrew text, which is an apparent repetition of the verb translated **leaving.** Probably it is a word play—a different verb with the same consonants meaning "loose." Thus the effect is somewhat like "not leave but relieve." These injunctions are motivated by social considerations rather than by consideration for the beasts, which would be exceptional in the ancient Near East.

23:6-9. These verses continue the injunctions about justice in verses 1-3. With verse 6 cf. verse 3. With verse 8 cf. 18:21 and Deuteronomy 16:19. With verse 9 cf. 22:21.

23:10-19. *Further Ritual Ordinances.* These are a continuation of 22:29-31. They are probably the fragments of a ritual code parallel to 34:14-26 (see comments). Here the injunction to let fields **lie fallow** in the **seventh year** is said to be for the purpose of providing food for the **poor**. Here alone also the sabbath is given a humanitarian rather than a religious explanation. Mentioning the **names of other gods** means invoking their presence. **Feast of harvest** is probably the original name of what is called the feast of weeks elsewhere in the Old Testament.

23:20-33. *Epilogue.* In this exhortation stressing God's conditional grace the law is related to the occupation of the promised land (see above on 20:12). Actually the section may be a conclusion to the whole Sinai episode which has been adapted as a conclusion to the Book of the Covenant. Here there are no curses on disobedience as in the epilogues to the law in Leviticus 26:14-39 and Deuteronomy 28:15-68. Rather there are both admonitions and assurance for the journey to Canaan and the settlement there.

23:20-26. Guidance is promised by an **angel**—that is, the presence of God, whose **name** indicates God's presence in character. The **voice** of the angel and his commands, however, indicate a human intermediary, a "messenger" (the literal meaning of "angel") such as Moses. On the other hand verse 23 suggests that the angel means the ark, which went before Israel in battle (cf. Numbers 10:35).

Possibly the passage shows several stages of elaboration. The familiar list of the inhabitants of Canaan, the prohibition against worshiping their gods, and the injunction to eradicate their worship and to make no covenant with them suggest expansion by a D editor.

Pillars were stones set on end either to symbolize the presence of a deity at the place where the deity had been manifested or to commemorate a noted or favored ancestor.

23:27-33. The **terror** of God is the supernatural panic which causes the enemy's morale to break in the crisis of battle, a familiar concept in the idea of the holy war (see comment on Deuteronomy 20). The partial settlement of Israel in Canaan, frankly admitted here, is explained theologically as according to the divine economy to keep the land in cultivation. Contrast Judges 2:20-23, where the survival of the Canaanites is explained as for the discipline and training of Israel.

Here only in the Old Testament the land occupied by Israel is defined as **from the Red Sea,** i.e. the Gulf of Aqaba (see above on 13:18*a*), **to the sea of the Philistines,** i.e. the Mediterranean, **and from the wilderness,** i.e. the southern desert, **to the Euphrates**—the extent of David's control if not occupation.

D. THE MAKING OF THE COVENANT (24:1-18)

Two accounts of the covenant are combined here. In the J account (verses 1, 9-11) **Moses with Aaron, Nadab, and Abihu, and seventy . . . elders** representing Israel celebrate a communion meal on the mountain in the presence of God. This effects the covenant. Contradicting this are the words **and worship afar off** in verse 1 and all of verse 2 which declare that Moses alone is to **come near** God. Therefore this must be a later addition.

The E account is in verses 3-8. It is more circumstantial and also includes a communion meal shared with God, the **peace offerings.** This tradition differs from that of J in that it is celebrated at a regular sanctuary with an **altar at the foot of the mountain** and **pillars** and involves a public recitation and endorsement of the **book of the covenant.** Possibly some of these elements were originally included in the J account but were omitted by the editor to avoid duplication.

24:3-8. *Ritual at an Altar.* This account reflects in several details the tradition of the sacrament of the renewal of the covenant in the period of the judges at Shechem. But there are older traditions here also. **All the words of the LORD** probably denotes a short collection of laws like the Ten Commandments in their original form. **And all the ordinances** is a later addition after the Book of the Covenant was composed.

The formal endorsement of the terms of the covenant (verse 3*b*) is a regular element of the ritual which is found in the Hittite vassal treaties (see above on 20:1-21). Moses' recording of the law in verse 4 is also paralleled in the Hittite vassal treaties. Without the recording the treaty was not valid. Cf. the recurrent tradition of the recording of the law in the covenant ceremony at Shechem (Deuteronomy 27:3 and Joshua 8:32; 24:26). The **twelve pillars** (see above on 23:20-26) are probably an anachronism reflecting the twelve-tribe confederacy in Palestine. A single stone was witness to the covenant at Shechem (Joshua 24:27 and Judges 9:6).

24:5-8. That **young men of the people of Israel** instead of priests killed the sacrificial victims clearly indicates an early tradition in this account. Its antiquity is further suggested by the fact that here only is the rite of sprinkling **blood** mentioned in connection with the covenant ceremony. The blood is dashed on the **altar,** symbolizing the presence of God, and on the **people** as the parties to the covenant. This unique tradition may reflect the formal adoption of members into the covenant community. Certainly it is not a literary composition merely written as an epilogue to the Book of the Covenant.

24:9-11. *A Communion Meal.* The simpler tradition in this J account may reflect the covenant ceremony at Kadesh in which southern groups of the Hebrews were involved with the Midianites or Kenites (see above on 18:12). **Nadab** and **Abihu** are introduced abruptly here and not mentioned elsewhere in J or E. In P they are identified as the two older sons of Aaron (6:23), who were later destroyed for offering "unholy fire" (Leviticus 10:1-2). They may represent a priesthood displaced by Aaron. Their presence here with Moses, Aaron, and the elders of Israel possibly indicates that they were representatives of the Kenites.

Though it is twice stated that the whole company **saw . . . God,** his appearance is not described except for the **pavement** under his feet. **Sapphire** probably refers to the blue sky. **Chief men** means literally "corners," hence "supports."

24:12-18. *Moses Alone on the Mountain.* In this passage P reappears for the first time since 19:1-2a. Verses 15b-18a evidently are the P version of the theophany on **Mount Sinai**

described by J and E in 19:16-19 and 20:18-21. The rest of the passage has generally been attributed to E as an introduction to the golden calf story in chapter 32.

Certain elements that seem unrelated to the E narrative have been explained by some scholars as coming from a second J source. These are probably due, however, to development by a P editor, who used the passage as an introduction to the account of the tabernacle and its service in chapters 25–31; 35–40. There the concern is to associate the reestablished cult of the temple after the Exile with the Mosaic tradition.

The **tables of stone** inscribed with the law may reflect the tradition of a monument inscribed with a summary code at a central sanctuary in the time of the judges. The assignment to **Aaron and Hur** of judicial duties during Moses' absence adds to the evidence that the appointment of judges at Jethro's suggestion (18:13-27) originally came later in the narrative.

24:15-18. In the P version of the theophany the **cloud** is the symbol of the divine presence. The anthropomorphisms of the earlier sources are carefully avoided (cf. 13:21; 14:24; 19:9; 20:21). P still retains, however, the traditional symbolism of **fire** as the sign of the theophany as well as the old narrative convention of **six days** before the climax on the **seventh.** Possibly **forty days and forty nights** is also a typical P statistic. More probably this detail is part of the E narrative providing time for the making of the golden calf (32:1-6).

IV. INSTRUCTIONS FOR THE SANCTUARY AND THE SERVICE (25:1–31:18)

Chapters 25–31 are all characteristically P in both content and style. They are nevertheless composite, as is evident from doublets and discrepancies. Yahweh alternates between first and third persons in the references to his person. The belated descriptions of the incense altar and the laver logically belong in chapters 25 and 27 respectively (see below on 30:1-38). Various theories of editorial change have been proposed, but the most plausible explanation is that two independent versions have been combined by an editor, who added supplementary material.

The tabernacle is generally regarded as the placing back in the desert period a later shrine which housed the ark. This is generally assumed to be Solomon's temple, though the dimensions and some other details are different. The differences may be due to fusion of the conception of the temple with that of the genuine old tradition of a much simpler tent of meeting (33:7-11), which is an oracle shrine where God condescends to meet man occasionally. The P description preserves continuity with the old tradition by continuing to use the term "tent of meeting" and specifically elaborates on the idea that God will meet with his people there (25:22).

The word for "tabernacle" is derived from the verb translated "dwell" in 25:8 and 29:45-46. Evidently the promise of God's dwelling in the tabernacle is to be understood in this sense of his occasional presence in the place of meeting. It would not be a localization of the transcendent God of postexilic Judaism (cf. I Kings 8:27).

A. THE SANCTUARY AND ITS FURNITURE (25:1–27:21)

25:1-9. *The Materials.* The tabernacle is to be provided by a freewill **offering,** as in the rebuilding of the temple after the Exile (Ezra 1:4; 2:68-69)—in contrast to the forced labor used by Solomon (I Kings 5:13-18).

Dyes of **blue and purple** were respectively bluish and reddish purple, the classical royal purple. Both were obtained from a Mediterranean shellfish, the murex, at various stages of decomposition. **Scarlet** dye comes from the cochineal insect, which lives on the Syrian evergreen oak. All were unlikely in the desert. Also unlikely were olive **oil** and balsam **spices,** i.e. perfumes, and Egyptian **linen** and dressed leather, which is probably denoted by the rare word translated **goatskins.** On the òther hand the webs of **goats' hair,** the framework of **acacia**

wood which grows in the desert, and the **tanned,** literally "reddened," **rams' skins** may have pertained to the primitive tent of meeting (33:7-11). On **ephod** and **breastpiece** see below on 28:6-35.

25:10-22. *The Ark.* That the first article in the tabernacle to be described is the ark reflects its significance in the temple, where it was the only object kept in the inmost shrine. In the older narrative sources in the Pentateuch the ark is mentioned only twice (Numbers 10:35-36 and 14:39-45) and in neither passage is it associated with the tent of meeting. In the narrative of Eli and Samuel at Shiloh in I Samuel 1-3 the ark is housed in a temple, and the mention of the tent of meeting in I Samuel 2:22*b* is an obvious later insertion. In the detailed history of the ark in I Samuel 4:1-7:2 and II Samuel 6:1-19 there is no reference to a tent until David provides one in Jerusalem. Therefore it seems probable that the ark and the tent of meeting belong to two independent traditions originally related to different tribal groups (see below on 33:7-11). For an alternative suggestion see below on 33:1-6.

The construction of the ark can only be surmised from the earlier sources. This is the only detailed description and it is unfortunately late and idealistic. Obviously nomadic Israel would not have this profusion of **gold.** The dimensions are credible—about forty-five by twenty-seven by twenty-seven inches according to the common **cubit** of about eighteen inches, though possibly a longer cubit of up to twenty-one inches is meant. But these dimensions may be no more reliable than many other P statistics.

The developing theological interpretation of the ark is noteworthy. In Numbers 10:35-36; 14:39-45 and I Samuel 4 it symbolizes the divine presence and activity in battle; cf. the Philistine reaction, "a god has come into the camp" (I Samuel 4:7).

Deposited in the temple built at Shiloh and later in the temple at Jerusalem, it is considered the throne of the invisible God. **Cherubim**—winged sphinxes—indicate a throne. These are familiar to archaeologists as side supports of thrones in Palestine and Syria.

In the ark narratives in I Samuel 4:1–7:2 and II Samuel 6:1-17 it is regularly called the "ark of God," sometimes "of Yahweh." But in the D writings it is termed "ark of the covenant," no doubt because it reputedly contained the two stone tablets on which the Ten Commandments were written. This may be the revival of a genuine old tradition; cf. the deposit of agreements in sanctuaries beneath the feet of statues of Hittite and Egyptian gods.

In the P material the ark is the repository of the **testimony**—that is, the two tables of the law (31:18)—and is accordingly called the **ark of the testimony.** The tabernacle as the shelter for the ark is sometimes called the "tabernacle of the testimony." Here God at his own discretion meets with and declares himself to human beings in revelation, and in mercy. The lid of the ark is called the **mercy seat,** and on it the blood of atonement was to be sprinkled by the high priest on the Day of Atonement (Leviticus 16:2-16).

25:23-30. *The Table.* The table was provided to hold the **bread of the Presence.** According to Leviticus 24:8, this was a symbol of the everlasting covenant between God and Israel. The twelve cakes (Leviticus 24:5-9) possibly symbolized the twelve tribes. They remained with **incense** on the table for six days and then were eaten by the priests on the sabbath while the incense was burned as an offering. The purpose of the rite was evidently either to make the presence of God real by mentioning God's name or to keep God mindful of Israel in a symbolic communion meal. Its antiquity is indicated by David's eating of the holy bread (I Samuel 21:4-6). The table with two incense vessels (verse 29) is depicted among the spoils of Herod's temple on the Arch of Titus in Rome.

25:31-40. *The Lampstand.* The seven-branched lampstand (*menorah*) shown on the Arch of Titus agrees with the description here. Thus it is evidently based on that used in the postexilic temple. In Solomon's temple there were ten single lampstands (I Kings 7:49), and Zechariah 4:2 describes a lampstand shaped like a bowl with spaces for seven lamps around its rim. A **talent of pure gold**—not less than 62½ pounds—is unlikely in the desert.

26:1-37. *The Tabernacle.* On the relation of the tabernacle to the tent of meeting and to Solomon's temple see above on 25:1–31:18. On the materials see above on 25:1-9.

The dimensions total thirty by ten by ten cubits (see above on 25:10-22). The length and width were exactly half those of Solomon's temple (I Kings 6:2). A few details of the structure remain obscure, but Arabic etymology has authenticated that the **frames** are to be understood as sections of trelliswork.

As in the temple, the interior is to be divided into two rooms. That farther from the entrance, corresponding to the room in the temple which in I Kings 6:16-31 is called the "inner sanctuary," is in P invariably termed the **most holy place,** whereas the other room is called the **holy place.** Only the **ark of the testimony** is to be placed in the most holy place. The **table** for the bread of the Presence (25:23-30) and the **lampstand** (25:31-40) are to be placed in the holy place. Separating the two rooms is to be a **veil,** which was given a theological significance in early Christian allegory (Hebrews 6:19; 9:3; 10:20; cf. Mark 15:38).

27:1-8. *The Great Altar.* This description is evidently intended to portray a portable model of the great "bronze altar" in the court of Solomon's temple (I Kings 8:64; cf. 38:30; 39:39). Probably it is based on a description of Solomon's altar originally included in I Kings 7:15-44 but later deleted or inadvertently omitted (with verse 3 cf. I Kings 7:45).

The construction of **acacia wood** encased in sheet **bronze** would hardly be fireproof, and it is incompatible with the ordinance requiring earth or undressed stone (20:24-25). The **horns** were upward protuberances at the corners. They were smeared with the blood of the sin offering (29:12) and a refugee from blood revenge grasped them to claim the sanctuary of the altar (see above on 21:13-14). Perhaps this feature was the survival of the horns of a sacrificial animal as the point of contact between God and man. The reference to the **ledge** apparently means that the upper half of the altar was to be smaller and that the **network,** or grating, was to surround the larger base.

27:9-19. *The Court.* The sacred area surrounding an ancient Semitic sanctuary is so regular a feature that it is often synonymous with "temple" in the Old Testament. Here the court is described as measuring 100 by 50 cubits—about 150 by 75 feet. It is to be fenced by **hangings** 5 cubits, i.e. about 7½ feet, in height. The number of **pillars** on each side is simply a fifth of the number of cubits—evidence that the author did not test his theory by drawing a plan.

27:20-21. *Oil for a Constant Light.* This instruction substantially duplicates Leviticus 24:2-4 (see comment) and is probably a late editorial insertion.

28:1-4. *The Priestly Family.* The selection of **Aaron . . . and his sons** to be **priests** reflects the hereditary high priesthood of the family of Zadok and especially the status of the high priest as the head of the Jewish community after the Exile. Restriction of the priesthood to the descendants of Aaron is characteristic of P. Descent from Levi is emphasized in D. On **Nadab and Abihu** see above on 24:9-11.

The family of **Ithamar** served as custodians of the ark at Shiloh. After its capture and the death of Eli they were priests at Nob until massacred at the order of Saul. Abiathar escaped and became David's priest but was later deposed by Solomon in favor of Zadok, who had supported his succession to the throne. According to the Chronicler (I Chronicles 6:4-8, 50-53; 24:3; Ezra 7:2-5) Zadok was a descendant of **Eleazar.** But since there is no mention of his origin in the early sources some scholars question his Aaronite descent and suggest instead that he may have been the hereditary Jebusite priest of Jerusalem when David captured the city. According to I Chronicles 24:1-4 the priesthood consisted of sixteen families descended from Eleazar and eight from Ithamar.

The word "priest" is here first mentioned in Exodus. It is probably related to an Arabic word denoting a functionary who might officiate at sacrifices but was better known as the medium of oracles and divination. In view of the association of the primitive tent of meeting with oracles Moses may have had such a function. The tradition of the consecration of Aaron as priest may reflect the divergence of the sacrificial office from that of the agent of oracles represented by Moses.

28:5-14. *The Ephod.* References to the ephod as a priestly vestment in the historical texts (cf. especially I Samuel 2:18; II Samuel 6:14, 20) indicate that it was a ritual loincloth, such as was worn also by Egyptian priests (cf. I Samuel 2:18 and II Samuel 6:14, 20). The ephod of the high priest described here is a relic of this, now worn over other vestments, perhaps as a sort of apron. Gradual enlargement no doubt led to the later development of **two shoulder-pieces** and a **band** around the waist. **Two onyx stones** engraved with the names of the twelve tribes are to be attached to the shoulder straps. The idea that the priest thus will **bear their names before the LORD** may reflect the calling of the tribal names in the common assembly in the time of the judges. On the materials and colors see above on 25:1-9.

28:15-30. *The Breastpiece of Judgment.* In other passages in the historical texts **ephod** evidently refers to an article used in divination which contained a receptacle for the sacred lots, **the Urim and the Thummim.** Possibly this was some sort of sacred robe, which might be a casing of sheet metal, if not something more substantial. The significance of this meaning of the term possibly survived in the high priest's **breastpiece of judgment,** better "decision," which apparently included a bag for the sacred lots. The **twelve stones** engraved with the names of the **twelve tribes** may be a variant tradition of the two stones so engraved on the shoulder straps in verses 9-12. The Hebrew names of the stones evidently refer to semiprecious stones, some of which cannot now be identified.

28:31-35. *The Robe of the Ephod.* The outer vestment worn immediately under the breastpiece and ephod is to be **blue,** i.e. bluish purple (see above on 25:1-9). The immature **pomegranate** was a fertility symbol in Canaanite art; cf. the capitals of the pillars Jachin and Boaz in front of Solomon's temple (I Kings 7:18-20). On the **skirts** of the priest's robe, however, they may simply denote tassels. The **bells** may have been originally designed to scare off evil influences—**lest he die**. Practically they warned the laity of the priest's approach and prevented the dangerous contact with the holy.

28:36-39. The Sacred Emblem. Verses 36-38 logically belong after verse 39, where the instruction to make a **turban** appears. It is possible that they may originally have followed verse 40 (cf. 39:27-31). The Hebrew word translated as **plate** usually means "flower" and here probably denotes a representation of a flower. The word translated **crown** in 29:6 evidently refers to this emblem, or possibly to its mounting (cf. 39:30; Leviticus 8:9). That it was a symbol of dedication is further indicated by the inscription **Holy to the LORD**. Almost certainly it was inherited by the high priest from the king.

28:40-43. Vestments for Other Priests. The instruction for the dress of **Aaron's sons** is that applicable to priests in general in the postexilic period. On verse 41 see below on 29:1-26. On verses 42-43 see above on 20:22-26.

29:1-37. The Consecration of Priests. This passage is apparently based on the account of the consecration of Aaron and his sons in Leviticus 8 and assumes the sacrificial regulations of Leviticus 1–7. There is no detailed account of the installation of a priest before this postexilic passage. The only feature in common with earlier passages—for example, Judges 17:5–12 and I Kings 13:33—is the idea expressed in the word translated **ordain**, literally "fill the hand." This may mean either the handing over of a sacrificial victim to the priest (verses 24-25), or the assignment of perquisites as reward for service (cf. verses 27-28).

The limitation of the hereditary priesthood to the family of **Aaron** reflects the postexilic period. Throughout the historical period up to the Exile the priestly status of the Levites was recognized, but the office was not limited to them. Samuel, for example, was an Ephraimite, and the highest priestly office was held by the king.

29:4-9. After ceremonial washing of all the candidates, **Aaron**—meaning the candidate for high priest—is to be invested with the high priestly **garments** (cf. chapter 28). He is then annointed as a symbol of his being set apart from common associations. His **sons**—meaning those to be lesser priests—are then to be invested in their garments (cf. 28:40). On **crown** see above on 28:36-39.

29:10-14. A young **bull** is then to be sacrificed. The **blood** is partly smeared on the **horns of the altar** (see above on 27:1-8) and partly poured **at the base of the altar** as in the sin offering for the community (Leviticus 4:25, 30, 34). The **flesh** is to be burned **outside the camp** since it is a **sin offering** for the priestly candidates, who are not yet fully consecrated (cf. Leviticus 4:11; 9:11). Their ritual impurity is communicated to the victim by their placing their **hands** on its **head** (cf. Leviticus 4:4).

29:15-18. The first **ram** is offered as a **burnt offering**—that is, one made wholly over to God in smoke and **pleasing odor.** This was probably considered as a gift to put God in a good humor with Aaron and his family.

29:19-25. The second ram is properly the **ram of ordination.** The **tips of the right ears** and **thumbs** and **great toes** of the ordinands are to be touched with the **blood,** which is then to be dashed **against the altar.** The priests will thus be attached to God. Supernatural influences were thought to have access to the extremities—as in the case of a cleansed leper in Leviticus 14:14. The application of blood to the extremities thus indicates a prophylactic rite. The smearing of the **garments** with blood and oil is surely a later elaboration, for contact with the sanctified person would itself sanctify the vestments.

29:26-37. *Priestly Perquisites.* Verses 27-28 are a secondary expansion on the **priest's portion.** Verses 29-30 provide for the hereditary high priesthood by specifying that Aaron's **holy garments** are to be passed on to his sons in an act of consecration lasting **seven days.**

The instructions of verses 1-26 are resumed in verse 31. The sudden mention of the atoning significance of the second ram and of the repeated **sin offering** indicates a later expansion. This would reflect the atonement for the imperfection of the priest and the **altar** on the Day of Atonement (cf. Leviticus 16).

29:38-42a. *The Daily Offering.* The custom of a **burnt offering** every **morning** and a **cereal offering** every **evening** was already established in preexilic times. Described here is a more elaborate practice of postexilic times. **Fine flour** was that ground from the inner kernels of the wheat. **Beaten oil** was the finest grade, the olives being patiently pounded in a mortar rather than squeezed in a press. The pulp was strained into water, from which the oil was skimmed after settling and hence was called "washed oil."

29:42b-46. *The Divine Presence.* The sudden divine address in the first person, in contrast with the third person **before the LORD** in verse 42a, indicates literary disunity. The P editor expresses the theological conception that God's presence is evoked by the daily offering, which is symbolic of the receptive and submissive spirit of the inquirer. Thus he will **meet** with his people in this place. In this sense he may be said to **dwell** in the sanctuary even though not restricted to it (see above on 25:1-31:18). This assurance, reflecting the covenant formula (verse 45) and Israel's historical confession (verse 46), forms a natural conclusion to the ritual ordinances.

30:1-10. *The Incense Altar.* The omission of this altar from the furniture of the sanctuary in chapter 25 and 26:35 indicates that the instruction for it is a later addition. The proportions—one and a half feet **square** and three feet high—and the **horns** are illustrated in incense altars from achaeological sites in Syria and Palestine. This fact and the apparent correspondence with the "golden altar" in Solomon's temple (I Kings 6:22; 7:48) suggest that it may have been revived in later postexilic times because of a tradition of its earlier use. The ritual involving this altar on the Day of Atonement (verse 10) is probably also described in Leviticus 16:15-19.

30:11-16. *The Poll Tax.* The numbering of the people would focus the divine attention on every individual, the moral or ritual defect of any one of whom would impair the community. Therefore it was always dangerous. Hence atonement for the community was required in order to divert God's wrath to the expiatory sacrifice, for which the poll tax is to be levied.

This explanation is apologetic and secondary. The actual purpose was to provide for the regular cult (verse 16). All alike eventually paid a **half shekel**; there was neither pauper nor patron in the cult in Israel. **Shekel** and **gerah** refer to weights of silver.

30:17-21. *The Laver.* The inclusion of this instruction here rather than with the description of the bronze altar and its accessories (27:1-8) indicates that it is a later addition. Solomon's temple had a "molten sea" and ten lavers, or basins, for priestly ablutions (I Kings 7:23-39).

30:22-38. *Holy Oil and Incense.* The ingredients of both these recipes are perfumes which were highly valued in ancient times. Except the Arabian myrrh they came from India and the Far East, probably by way of southern Arabia. The anointing of the **tent** and its furnishings indicates that the rite signified separation rather than delegation of authority (see above on 29:4-9).

The instruction that not only **Aaron,** but **his sons** also are to be anointed shows that this is a later addition (cf. 29:7). Probably the difference is due to the symbolism used by the respective authors rather than a reflection of a change in practice. In 29:7 the sons symbolize priests in general as distinguished from the high priest, symbolized by Aaron himself. Here they symbolize Aaron's hereditary successors in the office of high priest.

31:1-11. *The Craftsmen.* This passage was probably derived from 35:10-19 and 30–36:1. It was inserted here by an editor with antiquarian interests. Included are the **altar of incense** and the **laver** which were added later to the instructions of chapters 25–29 (see above on 30:1-10, 17-21).

The skill and intelligence of the craftsmen are attributed to the **Spirit** of God, that invasive divine influence which is the source of initiative and preeminence in thought and action in all fields. It is typical of the practical interest of the Hebrews and their wholesome integrated view of life that they related the skill of the craftsman, no less than the wisdom of the sage, the artistry of the poet, and the insight of the prophet, to the Spirit of God.

31:12-18. *The Sabbath Ordinance.* Insertion here of this P version of the sabbath commandment (cf. 20:8-11) was no doubt suggested by the instruction for work on the sanctuary. The passage is loosely constructed. Verses 15 and 17*b* are later expansions, as shown by the naming of Yahweh in the third person. Noteworthy features are the sabbath as the distinctive **sign** of the covenanted community, the penalty of **death** for its breach, and the relation to the P account of creation (cf. Genesis 2:2-3).

Verse 18 brings to a close the P version of the instructions given to Moses on **Mount Sinai** (chapters 25–31). On **tables of the testimony** see above on 25:10-22. The concluding phrases are probably a fragment of E linking the material in 24:12-18 with the golden calf narrative of chapter 32.

V. CONCLUSION OF THE EARLY SINAI NARRATIVES (32:1–34:35)

Having presented all of the P material alleged to have been revealed to Moses on Mt. Sinai (chapters 25–31), the compiler returns to the remainder of the JE Sinai narrative. Both literary analysis of this section and recovery of the complex traditions underlying it are very difficult.

32:1-6. *Making of the Golden Calf.* The bull was the cult animal of the Canaanite god Baal. His season of triumph was the new year festival on the eve of the early winter rains, at which time he was worshiped as king. The enthronement of Yahweh as King, an important element in the autumn festival in Jerusalem and in Bethel (cf. I Kings 12:32), was an adaptation of this Canaanite festival.

The centering of apostasy in a **molten calf,** i.e. bull, and especially the saying in verse 4*b* suggest that the story reflects the opposition to the establishment by Jeroboam I of Yahwist shrines at Dan and Bethel which included bull images. On the other hand the unfavorable role of Aaron in the story points to an underlying authentic tradition of the Mosaic age which involved a cult object in the form of a bull—cf. the serpent image of Numbers 21:8-9 (see above on 20:4-6).

Play refers to sexual license, reflecting Canaanite fertility rites and similarities of imitative magic practiced at some Yahwist shrines—at Bethel, for example (cf. Amos 2:7).

32:7-14. *Moses' Intercession.* The author who so skillfully composed the dramatic scene of Moses' discovery of the calf (verses 17-19) obviously never intended that he should be forewarned of the situation. Probably, therefore, this passage comes from a J parallel to the tradition of apostasy immediately following the covenant.

Editorial elaboration is evidently responsible for the summary of verses 1-6 in verse 8*bc* and the use of phrases from Genesis 22:17, a late passage, in verse 13. Some scholars have viewed the whole passage as a late insertion; but the differences of form and argument here and in verses 30-34, as well as of divine retribution in verses 25-29 and 35, indicate variant traditions. Moses' appeasing of the divine wrath by his mediation exemplifies an important aspect of the prophetic office.

32:15-24. *Destruction of the Calf.* This is the dramatic continuation of the E narrative begun in verses 1-6. The P phrase **tables of the testimony** (see above on 25:10-22) indicates editorial expansion of verse 15. Moses' words in verse 18 are in poetry and may come from a saga.

The breaking of the **tables** probably expresses the idea that apostasy abrogates the covenant. The Hittite vassal treaties (see above on 20:1-21) state that destruction of the record will invalidate the treaty. For the editor who combined J and E the breaking provided an opportunity to use the J account of the making of the tables (chapter 34) as a restoration.

Moses' compelling the people to **drink the water** with the powdered gold seems to involve a confusion of motifs. (1) The first is an ordeal to discriminate between the innocent and the guilty, of which the plague of verse 35 seems to be the immediate consequence. The second motif is the ritual of the sin offering, which involved the destruction of the offending object by powdering and mixing with water to carry it away. The absence of any reply by Moses to Aaron's very lame excuse suggests a glossing over of Aaron's part in the episode out of respect to the established Aaronite priesthood. Possibly a part of the narrative which linked it to the following verses was suppressed.

32:25-29. *The Massacre by the Levites.* The loose connection of the passage with its context suggests that it represents an independent tradition. For this reason some scholars have attributed it to the J source. Certain details of phraseology, however—especially its affinity with the folk oracle on Levi in Deuteronomy 33:9, which probably comes from northern Israel—make the E source more probable.

Viewed in the light of the ancient poem in Deuteronomy 33:8-11 both this account and the preceding calf story seem to preserve traditions of a conflict at Kadesh between two Levitical groups led respectively by Moses and Aaron. It has been suggested that Aaron and his adherents had not been in Egypt and had adopted Yahwism from the Kenites separately from Moses and his followers (see above on 18:12).

32:30-35. *Another Intercession.* This is probably the E parallel to verses 7-10. Some scholars, however, hold that the concept of Yahweh's **book** represents the theology of a later time (cf. Psalm 69:28 and Malachi 3:16). The thought here is not necessarily that of judgment in an afterlife. It may simply imply foreordination for life or death within the normal life span.

Moses' willingness to be sacrificed for the sake of his people expresses a concept of vicarious atonement that is developed later in the suffering servant of Isaiah 52:13–53:12. Instead Moses is given the practical task of leading his people to the promised land. The guiding **angel** (cf. 23:20) seems to come into the context as an afterthought and may be a later insertion. Verse 35 indicates variant tradition not only about the divine retribution but also about who made the calf—the awkward structure is no doubt due to an editor's effort to harmonize.

33:1-6. *Preparations for Departure.* The J source introduces this new phase of the narrative by recalling the promise to the

174

patriarchs (cf. Genesis 12:2). Verse 2, which is contradicted by verse 12a, seems to be a later elaboration based on 23:23.

Different sources are indicated by the two explanations of the discarding of the **ornaments.** According to J this is a mourning rite after Yahweh's refusal to go with Israel (verses 3-4). According to E it is in obedience to a divine command (verses 5b-6). The latter probably visualizes the ornaments as amulets or even figurines of gods such as are familiar from archaeological sites. This and the reference to Jacob's burying such ornaments at Shechem before his pilgrimage to Bethel (Genesis 35:4) may point to a regular rite of renunciation corresponding to the divine claim to purity of worship in the sacrament of the covenant. The association of this with the problem of the continuing **presence,** literally "face," of God on leaving his cult place has suggested to some scholars that originally the ornaments were used in construction of the ark and that this account was omitted in favor of that in 25:10-22. Another theory is that later orthodoxy has suppressed here a genuine old tradition of their use in the making of a cult mask to be worn by Moses in communicating the divine oracle, later communicated through the ephod and sacred lots (see below on 34:29-35).

33:7-11. *The Tent of Meeting.* The tent sanctuary of this passage is quite different from the P tabernacle described in chapter 26 but not yet constructed (cf. chapter 36). Unlike the tabernacle it is pitched **outside the camp.** It is used for oracles and is served, or kept, by **Joshua** alone. The contrast of this simple tent with the elaborate P tabernacle is strong evidence of its genuine antiquity, though Joshua's connection with it may be a secondary tradition.

The P concept of the tabernacle as the housing for the ark is obviously based on the place of the ark in Solomon's temple. Before the building of the temple, however, David placed the ark in a tent on bringing it to Jerusalem (II Samuel 6:17). Some scholars have taken this to be a revival of an original association of the ark with the tent in the desert. But this is by no means certain. The early traditions of the Pentateuch speak of them only separately. Indeed the ark as the symbol of the permanent presence of Yahweh is counter to the concept of Yahweh's occasional presence in the tent of meeting. Thus the ark and this oracle tent may belong to the traditions of different groups in the Israelite confederacy. The ark was associated with the tribes which settled near Shechem, Bethel, and Shiloh. The tent no doubt was associated with those in the south whose center was Hebron (see above on 25:10-22). The references in Joshua 18:1 and 19:51 to a tent of meeting at Shiloh are the work of a P editor who had in mind the tabernacle. On this assumption David's bringing the ark to Jerusalem and housing it in a tent would be, not the revival of an older association, but the new idea of a political genius for uniting the religious symbols of north and south.

This passage has characteristics of the J source. That it is independent of its present J context is indicated both by Yahweh's presence in the pillar of cloud, in contrast with the problem about the presence in verses 12-16, and by Moses' speaking with Yahweh **face to face**, in contrast with his being allowed in verses 22-23 to see only the back of God. Accordingly this and other early references to the tent (Numbers 11:16-17, 24b-30; 12:1-16; Deuteronomy 31:14-15) have often been attributed to E.

On the other hand the passage may well be editorially displaced, as the abrupt beginning suggests. In another position it would be no more inconsistent than certain other traditions assembled in J—for example, 24:9-11, where not only Moses but all his companions see Yahweh. Probably the tent of meeting tradition, whether from Hebron or elsewhere, was originally independent of the main tradition of both J and E. It came into association with one or the other through connection with David's tent.

33:12-17. *The Continuing Divine Presence.* This J passage is loosely connected with verses 1-4 through the theme of the departure. Perhaps a closer link containing the assurance quoted by Moses in verse 12b has dropped out. Some have suggested that verse 17 should precede verse 12, but then an antecedent for **this very thing** would be lacking. Another suggestion is that 34:9 should precede verse 14.

Moses' request for the divine **presence,** literally "face," to accompany Israel probably meant originally a concrete token. If this does not refer to the ark (see above on verses 1-6) it may anticipate sanctuaries of Yahweh in Palestine where one might see the "face" of God. Thus the theme of Yahweh's accessibility once his cult place in the desert has been left behind would be continued.

33:18-23. *Moses' Vision.* The revelation of God's **glory** or his **back is not the assurance of his continuing presence Moses has been requesting. Therefore it is probable that this very thing** originally introduced a story of the giving of a concrete token. It is also probable that the sight of the back of God represents an effort to modify the cruder concept of an earlier time.

As indicated by the threefold introduction to the speech of Yahweh, the passage is not a unity. Later modifications are the vision of the divine **glory,** i.e. worth or honor, and the declaration of the **name** Yahweh, with its implication of divine self-disclosure in the crises of history (see above on 3:14-15). The tradition of the revelation in verses 21-23 is certainly reflected in the tradition of Elijah at Horeb (I Kings 19:9*a*, 11-13*a*). Perhaps the passage is continued in 34:6-9.

34:1-5. *The Tables of Stone.* No doubt E included some notice of replacement of the tablets broken by Moses (32:19). Possibly phrases from the E account helped the editor who turned the J account of the making of the tablets into this story of their remaking.

In contrast to the E emphasis on their total divine manufacture (24:12; 31:18*b;* 32:16) the J tradition was that Moses both **cut** the tablets and **wrote** the words on them at Yahweh's instruction (verses 27-28). Originally the making of the tablets must have come earlier in J—certainly before the order to depart (33:1). The restrictions in verse 3 suggest closer connection to 19:12-13*a,* 20-22 than to the covenant meal in 24:9-11.

Some scholars have separated verse 5*b* from what precedes

and joined it to verse 6, but this proclamation of the **name** Yahweh is needed to introduce the **covenant** of verses 10-28. The initial element in the vassal treaties of the ancient Near East was a declaration of the name of the suzerain who imposed the treaty (see above on 20:1-21).

34:6-9. *Yahweh's Mercy and Justice.* This passage is probably from J. It has been transposed into the context, perhaps because of the similar wording in verses 5*b* and 6. It is connected rather with 33:12-23 by the dominating themes of Yahweh's presence, the favor Moses finds in his sight, and especially his discretionary mercy (cf. 33:19). This last is expanded to emphasize his retributive justice as well as his **love**.

The close analogy with 20:5*b*-6 suggests that this is the language of the liturgy of the covenant. Israel's incompatibillty with God prompts Moses' prayer for pardon (see above on 33:12-17) as the basis for the renewed covenant—a prayer which probably reflects actual usage in the sacrament of the covenant.

34:10-16. *Announcement of the Covenant.* Verses 10-28 continue verses 1-5. They consist of J material with D expansion. The framework is the making of a covenant that, like the Decalogue, follows the literary scheme of Hittite vassal treaties of the fourteenth and thirteenth centuries (see above on 20:1-21). In such a treaty the suzerain proclaims his name (cf. verse 5) and declares that he makes a covenant with his vassals (cf. verse 10*a*). He then lists his past exploits to remind them of his benefactions and his power to punish. Departing at this point from the usual pattern (cf. 20:2) verse 10*b* instead promises future display of Yahweh's **marvels** and **terrible** deeds.

34:11-16. The suzerain demands of his vassals absolute obedience to the terms he imposes (cf. verse 11*a*). The first of these terms is exclusive allegiance (cf. verse 14*a*; see above on 20:3, 5). The rest of verses 11-16 is D exhortation to obey this command by avoiding any **covenant** with the Canaanites—for example, to secure rights of seasonal grazing and sojourn in the settled land. Their **altars** and **pillars** (see above on 23:20-26) are to be destroyed. Also to be destroyed were their **Asherim**— probably trees, which symbolized the tree of life and ultimately the mother goddess Asherah. Lest they be drawn into participation in the local cult with its sexual rites of imitative magic, Israelites must especially avoid making marriage contracts with the Canaanites.

34:17-26. *The Ritual Code.* In the vassal-treaty pattern the comprehensive first command of exclusive allegiance is followed by a list of specific demands. Here the series constitutes a Ritual Code. The items in the code are parallel to the ritual ordinances of the Decalogue, the Book of the Covenant, and the sequel to the passover ordinance, as follows:

vs. 14*a*————————20:3	vs. 20*c*—————————23:15*b*
vs. 17————————————20:4	vs. 21———————————23:12*a*
vs. 18———————— 23:15*a*	vss. 22-23————————23:16-17
vss. 19-20*b*———— 13:12-13	vss. 25-26————————23:18-19

These ritual ordinances in the covenant sacrament are designed to preserve the distinctive cult and community of Yahweh against assimilation to Canaanite cult practices, especially at the three agricultural festivals. Therefore they must have arisen in Palestine rather than at Kadesh. "Yahweh the God of Israel" (verse 23) seems to have been a form of address used at the early tribal center at Shechem and transferred to the shrine at Shiloh. This had led to the suggestion that the Ritual Code originated at Shiloh during the time of the judges. On the other hand it may reflect the period of the early monarchy, when Canaanite areas were incorporated under David and the danger of assimilation became acute.

34:17-20. On verse 17 see above on 20:4-5 and 33:1-6; cf. Leviticus 19:4. On verse 18 see above 12:1–13:16. On verses 19:20*b* see above on 13:1-2, 11-16.

Appear before me, literally "see my face," indicates a concrete symbol of Yahweh's presence, probably the ark, at the central shrine. The pilgrimages **three times** a year with offerings were an economic necessity for the support of cult and priesthood.

34:21-24. On verse 21*a* see above on 20:8-10 and 23:10-19.

179

The addition here of specific mention of **plowing and harvest** safeguards the observance even in the busy seasons when urgency might encourage its suspension.

The second pilgrimage festival, at the end of the **wheat harvest,** took its name from being seven **weeks**—or fifty days, whence the Greek name Pentecost—after the feast of unleavened bread, which inaugurated the barley harvest. Thus it was the time for offering **first fruits.**

The third pilgrimage festival—the greatest and probably earliest—celebrated the autumn **ingathering** of all fruits, including the last of the grapes, olives, and grain from the threshing floor, **at the year's end** (see above on 12:1–13). The occasion thus came to be both harvest festival and new year festival. It is also called the feast of booths or tabernacles (Leviticus 23:34; Deuteronomy 16:13).

Desire is the same Hebrew verb translated "covet" in 20:17. Obviously it has here a stronger meaning than either English word denotes. The assurance, which surely stems from the early period of the occupation of Canaan, reflects the reluctance of the seminomadic settlers to leave their **land** for pilgrimages lest the dispossessed take advantage of their absence.

34:25-26. Leaven is old dough, contaminated by common use (see above on 12:14-20). The ban on leaven in bread offered with a **sacrifice** involving effusion of **blood** was known to Amos (4:5).

The following **passover** regulation has the same purpose of delimiting strictly the holy and the profane (see above on 12:7-10). However, it is evidently a later modification, for the passover was not an established **feast,** or pilgrimage festival, till the time of Josiah (see above on 12:1–13:16). Cf. 23:18, which probably preserves the original ordinance applying to the pilgrimage feasts.

First fruits of your ground may mean the first crop of freshly broken, or occupied, land rather than an annual offering as in verse 22. **The house of the LORD your God** probably refers to the temple at Shiloh or another early central sanctuary.

The injunction not to **boil a kid in its mother's milk**—the basis for orthodox Jewish maintenance of two sets of cooking utensils to segregate meat and dairy products—was probably directed against a Canaanite practice. Its association with first fruits suggests that the first kid may have been sacrificed in this way to insure the future fertility of the mother. Adoption of this rite would infringe the dedication of the firstborn to Yahweh. Israel's prosperity depends on Yahweh's grace rather than on manipulative magic.

34:27-28. *Recording of the Covenant.* The Hittite vassal treaties (see above on verses 10-16) were given final validity by being recorded. Moses is therefore instructed to **write** the terms of the covenant on the **tables** he has prepared (verses 1, 4). The process visualized may be simply application of ink with a brush rather than the divine engraving of the E tradition (32:16).

The covenant is said to be based on **these words,** identified as the **ten commandments.** Accordingly various attempts have been made to arrange the ordinances of verses 14-26 into a "Ritual Decalogue," which some scholars have viewed as more primitive than the "Ethical Decalogue" (20:1-17). But since the Palestinian origin of the Ritual Code is obvious (see above on verses 17-26) it could not have been the basis of the Sinai covenant. More probably it was modeled on the Decalogue as a priestly summary of the cultic duties of the laity. Possibly the compiler of JE, having used the Decalogue earlier, omitted a J version of it here and substituted the Ritual Code. If not, the final phrase may be a later addition by one concerned to make clear that the Ten Commandments were the basis for the covenant.

34:29-35. *The Shining of Moses' Face.* The verbs in this curious passage indicate two parts. Verses 29-33, the P continuation from 31:18*a,* describe what happened once at the conclusion of the Sinai theophany. Verses 34-35 are a genuine old tradition of a continuing custom of Moses, probably connected with the tent of meeting (33:7-11).

The word translated **veil,** used only here, probably means a cult mask which Moses used when speaking an oracle from Yahweh. Since the tradition was embarrassing to later orthodoxy (cf. Ezekiel 13:18) the P author explains the mask as worn on only one occasion. It was meant to cover the awesome afterglow on Moses' face resulting from the divine encounter (cf. Paul's explanation, II Corinthians 3:13). The Septuagint, however, omits **the skin of Moses' face** in verse 35a. This suggests that these words were repeated by an editor from verses 29-30 and that the meaning is rather that the **face of Moses . . . shone** when he was wearing the mask. No doubt it was made of burnished metal or decorated with metal pieces, perhaps from the ornaments contributed by the people (see above on 33:1-6). **Shone** translates a rare word which contains the consonants of "horn" and was so rendered in the Vulgate—whence Michelangelo's famous statue of Moses with horns. Possibly verse 35a originally described the mask as having horns.

VI. EXECUTION OF THE INSTRUCTIONS FOR THE SANCTUARY AND THE SERVICE (35:1–40:38)

This account of the establishment of the cult largely repeats in narrative form the detailed instructions which according to P were given to Moses on Mt. Sinai (chapters 25–31). There are a few summary abridgments and secondary elaborations. Items added in chapters 30–31 are here included in their proper order, indicating that most of this section is also a later addition.

35:1-3. *The Sabbath Ordinance.* See above on 31:12-18. Unique here, though implied in 16:23, is the prohibition of **fire** on the sabbath. It has been suggested that this may be a vestige of the religion of the Kenites, desert smiths (see above on 18:27), who were no doubt forbidden to smelt or work metals on the sabbath.

35:4–36:7. *The Contributions.* This section is an elaboration of 25:1-9, mostly by repetition and summary. Added is the enlistment of **every able man** to contribute labor, under the leadership of **Bezalel and Oholiab** (see above on 31:1-11). Added also is the account of having to stop the contributions because the people have offered **much more than enough**—the depiction of an ideal situation, obviously as a stimulant rather than as a narration of fact.

36:8–38:20. *The Sanctuary and Its Equipment.* Departing from the order in the instructions of chapters 25–27, the narrative describes first the construction of the **tabernacle** (36:8-38; see above on 26:1-27). An added detail is that the **pillars** have **capitals** (cf. 26:32, 37), presumably of carved work (cf. I Kings 7:16-20). On the **ark** (37:1-9), **table** (37:10-16), and **lampstand** (37:17-24) see above on 25:10-22, 23-30, 31-40.

The **altar of incense** and **anointing oil** and **incense** (37:25-29), the instructions for which are later additions (cf. 30:1-10, 22-38), are here included with the furnishings of the tabernacle. Because of inclusion of the incense altar the main altar is not identified as the **altar of burnt offering** (38:1-7; see above on 27:1-8).

In the mention of the **laver** (38:8; see above on 30:17-21) the reference to **women** serving **at the door of the tent of meeting** does not fit this context, since the tabernacle is not yet in use (cf. 40:17). Neither does it fit the early tradition of a simple tent for oracles to which only Moses and Joshua have access (33:7-11). It is apparently related to I Samuel 2:22*a*, also an insertion into its context. Possibly female singers of the temple are visualized. In the **court** (38:9-20; see above on 27:9-19) **capitals** for the **pillars** are also added.

38:21-31. *A Statistical Summary.* That this section is a late expansion is indicated by the mention of **Ithamar** as supervising the service of the **Levites** in the sanctuary (cf. Numbers 4:28, 33; 7:8) and by the calculation on the basis of the poll tax (see above on 30:11-16) and the **census** (Numbers 1:1-46). The census total (see above on 12:37-39), taken from Numbers 1:46, was probably calculated from the phrase "the children of Israel" by gematria—that is, by giving each letter its numerical significance.

39:1-43. *The Priestly Vestments.* See above on 28:5-43. The most significant variation is the omission of the Urim and Thummim from the description of the **breastpiece**, which accordingly is not called the "breastpiece of judgment." On **plate of the holy crown** see above on 28:36-39.

40:1-38. *Consecration of the Tabernacle*. Construction of the tabernacle with its appurtenances having been completed, it is now erected and consecrated and occupied by Yahweh's **glory**. The separation from common use is effected by anointing with the holy **oil** (see above on 30:22-38). The **cloud** covering the tabernacle, signifying the presence of Yahweh according to the promise of 29:43-45, sets the seal on the final episode of the book. The note on the cloud's significance for the **journeys** is really supplementary, anticipating the next phase, the desert wandering.

THE BOOK OF LEVITICUS

Jacob Milgrom

INTRODUCTION

Leviticus forms the third book of the Pentateuch (see the Introduction to Genesis). The name comes from the Latin Vulgate, based on the Greek Septuagint title meaning "The [Book] of the Levites" or, as the rabbis more accurately described it, "The Priests' Manual." By its own definition the priests here teach the distinctions "between the holy and the common, and between the unclean and the clean" (10:10).

We would be mistaken, however, to expect just a book of ritual. On the contrary in Leviticus the ethical underlies and fuses with the ritual so that we are justified to assume a moral basis behind almost every ritual act. This is so because Israel's cult is the product of the monotheistic revolution. Even though its outward expression is often similar to the surrounding pagan world, its spirit is ethically different.

Leviticus is not the whole of "The Priests' Manual." This actually begins in Exodus (chapters 25–31 and 35–40) and continues through most of Numbers. Moreover it is part of a larger historical narrative that runs from Genesis through Numbers, with a brief conclusion in Deuteronomy or perhaps Joshua. This narrative and the legal material which it contains is the latest of the four literary sources of the Pentateuch. Because of its content and viewpoint it is known as the "Priestly" (P) source.

Literary analysis of Leviticus and the other parts of P reveals evidence of strata—especially the unit known as the Holiness Code (chapters 17–26). However, all the material has been so thoroughly assimilated to the P viewpoint and is so indistinguishable in ideology that such study offers little help in interpreting the book. Because the text has been so excellently preserved, textual study has likewise been of comparatively little value.

The significant problems of interpretation lie in the one area of terminology. We are dealing here with the cult, a hoary institution with its peculiar vocabulary, the meaning of which was sometimes lost on those of the postexilic age, not to speak of later generations. It is a wonderful paradox that we today understand more of the older terminology of Leviticus than they did. This is due to recently unearthed cultic and legal texts of other ancient Semitic peoples of the second millennium. The most notable of these come from Mari on the middle Euphrates, Nuzi in eastern Assyria, and Ras Shamra in northern Syria, site of the old Canaanite city of Ugarit. In view of these discoveries it may be safely hazarded that most if not all of the peculiarities of vocabulary and style in Leviticus will prove to be obsolete technical terms from Israel's early history.

It is clear, therefore, that the legislation of Leviticus is old. That this is invariably true is indicated by the fact that no part of it can be identified as reflecting a postexilic innovation. Though the book in its present form is the work of the late P school, its members have here done little more than fit the older material into their narrative framework. This material is presented as instructions given to Moses for the service of Aaron and his sons, representing the high priest and his assistants, at the tent of meeting, representing the temple.

I. The Sacrificial System (1:1–7:38)

The sacrifices described here are to be voluntarily brought by the individual Israelite. They must be sharply distinguished from the mandatory requirements of public feasts and fasts in chapters 9, 16, and 23, and in Numbers 28–29. Even when the people's motivation is clearly recognition of wrongdoing (4:1–6:7) no outside force compels them—only the urging of conscience and a sense of guilt. The emphasis is on offenses committed involuntarily. Even in cases of premeditation (6:1-7) there is no indication that the offender is in fear of being apprehended. His desire for atonement is assumed to be spontaneous, and his sacrifice is the culmination of a penitential process of contrition, confession, and compensation. Thus the sacrificial system practiced by the ancient Israelite is a tribute to his moral sensitivity.

It is surprising that the sacrificial regulations are incorporated here. In the pagan world this could not have happened. Sacrifices were exclusively a priestly prerogative and their laws a jealously guarded secret. But in Israel, certainly by postexilic times, they were exposed and taught to the laity (cf. 10:10-11). There were no esoteric mysteries to frighten the people into obedience to the temple cult and its functionaries. Priests and laity alike learned and practiced their respective responsibilities as partners. To judge by the witness of scripture (for example, Psalms 43; 65; 84) they effected a ritual of worship that fully answered the people's spiritual needs.

A. INSTRUCTIONS FOR LAITY (1:1–6:7)

That the emphasis of this section is on the layperson is shown by the pronouns, which consistently refer to the donor of the sacrifice. A difference in the Hebrew conditional particles suggests that chapters 1 and 3 were originally a unit—as confirmed by the linking of their two offerings in the oldest records. Chapters 2 and 4–5 were added later.

1:1-2. *An Invitation to All.* In the P narrative the **tent of meeting,** i.e. tabernacle, houses the ark, from above which God speaks to Moses. The conditional construction **When any man of you brings an offering** underscores the voluntary basis of these individual sacrifices. Though the instructions are addressed to **Israel**, we know from this book (e.g. 17:8) and elsewhere (e.g. I Kings 8:41-43) that the sacrificial system was made available to the sojourner, i.e. resident alien, and even the foreigner. **Offering** means literally "that which is brought near"—that is, near to God. It is not always placed on the altar.

1:3-17. ***The Burnt Offering.*** The Hebrew word translated **burnt offering**—literally "that which goes up," that is, in smoke—is used exclusively of a sacrifice entirely consumed on the altar. To distinguish it from other offerings of which only a part is burned this sacrifice might better be called a "whole burnt offering" or simply "whole offering." Within Israel, both for individuals and for the community, it is the oldest and most typical sacrifice.

1:4. The laying of the **hand upon the head** designates the animal as representative of the worshiper. Involved is the transmission of power—or, in this case, of sin (cf. 24:14). Though the whole burnt offering can have connotations of a tribute, here its expiatory function is emphasized. Indeed expiation is the fundamental purpose of the sacrificial system as a whole (cf. 14:18-20; but see below on 3:1-17). Thus **atonement** is better translated "expiation."

1:5-9. The text does not identify who is to **kill the bull** and **flay** and **cut it into pieces.** Apparently anyone could qualify, even a foreign slave. Slaughter by priests and also Levites was limited to their personal and public sacrifices. But the priests only were permitted to "go up to my altar" (I Samuel 2:28) and therefore to **present the blood** (see below on 17:10-16), prepare the **fire,** and **lay the pieces on it.** For his service the priest received the hide of the animal (7:8). **Pleasing odor** harks back to an era when sacrifices were thought to be food for the gods.

1:14-17. For the poor (cf. 5:7; 12:8) a whole burnt offering of **birds** is provided, without the requirement that they be male and unblemished (cf. verses 3 and 10). Since this is not mentioned in verse 2, it may be a later addition. **Turtledoves** and **pigeons** were especially abundant in Palestine.

2:1-16. ***The Cereal Offering.*** The word translated **cereal**

offering denotes a gift to gain favor or a tribute of subjects to their overlord. Such tribute to the divine Overlord might be either animal or vegetable, but in time the term came to be used specifically of an offering of grain or its products. This restriction of the meaning emphasizes a person's tribute to God brought from the fruit of their labors on the soil which God has entrusted to their care. In practice the aspect of a gift for appeasement may also have been present.

As Israel developed from a pastoral to an agricultural community, the tribute offering of grain may have largely replaced the private whole burnt offering of an animal. The cereal of the tribute offering may take three forms: **fine,** i.e. choice, **flour, cakes** or **wafers** cooked from such flour, or roasted **grain.** For other cereal offerings cf. 5:11-13; 6:20-23; 23:13; and Numbers 5:15; 15:1-12.

2:2b-3. By definition a tribute offering belonged to the deity and originally was entirely consumed on the altar as food for God. This is suggested by the equivalence of **offerings by fire** with "bread of their God" (21:6). For the pagan the cereal tribute was the staple of the divine diet. But in Israel—as an example of the changes wrought by the monotheistic revolution—all but a **memorial portion,** i.e. a token, of the food was transferred to the **priest.**

A similar development took place with the bread of the Presence (24:5-9). The priest's portion of this and certain other offerings is **most holy** (cf. 6:17), meaning that it may be eaten only by priests within the sacred precinct near the altar. Merely "holy" perquisites may be eaten by all clean members of the priest's household in any clean place. The Hittites made the same distinction.

2:11-13. The prohibition of **leaven,** i.e. old dough containing yeast, and **honey,** a term including fruit syrup, is probably based on their fermentation. **First fruits** in verse 12 translates a different Hebrew word from that in verse 14; since these are not **offered on the altar** leaven and honey are permissible. On the other hand **salt** is a preservative and thus a symbol of the abiding. It was used in sealing a **covenant** (cf. Numbers 18:19), as among the Arabs to this day.

2:14-16. Because **first fruits** had to be offered up before the new grain crop could be eaten (23:14), they were brought roasted rather than milled.

3:1-17. *The Peace Offering.* The Hebrew word for "peace" meant much more than absence of conflict. It included health, prosperity, and general well-being. This broad meaning should be understood in the designation **peace offering**. Because this offering is shared by the deity (verses 3-5, 9-11, 14-16), the priest (7:31-34), and the worshiper (7:11-18), it is often said to be for the purpose of bringing about unity with God. The scriptural language, however, gives no basis for any notion of mystical union with God—one is to "eat before the LORD" (Deuteronomy 12:7), not with him.

Rather the original function of the peace offering, as is clear from chapter 17, was simply to permit the eating of meat. Since quick spoilage required consumption of an entire animal within two days, beef and mutton were luxuries all too rare for any but the most wealthy in ancient times. Such a sacrifice would usually be prompted by some special occasion for rejoicing. Three types of such occasions are cited in 7:11-18: thanksgiving, fulfillment of a vow, and freewill sacrifice, which is always mentioned in a happy context (cf Numbers 15:3 and Deuteronomy 16:10-11).

In view of the joyous character of such occasions it is not surprising that in P the word "atonement," i.e. "expiation," which is regularly used of the other four private offerings, never occurs in connection with the peace offering. True, in Ezekiel 45:15, 17 the peace offering is included in a list of sacrifices said to be for atonement. And among the many historical references to it a few are in times of crisis—even in a situation that elicits wailing and fasting (Judges 20:26). In each of these cases, however, the peace offering follows a whole burnt offering (see above on 1:3-17) and thus may be recognized as the joyous conclusion to a series of propitiatory rites (cf. II Chronicles 29:31-36). It becomes a festive meal enjoyed in gratitude, or at least hope, that a reconciliation with God has finally been effected.

The sacrificial rules enumerated here are similar to those for the whole burnt offering (chapter 1) with certain exceptions. The victim may be either **male or female,** and the requirement here that it be **without blemish** is modified in 22:23 for a freewill offering. There is no provision for the poor to present birds (cf. 1:14-17) for a peace offering. Some of the internal organs and the internal **fat**—i.e. suet, which should be understood throughout in distinction from the muscular fat—including the broad tail of the sheep, are burned on the altar, for **all fat is the LORD's.** Deuteronomy 32:37-38 gives biblical attestation to the universal pagan belief that animal suet, as well as blood (cf. 17:11), was a source of cosmic vitality and nourishment for the gods. The reference to divine **food,** like that to **pleasing odor,** is a linguistic vestige of such belief that survived in Israel's cult.

4:1-21. *The Public Sin Offering.* The most common Hebrew verb for "sin" in some of its forms has the reverse meaning "cleanse," "purge," or "purify." Its noun form also has this sense in the phrase translated "water of expiation" (Numbers 8:7), where a purificatory function is clear. That this is the sense of the word likewise in its application to the **sin offering** is shown by the purposes for which this sacrifice is specified: to mark recovery from childbirth (12:6-8), leprosy (14:19, 22*b*, 30-31), and gonorrhea (15:14-15); to complete the Nazirite vow (Numbers 6:13-17); to sanctify new objects (8:14-15; Exodus 29:35-37); and to consecrate new priests and Levites (9:8-11; Exodus 29:10-14; Numbers 8:8, 12). The name might therefore be more accurately rendered "purification offering."

4:2. The sin which this offering is intended to remove is "uncleanness" (cf. 14:19)—that is, ritual impurity, rather than any ethical offense. Thus **any of the things which the LORD has commanded not to be done** (cf. verses 13, 22, 27) refers to the prohibitive commandments between persons and God, not those between human beings. The sacrifice is efficacious for such violations committed **unwittingly**—better "inadvertently" or "unintentionally," for one is aware of them and acknowledges them. The point is that—as the root meaning, "miss," of the word "sin" suggests—they are errors or shortcomings rather than deliberate misdeeds. Sacrifice cannot expiate what one does "with a high hand" (Numbers 15:30).

4:3. The first situation for which this offering is prescribed presumes that the **anointed priest,** i.e. the high priest, has inadvertently erred and thereby caused harm to his **people.** Normally he is able to "take upon himself any guilt [i.e. unintentional ritual error] incurred in the holy offering which the people of Israel hallow as their holy gifts" (Exodus 28:38). That is, while officiating he possesses the holiness to absorb all the accidental impurity of the people. But if the impurity is due to his own error, only his personal purification offering can expiate for him, as well as for his fellow priests (cf. 16:6, 11).

4:4-12. The distinctive features of the procedure for this sacrifice are the smearing of **blood** on the **horns of the altar** and the removal of all but the blood and suet of the victim to be burned **outside the camp**—or, in the case of an individual's sacrifice, to be eaten by the priests under special safeguards (see below on 6:24-30).

The smearing of blood purifies the sanctuary of the impurity transmitted to it by the worshiper's inadvertent error and immunizes it against future contamination. It is clearly akin to the application of blood to lintel and doorposts in Egypt to keep away the "destroyer" (Exodus 12:23).

The unique disposition of the victim, considered along with the detailed descriptions for two other specific purificatory rites—the sanctuary purification (16:26-28) and the red heifer (Numbers 19:6-10, 21-22)—leads to the deduction that this offering causes defilement to its handlers.

From both these distinctive features, therefore, we must conclude that the purificatory sin offering has its roots in an apotropaic rite—that is, a magical procedure for warding off evil. It has come down from an era when the domain of evil was believed to be so powerful and pervasive that it could even invade and overwhelm the temples of the gods.

Though the forms of such a rite have persisted, there is no

longer any trace of the belief in an independent, primordial evil. Here the only demonic influence is with a person—his own error. It is human sin which impairs the holiness of the camp and the sanctuary and even necessitates cleansing of the Holy of Holies (cf. chapter 16). The rite now follows awareness of the sin and acknowledgment of it. Because the sin, though inadvertent, has been committed, a miasma of impurity has been released to defile the community and the sanctuary. Purification is thus required before forgiveness is assured (cf. 14:19-20).

4:13-21. These instructions assume that the offering of the **whole congregation** or **assembly,** i.e. community, is to follow that of the high priest (verses 3-12). This is shown by:

(1) the emphasis on identical procedure (verses 20-21);
(2) the specification of a **bull** rather than a goat (cf. 9:15; 16:5; Numbers 15:24); and
(3) the inclusion of the concluding formula **shall make atonement . . . shall be forgiven** only at the end of the people's sacrifice (cf. verses 26*b*, 31*c*, 35*c*; 5:10*b*, 13*a*).

No doubt the reason is recognition that the **sin,** i.e. ritual error, committed **unwittingly** by the people is probably the result of the high priest's improper guidance.

4:22–5:13. *Private Sin Offerings.* The impurity resulting from the inadvertent error of high priest and community penetrates to the sanctuary and requires purificatory action there. But that involving the laity requires smearing **blood** only on the **horns of the altar of burnt offering** in the outer court. Furthermore, whereas the sin transferred to the victim by the high priest or the elders of the community can be removed only by destroying it at a distance, the priests can absorb that of the layman's offering and therefore may eat the flesh of the victim as something "most holy" (6:24-30; see above on 2:2*b*-3; 4:3).

The general term **ruler** in the P material is the archetype and synonym of the king. The goat he offers must be **male,** but **one of the common people** offers a **female,** either **goat** or **lamb.** Offerings of money are mentioned in II Kings 12:16. The poor may offer **two turtledoves** or **pigeons** or even **flour.** The fact that only this and the whole burnt offering (1:14-17) have such alternatives is further indication of their similar purpose—expiation of sin, a need that had to be made available to all levels of the populace.

5:1-6. There is apparent confusion in the terminology here, in that the same sacrifice seems to be called both a **guilt offering** and a **sin offering.** A possible explanation is that the P editors introduced the confusion because they no longer understood the distinction between the two sacrifices. More probably, however, they accurately transmitted an older text which is confused only in translation.

The verb translated **be guilty** in this passage has the extended meaning "suffer guilt" and its consequence, "punishment." With a personal indirect object the verb has the further meaning "incur liability" to that person—for example, in Genesis 42:21, where these two senses are combined: "In truth we are guilty concerning our brother," i.e. "we are being punished for our liability to our brother." In this sense the noun form refers to liability and its cost, i.e. a payment or restitution of reparation—for example, in Numbers 5:6-7, where the word in verb and noun forms appears three times: "When a man or woman . . . *is guilty* . . . he shall make full *restitution* . . . to him to whom he *did the wrong.*" The noun also sometimes has the specific meaning **guilt offering** (see below on 5:14–6:7). But the confusion of terminology is cleared up if we recognize that in verse 6 as well as verse 7, the meaning is instead "his reparation to the LORD."

There is also apparent confusion of function. At least some of the cases in verses 1-4 seem not to fit the specification in 4:27 of **sins** committed **unwittingly.** No doubt it is precisely because these are borderline cases that they are included here as an appendix to the procedures for this sacrifice.

Since one who **utters . . . a rash oath** knows it at the time, the phrase **hidden from him** must refer in this case to a lapse of memory. Probably it has the same meaning in verses 2-3. Simply becoming **unclean** as described in these two cases requires no sacrifice but merely washing (cf. 11:24-40; 15:1-12, 16-27). The offense requiring sacrifice lies in forgetting the uncleanness and taking some action permissible only for one who is ritually clean—for example, touching holy things, thus allowing his impurity to contaminate the sanctuary.

An **adjuration**, literally "curse," if assented to by the **witness,** or even if directed to him specifically, would make him guilty of perjury if he should keep silent. Indeed in an earlier time such a curse would be considered effective without his assent or even awareness (cf. I Samuel 14:24-28, 36-45). Here, however, his ignoring of the adjuration, like the forgetting of an oath, is classed as a profanation of the name of God (cf. 19:12) for which confession and purification are needed.

5:7-13. These provisions for the poor are presented as relating only to the cases of verses 1-4 (cf. verse 13 with verse 5a). On the other hand the lack of a special introduction to verse 1 (contrast 6:1) may indicate that 4:27–5:13 should be considered as a single unit. The scaled sacrifices would thus apply to the general statement of 4:27.

On **guilt offering** see above on verses 1-6. **Two** birds are required so that one may be treated as a **burnt offering** to take the place of the suet available in a larger victim. For an offering of **flour** the procedure is the same as for a cereal **offering** except that **oil** and **frankincense** are to be omitted. An **ephah** is half a bushel.

5:14–6:7. *The Guilt Offering.* "Guilt" is the root meaning of the Hebrew word translated **guilt offering.** However, it does not convey the distinctive function of the sacrifice, since guilt is a prerequisite also of the purificatory sin offering (cf. 4:13, 22, 27; 5:2-5). The sense of the word as it is applied to this offering is more accurately expressed by the name "reparation offering." In every case its purpose is to discharge liability for material damage or loss, either to God or to other persons (see above on 5:1-6). Restitution for the damage, plus 20 percent, must be supplemented by a sacrificial fine in expiation (cf. Numbers 5:6-8).

That the offering is a sacrificial fine that can be converted into **silver** (see below on 5:15) is evidence of its antiquity. The Nuzi texts from eastern Assyria reflect customary law that goes back at least to the middle of the second millennium. These state that in certain cases fines are to be imposed in terms of fixed ratios of animals for which specified amounts of precious metal may be substituted. In the story of the Philistines' return of the ark (I Samuel 6:2-18) a guilt offering of gold is described. In connection with Jehoash's repair of the temple guilt offerings of money are mentioned (II Kings 12:16).

The distinction between the sin offering for purification and the guilt offering for reparation is illustrated in the regulations for the Nazirite, one who takes a vow of temporary "separation to God" (Numbers 6:1-21). If during his period of holiness he touches a corpse he becomes defiled and the time he has spent is voided. Thus a sin offering is required to purify his defilement and a guilt offering to compensate for the loss he has inflicted on God by thus depriving him of the promised term of service. A Nazirite who completes his period of separation brings a sin offering for purification. But, having fulfilled his vow, he is not liable for a guilt offering.

5:15. The Hebrew word translated **breach of faith** is usually rendered "faithlessness" or "treachery" in the Revised Standard Version. Here, however, it is defined as sinning **unwittingly in any of the holy things of the LORD**—that is, withholding, misappropriating, or profaning his sacred property (cf. 22:14-16). This may involve material objects (e.g. Joshua 7:1), the temple (e.g. II Chronicles 26:16-18), his chosen people (e.g. Ezra 9:2), or the loyalty due him (e.g. Numbers 31:16 and Ezekiel 20:27). All are holy things of God whose misuse requires reparation. The word is used exclusively of a sin against God except once (Numbers 5:12, 27), where it is applied to the wrong an adulterous wife does her husband. Thus the older translation "trespass," as in the King James Version, comes closer to the true meaning as the sort of offense against God to be expiated by a guilt offering.

The procedure for sacrificing the **ram** is described in 7:1-7. The obscurity of **valued by you in shekels of silver** may be due to postexilic ignorance of the ancient ordinance. In view of the history of the guilt offering as a sacrificial fine (see above on

5:14–6:7) and the similar regulations in chapter 27, the meaning is evidently that an equivalent monetary payment may be substituted for the sacrifice.

Until the Persians introduced coins into Palestine after the Exile **silver** used as currency had to be weighed in balances. The **shekel of the sanctuary** had a different weight from the commercial shekel adjusted to foreign trade.

5:16. Though the word **also** is not in the Hebrew, its insertion is justified to make clear that the sacrificial fine of verse 15 is in addition to the **restitution.** To this is added a **fifth** penalty, due to God for the loss or damage just as in the case of a wrong done to a neighbor (6:5). The restitution is made to the **priest** because ordinarily the **holy thing** involved would be a priestly perquisite.

5:17-19. The language of verse 17 is almost the same as that describing the occasion for a sin offering for purification (4:1, 22, 27). The significant difference is that, whereas the sin offering is predicated on later discovery of the cause of guilt (4:14, 23, 28), here the person still **does not know it.** Nevertheless he feels **guilty,** usually because suffering **his inquity,** i.e. punishment. For example, illness is viewed as the result of sin. To obviate the possibility of further divine wrath he beings a guilt offering.

This provision is witness to the psychological truth that anyone who does not know the exact cause of their suffering will imagine the worst. They will assume that they have incurred liability for damage or loss to holy things rather than mere ritual error. Therefore they will make the more expensive reparation offering.

6:1-7. The sacrificial laws here reach their ethical summit. The same reparation due for damage to God's property is specified for one's neighbor—with the significant priority that only after rectification has been made with the other person can it be sought from God.

Though the guilt offering originated as a fine for civil damages, it is here clearly outside the jurisdiction of the court—a voluntary sacrifice like the others of chapters 1–5. The crime could not be proved and the offender has escaped the usual penalty for embezzlement or theft (cf. Exodus 22:1-4, 7-13). Nevertheless he has **become guilty** (see above on 5:17-19) and in contrition comes forward to **restore** his wrongful gain, with an added **fifth,** and offer a reparation sacrifice to God.

Probably **swearing falsely** should follow the dash in verse 3 and be joined to the following phrase (cf. verse 5*a*) as the common element in all the examples cited. Violation of an oath before God (cf. 19:12) constitutes a **breach of faith** (see above on 5:15) **against the LORD** which needs expiation by guilt offering.

B. SUPPLEMENTARY INSTRUCTIONS FOR PRIESTS
(6:8–7:38)

The reference to these laws as given **on Mount Sinai** (7:38) shows that they are independent of 1:1–6:7, which is said to have been spoken "from the tent of meeting" (1:1). They are addressed to the officiating priest. The series groups together the cereal, sin, and guilt offerings, of which all not burned on the altar is "most holy" and must be eaten by the priests themselves in the environs of the sanctuary. It places last the peace offering, of which the priest's limited portion is merely "holy" and may be taken home to his family. Included with this last is an appendix addressed to the laity (7:22-36).

6:8-13. *The Burnt Offering.* These instructions especially concern the daily whole burnt offerings of the community (Exodus 29:38-41). The **fire of the altar** is to be **kept burning** and the fat-saturated **ashes** are to be cleared each morning. The **linen garment** worn for this chore is perhaps the coat of Exodus 28:40; on the **breeches** cf. Exodus 28:42-43. The clothing worn while approaching the altar is holy and must be changed before a trip outside the sacred precinct.

The altar is thus prepared for voluntary offerings (verses 14-18, 24–7:36; cf. 1:1–6:7) whenever brought by individuals. Of these only **peace offerings** are mentioned—perhaps because of their ancient affinity with whole burnt offerings (see above on 1:1–6:7) or perhaps because of their greater frequency.

6:14-23. *The Cereal Offering.* This explains what **most holy** means as applied to the priestly portion of cereal offerings brought by the laity (see above on 2:2b-3). It must be **eaten unleavened** by **male** descendants of **Aaron,** i.e. priests, **in the court of the tent of meeting**. On the other hand cereal offerings brought by priests—both those of the high priest which accompany the daily public burnt offerings and voluntary offerings of ordinary priests—must be **wholly burned** on the altar. **On the day** in verse 20 should be translated rather "from the day" (cf. 7:35-36).

6:24-30. *The Sin Offering.* On **most holy** see above on verses 14-23. The resemblance of verses 27-28 to the laws of uncleanness of 11:32-33 shows that holiness and ritual impurity, though opposites, are alike in their contagion. Not only does the **flesh** of this purification offering render **holy**, that is withdrawn from ordinary use (cf. 27:9-10), all objects it touches but it infects the **vessel** in which it is cooked and the **garment** on which its **blood** is splattered. The contagion must be washed out; and porous earthenware, from which it cannot be extracted, must be **broken.**

No other passage so clearly indicates both the pagan background of Israel's sacrificial system and severance from it. The contamination which in paganism was an active demon has been transformed into a "most holy" substance. Thus apotropaic magic (see above on 4:4-12) has emerged as ritual purification. Verse 30 reinforces the distinction between the sin offerings of priest (4:3-21) and laity (4:22–5:13).

7:1-10. *The Guilt Offering.* The procedure omitted in 5:14–6:7 is described here It is the same as that for the **sin offering** (cf. 4:27-31; 6:25-26, 29) except that it lacks the purificatory ritual with the blood of that offering.

The references to the officiating **priest** in the singular reflect the early days when a single priest would see the sacrifice through from beginning to end. The failure of Josiah's effort to bring the country priests into the centralized worship of the temple (II Kings 23:9) indicates that there were no vacancies in the Jerusalem priesthood at that time. Perhaps by then the priests were already organized into "divisions" and "fathers' houses" (I Chronicles 24) which multiplied the number of officiants at each sacrifice.

7:11-36. *The Peace Offering.* These instructions make clear what is assumed but never explained in chapter 3, that the peace offering is essentially a feast of the worshiper and his family and guests. After the sprinkling of the blood and the burning of the suet on the altar, and the payment of certain choice pieces to the officiating priest, the rest of the flesh of the victim is to be **eaten.**

7:12-15. The motivation for such a feast would nearly always include gratitude to God. But if the worshiper specifically calls it a **thanksgiving** he must observe certain additional formalities. The **bread,** which in any case he would certainly provide for the feast, must include four specified types, from each of which he must give the officiating priest **one cake.** His guest list must be large enough to consume all the meat **on the day of his offering.**

7:16-18. For a less formal offering—whether **votive,** i.e. in fulfillment of a vow, or **freewill,** i.e. without the compulsion of a previous promise (cf. 22:23)—the donor and his guests may take two days to consume the meat. **On the third day** any leftover is an **abomination,** literally "stinking thing." It is putrescent, and must be **burned.** Eating any of it would make the whole sacrifice unacceptable.

7:19-21. Anyone who is ritually **unclean** (cf. chapters 11–16) must not participate in the feast. **Cut off from his people** probably means, not banishment or ostracism by the community, but an early death by divine action (see below on 20:2-9). One who joins in without recognizing his uncleanness until afterward, however, can obtain purification and forgiveness by a sin offering (cf. 5:2-3).

Abomination—literally "filthy thing," a different word from that in verse 18—is evidently a scribal error for "swarming thing" (cf. 5:2), found in several manuscripts and the ancient versions.

7:22-27. The general prohibition of eating **fat,** i.e. suet, and **blood** stated in 3:17 is here made more explicit for the benefit of the **people of Israel,** meaning the laity. The detailed statement fails to cover all species—for example, the suet of birds and game (cf. 17:13) and the blood of fish, which inferentially might thus be exempted.

The negative implication of verse 24 is that the suet of a slaughtered animal must not be **put to any other use**. Therefore, since it cannot be eaten either, it must be burned on the altar. If so, this is another vestige of the days before Josiah's adoption of the D law (Deuteronomy 12:15-16, 20-25) permitting slaughter of animals without sacrifice. Inclusion of these prohibitions in this context indicates that before that time all meat of domestic animals was prepared as a peace offering.

7:28-36. These instructions are also addressed to the laity. They emphasize the worshiper's obligation to make all the preparations for the sacrifice himself up to the point of delivering the suet for the priest to burn on the altar and the choice of pieces which are the priest's perquisites.

In the Canaanite temple at Lachish in southwest Judah archaeologists found the bones of four animals clustered about the altar: sheep or goat, ox, and two wild species, either gazelle or ibex. All identifiable bones were from the upper part of the right foreleg. In Israel this desirable portion is here reserved for the priests.

Offered in verse 34 means literally "lifted up" and has been thought to refer to a specific gesture of the sacrificial ritual in contrast to another gesture represented by **waved**. More likely, however, since the two terms are used interchangeably they are simply synonyms for "offered." In verses 35-36 **on the day** should be translated "from the day" (cf. 6:20).

7:37-38. *A Summary.* This list corresponds exactly to the order of the sacrifices in 6:8–7:36 except that **consecration**, that is the ordination offering, is added. The addition has been generally assumed to be a marginal notation which a scribe erroneously copied into the text. However, it may be evidence that the instructions about the peace offering in verses 11-36 were originally preceded by similar instructions about the ordination offering. The inclusion of such material here would give the references to ordination in 6:20 and 7:35-36 more point.

Adaptation of it by the author of Exodus 29 would help explain the parallels between that chapter and verses 11-36, as well as its omission by the compiler of Leviticus. On **Mount Sinai** see above on 6:8–7:38.

II. THE INAUGURAL SERVICES AT THE SANCTUARY
(8:1–10:20)

This section of P narrative resumes the story following the interruption of the legal material in chapters 1–7 after the construction of the sanctuary and its appurtenances (Exodus 35–40). The priests are inducted into service and perform their initial sacrifices. It is noteworthy that Moses rather than Aaron dominates the scene. It is he who conducts the inaugural service, consecrates the priests, and assigns all tasks. Aaron is clearly answerable to him, as seen from their confrontation in 10:16-20. Thus a P author insists on the superiority of prophet over priest.

8:1-36. *The Installation of the Priests.* This account of the ordination of Aaron and his sons largely duplicates in narrative form the instructions in Exodus 29, as indicated by the repeated reminder **as the LORD commanded Moses.** On the priestly vestments mentioned in verses 7-9 see the comment on Exodus 28.

8:10-13. Middle Assyrian laws of the second millennium dealing with the marriage of patricians mention pouring **oil** on the head of a prospective daughter-in-law as a sign of betrothal. In Israel this ancient custom indicated the consecration to divine use of both things and persons—prophets and kings as well as the high priests symbolized by Aaron. **Aaron's sons** are clothed in the vestments of ordinary priests. Though only Aaron is anointed, the sons participate in all other elements of the ordination.

8:14-30. On the **sin offering** see above on 4:1-21. On the **burnt offering** see above on 1:3-17. The procedure for sacrificing the **ram of ordination** is quite similar to that for a peace offering for thanksgiving (see above on 7:37-38). Here Moses is in the role of the officiating priest, who receives his portion, and Aaron and his sons correspond to the lay donor of a peace offering. As priests, however, they may offer only **unleavened bread** (contrast 7:13). On the special rites with the **blood** and the **anointing oil** see the comment on Exodus 29:19-25.

8:31-36. The **flesh** and the **bread** of the ordination offerings brought by Aaron and his sons are viewed as "most holy" (see above on 2:2b-3). They are therefore to be eaten **at the door of the tent of meeting**, where the priests are required to stay for **seven days**.

The Hebrew phrase translated **ordain** means literally "fill the hand of" and is used exclusively of the ordination of priests. In archives from Mari on the middle Euphrates dating from early in the second millennium this idiom is used of the distribution of booty taken in battle. Thus the original sense as applied to priests was that their ordination entitled them to a share of the sacrifices brought to the sanctuary. That such a priestly share was an ancient custom in Israel is shown by the story of Eli's sons (I Samuel 2:13-14).

9:1-24. *The Priests' Initiatory Sacrifices.* Following the week of consecration, during which Moses has officiated, the priests begin their official duties. Aaron now officiates in offering special sacrifices for the people, with Moses' promise that God's presence will be revealed. Thus the **eighth day** is a climax to the ordination (cf. I Kings 8:66–9:2 and Ezekiel 43:27). Indeed the whole purpose of the sacrificial system is revelation, the assurance that God is with his people. But here there is no pagan idea of the cult as controlling the revelation. Rather God's presence is recognized as always an act of his grace.

9:8-21. The procedure narrated here departs from the prescriptions of chapters 1–7 in two details:

(1) The people's sin offering is a **goat** instead of a bull (cf. 4:14).

(2) The **blood** purification rite is performed at the main **altar** rather than in the "inner part of the sanctuary" (10:18; cf. 4:5-7, 16-18).

The first of these, at least, probably indicates strata in the P material reporting the practices of different periods. But purifying the sanctuary (see above on 4:4-12) may have been omitted from these initiatory sacrifices on the assumption that following its consecration (8:10) no impurity has entered it.

9:22-24. Aaron's blessing of the people is an invocation of God's presence with them. Such a blessing regularly concludes the offering on the altar and precedes the sacrificial meal (cf. I Samuel 9:13). In this case, however, Moses and Aaron enter the sanctuary, presumably for a further prayer that God will reveal himself. Then before the people they again invoke God's presence in a final blessing, after which the revelation occurs.

Glory generally refers to a cloud, which often contains **fire**. Because the usual fire on the altar is implied throughout the narrative, some have taken verse 24 to be an interpolation based on earlier accounts of divine igniting of a sacrificial flame (Judges 6:21; I Kings 18:38). Here, however, the **fire . . . from before the LORD** is an essential climax of the promised revelation. It is to be understood as a supernatural flame which immediately **consumed** and totally reduced to ashes, the offering being slowly burned by the ordinary process.

10:1-11. *The Sin of Nadab and Abihu.* The reason for the death of Aaron's two older sons (cf. Exodus 6:23) is not clear and has been variously interpreted. Probably they are punished for offering **fire** which is **unholy,** literally "alien," because taken from elsewhere than the altar (cf. 16:12).

Other suggestions are:

(1) that their **incense** is improperly prepared (cf. Exodus 30:9, 34-38);

(2) that these two sons, though specially privileged (cf. Exodus 24:1, 9-11), are not authorized to offer incense **before the LORD,** i.e. in the Holy of Holies (cf. 16:1-2);

(3) that the two are drunk, as indicated by the injunction against drinking intoxicants before the service (verses 8-9), which otherwise seems irrelevant in the context.

That the destroying fire comes **from the presence of the LORD** may mean that it shoots out from the Holy of Holies. Perhaps it is to be understood as the same fire which consumes the offerings on the altar (9:24).

10:4-7. Aaron and his two remaining sons are forbidden to show their grief lest it appear as a protest against God's justice and bring further punishment.

10:8-11. On verse 9 see above on 10:1-11. The priests are more than officiants at sacrifices; they are to be Israel's chief teachers. The Hebrew word translated **teach** is the verbal form of *torah*, the usual term for the divine law. The priestly educational duty includes not only ritual (verse 10) but also ethics, as implied in **all these statutes** and confirmed by the prophets.

10:12-20. *The Eating of the Initiatory Offerings.* Moses' instructions for the eating of the **cereal offering** and the **peace offerings** repeat in substance those of 6:16 and 7:28-34. In verses 16-20 a genuine part of the Nadab and Abihu tradition has been elaborated by an editor concerned to justify the discrepancy between this narratve and the rules of 6:24-30. He also wished to emphasize the duty of the high priest to **bear the iniquity of the congregation** (see above on 4:3).

In 9:15 it is implied that the **goat of the sin offering** was treated in all respects **like the first sin offering** and thus that the flesh was **burned** immediately **outside the camp** (9:11; cf. 4:21). Here it appears, however, that the meat was originally retained for eating by Aaron and his sons (cf. 6:26). It was only after the death of the two older sons that Aaron followed the more stringent procedure of destroying rather than eating it. Moses' objection to this implies that the meat must be **eaten** for the **atonement**, i.e. expiation, to be complete. In reply Aaron points out that in spite of the purificatory and expiatory sacrifices just completed his two older sons died. Fearing that their ritual error has added priestly sin to the lay sin with which the flesh of the goat is laden, he has not dared to eat it lest it not be **acceptable**. The emergency purgation rites necessitated by the dangerous defilement of the sanctuary are described in chapter 16, which at one time probably followed immediately.

III. THE LAWS OF UNCLEANNESS (11:1–15:33)

On the meaning of "unclean" see above on 4:2, 3, 4-12. A working knowledge of contagion must be credited to biblical people. For example, though the symbolism of cleansing may have influenced the use of washing as a part of purificatory rituals, the ways it is used reveal some recognition of its practical value. Washing is prescribed only for those types of impurity arising from dead bodies (11:25, 28, 40; Numbers 19:11-19) and from certain skin diseases (chapters 13–14) and discharges (chapter 15)—all prime sources of putrefaction and infection. Contact with an animal carcass or a diseased person calls for washing immediately—such antisepsis would be effective only during the first hour or so—rather than at nightfall when the impurity ends, as symbolism would suggest. On the other hand the one afflicted with a disease is quarantined and washes only after he has been healed—washing would serve no medical purpose once infection has set in.

11:1-47. *Unclean Animals.* The food prohibitions are certainly older than the rationale given them in scripture. No doubt their origins were quite varied. Some creatures were disgusting in appearance or habits, while others were discovered from experience to be carriers of disease—attributed to demonic forces. Taboos against some were no doubt the remnants of long-forgotten associations with tribal enemies. Recent research has pointed to the possibility that some dietary prohibitions were directed against the cultic practices of pagan neighbors.

Regardless of individual origins, however, the development within Israel of the diet laws as a total system must be attributed to the one reason offered by all four scriptural passages referring to these laws, namely holiness (verses 44-45; 20:22-26; Exodus

22:31; Deuteronomy 14:21). It is noteworthy that no punishment for violating these laws is ever mentioned. The prohibited foods are simply declared **unclean.** It is understood that anyone absorbing their impurity would be cut off from all contact with the **holy** and therefore from God. The concept of holiness bears a dual connotation: not only separation from impurities—especially those of the pagans (cf. 20:23-26)—but also sanctification, the emulation of God's nature (verse 44*a*; see below on 18:1–20:27).

The food prohibitions taken together with the blood prohibition (see below on 17:1-16) form a unified dietary code whereby persons may indulge their appetite for meat and not be brutalized in the process. At creation human beings were meant to be vegetarians (Genesis 1:28-29). Later the sons of Noah, i.e. all races of men, were permitted meat on the condition that they not eat the blood (Genesis 9:3-4). Now the sons of Jacob, as a "holy nation" (Exodus 19:6*a*), are directed to a higher level of holiness. They are to narrow their menu to a few living creatures of the tame, herbivorous species. They are to recognize that the taking of animal life is a divine concession and that the spilling of its life source, the blood, is a divine injunction. Thus they are disciplined to revere all life.

The **living things** covered by the regulations about food are classified into four categories (cf. verse 46):

(1) **animals,** i.e. larger mammals, the same word as **beast** in verse 46;

(2) aquatic creatures;

(3) **birds,** a term that takes in all flying creatures;

(4) **swarming things,** i.e. small creatures, including mammals (cf. verse 29), **upon the earth.**

Interrupting the food laws is a passage on impurity from contact with animal carcasses (verses 24-40). This is evidently inserted from another source.

11:2-8. Here the rule for distinguishing clean from unclean **animals** is given but only those forbidden are named. Contrast the parallel in Deuteronomy 14:4-8, where those permitted are named also. The **rock badger** is the hyrax, which looks rather like a groundhog but does not burrow. Like the **hare**, it frequently moves its jaws in a way that gives the appearance that it **chews the cud.**

11:9-12. That no aquatic creatures are named, either here or in Deuteronomy 14:9-10, may be explained by the little contact Israel had with the sea.

11:13-23. No classification is given for **birds**, probably because none was known. Identification of a number of the species named is uncertain. **Winged insects**, literally "swarming birds," are included in the same category. For these a rule is given to permit the eating of certain varieties of **locust.**

11:24-40. This interpolation into the food laws deals with the impurity arising from touching the dead body of an animal. No living animal is unclean to the touch. Among larger mammals the distinction is like that of the food laws (cf. verses 3-7)—that is, the **carcass** of one forbidden as food transmits impurity on contact. So too does the body of a permitted animal if it died naturally (verses 39-40). Nevertheless a carcass must be removed, and so touching it is not prohibited (contrast verse 8); instead one who **carries** it away must go through the ritual of washing and avoid contact with holy things until nightfall.

Apparently no impurity attaches to the bodies of aquatic or aerial creatures, or of earthbound **swarming things** other than the eight named in verses 29-30. **Mouse** was a general term for mice, rats, moles, hamsters, etc.; and **weasel** was similarly inclusive. Nonporous articles defiled by the carcasses of these eight household pests must be washed; but absorbative pottery, including the usual earthenware **oven or stove**, must be destroyed (cf. 6:28). **Food** and **seed** grain are immune to the impurity when dry but absorb it if moist.

11:41-47. This is the original continuation of verse 23, completing the food laws with the fourth category and a summary. Isaiah 66:17 has been taken by some to refer to a pagan cultic practice of eating "mice"—perhaps rats or some other rodents. Possibly the extra emphasis given to the ban on eating **swarming things** is due to their involvement in pagan sacrifice. More likely it grew out of experience of their transmission of disease. On **holy** see below on 19:1-37.

12:1-8. *Uncleanness from Childbirth.* For the mother of a newborn son a period of impurity lasts for forty days. During the first **seven days** no conjugal relations are allowed (verse 2c; cf. 15:19-24). During the rest of the time she must not **touch any hallowed thing**—for example, meat (cf. 7:19-21). If the child is a girl the periods are doubled. That her sacrifices are brought after her defilement has passed is evidence that their purpose has become purificatory rather than magical (see above on 4:4-12); the childbirth period is no longer feared as under demonic control. There remains only ritual impurity, which time alone removes, and which a purification rite certifies. The offering is scaled to economic circumstance (cf. 5:7-13).

13:1–14:57. *Uncleanness from Skin Diseases.* Considering the ancient view of illness as a punishment for sin, we might expect the priest in Israel to be a physician, as was his pagan counterpart. He does officiate in sacrificial rite which include special public offerings in time of epidemic and private voluntary expiations motivated by illness. Aside from this the only responsibility for health assigned him in scripture is that described here in connection with contagious skin diseases. Here the priest's role is that of a quarantine officer. He is an ecclesiastical minister of public health, who determines whether the afflicted person is a menace to the community.

Only God can cure. The sufferer on his own initiative must pray and fast to win healing from God, who may act either directly or through a prophet. It is only after the disease has passed that the priest imposes sacrificial rites (14:1-32). These are not for healing but for purification—to purge the convalescent and the sanctuary of their ritual impurity—and immunization against future incursions.

13:1-44. The word translated **leprosy** covers a variety of skin diseases in addition to Hansen's disease, to which "leprosy" refers in modern usage. Most of the afflictions apparently described are curable. Comparatively few cases would actually warrant separation from society.

13:45-46. The unfortunate **leper,** as determined by the priest's diagnosis, must be removed from the community and live **outside the camp,** i.e. city. He must give notice of his impurity by dressing as a mourner and by a voiced warning.

13:47-59. The symptoms of a **leprous disease in a garment** are probably the effects of mildew or other fungus.

14:1-32. *Purification of a Healed Leper.* Recovery from some of the skin diseases described in 13:1-44, even without special treatment, was common enough that a method of restoring the person to the community became established. The procedure involves three separate ceremonies, on the first day (verses 4-8), the **seventh,** and the **eighth.**

14:4-9. The ritual of the first day is also applied to "leprosy" of houses (verses 48-53). Originally it was no doubt the method of exorcising the demon responsible for the disease by means of **blood** and **scarlet** dye and a flying **bird** to carry the demon away. Now that monotheism is established the demonic element is gone and the rite is entirely purificatory (see above on 4:4-12). After this partial purification the healed leper is admitted to the **camp** but cannot yet enter his **tent.** The ritual of shaving and washing on the seventh day resembles the purification of the Levites before their ordination (Numbers 8:7).

14:10-20. The sacrificial ritual of the eighth day is quite similar to that for the consecration of priests (chapter 8). Even the differences between them underscore the purificatory purpose underlying both. The healed leper brings a **guilt offering** as reparation for the trespass against God which must be presumed as the cause for his punishing affliction (see above on 5:17-19). In contrast the new priest has no such taint, and so his ordination ram is treated as a thanksgiving offering to be climaxed by a joyous feast.

The smearing of **blood,** common to both rituals, is probably apotropaic in origin (see above on 4:4-12). The priest needs protection against harm during his ministry and the leper against a recurrence of his disease. The daubing of the healed leper with **oil** reemphasizes the purification motif. In ancient Ugarit a female slave was freed when the officiant announced: "I

have poured oil upon her head, and I have declared her pure."
The **ephah** was half a bushel and the **log** a little over half a pint.

14:21-32. The **poor** are permitted a less costly sacrifice, but
only for the **sin offering** (cf. 5:7-13). The reparation of the **guilt
offering** cannot be reduced.

14:33-57. *"Leprosy" in a Building.* The appearance of a
leprous disease in a house might be due either to chemical
action—saltpeter, for example—or the growth of a moss or
fungus. Unusual consideration for property is reflected in the
provision that the priest should clear the house before his
inspection lest the contents be condemned along with the
building. The procedure for purifying a house that has been
healed is adapted from the first ritual for purifying a healed
person (verses 4-7).

The separation of this section from the section on leprous
garments (13:47-59) has been taken to indicate it was inserted
later, but inclusion of the purificatory ritual would explain its
placement after the rituals of verses 1-32 (cf. verse 55).

15:1-33. *Uncleanness from Genital Discharges.* In this
chapter **body,** literally "flesh," is a euphemism for the genital
organs. A discharge from any other part of the body, for example
the nose or ear, is not **unclean.**

The regulations apply to four cases:

(1) male pathological discharges, usually due to gonorrhea;

(2) normal **emission of semen**;

(3) normal menstruation;

(4) female pathological discharges.

The impurity from a pathological discharge is presumed to
have contaminated the sanctuary, which thus requires sacrificial
purification after recovery (verses 14-15, 29-30; cf. 5:7-10).
Impurity from normal discharges or from contact with another
person having a pathological discharge is a lesser matter and is
removed by washing and passage of the specified time.

On verse 12 see above on 11:24-40. The effect of verse 18 is to
prohibit marital relations on the eve of worship at the sanctuary
(cf. verse 31). The language of verse 24 appears to mitigate the

absolute prohibition of the Holiness Code (cf. 18:19; 20:18) but may refer to accidental contamination from mere proximity.

IV. THE PURIFICATION OF THE SANCTUARY AND THE NATION (16:1-34)

Verse 1 identifies this chapter as a sequel to chapter 10. Nadab and Abihu create double defilement of the sanctuary (10:1-2)—in life by their sin, in death by their corpses. Thus purification of the sanctuary, including the Holy of Holies, is required. Instruction for this emergency rite is given in verses 1-28. Verses 29-34 then transform this into a yearly procedure. Chapters 11-15 were no doubt inserted by an editor who viewed them as a relevant listing of specific impurities which inhibited contact with the sanctuary (15:31) and its holy things (12:4b). All these impurities would be expiated by the ritual described.

16:1-28. *The Purificatory Ritual.* This procedure represents a fusion of two rites:
   (1) purging the sanctuary of priestly and lay defilement through sacrifices (cf. 4:3-21);
   (2) expiating the sins of the people through their confession and transfer to a live animal banished into the desert.

The first of these rites seems to have been performed without the other in Hezekiah's purgation of the temple (II Chronicles 29:15-24; cf. Ezekiel 45:18-22). The sins expiated by both rites are clearly of the same character and thus are exclusively within the religious sphere—that is, between persons and God (see above on 4:2). Ethical violations would require rectification with the person wronged before God's forgiveness could be expected (see above on 6:1-7).

16:2-5. The **mercy seat** is the cover of the ark containing the **testimony,** the tablets inscribed with the Ten Commandments. It represents God's throne in the Holy of Holies. Here the **cloud** over it is apparently not the divine revelation of 9:23-24 but a **cloud of incense** brought in by Aaron to hide the symbol of God's presence from his human gaze.

Instead of his usual elaborate vestments Aaron is to wear the simple white **linen** garments prescribed for a priest tending the altar (cf. 6:10). White linen is assumed to be worn by divine beings (cf. Ezekiel 9:2; 10:2 and Daniel 10:5; 12:6) and symbolizes the highest degree of purity.

16:6-28. On the **goat** rather than a bull for the people's **sin offering** see above on 9:8-21.

Some interpreters take **Azazel** to be the name of a place east of Jerusalem where in later times it was customary to push the second goat off a cliff. But the parallelism of **for Azazel** with **for the LORD** and the instruction to **let the goat go in the wilderness**—that is, set it free rather than kill it—favor the view of most scholars that Azazel is the name of a demon. Originally the rite may have been for the purpose of driving away a demon of this name in the goat. Now Azazel has come to be merely a symbol of a no-return to which the people's impurities are consigned. During the Babylonian spring new year festival an animal loaded with the temple's exorcised evil was thrown into the Euphrates, and those who handled it were rendered impure. Other temple purification rituals of the ancient Near East are also known.

16:29-34. *The Annual Day of Atonement.* The purpose of the merger of the two rites in verses 1-28 is now given. It is the joint purification of sanctuary and nation on a specified day in the autumn of each year (cf. 23:27-32; Numbers 29:7-11). Thus the editor tacitly admits that an emergency rite of purgation prescribed for such extraordinary cases of defilement of the sanctuary as the sin of Nadab and Abihu has later become a regular part of Israel's cultic calendar.

Afflict yourselves refers to fasting and other forms of self-denial. **Sabbath** here has its root meaning of cessation from ordinary pursuits (see comment on Exodus 20:8-10).

V. THE HOLINESS CODE (17:1–26:46)

This lengthy insertion into the P material seems to be an independent legal code. Because of its repeated call for Israel to be **holy,** as God is holy, it has become known as the Holiness (H) Code. Like the Covenant Code (Exodus 20:22–23:33) and the Deuteronomic Code (Deuteronomy 12–28) it opens with a law about the place of sacrifice and closes with an exhortation. Also like them it contains a mixture of ethical and ritual laws and appears to be a compilation of several older collections.

The closing exhortation seems to point to a date of compilation in preexilic times (see below on 26:3-46). This is supported by the apparent allusions in Ezekiel 22 to laws found in chapters 18–20. Aside from the compiler's hortatory contributions the content is essentially similar to the other legal material incorporated by the P editors.

In Semitic polytheism **holy** referred to what was separated from common use by a supernatural quality that made it dangerous to touch or even approach except under certain conditions. Material objects—for example, specific trees, stones, rivers—were believed to have this quality. For Israel, however, holiness stems solely from God. Certain things—the land, the sanctuary, the fesitvals, the priests—are holy by divine dispensation.

Only for Israel is holiness known to have been enjoined on a whole people. Humanity, Israel, and the priesthood form three concentric rings of increasing holiness about the center, God. The scriptural ideal is that all Israel shall be "a kingdom of priests and a holy nation" (Exodus 19:6). Israel is to observe a more rigid code of behavior than other nations, just as the priest lives by stricter standards than his fellow Israelites. Holiness therefore requires separation from all defiling contact with other persons—for example, through sharing in idolatrous practices (cf. 20:6-7, 23-24)—or with beasts—for example, through eating forbidden meats (cf. 11:43-45; 20:25-26).

Holiness for Israel means more than separation, however. It is a positive concept, an inspiration and a goal associated with God's nature and his desire for all persons: **You shall be holy; for I . . . am holy** (19:2). What people are not and can never fully be, yet what they are commanded to emulate and approximate—this is the life of godliness called "holy."

A. LAWS ABOUT MEAT (17:1-16)

17:1-14. *Slaughter of Animals.* This passage presents two related laws:

(1) All slaughtered domestic animals must be brought to the altar as **peace offerings** (see above on 3:1-17; 7:22-27).

(2) The **blood** must not be eaten.

The centralization of worship demanded in the Deuteronomic Code was practical only if slaughter for food was permitted without sacrifice (Deuteronomy 12:15-25). Before Josiah's adoption of this code (II Kings 23) there were many local shrines to which anyone desiring to slaughter an animal could bring his peace offering (cf. Exodus 20:24). Since **to the door of the tent of meeting** is characteristic P language adapting to the setting of Moses' day, this law may originally have commanded bringing the animal to an established shrine with a priest in attendance rather than slaughtering at an improvised altar with a non-priest officiating.

Bloodguilt, i.e. murder, is charged against anyone who kills an animal without sacrifice. On **cut off from among his people** see below on 20:2-9. The **atonement,** i.e. expiation, gained by bringing the blood to the **altar**—or, in the case of game, by draining it and covering it with earth—is not for general sin but for the slaughter which without such expiation would be murder.

17:15-16. *Uncleanness from Eating Carrion.* In P the carcass of an animal that dies naturally or by mishap is not forbidden as food, except to priests (22:8). But it transmits impurity (cf. 11:39-40), even to the **sojourner,** or resident alien. That the absolute prohibition of Exodus 22:31 and Deuteronomy 14:21 was not obeyed may be inferred from Ezekiel 4:14 and the laws of Exodus 21:28, 34-36.

B. ETHICAL AND RITUAL LAWS (18:1–20:27)

18:1-30. *Illicit Sexual Relations.* The laws of this chapter are framed by opening and closing exhortations by the H compiler which castigate the Egyptians and Canaanites for the depravity of their sexual mores. The pagan world of the ancient Near East worshiped and deified sex. It reserved the term "holy ones" for its cult prostitutes. No wonder Israel is charged with an exacting code of family purity whose violation means death (cf. 20:11-16).

18:6-18. In these laws against incest, relation by marriage has the same force as blood relationship. Each partner in the marriage transfers his set of incest taboos to the other. The list prohibits unions that were customary in patriarchal and Mosaic times and even during the early kingdom.

18:19-23. Amid the prohibitions of sexual aberrations is the condemnation of subjecting **children** to the cult of **Molech,** literally "the King." The Hebrew text here omits **by fire** from the usual formula referring to a god with this title (see comment on Deuteronomy 18:10). It is possible that a different meaning is intended—that **devote them . . . to** should read "serve" as in the Septuagint. If so, in this context cultic prostitution might be meant.

More probably, however, this is the usual reference to the child sacrifices practiced by certain neighbors of Israel (cf. II Kings 3:27). With the approval of some of Judah's later kings an apparatus for this practice was set up in the valley on the southern side of Jerusalem (II Kings 16:3; 21:6; cf. Jeremiah 7:31; 32:35), but it was never incorporated into Israel's worship and did not spread beyond this solitary shrine.

18:24-30. The Holiness Code is the only source which proclaims the holiness of the **land** of Palestine. This doctrine explains the equal responsibility of both Israelite and **stranger,** that is resident alien, to maintain its sanctity (cf. 20:2; see below on 19:1-37) as well as the moral justification for its conquest (cf. 20:22-23). But Isarel's ideological sword is two-edged. If it is guilty of the same infractions it too will be **vomited out.** On **cut off from among their people** see below on 20:2-9.

19:1-37. *Positive Holiness.* How can one imitate the holiness of God? The answer of this chapter is given in a mixed series of ethical and ritual commands; no distinction is made between them. Throughout the ancient Near East morality was inseparable from religion. Indeed it is precisely within a ritual context that scriptural ethics rise to their summit.

The Decalogue is incorporated here—the first half in verses 3-8, the second in verses 9-22. Soaring above it all is the commandment to **love** all men, fellow Israelites and aliens alike. This leveling of society stems partly from the sanctity which, in the view of the H compiler, God's **land** imposes on all its inhabitants (see above on 18:24-30).

But there is more. The law of love is probably not one of the older laws assembled by the H compiler but his own composition—his generalization of the meaning of the laws. Yet it is no mere verbal ideal of one man. It is the principle underlying many of the laws collected not only in the Holiness Code but throughout the P material and indeed the whole Pentateuch. The law of love must be expressed in deeds: equality in justice, both civil and religious, and equality in mercy, e.g. free loans (25:35-55) and free gleanings. That the law of love may be implemented, callousness and hatred are also proscribed.

19:5-18. On verses 5-8 see comments on 7:16-18 and 20:2-9. On verses 9-10 cf. 23:22 and Deuteronomy 24:19-22. Since the **sojourner**, i.e. resident alien, was not permitted to own land, he had to subsist by hiring out his services (cf. Deuteronomy 24:14). He is often classified with the **poor** as a ward of God, for whom Israel must provide.

The context in verse 16 favors the translation **stand forth**—that is, stand up to make a false accusation. But the Hebrew verb, literally "stand," may mean here "stand still," to fail to take action to help one in peril. Another possibility is "profit by the blood of your neighbor" (Jewish Publication Society translation). Also obscure is **bear sin** (cf. 22:9 and Numbers 18:32). On verse 18b see above on verses 1-37.

19:19-25. A cloth made of two kinds of stuff, wool and linen, is prescribed for the curtains of the tabernacle (Exodus 26:1, 31, 36) and the vestments of the high priest (Exodus 28:5-6, 8, 15). Such a mixture is holy and therefore forbidden to the laity. Similarly a field sowed with two kinds of seed becomes holy

(Deuteronomy 22:9*b*) and cannot be used by the lay owner. Though the prohibition against cross-breeding animals was no doubt observed, mules were imported and used.

The Hebrew word for **betrothed** is not that used of a free woman but means rather "assigned" or "designated," as in Exodus 21:7-11. **An inquiry shall be held** should be translated "an indemnity shall be paid." The case involves a two-fold offense:

(1) Since the woman is no longer a virgin her value as a concubine has been reduced and her owner is entitled to damages.

(2) Since the designation included a vow before God, its violation is a trespass against him requiring a **guilt offering** (see above on 6:1-7).

19:26-37. The juxtaposition in verse 26 of eating **blood** and practicing **witchcraft,** i.e. divination, is not accidental. These pagan practices rank with idolatry and homicide. Shaving the head and face except for a circle of hair as a magical rite was also a pagan practice. Removing hair and beard and gashing the flesh were common ancient ways of mourning and were a prominent part of the annual rites in observance of the seasonal death of Baal (cf. I Kings 18:28). **Mediums** and **wizards** (cf. 20:6, 27) practiced divination by communication with the dead. On verses 33-34 see above on verses 1-37, 5-18. The **ephah** was a measure for grain (half a bushel), the **hin** for oil and wine (three and a third quarts).

20:1-27. *Penalties for Certain Infractions.* In this chapter a number of the absolute commands of chapters 18 and 19 are duplicated in conditional form with punishments specified. Evidently the H compiler here turned to a different source.

20:2-9. On the giving of **children to Molech** see above on 18:19-23. One who commits this sin is to be **stoned** by the **people,** but if they fail to act God himself will **cut him off from among his people.**

Elsewhere in the P writings this expression appears in passive form and is often taken as a demand that the religious community banish the guilty person (cf. Ezra 10:8). The usage here, however, suggests that in all cases the idiom refers to divine rather than human punishment, namely an early death through sickness or accident. The offenses for which this punishment is threatened involve ritual impurity—**defiling my sanctuary and profaning my holy name.** Verses 4-5 are not a mere repetition but add that all who do not bring the Molech worshiper to judgment are likewise implicated and will suffer the same punishment. So too will those who consult **mediums and wizards** (see above on 19:26-37). On verse 9 see comment on Exodus 21:15-17.

20:10-21. These sexual prohibitions duplicate those in chapter 18 except for the cases of grandchild, stepgrandchild, and marriage with two sisters (18:10, 17*b*, 18). No doubt the difference in form, and especially the inclusion of penalties in this series, induced the H compiler to include both collections. In verses 10-16 the penalty is death by human agency, but in verses 17-21 it is to be **cut off** by divine action (see above on verses 2-9).

Most of the offenses noted in verses 17-21 involve marriages known to have been acceptable in Israel's early history (see above on 18:6-18). With such notable precedents the ordinances could not be humanly enforced and must be left to God's action. To the ancient Israelite to **die childless** was the supreme penalty.

20:22-27. The H compiler's exhortation in verses 22-24 largely repeats 18:24-30. Verse 25 seems closely related to 11:43-45, which perhaps at one time was included here along with a set of diet laws. The **medium** or **wizard** (see above on 19:26-37), as distinct from the one who merely consults such a person (verse 6), must be **stoned.**

C. Laws About Priests and Sacrifices (21:1–22:33)

The priest, ranking highest in human holiness, could enter the sanctuary to handle its objects and eat of its gifts. These privileges had corresponding restrictions, the more so for the high priest. They were intended as safeguards against moral and ritual defilement which might inflict dire consequences on him and his people (22:9, 15-16; cf. 15:31).

21:1-15. *Mourning and Marriage.* In marked contrast to modern clergy the ancient priest was virtually isolated from death in the community and even among his relatives. The Israelite view, indeed obsession, was that death imparted a most severe impurity (cf. Numbers 19:11-19). Probably this was a violent rejection of Egyptian belief that the dead and their burial place were equal to the temple in sanctity.

Verse 4 is obscure and perhaps textually corrupt. Probably **as a husband among his people** means "as a kinsman by marriage" (Jewish Publication Society translation). On verse 5 see above on 19:26-37.

21:7-9. The priest's household must be protected from any sexual defilement through either his wife or his daughter. Marriage with a woman whose husband has died is not forbidden to the ordinary priest. But he must not marry a woman who has been **divorced,** "driven away," by her husband—perhaps on the assumption that her dismissal would probably be due to "some indecency" (Deuteronomy 24:1).

21:10-15. The high priest is identified as **chief among his brethren** by his anointment and special vestments. His greater holiness requires more severe restrictions. He is forbidden any show of mourning or any contact with the **dead,** even his closest relatives. He must not even **go out of the sanctuary** to attend burial rites (cf. 10:6-7). He is prohibited from marrying a **widow.** His wife must be a **virgin of his own people**—that is, from a priestly family.

21:16-24. *Physical Disqualifications.* Like the sacrificial victim the officiating priest must be **without blemish.** The exact meaning of some of the blemishes is uncertain; **mutilated face** may mean "limb too short" (Jewish Publication Society Translation; cf. 22:23). The disfigured male descendant of a priestly family is permitted to share in eating the priests' portions of offerings, even the **most holy** (see above on 2:2b-3).

He is, however, forbidden to enter the sanctuary or have access to the altar.

22:1-16. *Eating of Holy Food.* The priest is subject to the same laws of uncleanness as the lay person (cf. chapters 11-15). While he is in a state of impurity he must avoid **holy things**—specifically, must not eat the priest's portion of offerings (cf. 7:19-21; 15:31). Obviously a qualification such as **while he has an uncleanness** is to be understood with **keep away** in verse 2. On verse 8 see above on 17:15-16.

22:10-13. The priestly perquisites, except those classified as "most holy" (see above on 2:2*b*-3), are to be eaten by all members of the priest's family. This includes a **slave** but not an **outsider** (guest who is not a priest) or a **sojourner** (resident alien) or other **hired servant.** A **widow** with a **child** would be supported by her husband's relatives and therefore not qualify as a member of her father's family.

22:14-16. These verses are somewhat obscure. A layperson who unintentionally **eats of a holy thing** can scarcely thereafter give it to the priest. The sense is evidently that they are to give its equivalent, plus an added **fifth.** They are also to bring a guilt offering, which should be the translation of **guilt** in verse 16; (see above on 5:1-6, 16).

Looking for his own gain, an unscrupulous priest might deliberately allow an unsuspecting layperson to eat holy food and thus commit a profanation. The priest would thus receive repayment with an extra fifth and a guilt offering for himself. Verses 15 and 16 forbid such venality.

22:17-33. *Sacrificial Animals.* The regular rule that an animal offered for sacrifice must be **without blemish** is here elaborated and some of the unacceptable blemishes are specified. Though only a **burnt offering** and **peace offerings** are mentioned, it is to be understood that other offerings would require a stricter standard. Some exception is made for a **freewill offering** but is not permitted for **votive offering,** since a perfect animal is assumed to have been promised by the vow.

Castration of edible animals is effectively forbidden by verse 24. Before adoption of the Deuteronomic Code, which permitted slaughter without sacrifice, an animal not eligible for sacrifice could not be eaten (see above on 17:1-14).

22:26-33. On verse 27 cf. Exodus 22:30. On verse 28 cf. Deuteronomy 22:6-7. On verses 29-30 see above on 7:12-15. Verses 31-33 are the compiler's concluding exhortation for this section.

D. THE FESTIVALS (23:1-44)

These instructions are addressed to the **people of Israel,** that is the lay farmers, rather than to the priests. Thus except in the later interpolations in verses 13, 18-20 only the offerings of the individual farmer are enumerated. The new moon observance (cf. Numbers 28:11-15) is not mentioned here, probably because the lay Israelite had no special duties or prohibitions on that day.

That this chapter is composite is obvious from the new beginnings in verses 9 and 39. Closer analysis suggests that the component introduced by verses 2 and 4 and summarized by verses 37-38 includes verses 5-8, 21, 23-36. The connection of verses 26-32 with chapter 16 suggests further that this component comes from the P narrative source.

Verse 3 is probably a later interpolation; most of verses 13, 18-20 seem to be variants of Numbers 28:5, 7, 27-30. Verse 22 is a duplication of 19:9-10. The rest is presumably from the Holiness Code and was taken by the compiler from a preexilic source.

23:5-14. *The Feast of Unleavened Bread.* The **passover** and unleavened bread observances were originally quite separate. The former was a pre-Israelite nomad shepherd rite and the latter an agricultural holiday of Canaan marking the beginning of the barley harvest (see comment on Exodus 12:1-13:16). The two fell at the same season. Early in Israel's history they came to be linked to each other and to the Exodus.

Bread was leavened by including a piece of dough from an earlier batch in which yeast had developed. The first bread of the new crop is to be eaten **unleavened**—that is, without anything from the previous year's crop in it (verse 14). The **first month** is numbered according to the Babylonian calendar, in which the year began at the spring equinox (see below on verses 23-25).

23:9-14. According to the older law in the Holiness Code the first **sheaf** of the barley **harvest** is to be brought to the local sanctuary. There is no fixed date; it is to be brought on the first day of reaping (cf. Deuteronomy 16:9). The **priest** is to **wave** it as a thank offering for the new crop (see above on 7:28-36). The obvious agricultural setting of this ordinance is evidence of its antiquity. Verse 13 is a later interpolation based on the public cult. On **ephah** and **hin** see above on 19:26-37.

23:15-22. *The Feast of Weeks.* This festival, unnamed here is called the feast of harvest in Exodus 23:16—a recognition that it celebrates the harvesting of the wheat, the last grain to ripen. It comes **fifty days** after the ceremony of the first sheaf of the barley harvest—hence the name Pentecost, from the Greek for fifty. An offering of **loaves of bread** is to be brought in thanksgiving—**leavened** to indicate that the new crop is sanctioned for ordinary use. On verses 18-22 see above on verses 1-44.

23:23-25. *The New Year.* For the postexilic P authors the year began in the spring, according to the Babylonian calendar, which was followed also by the Persians. Thus the first month fell in the spring and the **seventh month** in the autumn. This numbering of the months seems to have been used in Judah before the Exile, perhaps for commercial convenience, even though its own new year came in the fall (cf. II Kings 22:3; 23:23).

In early times the feast of booths (cf. verse 34), or ingathering, apparently marked the "end of the year" (Exodus 23:16). Development of a more precise calendar fixed the opening of the new year before that festival (cf. I Kings 8:2; 12:32-33), with an observance of its own. In postexilic times this observance was continued at the traditional time but without the new year designation, which was revived only at a later time.

The observance includes **rest,** special **blast of trumpets,** and additional public offerings (Numbers 29:1-6). Perhaps psalms in which trumpeting is prominent (for example, Psalms 47; 95–100) may have been used on this day. The theme of cosmic judgment, "he comes to judge the earth," became a permanent feature.

23:26-32. *The Day of Atonement.* The essential purpose of this day is to purify the sanctuary of its year-long defilement by humans (see above on 16:1-34). Since the expiation rituals are confined to the sanctuary and performed exclusively by the priests this lay calendar omits the cultic aspects.

This day is often said to be a postexilic innovation because it is not mentioned in preexilic sources, especially Deuteronomy 16. But the obvious antiquity of the purification ritual from which it developed makes its early establishment as an annual occasion probable. The fact that it involves no participation by the laity would keep it from mention in such a passage as Deuteronomy 16, which describes the festivals requiring the people to bring offerings to the central sanctuary.

On this day they do not go to the temple. They **rest** from work, **afflict** themselves, i.e. fast, and rejoice that their year-long sins against God—the ritual sins causing the sanctuary's contamination—have been forgiven (cf. 15:31; see above on 4:2).

23:33-44. *The Feast of Booths.* This festival is also called the feast of ingathering (Exodus 23:16), the **feast of the LORD,** and simply "the feast" (Ezekiel 45:25)—indication that in preexilic times it was the most important of the festivals.

23:39-43. This description, placed after the P summary of verses 37-38, evidently represents a preexilic source copied by the H compiler (see above on verses 1-44). The date in verse 39 is an editorial harmonization, as is the reference to the **eighth day**—cf. the similar alteration of I Kings 8:66 in II Chronicles 7:9-10).

The four types of **branches—fruit** can mean "boughs"—are presumably for festal processions around the local altar (cf. Psalm 118:27). The people are to live during the week in the fields in **booths,** temporary shelters such as are put up to this very day in Palestine during the grape and fruit harvest. This strictly rural and neighborhood celebration of the end of the agricultural year was radically altered by the author of Deuteronomy 16:13-17. There a pilgrimage to the centralized sanctuary is enjoined, and there is no mention of branches and booths. Nehemiah 8:14-17, reflecting an age which probably had the complete Pentateuch, harmonizes the conflicting traditions of H and D. It calls for the use of branches—five in number, a variant tradition—as construction materials for the booths, which are to be built on the roofs of the houses in Jerusalem.

Like the passover this festival has been historicized as a memorial of the Exodus (verse 43). Numbers 29:12-38 gives the order of public sacrifices in the temple for each day.

23:44. This verse is either the sequel to the P summary in verses 37-38—cf. **appointed feasts** in verses 2, 4, and 37—or the insertion of a later editor. It is at odds with the viewpoint of the Holiness Code, which is represented as a continuous series of instructions given to Moses on Mt. Sinai (26:46).

E. MISCELLANEOUS LAWS (24:1-23)

This chapter is again composite. Only verses 15-21 and 22*b* appear to come from the Holiness Code. The rest is P material.

24:1-4. *The Lamp Oil.* Verses 2-3 substantially duplicate Exodus 27:20-21. The **lampstand of pure gold** is described in Exodus 25:31-40. Since it is inside the sanctuary, its greater sanctity requires **pure oil**—unlike the oil for anointing (Exodus 30:22-33). It must be lighted by **Aaron,** i.e. the high priest (cf. Exodus 30:7-8; Numbers 8:2-3); "his sons" in Exodus 27:21 probably symbolize his successors as high priests. The lamp is to burn **from evening to morning,** i.e. only through the night; **continually** means "regularly" rather than "continuously."

24:5-9. *The Bread of the Presence.* This bread, translated also as "showbread," consists of **twelve cakes,** made from the best wheat **flour,** probably without leaven. They are symbols of God's Covenant with the twelve tribes.

The loaves are to be placed along with **pure frankincense** in **two rows of six** on the **table** which stands before the Holy of Holies (cf. Exodus 25:23-30). Being within the sanctuary, they are to be tended only by **Aaron** the high priest. **Every sabbath** he is to renew the bread and incense, burning the previous week's incense as a token offering and joining with other priests in eating the old loaves as a **most holy portion** (see above on 2:2b-3). The bread is thus considered as the priestly share of **offerings by fire,** reflecting the probability that originally it was entirely burned on the altar.

It was a widespread pagan belief that the gods dined at the sanctuary table, as illustrated by the mockery in Isaiah 65:11 and Bel and the Dragon. That the rejection of this belief and the transfer of the eating from deity to humans took place early in Israel's history is shown by the account of David's eating such bread (I Samuel 21:6).

24:10-23. *The Penalty of Blasphemy.* Two laws about blasphemy in a brief series from the Holiness Code (verses 15-21) are here emphasized by a P narrative illustrating the enormity of this offense. The supreme blasphemy spotlighted by the narrative is not mere cursing of God but doing so while speaking the **name of the LORD**—that is, the unique name Yahweh by which he revealed himself to his covenant people. The elaboration in verse 16bc was probably added by the P editor, since **congregation** is a characteristic P term. Because of the derogatory context the P author dares not even write "Yahweh" and substitutes **Name.**

24:13-16. The power of the blasphemy affects not only the speaker but his hearers. Their contamination must be transferred back to the blasphemer by the ritual of laying **their hands upon his head** (see above on 1:4). The injunction to enforce this particular law against the non-Israelite **sojourner** may have been suggested by the identification of the culprit in the narrative as only half Israelite.

24:17-23. The remainder of the brief series from the Holiness

Code (verses 17-21) states the law of retaliation *(lex talionis;* cf. Exodus 21:23-25; Deuteronomy 19:21). This limits vengeance to punishment equivalent to the damage caused by the original crime.

The granting of the protection of this limitation to **sojourner** as well as **native** might well be attributed to the H compiler (see above on 18:24-30). But the statement of it is quoted from other P material (Exodus 12:49; Numbers 15:15-16, 29) and thus must be an insertion by a P editor. No doubt the insertion here was suggested by that in verse 16*c*, but it is noteworthy that the principle of the resident alien's equality before the law is stated for as well as against him. The extension of this justice to the sojourner is one of the great moral achievements of the P legislation. Not only is distinction eradicated between the powerful and the helpless but even between the Israelite and the non-Israelite.

F. THE SABBATICAL AND JUBILEE YEARS (25:1–26:2)

A number of commentators have taken the references to the jubilee year (verses 8-13, 15-16, 26-34, 40*b*-41, 44-46, 50-52, 54, with minor variations) to be a late P editorial insertion primarily because they assume the jubilee to be a utopian proposal rather than an actual practice (see below on verses 8-34). Yet Deuteronomy 15:1-11, which enjoins a similarly "utopian" cancellation of debts every seventh year, is clearly an integral part of the Deuteronomic Code. Thus there seems no strong reason to suppose that this material is not an original part of the Holiness Code.

25:2-7. *The Sabbatical Year.* Each **seventh year** is to be a **sabbath of solemn rest for the land** (see above on 18:24-30). Exodus 23:10-11 makes a similar provision, with the stated purpose of providing food for the poor. There it might be supposed that each plot of ground could have its own schedule, but here it is obvious that all Israel is to observe the same sabbatical year.

Leaving fields fallow was practiced in early times, and a seven-year cycle for it may be reflected in the seven years of plenty and of famine in the Joseph story (Genesis 41:25-36). There is no proof of early observance of a simultaneous sabbatical year for the land outside the codes. But 26:35, 43 (cf. II Chronicles 36:21) seems to indicate that it was recognized as an obligation before the Exile, even though not always faithfully observed. Its observance in later times is shown in Nehemiah 10:31*b* and I Maccabees 6:49, 53.

25:5-7. Verses 6-7 have been thought by some to be a later interpolation amending the strict prohibition of verse 5 (cf. verses 20-22). But the meaning may be that, though a harvest of **what grows of itself** is forbidden, eating from it from day to day is permissible.

25:8-34. *The Jubilee Year.* At the sound of the **trumpet**, i.e. the ram's-horn shophar—**jubilee** means ram or ram's horn—a year of **liberty** is to be proclaimed. The liberty includes:

(1) leaving the land fallow,

(2) restoring landed property to its original owner,

(3) setting free all Israelite slaves.

The basis for the jubilee is clearly stated: the land belongs solely to God (see above on 18:24-30) and so do the people of Israel. Absolute human ownership of either is forbidden.

Since the rabbinic literature indicates that the jubilee, unlike the sabbatical year, was not observed in later times, some scholars have viewed it as a theoretical scheme for alleviating poverty which was never actually put into practice. It is true that there are no early references to it. But in addition to the P references (27:18, 23-24 and Numbers 36:4) Ezekiel 46:17 takes it for granted and Isaiah 61:1-2 is a literary allusion to it.

The patrimonial system of land ownership which it reflects and the tribal inheritances which it protects (cf. Numbers 36:4) were outmoded institutions by the time of the early monarchy. They would hardly be useful in a new proposal in the time of the H compiler or the P authors. The exclusion of town houses from redemption (verses 29-31) is clearly an amendment to the original law to meet changing economic conditions. This is probably true also for the omission of the early limitation of an Israelite slave's service to six years, of which Deuteronomy 15:12-18 was no doubt a revival. Amendment is the sign of a living rather than a theoretical law.

It should be noted also that the jubilee year begins in the fall according to the preexilic calendar (verse 9; see below on verses 8-12) rather than in the spring according to the Babylonian calendar followed by the P authors (see above on 23:23-25).

25:8-12. There is uncertainty how the jubilee cycle is calculated. The most plausible theory is that the author figures from the standpoint of the Babylonian calendar with a spring new year (see above on 23:23-25). Thus the **day of atonement** inaugurating the jubilee year falls in the middle of this year. By the common ancient inclusive method of counting he takes the half year at the beginning as the first year and thus comes out at the end with a half year as the **fiftieth**—even though the actual interval has been only **forty-nine years.** Thus the jubilee year coincides with the seventh sabbatical year. This theory avoids assuming two successive fallow years, which would be impossible without famine. It is supported by the forty-nine-year cycles used in the apocalyptic Book of Jubilees, written in the Maccabean period, and in the Dead Sea scrolls.

25:13-17. Since all land reverts to the original owner at the jubilee, any sale is actually a lease for the remaining years of the cycle. The price is to be calculated accordingly.

25:18-22. The calculation here is probably to be explained on the basis that the author's numbered years begin in the spring (see above on verses 8-12) whereas the observance of the sabbatical year begins after the end of the harvest in the fall. Thus there is actually no problem about what to **eat in the seventh year.** The people **gather** during the spring and summer of that year the **crop** sowed during the **sixth year,** which must provide the food for parts of **three years.** The sabbatical year begins with the fall of the seventh year and extends through the summer of the **eighth year.** After this the people sow a crop that does not come to harvest **until the ninth year,** i.e., the first half of it.

25:23-28. All the **land** in Palestine belongs to God. He is assumed to have assigned it in the days of Joshua—by the casting of lots, believed to be divinely controlled—to the families of Israel. There is to be no absolute sale of this property. Any transfer of it is subject to **redemption** by the current heir of the family to which it was originally allotted. If he is too **poor,** it may be redeemed by **his next of kin**—a technical term for the member of his family obligated to be the avenger of blood as well as the redeemer of property and of the person from slavery. In view of the approaching jubilee the sale is just a lease (see above on verses 13-17), and so the redemption price is reduced year by year.

25:29-34. With the growth of urban life and an economic class engaged in trade rather than agriculture an exception has to be made for a **house in a walled city,** which cannot be kept in the same family indefinitely. An exception to the exception, however, is made for the **Levites.** In the beginning they were assigned the nonagricultural occupation of religious leadership and allotted special cities.

25:35-55. *Debt and Slavery.* The Israelite farmer who has had to sell his land must become a hired hand for one of his more fortunate neighbors. He thus falls to the status of a landless **stranger** or **sojourner**—technical terms for two classes of resident aliens, the sojourner having limited citizenship rights (see above on 24:17-23). If unable to pay his debts he has no recourse but to sell himself and his family into slavery. Exodus 21:2-6 (cf. Deuteronomy 15:12-18) limits the term of service of a Hebrew slave to six years unless he voluntarily chooses to remain for the rest of his life. No doubt that law was not always enforced (cf. Jeremiah 34:13-14). Perhaps it had become a dead letter when this passage was written.

25:35-38. Parallels to the terminology of this passage are found in Old and Middle Babylonian laws from the time of the patriarchs discovered at Alalakh in northern Syria and Nuzi in eastern Assyria. These help to clarify the obscurity in verses 35:36a. Probably they mean: "If your brother, being in straits, comes under your authority, and you hold him as though a resident alien, so that he remains under you, do not exact from him advance or accrued interest" (Jewish Publication Society translation). Cf. Exodus 22:25 and Deuteronomy 23:19-20.

25:39-55. An Israelite enslaved for debt is to be treated like a **hired servant** rather than a slave and is to be released in the jubilee year. But a non-Israelite slave, whether imported or born in the land, is not subject to the jubilee release. On the other hand a resident non-Israelite master must release an Israelite slave in the jubilee year. He must also let him be **redeemed** earlier by a **kinsman** (see above on verses 23-28), the amount depending on the **number of years** till the jubilee. Masters sometimes allowed slaves to earn income and keep part of it, so that in time a slave might save enough to **redeem himself.**

26:1-2. *Prohibition of Idols.* Cf. 19:3*b*-4. **Idols** here is literally "things of naught." **Pillar** is joined with **graven,** i.e. sculptured, **image** because it served not only as a commemorative monument but also as a cultic symbol of the deity. Such pillars have been found at various places in Palestine. One has been discovered in an Israelite sanctuary at Arad in Southern Judah, whose destruction is tentatively dated at the end of the seventh century, the time of Josiah's reform (cf. II Kings 23:14).

G. The Concluding Exhortation (26:3-46)

Like the promises at the end of the Covenant Code (Exodus 23:20-33) and the blessings and curses at the end of the Deuteronomic Code (Deuteronomy 28) this final admonition with both promise and threat follows a pattern common in ancient law codes.

26:27-45. They base this on the detailed threat of devastation and exile and the final promise to **remember the covenant,** as well as the parallels in thought and language to Ezekiel. A number of commentators date this passage, and accordingly the compiling of the Holiness Code as a whole, during the period of the Exile. On the contrary, however, the discrepancy between the description in verses 36-39 and the actual life of the exiles in Babylonia (cf. Jeremiah 29:5-7) shows that this passage must have been written before the event. Furthermore the plural **sanctuaries** in verse 31 points to a time before Josiah's centralization of worship.

From the middle of the eighth century on, the possibility of conquest and exile was never very remote. The parallels with Ezekiel, therefore, must come from the prophet's acquaintance with the code. It should be noted that the H compiler's view that children are punished **because of the iniquities of their fathers** is repudiated both by Ezekiel (Ezekiel 18) and by the P authors (Numbers 14:31 and 26:11).

26:46. This sentence declares what precedes to be the basis of the covenant on **Mount Sinai.** Many scholars have taken it to be the conclusion to the Holiness Code, but the parallelism with 25:1 indicates rather that it applies only to 25-26.

VI. COMMUTATION OF VOTIVE GIFTS (27:1-34)

A **vow** was a promise to God, usually of an offering, made contingent on his aid in response to some petition—for example, for success in achieving a goal or for recovery from illness or other distress. Originally a **vow of persons** called for a human sacrifice (cf. Judges 11:29-40). In very early times, however, substitution of an animal (cf. Genesis 22:13) or a payment of silver (cf. II Kings 12:4) became established (see above on 5:14–6:7). The word translated **valuation** is thus an ancient technical term for the equivalent in commutation (see above on 5:15).

27:9-25. A vow to sacrifice a specific clean animal must be fulfilled. An attempt to substitute another renders both beasts **holy,** i.e. subject to sacrifice. But an equivalent payment plus a **fifth** may be substituted for an **unclean animal,** e.g. an ass or camel, or for a **house** or **land.**

A **homer,** about 5 bushels, **of barley** would sow a vast area and make the land ridiculously cheap. It is likely that **seed** and sowing—the same word—here mean "grain" and refer to the yield (cf. verse 30). The land is subject to release in the **year of jubilee** and thus must be appraised on the basis of the number of years remaining (cf. 25:13-17).

27:26-34. Since a **firstling** belongs to God anyway it cannot be the fulfillment of a vow. On verse 27 cf. Exodus 13:13.

A **devoted thing** in early times was irrevocably condemned to death or destruction, usually in connection with holy war. Now it is **most holy,** the unredeemable property of the sanctuary and its priests (cf. Numbers 18:14). A devoted person, however, is still to suffer **death** without a way to be **ransomed.**

Like firstlings, the **tithe** already belongs to God and cannot fulfill a vow. But an equivalent payment plus a **fifth** may be substituted for it if it is **seed,** i.e. grain, or **fruit.** On the other hand an animal tithe—mentioned only here and in II Chronicles 31:6—cannot be **exchanged.** Verse 34 probably sums up this chapter rather than the entire book (cf. 1:1).

THE BOOK OF NUMBERS

Harvey H. Guthrie, Jr.

INTRODUCTION

Like the other books of the Pentateuch (see Introduction to Genesis) Numbers is designated in the Hebrew Bible by a word from its opening sentence, "In the wilderness." Its English title originated with the Septuagint and refers to the census described in its opening chapters.

Numbers is not a separate unit either in its final form or in any of the sources underlying it. It is part of a larger unit, and the division of this unit into books is largely arbitrary. The rationale by which Numbers is set off in this division is that it narrates the movement of Israel from Sinai to the borders of Canaan, beginning with the census of the tribes taken before the journey. In other words it covers the traditional forty years of wandering in the wilderness.

Sources

The literary sources J, E, and P (see Introduction to Genesis) are the basis of Numbers as they are of Genesis and Leviticus. The separation of J and E in Numbers is difficult, and there is no general agreement about it. The following commentary, for the most part, simply refers to JE sections. P is usually fairly easily recognized. Many of the P portions of Numbers are secondary supplements to the basic P work, inserted rather haphazardly into the narrative.

Tradition seems to have been vague about the wilderness period, and the era covered in Numbers became a convenient peg on which to hang presettlement traditions which editors wished to get into the record. A table of the sources appears below.

Behind the literary sources, and alongside them, lay traditions from various places and groups in Israel. As a larger unity Israel undoubtedly came into existence later than the period of which Numbers speaks, after constituent groups were established in Palestine. After this establishment the traditions of the Exodus and the Sinai covenant became the basis for the theology of the entire united federation of tribes that preceded the monarchy.

The experiences underlying the traditions, however, were originally undergone by the ancestors of only parts of united Israel, not by those of all the tribes and clans. Likewise the many other traditions later recounted and revered by the whole of Israel arose out of the past of only segments of the united people. If the narrative of Numbers seems disjointed and haphazard— especially in 10:11–20:29—it is due to the way in which a subsequently united people remembered and organized originally separate traditions as part of a common history. In the same way today a citizen of the United States thinks of the traditions of the Massachusetts pilgrims and the Virginia cavaliers as his heritage without considering when his own ancestors came to America. This process does not devaluate or discredit the biblical narrative. Rather it leads to an understanding of the real nature of Numbers and of what Israel's tradition meant to her.

Sources of Numbers

The early and late strands of tradition in Numbers are shown in the two columns below. Since the most prominent distinguishing marks of the two early strands, J and E, do not appear in Numbers, they can rarely be separated with assurance.

Accordingly probable J and E elements are noted in the commentary where recognizable but are not distinguished in this table. Strata apparent in the P material are indicated by the letter "s" to mark later additions. The combined initials after 32:1-42 and 33:1-49 point to the probability that traditions from all three sources have been combined by a later editor.

JE (early)	P (Priestly)
	1:1-47, 48-54s
	2:1-34
	3:1-13s, 14-51
	4:1-15, 16-20s, 21-49
	5:1–7:89s
	8:1-4s, 5-22, 23-26s
	9:1-14s, 15-23
10:29-33, 35-36	10:1-10s, 11-12, 13-28s, 34s
11:1–12:16	
13:17b-20, 22-24, 26b-31	13:1-17a, 21, 25-26a, 32-33
14:1b, 4, 11-25, 39-45	14:1a, 2-3, 5-10, 26-38
	15:1-41s
16:1b-2a, 12-15, 25, 26b, 27b-34	16:1a, 2b-11, 16-24, 26a, 27a, 35, 36-50s
	17:1–19:22s
20:14-22a	20:1-13, 22b-29
21:1-35	
22:2-41	22:1
23:1–24:25	
25:1-5	25:6-18
	26:1-65s
	27:1-11s, 12-23
	28:1–31:54s
32:1-42JEP	32:1-42JEP
33:1-49JEP	33:1-49JEP, 50-56s
	34:1–36:13s

Theological Significance

It is only through allegorical interpretation that readers today can receive inspiration and edification from the bulk of

Numbers. Its theological significance for the Christian lies simply in the fact that both the church and the civilization of which it is a part have arisen in the context of a history of which Israel and Israel's remembrance and interpretation of her past as found in Numbers are part. Furthermore the uniqueness of Israel and the church lies in their affirmation that it is precisely in this history that God has acted to reveal himself and to redeem his world. Thus, using the results of historical method as applied to the Bible, the Christian can read Numbers for what it really is. To read into Numbers relevance or edification that is not really there—or to reject Numbers because of the lack of those things—is to misunderstand what the Bible as a whole is really saying.

I. Final Days at Sinai (1:1–10:10)

This section is the conclusion of the P account of Israel's sojourn at Mt. Sinai, which began at Exodus 25:1 and, excluding Exodus 32–34, continues through Exodus and Leviticus. As elsewhere, P is obviously composite. Its basic account of Israel's sacred institutions has been expanded and supplemented. The dates in 1:1 and 10:11 indicate that P conceives of this section as covering a period of nineteen days.

1:1-46. *The Census of Israel.* The purpose of this census is military, but not in a secular sense. Israel in the days before the monarchy was an amphictyony (sacral league) consisting of independent tribes with allegiance to a common God, Yahweh. All were obligated to maintain his sanctuary and to send men to his army when holy war was declared.

1:1. The **wilderness of Sinai**—that is, the desert around Sinai—is traditionally located at Jebel Musa in the south of the Sinai Peninsula. But many scholars, for sound reasons, locate the holy mountain farther north near Kadesh-barnea (see comment on Exodus 3:1). Like J, P always refers to the mountain as Sinai, while E and D call it Horeb. This may indicate a more radical difference in traditions than is allowed by the usual simple equation of the two.

P generally uses the term **tent of meeting** for the sacred central shrine of the tribes, and speaks of the **tabernacle** (verse 50) as being inside the tent (Exodus 26:7) as a housing for the ark (3:31; 4:5). Both tent and ark are used in the present literary sources. But they may originally have been associated with the traditions of separate groups which came together within Israel only after the settlement in Palestine (see comments on Exodus 25:10-22 and 33:7-11).

1:2-16. Though usage is sometimes confused, the tribe consisted of a number of **families** ("clans" might be better), each of which consisted of a number of **fathers' houses,** which was the smallest social unit (cf. Joshua 7:16-18). **Company** and **clans** (literally "thousands") are military divisions.

1:20:46. The statistics are unbelievably large for this period and are generally considered artificial (see comment on Exodus 38:21-31). They may, however, represent the results of a census at some later point in Israel's history. Like much in P, these figures may be material much older than the finished document itself.

1:47-54. *The Levites.* P agrees with all early traditions in associating the Levites closely with Moses and the shrine of Yahweh. But this passage reflects their status in the postexilic temple in representing them as a group separate from and subordinate to the priests (cf. 3:5-10).

A long, complicated, and debated history of the Israelite priesthoods lies behind the situation assumed here, which is like that described in Chronicles. The Levites' function is said to be simply to care for and protect the **tabernacle.** They are not one of the twelve tribes (as in, for example, Genesis 35:23; 49:5-7 and Exodus 1:2) but a caste outside the tribes. The division of Joseph into two tribes (verses 32-45) brings the number back to twelve.

2:1-34. *The Sacred Encampment.* The plan of Israel's camp in the wilderness is pictured by P as quadrilateral. The twelve tribes are arranged, three on each side, to form the perimeter.

Inside, the priests are to the east of the tent, and the three divisions of the Levites are on the other three sides (cf. 1:50-53; 3:23, 29, 35, 38).

While the symbolism of God's presence in Israel's midst is significant to P, what is described here is probably not sheer invention from the exilic or postexilic period. Behind this chapter may lie very ancient, premonarchic cultic tradition. It has been held that the source of traditions such as this was the most ancient form of the feast of booths, an annual occasion on which the tribes would camp in the desert around the tent of meeting to recall their ancient days.

3:1-4:49. *The Levites and Their Duties.* In designating the Aaronic priests alone as those to whom the priestly office belongs (3:1-4) P differs from preexilic sources. Verse 4 refers to Leviticus 10:1-2. On verses 5-10 see above on 1:47-54.

3:11-13. A different tradition from that in the preceding verses claims that the Levites were taken from **among the people of Israel** as substitutes for the **first-born** sons of Israel, who belong to Yahweh. See below on verses 40-51.

3:14-39. These verses describe a census of the Levitical families (contrast 1:47-49) and the stations in camp and duties of the three divisions of the Levites. Verse 38 designates the priests' place in the camp. The discrepancy between the total of Levites in verse 39 and the sum of the figures in verses 22, 28, 34 may be due to an early scribal error dropping a letter from verse 28.

3:40-51. The count of **first-born males** of all Israel includes those **from a month old and upward** because it was at the age of one month that the parents of a first-born son were required to pay **five shekels** to the priests (cf. 18:16; on **shekel of the sanctuary** see comment on Exodus 30:13). A Mosaic origin for this requirement is here claimed.

In all this P, or a supplement to it, may be utilizing ancient tradition about the encampment, but cultic conditions of postexilic times are certainly read back into the account. Thus it is asserted that what Israel is, originated with Moses. There may have been polemical reasons for such an assertion at the time of writing.

4:1-49. Another **census** is made of men aged thirty to fifty in the three groups of Levites. The purpose is to assign their duties in the camp and on the march. Various tasks of the priests are also mentioned. Again premonarchic cultic traditions are read in the light of postexilic times. This accounts for discrepancies and inconsistencies in the passage. The results of the census are summarized in verses 34-49. We have no way of knowing the source or date of the figures.

5:1–6:27. *Various Laws.* This section logically follows what precedes it. Sacral army, camp and sanctuary, priestly and Levitical duties have been described. P now turns to the conditions of ritual purity incumbent on all Israel. This is the point of the bulk of Old Testament law.

5:1-4. Specified bodily disqualifications bar one from inclusion in the sacral congregation. Such ritual requirements have prevailed in Roman Catholic and Eastern Orthodox qualifications for physical soundness in members of the priesthood.

5:5-10. Ritual disqualification results when an oath or pledge is violated, and one must make **restitution.** Such a violation constitutes **breaking faith with the LORD**—sacred and secular are not distinguished (cf. Leviticus 6:1-7). In modern terms, ritual law is also ethical.

5:11-31. Adultery defiles the ritual purity of the congregation. A woman suspected of the offense must undergo an ordeal in connection with a sacrifice by her husband and her own oath of purgation. This is the only Old Testament specification of a trial by ordeal, an attempt to obtain a direct divine verdict in ambiguous cases, but the custom must have been used by Israel in other situations (cf. chapter 16). In verse 23 **book,** a general term for writing material, probably means a piece of pottery, stone, or wood from which the priest could wash the ink.

6:1-21. Regulations are laid down for the **Nazirite,** one separated from others by a **special vow.** The dietary and tonsorial customs of Nazirites, found all through Israel's history, may indicate that one of their motives was protest against agricultural, Canaanite society. P places the Nazirite under priestly authority.

6:22-27. This familiar priestly blessing might more logically have come in Leviticus 9:22. It is probably very ancient, and has continued to be used in temple, synagogue, and church. Its essence in Ancient Israel lay in the placing of the divine **name** (note its threefold repetition) on God's **people.**

7:1-89. *Offerings at the Dedication of the Altar.* This chapter is out of order chronologically (Exodus 40 has the altar anointed a month before the date in 1:1) and repetitive in its enumeration of the offerings by tribal leaders. It must be the product of a late supplementer of P. Its basis in fact may have been found in lists of temple equipment and offerings, and it may have been placed here because of the census lists in chapters 1–4, but it must be largely fancy. Possibly its writer thought of the ancient leaders as models of generous supporters of the sanctuary. Verse 89 is a fragment from a lost narrative; it has no connection with its context here (cf. Exodus 25:22).

8:1-4. *The Golden Lampstand.* This prototype of the well-known Jewish *menorah,* which stood before the table for the bread of the presence in the temple, is described in P at greater length in Exodus 25:31-40 and 37:17-24. The motive behind chapter 7 probably accounts for the allusion to it here.

8:5-26. *Consecration of the Levites.* Like the two preceding sections, this shows how P was expanded and supplemented. It repeats what is already found in 3:5-13. Verses 23-25 do not agree with 4:3. At several points it repeats itself (verses 6, 11, 13, 15). The original part is in verses 5-13, the procedure by which Levites were set apart for their service.

9:1-14. *The Supplemental Passover.* This passage is also a supplement in P. It provides for the keeping of the passover a month later than its regular date by those found ritually unclean at the appointed time. It was probably placed here by attraction to the date in 1:1, which places chapters 1–10 in the second month, the time of the supplemental passover it describes (cf. II Chronicles 30).

9:15-23. *The Fiery Cloud.* This section repeats Exodus 40:34-38. Again, it must be a supplement in P. In Exodus 40:35 the cloud is connected with the "glory" of Yahweh, i.e. his presence. P, Isaiah, and Ezekiel come from a tradition in which "glory" designates Yahweh's presence, Deuteronomy from a tradition emphasizing Yahweh's "name."

10:1-10. *The Silver Trumpets.* P holds that the last act before leaving Sinai was the manufacture of silver trumpets with which the tribes of Israel were to be summoned to various sacral functions. These are described to account for the trumpets mentioned in II Kings 12:13; Psalm 98:6; and often in Chronicles, Ezra, and Nehemiah. These instruments were straight tubes about two feet long. Their use in the postexilic cult probably was an elaboration of the solemn sounding of the rams-horn *shophar* in the preexilic, and even premonarchic, cult at the point of Yahweh's manifestation of his presence. Thus, this time with real warrant, P again attributes the institution of postexilic procedures to the time of Moses.

II. THE PERIOD IN THE WILDERNESS (10:11–20:29)

Any outline of Numbers is arbitrary. The final form of the book resulted from a sometimes haphazard combination of various traditions. Underneath it, however, seem to lie two traditions of how Palestine was entered by the tribes: (1) a push upward from the south, completed in Judges 1; (2) a movement north into Transjordan, completed in the account of the conquest in Joshua. The present form of Numbers combines these originally separate traditions—if such they are—into a unified narrative.

Tradition holds that the period covered in this section was forty years—a generation (cf. 14:33). The chronology of P strictly followed makes the exact figure thirty-eight years (cf. 10:11 with 20:23-29 and 33:38). Major attention is devoted to the beginning (10:11–14:35) and end (20:1-29) of the period.

In spite of the various places mentioned by P (cf. the catalogue in chapter 33), the traditions seem to indicate that actually the center of Israel's life in this period was the oasis-sanctuary of Kadesh-barnea. Massah and Meribah (cf. Exodus 17) were located here. Near this area, rather than at the site fixed on by postbiblical tradition, was Mt. Sinai (see comment on Exodus 3:1). Thus the traditions in chapters 1–20 have to do, not with "wandering," but with the life of an association of tribes at a common center.

A. The Departure from Sinai (10:11-36)

10:11-28. *The P Account.* P here recounts how instructions given previously are followed as the march from Sinai begins. The **cloud** (cf. 9:15-23) signals the time to move. The order of march specified in chapter 2 is followed, with the Levites (cf. chapters 3–4) and the tribes under their leaders (cf. 1:5-15) in proper place.

10:29-36. *The JE Account.* Here for the first time in Numbers the thread of narrative from the preexilic sources, J and E, is taken up, continuing from Exodus 34:28.

Though the wording here is ambiguous, the total evidence suggests that in the E tradition **Moses' father-in-law** was a **Midianite** who returned to his own land (cf. Exodus 18:27). In the J tradition he was **Hobab** the Kenite of the clan of **Reuel** and accompanied the Israelites, or at least part of them, into Canaan (cf. Judges 1:16; 4:11; see comment on Exodus 2:15b-22; 18:1-12). At any rate the traditions indicate that Moses, and therefore the origins of Israelite religion, were closely connected with a nomadic group, which was probably a part of the tribal complex to the south of Canaan before the occupation. This is one of the indications that behind the traditions of the Pentateuch lies a long and complex history not now recoverable in all its details.

10:33-34. JE calls the portable sanctuary the **ark of the covenant,** as opposed to the "tabernacle" and "tent of meeting" in P, and says that it **went before** the people on the march (contrast verses 11-28). Again variant traditions from groups which actually merged only later on in Palestine underlie the text. The second **three days' journey** seemed to be a scribal error duplicating the first. Verse 34 is probably a P supplement.

10:35-36. This is an ancient poetic invocation of Yahweh's presence with the ark, which led Israel in holy war until it was placed by Solomon in the Jerusalem temple.

B. PROBLEMS AND DISSENSION IN ISRAEL (11:1–12:16)

The traditions of the Pentateuch stress that the Israel being led by God to a homeland was by no means a cooperative people. The rebelliousness during the trek from Egypt to Canaan is the subject of a number of stories (cf. Exodus 16:1-3; 17:1-4; 32). Israel's sacred songs cited these stories as examples of the terrible decision demanded by God's election (e.g. Psalm 95:8-11). It is not reading later theology into the Old Testament to say that Israel stressed divine grace as opposed by human sinfulness. That is the theological motive behind the presence of such stories in the earliest strata of the Pentateuch. This whole section is from JE.

11:1-3. *Taberah.* Though the **fire of the LORD** can mean lightning, this story implies a direct divine act which punishes Israel's complaining. The story gives an explanation of the name of a place—though Taberah could mean "pasture" as well as "burning." It also serves as an example of the effectiveness of prophetic intercession, a motif stressed in E (cf. Genesis 20:7, 17). Deuteronomy 9:22 indicates that this place, along with Massah, was in the vicinity of Kadesh.

11:4-35. *The People's Craving for Meat.* Two stories are now interwoven in these verses. The account of Israel's complaint about having to subsist only on the manna of the desert is a parallel to the story from P in Exodus 16. Aside from being the JE account of Yahweh's provision for Israel in the desert, the story explains the name of a place (verse 34). It has been generally attributed to J but may contain fragments from E.

Verses 11-15 especially seem to manifest the interest of E in the power of prophetic intercession.

11:4-6. The word **rabble** comes from a root meaning "gathering" (a different term is used of this group in Exodus 12:38). The traditions are conscious that groups not later considered part of Israel were involved in her preconquest history (see above on 10:29-32). The catalogue of Egyptian food is accurate. The preexilic sources seem to have had an acquaintance with Egypt and its ways.

11:7-9. This story does not suggest, as does Exodus 16, that the manna was miraculous, but sees it as a natural product of the desert. The miracle is rather in the provision of quail.

11:16-25. The interwoven story of **seventy . . . elders of the people** and the prophetic **spirit** (verses 16-17, 24b-30) shows the interests of E. As in Exodus 18 and 24 the elders are associated with Moses in his leadership of Israel—E seeming to reflect the more antimonarchic tendencies of northern tradition. Present also is E's tendency to stress Moses' great spiritual powers, as well as its interest in prophecy.

Though it has been maintained that the story here is only a variant of that in Exodus 18, or that in Exodus 24:1-11, its motive seems to be different. The endowment of the elders with the spirit of prophecy is only the setting for the Eldad-Medad incident in verses 26-30.

Prophesied here refers to the ecstatic behavior implied in I Samuel 10:9-12 and 18:10 (where "raved" is in Hebrew the same verb). This behavior was the outward sign of the elders' possession of divine power (**spirit**). The conclusion of verse 25 implies that it took place on only one occasion.

11:26-30. The point of the story is Moses' attitude toward the two men who prophesy **in the camp** while he and the elders are at the sanctuary (note that E, contrary to P in chapters 2–3, places the **tent** outside the camp). Moses' reply to Joshua's indignation is more than a claim for magnanimity. In it is expressed an ideal which Joel 2:28-29 declares will be realized in the final time, and which finds expression in a different way in Jeremiah 31:31-34.

11:31-35. Large flocks of migrating **quails** often stop to rest in this region. Exhausted from flight, they can be easily caught.

Deuteronomy 9:22 indicates that **Kibroth-hattaavah** was near Kadesh, but its exact location is not known. The location of **Hazeroth** is also unknown.

12:1-16. *The Rebellion of Miriam and Aaron.* The point of this story, probably from E (except verse 16 from J), is quite simple. It is easy to see how it was preserved in close connection with the Eldad-Medad story in 11:26-30. Miriam and Aaron question Moses' unique, divinely granted authority. They are solemnly reproved by Yahweh, who proclaims Moses' authority in a poetic oracle and punishes Miriam with leprosy.

The story is one strong indication of a rift that developed among the Israelites at Kadesh. Hints of the same thing are given in the accounts all through chapters 11–16 of discontent, differences over entering Canaan from the south, and challenges to Moses' authority. Combined with traditions of two entries into Canaan, one from the south and one from Transjordan (cf. Judges 1 with Joshua 1–12), all this may indicate some kind of split into separate groups. These groups were reunited tenuously later on in Canaan only to break up once more after Solomon's reign.

If this is what happened, however, later tradition has forgotten it. Numbers now treats the past as a series of successive events involving all the ancestors of the Israel of later times.

12:1-2. Though **Cushite** usually means Ethiopian or Kassite (see comment on Genesis 10:8-12), Habakkuk 3:7 suggests that here it may mean Midianite and refer to Zipporah (cf. Exodus 2:15-22; see comment on II Chronicles 14:9-15). There is no mention elsewhere of a tradition that Moses had a second wife, and verse 1*b* probably is a later insertion. In any case the reference is a puzzle. Verse 2 locates the root of the incident in offended pride.

12:6-8. The semipoetic form of this pronouncement argues for its antiquity. The lines may come from the premonarchic cult in which Moses' "covenant mediator" successors played a central role.

C. Spies Sent into Canaan (13:1–14:45)

The account is presented in such a way as to show why Israel journeyed around the eastern side of Canaan to enter across the Jordan. Here the traditions may indicate that the groups that formed the later Israel entered the land in various ways and at various times (see above on 12:1-16).

The present account, with its incongruities and repetitions, is clearly composite. Scholars differ in their analyses of J and E, but there is substantial agreement on what is JE and what P.

According to JE, Moses sends men to enter Canaan from the south for reconnaissance (13:17b-20). Through the Negeb they penetrate as far as Hebron and obtain samples of the excellent crops of the country (13:22-24). They report to Moses at Kadesh the desirability of the land and the forbidding strength of its inhabitants, but Caleb insists that it can be taken (13:26b-31).

Discouraged and disappointed at this frustration (14:1b), the people advocate overthrowing Moses and returning to Egypt (14:4). Yahweh is enraged at the people's response. Yahweh is ready to reject them and reserve election for Moses and his descendants. Yahweh accedes to Moses' plea for pardon, but says that of those concerned only Caleb shall enter Canaan, and commands Israel to turn back into the desert in order to circumvent southern Canaan (14:11-25). Reversing their former reaction, the people insist on an invasion, only to be defeated and routed (14:39-45).

The P account states that the spies include a representative from each of the twelve tribes (13:1-17a) and that they explore the whole of Palestine (13:21). After forty days they return to Paran (13:25-26a) with a discouraging report of the land itself and of the size of the inhabitants (13:32-33), which causes the people to complain (14:1a, 2-3). Joshua and Caleb declare that the land is good. They claim that with Yahweh's help they can conquer it, but the people reject their counsel (14:5-10). Therefore Yahweh decrees that Israel must wander in the desert for forty years, until all the murmurers have died. Only Joshua and Caleb will be left to lead the new generation into the Promised Land (14:26-38).

13:1-16. The listing of the twelve spies as representatives of their tribes agrees with the constitution of the tribal league described in chapters 1, 26, and 34. It shows the usual interest of P in genealogy.

13:17-21. According to JE the spies are to explore simply the **Negeb,** the arid country south of Beer-sheba, and the **hill country,** the rough, mountainous area of Judah. In the P account, however, they survey the whole land from **the wilderness of Zin** surrounding Kadesh to **Rehob,** i.e. Bethrehob near Dan. This illustrates the P tendency to emphasize the nation as a whole and play down local and tribal traditions.

13:22-29. The JE traditions contain probably accurate remembrance of which clans were pre-Israelite inhabitants of the **Hebron** area and of the **Negeb** and the **hill country.** On **Zoan** see comment on Exodus 1:8-14. On **Anak** see below on verses 32-33.

The **Amalekites** were desert nomads remembered by Israel as archetypal enemies (cf. Exodus 17:8-16 and I Samuel 15:1-33). The **Hittites** were remnants of an empire in Asia Minor that had penetrated into Palestine before the Israelite occupation. The **Jebusites** were the Canaanite group still holding Jerusalem in David's time.

The **Amorites,** mentioned often in various areas both in the Old Testament and in other ancient sources, were desert peoples who penetrated into all parts of the Fertile Crescent in the eighteenth and seventeenth centuries B.C. E regularly uses the name instead of **Canaanites** as the general term for the pre-Israelite inhabitants of Palestine. Note the characteristic interest in telling the supposed origin of a place name, **Eshcol** in verses 23-24.

13:30-31. Caleb is depicted in the JE account as the one spy expressing confidence in Israel's ability to **overcome** the land.

This seeks to explain why elements of Judah, including Calebites (cf. Judges 1:10-20), occupied the Hebron area long before the conquest of central and northern Palestine.

13:32-33. In contrast to the JE report of fertility (verses 23-24, 26b-27) the spies in the P account declare that the country **devours its inhabitants,** apparently meaning that it starves them.

Verse 33 is probably from P though many scholars attribute it to JE. It expands the tradition that the **sons of Anak** (cf. verse 22) were of unusual size by interpreting them to be descendants of the **Nephilim** (cf. Genesis 6:1-4). This probably represents a legendary or mythological tradition that the original inhabitants of Israel's land were more-than-human giants.

14:6-9. P portrays not only Caleb but also **Joshua** in a good light. This is in line with P's emphasis on the unified movement of the tribes in the wilderness until the conquest led by Joshua and on the inclusion of the northern tribes (Joshua) in the favor with which Yahweh looks on the southern tribes (Caleb) in the JE account. It is also in line with a tendency to emphasize an orderly, divinely ordained chain of command, since tradition claimed Joshua as Moses' valid lieutenant.

14:11-20. Once again the JE account stresses the divine approval of Moses and the power of his intercession as a prophet. Moses claims that Yahweh's reputation demands an action which seemingly violates his justice. This touches on a problem present also to later prophets (cf. Ezekiel 36 and Isaiah 48). The real basis of pardon is Yahweh's **steadfast love,** his abiding, loving loyalty to his covenant with his people (cf. Exodus 34:6-9).

14:21-38. The purpose of the story of the spies in both JE (verses 21-25) and P (verses 26-38) is to explain why tradition held that Israel, after escaping so successfully from Egypt, spent a generation wandering in the wilderness between Sinai and the Conquest. The answer here is that those who came out of Egypt failed to trust Yahweh to lead them to victory and were punished by being forbidden to enter the Promised Land. Only Caleb, one who trusted (and Joshua, according to P), is permitted to survive and enter with the new generation. On **the way to the Red Sea** see below on 21:4-9.

14:39-45. In contrast to the Calebites (see above on 13:30-31) other Israelite groups did not succeed in occupying the hill country of Judah (on **Hormah** cf. 21:1-3). Again there is indication of differences among the groups at Kadesh. There is indication also of a more gradual possession of Canaan than the finished biblical tradition recognizes.

D. Various Ritual Laws (15:1-41)

This section as a whole bears no perceptible relation to its context, and the four laws and an incident of which it consists bear no relation to one another. It probably represents additions to P which were included after the completion of that document simply because they were not found elsewhere in it. Why they were inserted at this point is hard to say, though verse 1 provides a link with what has gone before.

15:1-16. The amounts of **fine flour** (ground from the hearts of the wheat kernels), **oil,** and **wine** to be offered with various kinds of sacrifices are specified. An **ephah** is half a bushel and a **hin** is three and a third quarts. Similar regulations are found in Ezekiel 46:5-7, 11, 14. Verses 14-16, in line with may other passages in P, assert that this law applies to the **stranger** or **sojourner** (resident alien) as well as to the native Israelite. Such passages indicate that even at a very late time Israel consisted of various elements. Membership in the worshiping congregation was not simply hereditary.

15:17-21. The meaning of the key word in this instruction about an offering is unknown. **Coarse meal** is only a guess at translation.

15:22-31. Propitiatory offerings are provided for those breaking the law **unwittingly** (cf. Leviticus 4:2-21). It should be noted, however, that sins committed **with a high hand** (i.e. intentionally) are not covered by any sacrifice. Properly understood, Israel's complicated system of sacrifices was not mere ritualism but expressed the gracious provision of a forgiving God for those who sincerely sought to obey his law.

15:32-36. This narrative is apparently introduced to underline the fact that there is no atonement for sins committed "with a high hand."

15:37-41. This provision, also found in Deuteronomy 22:12, is still followed by Jews in the wearing of the tallith, or prayer shawl, with **tassels on the corners.** Verses 39-40 give a rationale for a custom which undoubtedly originated in ancient superstition. Verse 41 concludes the section with the divine assertion characteristic of the Holiness Code (Leviticus 17–26).

E. Rights and Duties of Levites and Priests (16:1–18:32)

The purpose of this section in P is seen in chapter 18, which outlines the duties of Levites and the sources of income reserved for priests and Levites. The stories in chapters 16–17 are illustrations of the exclusive claims of these orders to the tasks appointed them. While P (undoubtedly supplemented) is wholly responsible for chapters 17–18, a story from JE has been worked into the narrative in chapter 16.

16:1-50. *The Rebellion of Korah, Dathan, and Abiram.* That this chapter is composite in origin is indicated not only by repetitions and inconsistencies but by the fact that the two basic elements in it are elsewhere referred to separately (27:3; Deuteronomy 11:6). In its present composite form the story was well known (cf. 26:9-11; Psalm 106:16-18; Jude 11).

The JE element (verses 1*b*-2*a*, 12-15, 25, 26*b*, 27*b*-34) seems to be the conflation of a J narrative about **On the son of Peleth** with a brief E account of **Dathan and Abiram.** The P story of **Korah** (verses 1*a*, 2*b*-11, 16-24, 26*a*, 27*a*, 35-50) is likewise itself composite. A supplement by a later P author or authors has changed a story of general rebellion into a challenge of priestly authority by the Levites.

16:1-2*a*. This introduction contains bits from all four sources. **Korah** from the basic P account is given a genealogy making him

251

a Levite by the P supplement. **On,** if not a corruption in the text, is perhaps a fragment of the J story. **Dathan and Abiram** are identified as **sons of Reuben** who **rose up before Moses**—indicating that in the E source, and probably also in J, the revolt centers in the tribe of Reuben (cf. the tradition of loss of primacy of this tribe in Genesis 35:22; 49:3-4). This represents a challenge to Moses' authority as leader of the tribal league.

The constitution of Israel before the monarchy was that of an amphictyony, a league of independent tribes to which the constituent tribes owed certain duties and by whose laws certain boundaries were set around their own independence. This story in JE recalls some occasion on which the tribe of Reuben refused to submit to the league's authority and perform its appointed duties.

16:2b-11. The basic P story has to do with a sort of "laymen's revolt" against the religious leadership of Moses and Aaron. Korah's contention is that **all the congregation are holy** and that sacred functions should therefore not be reserved to a few. Moses proposes a way to test the objection by having the **two hundred and fifty** rebels offer incense so that Yahweh can choose **the holy one.**

The P supplement has added verses 7b-11 to change the basic P story of a revolt by **leaders** from all the tribes into an account of the challenge of priestly authority by the Levites. Some controversy, probably postexilic, in the long and complicated history of the Israelite priesthoods must underlie this version.

16:12-15. The JE story is here continued from verse 2a. **Come up** is probably a technical term referring to the tribal obligation (see above on verses 1-2a). **Put out the eyes** means "deceive." Verse 15 perhaps refers to a part of the story omitted by the editor.

16:16-24. In verses 16-17, from the P supplement, the **company** of Korah is actually the same Hebrew word as **congregation.** Here it is applied only to the group of Levites joined with Korah in his rebellion. In the basic P story, on the other hand, **all the congregation**—that is, all the Israelites except Moses and Aaron—are sympathetic to Korah, as shown by the intention of Yahweh to consume them all. In response to the intercession of Moses and Aaron, however, Yahweh tells them to instruct the people to leave so that they may be saved. **Dwelling** in verse 24 means the tabernacle (cf. verse 19); **of Korah, Dathan, and Abiram** is an editorial addition.

16:25-35. In these verses the climaxes of the JE and P stories are confusingly interwoven. The P story of the assembly before the tabernacle is continued in the words **And he said to the congregation** (verse 26a). But Moses' warning has been omitted by the editor in favor of the similar order from the JE story (verse 26b). The people leave the **dwelling,** i.e. the tabernacle (verse 27a; **of Korah, Dathan, and Abiram** is another editorial addition), and those presuming to offer **incense** are **consumed** by **fire** (verse 35).

The JE story into which these bits have been inserted portrays a solemn gathering of the tribal league, with **all Israel** present (verse 34). Moses is accompanied by the **elders of Israel** (verse 25) as he confronts the offending Reubenite clans represented by Dathan and Abiram. At his word a miraculous divine judgment descends on them—**the ground opens its mouth, and swallows them up.** A misguided editorial insertion in verse 32b includes Korah and his followers in this catastrophe so that they are killed twice (cf. verse 35). This JE story thus goes back to very ancient times and institutions (also recalled in Judges 19–20), in spite of its present position in a narrative with a different point to make.

16:36-40. This is a further addition by the P supplement. The **censers** of the rebels are made into a **covering for the altar** to act as a continual warning to anyone not a priest—a Levite, for example—not to approach it.

16:41-50. In the conclusion of the basic P story **all the congregation** continue the complaint begun by Korah. They are saved from total annihilation by Yahweh only when Moses and Aaron again intervene. In contrast to the offering of the 250 laymen the **incense** carried by Aaron is effective to halt the **plague** and save Israel. The story thus drives home the reservation of sacred acts for Moses and Aaron as representatives of the Levites. It is typical of the P viewpoint.

17:1-13. *Authentication of Aaron's Authority.* The close connection of this story with the P narrative in chapter 16 is evident—the Hebrew Bible even begins chapter 17 with 16:36. This story must come from P itself rather than from the later supplement in chapter 16, for its point is the vindication of the Levitical claims. Here, in contrast with chapters 1 and 26, Levi is apparently reckoned as one of the twelve tribes, not as a separate caste. Thus P maintains a confusion present in early traditions (cf. Genesis 29:31–30:24 and 49).

18:1-32. *Duties and Income of Levites and Priests.* This chapter is more logically connected with the narrative than many laws in Numbers. It forms a conclusion to chapters 16–17 by giving specific regulations concerning Levites and priests. It is a valuable source of information for compiling a history of the Israelite priesthoods.

18:1-7. In view of the preceding stories it is provided that only the priests shall directly approach the sanctuary, in order that the rest of Israel may be saved from perishing. In accord with postexilic practice, the Levites are assistants to the priests.

18:8-20. The priests and their families are to be maintained from the various offerings to Yahweh. As he has allotted the land as the **portion** of the tribes, so he allots what is offered to him as the priests' portion. Various regulations to be observed in the practice of this allotment are set down. On the **redemption** of the **first-born** see above on 3:40-51.

8:21-24. The **tithe** (cf. Leviticus 27:30-33 and Deuteronomy 14:22-29; 26:12-15) is to provide the income for the Levites, who like the priests have no inheritance of land.

18:25-32. The Levites must give to the priests a tithe of their income from the people's tithe—**a tithe of the tithe** (cf. Nehemiah 10:38).

F. PURIFICATION OF UNCLEANNESS FROM CONTACT WITH THE DEAD (19:1-22)

This chapter is from P, parts of it probably from a supplement to the basic work. Verses 1-10 and 20-22 provide for a ritual washing in a solution of which the basic ingredient is the ashes of a red heifer. Verses 11-19 describe the various ways in which ritual uncleanness is contracted through contact with the dead.

The chapter represents late priestly regulation of a practice which must have been very ancient. The belief that pollution results from contact with a corpse is common in many cultures. It is difficult to see why the chapter is inserted at this point. It may have been that the large number of deaths reported in chapters 16–18 brought the subject to an editor's mind. For other discussion of the subject see Leviticus 5:2; 11:8, 24–28; 21:1-4, 10-11; Numbers 5:2; 6:6-12; 9:6-14. Cf. also 31:19-24.

G. END OF THE STAY AT KADESH (20:1-29)

This chapter marks the transition from the stay in the wilderness to the journey through Transjordan to the point where the tribes enter Canaan under Joshua.

20:1. *The Death of Miriam.* In spite of the tradition that Israel "wandered" in the wilderness for forty years after the events of chapters 13–14, the narrative is almost completely silent about what happened during such a period. It is P that holds this theory, and its difficulties may be the reason P cites here only **the first month** without specifying the year. On the other hand, P supposes that Israel only now arrives in the **wilderness of Zin,** the region in which Kadesh is located. This had led some scholars to suggest that an editor may have omitted the year to avoid contradicting the JE account of an earlier arrival in this area. The older sources, J in particular, remember Kadesh as the center of Israel's life all through this period. For this reason the geography of chapters 1–20 is confused. The latter half of this verse, naming **Kadesh** and reporting the death of **Miriam,** of whom P has not recounted any incidents, is probably from JE.

20:2-13. *Water from the Rock.* The arrival at the wilderness of Zin is no doubt the reason for the inclusion here of this incident associated with Kadesh. A JE version is found in Exodus 17:1-7. This account is mostly from P but seems to contain some fragments from a J story.

As in the earlier version, the name of a spring, **Meribah** ("contention"), is accounted for by this ancient tradition. This is another indication that controversy at Kadesh resulted in some kind of division there among the Israelites. The wording of verses 12-13 suggests that originally the story also accounted for the name Kadesh, the root of which is **sanctify** or **holy.** But for P it serves as an explanation of the fact that both Moses and Aaron died without entering the promised land. The obscurity of this explanation is due to the attempts of later editors to soften criticism of such holy men. It may be that **did not believe** in verse 12 refers to the question of verse 10, which was perhaps originally addressed to God.

20:14-22a. *Rebuff by Edom.* This JE narrative begins the account of Israel's trials and battles on the journey from Kadesh to the Jordan. It tells how the Edomites refused passage through their territory. **Your brother** indicates Israel's consciousness of kinship with Edom (cf. Genesis 25:21-34; 27; 36), but the story also illustrates the traditional enmity between the two.

The King's Highway is the road from Damascus to the Gulf of Aqaba in use from time immemorial, known still by that name in Arabic. Verse 22a is the transition in JE to the incidents in chapter 21.

20:22b-29. *Death of Aaron.* This section of P concludes with an account of Aaron's death and his replacement by his son **Eleazar.** P locates **Mount Hor on the border of the land of Edom.** Tradition locates it near Petra, but the antiquity and obscurity of the tradition make exactitude impossible. P takes no interest in Israel's subsequent adventures on the march to Canaan. The continuation of the P narrative is found in 22:1.

III. The Occupation of Transjordan (21:1–36:13)

Entry into Canaan from the south having failed and permission to pass through Edom having been denied, Israel skirts Edom and Moab through the desert to the south and east. It then conquers an Amorite kingdom across the Jordan from central Palestine and the kingdom of Bashan just to its north. Numbers closes with Israel in the **plains of Moab** in that conquered territory. The narrative presupposes that the Moabite kingdom is east of the Dead Sea, with its northern border marked by the river Arnon. It assumes that the plains of Moab actually lie in the territory of the Amorite kingdom.

Here as elsewhere the narrative is composite, the result of the preservation, modification, and combination of various traditions through more than seven centuries. Even the earliest written document is some two centuries younger than the events here reported.

A. The Battle at Hormah (21:1-3)

This isolated piece of tradition from JE does not belong with the main narrative in this section. Probably it originated with the group that entered Palestine directly from the south (cf. Judges 1:17, where important differences in associated place names complicate a simple equation of the two places). **Arad** apparently lay between Kadesh and Hebron, and 14:45 locates **Hormah** in the same area. Its name is explained here by its connection with **utterly destroy**, the technical term for laying a place under a sacred ban.

B. From Edom's Border to the Region of Moab (21:4-20)

In a short space, and with only two incidents briefly recounted, JE brings the Israelites from the southern desert around inhabited Transjordan to the area adjacent to central Palestine.

21:4-9. *The Bronze Serpent.* The opening words of verse 4 are from a P editor, connecting this part of the finished narrative with 20:22*a*-29. But the account itself is from JE and continues from 20:14-21.

The Israelites are setting out from Kadesh (20:16) to **go around the land of Edom** to the south before going east and north. Thus **the way to the Red Sea** obviously means the caravan route from Kadesh to the head of the Gulf of Aqaba. The same Hebrew name, literally "Sea [or "Lake"] of Reeds," elsewhere designates the body of water miraculously crossed by Israel in escaping from Egypt (see comment on Exodus 13:18*a*). Its use here indicates that at the time of this writing the two bodies were thought to be the same—that is, the exodus tradition had already been interpreted as describing a crossing of some part of the arm of the ocean between Africa and Arabia (cf. 33:10-11). The English "Red Sea" comes from the Septuagint, where the Greek name for these waters replaced the Hebrew term.

Though the incident here described displays motifs present in many of the stories in Numbers (the people's complaints, Yahweh's punishment of them, relief at Moses' intercession), it has been preserved to account for the **bronze serpent** in Solomon's temple (cf. II Kings 18:4).

21:10-20. *Progress Through Transjordan.* This section seems to consist of bits and pieces from various sources and traditions. Its list of stations on Israel's trek is not as complete as the one in chapter 33 and is rather confused because of the combination of sources. It could be derived from lists of pilgrimage sites existing in the period of the judges and into the monarchy. The confusion indicates that the movements of the Israelites were not as unified as the finished narrative assumes.

21:10-13. Verses 10-11*a* about **Oboth** and **Iyeabarim** are apparently a misplaced duplication of a bit from P (cf. 33:44-45). Verses 11*b*-13 are probably from E. They seem to view the route of Israel as skirting Edom on the south and east. They then go north through the desert east of **Moab,** across the **Zered,** which flows into the southeastern end of the Dead Sea. They make a stop somewhere near the **Arnon,** which flows into the eastern side of the Dead Sea. **Other side** probably is to be understood from the viewpoint of the author in central Palestine—that is, on the southern side of the Arnon, in Moab.

21:14-15. This very ancient fragment of a poem is cited to show that the Arnon was indeed the border of Moab in a much earlier time. When this account was written Moab extended farther to the north.

The poem is said to come from the **Book of the Wars of the LORD.** Like the Book of Jashar (Joshua 10:13; II Samuel 1:18), this must have been an ancient collection of poetry. The wars of Yahweh were sacral affairs for the tribal league, and this collection must have been a sacred book of premonarchic Israel. **Ar** (cf. verse 28) was evidently a major city of Moab on the southern bank of the Arnon, but its site has not yet been identified.

21:16-18c. Another ancient piece of poetry is this song at the digging of a **well.** Verse 16 preserves a tradition that the song originated in the time of Moses when water was sorely needed in the desert. **Beer** simply means "well" and is too general a term to permit any location of a place.

21:18d-20. This fragment of itinerary records Israel's movement north into Sihon's kingdom. **Mattanah** has been identified with El-Medeiyineh east of the Dead Sea. **Nahaliel** could denote either a stream or a town. **Bamoth** simply means "high places," but probably refers here to some specific place (cf. 22:41; Joshua 13:17).

None of these places is mentioned in chapter 33, and their identification is uncertain. Again there is reason to believe that the different groups that formed Israel brought different traditions from different places into the common heritage. Verse 20 agrees with 33:47 in locating the final stop in Sihon's territory in the headlands of the Moabite plateau (**Pisgah** and Nebo; see comment on Deuteronomy 3:23-29) opposite the northern end of the Dead Sea. **Desert** is probably a proper noun, Jeshimon, referring to the waste area of the Jordan where it enters the Dead Sea.

C. CONQUEST OF THE AMORITE KINGDOM (21:21-31)

Israel's earliest possession was the territory associated with the tribes of Gad and Reuben. This was bordered by the **Arnon** on the south, the Jordan on the west, the **Jabbok** on the north, and the **Ammonites** on the east. This territory had been controlled by **Sihon** from his city-kingdom of **Heshbon.** He had won it from the Moabites, so that part of his territory could continue to be called **the region of Moab. On Amorites** see above on 13:22-29.

21:21-25. Israel's request to Sihon is described as like the one to Edom (cf. 20:17). The exact location of **Jahaz,** site of the decisive battle, is not known, but other references indicate that it was near the desert to the east (cf. Deuteronomy 2:32; I Chronicles 6:78; Jeremiah 48:21).

The Hebrew text of verse 24 says that the Ammonite boundary was "strong." It has been defended as showing why Sihon's territory extended no farther to the east. But the Revised Standard Version **Jazer,** following the Septuagint, must be correct. Jazer was evidently a few miles west of the Ammonite capital, Rabbah.

21:26-31. Verse 26 betrays that this narrative has to do with more than a mere incident on the way to Canaan. Like many of the Pentateuchal traditions, this one undoubtedly belonged originally to only one part of the Israelite tribal league. It nevertheless was revered by Israel as the record of the first victorious step in possessing a land of its own. Israel took over an ancient song in praise of the city of Heshbon, celebrating a victory over Moab, just as it later took over songs praising Jerusalem (cf. Psalms 46 and 48). The literature again and again recalls this victory (e.g. Deuteronomy 31:4; Joshua 2:10; Psalms 135:11; 136:19).

On **Ar** see above on verses 14-15. **Chemosh** was the god of the

Moabites, here said to have let his children be defeated. **Dibon**
and **Medeba** were between Heshbon and the Arnon.

D. CONQUEST OF BASHAN (21:32-35)

Apparently much of Transjordan was held by **Amorites.** Verse
32 records the conquest of Jazer (see above on verses 21-25),
perhaps another city-kingdom and its territory. Verses 33-35
record the conquest of **Og the king of Bashan.** Og was
apparently another Amorite (cf. Deuteronomy 31:4; Joshua
2:10), and Bashan lay east and north of the Jordan. **Edrei** lay in
the extreme northeast of Israel's territory. This account, also
originally concerning a part of Israel, seems to have been
incorporated into Numbers from Deuteronomy 3:1-2.

E. THE BALAAM STORIES (22:1–24:25)

The narrative now turns back to the Moabites, who occupied
the remaining territory to the east of the Jordan. That the stories
in Numbers came from the traditions of various groups is clearly
seen in the geographical confusion. While it has been stated that
Sihon's kingdom extended south to the Arnon (21:24; cf. 22:36),
some of the incidents recounted in this section as occurring in
Moabite territory (23:14, 28) are definitely located north of the
Arnon.

Moab's defeat is not really recounted but assumed in the
famous and fascinating stories about the diviner Balaam. They
are unlike anything else in Numbers. Very ancient material
from preliterary oral tradition is preserved here, and its
popularity is evident not only in the fullness of the parallel J and
E narratives but also in their agreement on the main points of
the story despite differences in details.

The evidences of the interwoven strands are rather clear even
in the English translation, and except in a few passages the
narrative threads can be traced. P is represented in this section

only by 22:1, which is the continuation of 20:22b-29 and 21:4a. Later allusions to Balaam in P (31:8, 16; see below on 25:6-18) reveal a quite different tradition about him.

In the view of E a non-Israelite would not know the divine name Yahweh which was revealed to Moses (Exodus 3:13-15). Accordingly E often uses Elohim ("God") in the narrative portions (e.g. 22:9-10, 38; 23:4, 27). But, as in Genesis, J regularly identifies the God who speaks to Balaam as Yahweh ("the LORD"). That this distinction is not consistent throughout may be due to the editor. It should be noted, however, that Balaam's oracles all contain both divine names, with Elohim predominating. These pronouncements are evidently very ancient poems which J and E have incorporated in their accounts.

22:2-21. *Balak Sends for Balaam.* Though closely intertwined in this part of the story, the J and E portrayals can for the most part be recognized.

According to the J account the Moabite king Balak sends **messengers** to summon the diviner Balaam to **curse** Israel (verses 5-6). These **elders of Moab** bring **fees for divination** (verse 7) and promise **great honor** (verse 17). But Balaam declares that even for a **house full of silver and gold** (verse 18) he cannot disobey Yahweh. Though the editor has evidently omitted part of the J narrative following this, we may infer that after the messengers leave, the thought of the fee becomes too great a temptation for Balaam to resist.

In E the representatives sent by Balak are **princes of Moab** (verse 8), and the inducement they offer is not mentioned. In this account Balaam does only what God commands. Balaam keeps the princes overnight while he receives divine instruction not to go and then sends them back to Balak (verses 8-10, 12-14). When Balak dispatches a larger and more honorable delegation of princes (verses 15-16), Balaam keeps them waiting also until the divine word comes to him **at night.** The message is that he may go to Balak, but only to speak what God commands (verses 19-20). Accordingly Balaam sets out for Moab with the princes (verse 21).

22:4. Here and in verse 7 (where the phrase may be a harmonizing editorial insertion) **elders of Midian** are associated with Moab in sending for Balaam, but no further mention of them occurs. Such an association was entirely possible, as Midian ranged over the southern and eastern desert (cf. Genesis 36:35). But the reference is curious. It may have come in under the influence of 31:8, or it may be a remnant of something more prominent in one of the sources.

22:5. Balaam is said to have lived **at Pethor, which is near the River** (i.e. the Euphrates), **in the land of Amaw.** Pethor apparently is a site in Upper Mesopotamia where the Sajur joins the Euphrates, near Carchemish. Amaw has been found in inscriptions as a name for this region. This area is some four hundred miles from Moab.

On the other hand instead of Amaw several Hebrew manuscripts and most ancient versions read "Ammonites," which would put Balaam's home much nearer Moab; and in 23:7 he says he has come from **Aram** (i.e. Syria). It has been suggested that Amaw may be a scribe's harmonizing of the J and E accounts. At any rate the traditions have Balaam come from some place in the northeast.

22:22-35. *The Talking Ass.* This colorful account seems to be entirely from J except in verse 35, where the editor has inserted an adaptation of E material. This leaves the original J conclusion of the episode in some doubt.

There is some uncertainty about the original beginning also (see above on verses 2-21). In verse 18 Balaam has refused the offer of Balak's messengers, declaring that he must obey Yahweh's command. But in verse 22 he is setting out with his **two servants,** apparently after the messengers have left and without the permission of Yahweh. It is clear enough, however, that he is strikingly reminded that he must obey and declare the word which Yahweh gives to him.

The theme that God has his way in spite of the recalcitrance of his spokesman underlies this whole story. It arises out of Israel's conviction of its election and accounts for Balaam's prominence in later tradition (cf. Deuteronomy 23:3-5; Joshua 24:9-10; Nehemiah 13:1-3; Micah 6:5).

22:36-40. *Meeting of Balaam and Balak.* This part of the story is hard to follow because of the fusion of J and E, which here cannot be isolated with certainty. The **city of Moab** probably means Ar (see above on 21:14-15), since it is said to be on the Arnon. But the rest of the story, at least in the E account, seems to take place farther north near Mt. Pisgah (cf. 23:14). **Kiriath-huzoth** is otherwise unknown.

22:41–23:12. *Balaam's First Oracle.* This part of the story seems to be entirely from E. The exact location of **Bamoth-baal** (literally "high places of Baal") is not known, but it must have been in the mountainous area east and north of the Dead Sea. The point is that the diviner is being brought in sight of those he is to curse. Verses 1-4 relate preparations calculated to dispose God favorably toward the cursing.

In some ancient versions Balak alone offers the sacrifices in verse 2. It has been suggested that originally verse 4*b* may have followed this as his report to Balaam of what he has done. The poem of verses 7-10 must be at least as old as the tenth century. It illustrates Israel's fierce conviction of the involvement of divine revelation in her own historical destiny—note especially verse 9*cd*. Verses 11-12 reemphasize the chief motif of this story, that regardless of all efforts to the contrary Balaam must speak the word of Yahweh (cf. verse 5).

23:13-26. *Balaam's Second Oracle.* The humor of Balak's repeated frantic efforts to obtain a curse on Israel in both the J and E versions is no doubt one reason for the story's popularity. This portion seems to be a continuation of the E account. Balak takes Balaam to another place where he can **see** the people of Israel (cf. 22:41). Perhaps this originally read "may see them all" but was modified by the editor to prepare for the J account in chapter 24.

Zophim (literally "watchers") is not otherwise known and may be a common noun here. On **Pisgah** see above on 21:18*d*-20. In the poem verses 18-21 are clearly an ancient companion to verses 7-10, but doubts have been raised about verses 22-24.

Verse 23 is obscure (**against** in the first two lines probably should be translated "in"), and verses 22 and 24 largely duplicate 24:8-9. Verses 25-26 bring to a close the Balaam story of E (though perhaps 24:25 is its final sentence) with a repetition of its theme.

23:27–24:13. *Balaam's Third Oracle.* The remainder of the narrative is taken primarily from J. Verses 27-30 seem to be largely a composition of the editor to fit the new source into the pattern of what has preceded. On **Peor** see below on 25:1-5.

The narrative which follows is the framework for an ancient poem, found in verses 5-9, with verses 3-4 as a poetic prelude. Verse 7 seems, however, to place this poem in the time of the monarchy. The reference to **Agag** is obscure, as the Amalekite king of I Samuel 15 was no model of royal power. On verses 8-9 see above on 23:13-16. The conversation in verses 10-13 refers to the beginning of the story (cf. 22:17-18). It emphasizes that in J also Balaam speaks, not for himself, but for Yahweh.

24:14-25. *Balaam's Fourth Oracle.* The J narrative continues with Balaam pronouncing a farewell oracle that Balak has not asked for. It predicts the future conquest of Moab by Israel. Verses 15-19, especially verse 17, clearly glorify the monarchy and are a prophecy after the event.

It may be no accident that both this poem and the one in verses 5-9 occur in the framework of J, the Jerusalemite source in which the Davidic monarchy is seen as the fulfillment of God's promise. Israel subdued Moab (as well as **Edom**) only in the time of David. This may explain why Moab is the framework for prophecy, whereas the stories about the Amorites tell of conquest. **Sons of Sheth** (literally "tumult," or perhaps "pride"; cf. Isaiah 16:6) seems to be simply a poetic designation of the Moabites. **Seir** is the mountain range covering most of the land of Edom.

24:20–25:24. These three brief oracles cursing other nations seem to have little relation to the context, and many scholars consider them a later insertion. The curse on **Amalek** is in line with tradition (cf. Exodus 17:8-16 and I Samuel 15). The curse on the **Kenite** is harder to understand since the Kenites are usually pictured as friends and allies of Israel. The reference of verse 22*b* to Assyria's capturing them is obscure, and the text is difficult to translate. Our distance from these lines makes it impossible to know what their meaning was.

The curse on **Asshur** (i.e. Assyria) **and Eber** (cf. Genesis 10:21-25; its association with Assyria is puzzling) must have originated in the eighth or seventh century. It seems to predict a defeat of the Assyrians by **Kittim**—that is, Cyprus, though the name later was applied generally to maritime peoples of the Mediterranean. Again the meaning is irrecoverable.

F. APOSTASY AT PEOR (25:1-18)

This chapter recounts two originally separate pieces of tradition—one from JE (verses 1-5), the other from P (verses 6-15). They have been linked together by a P editor in verses 16-18.

25:1-5. *Baal of Peor.* Israel is now in **Shittim,** or Abel-Shittim (33:49), the place in Transjordan from which was made the final move across the Jordan. Its location is not certain, but it must have been in the territory taken from Sihon. The appearance of the **daughters of Moab** is evidence that boundaries fluctuated and that formerly dominant groups would remain in a conquered territory—as the Canaanites did when Israel dominated Palestine. The incident recounted here previews the pattern repeated in the stories in Judges—Israel's apostasy to the gods of the land. The meaning here is that Moabite women led their Israelite lovers into worship of the local deities.

Baal is a general title meaning "lord." **Peor** here may refer to a mountain near Pisgah and Nebo (cf. 23:27-28), or it may mean a city named Beth-peor (cf. Deuteronomy 4:46; Joshua 13:20). The Moabites may have identified the god of Peor with their national god, Chemosh. Two traditions of the punishment meted out to the offenders seem to be represented in verses 4 and 5. The incident is frequently cited as an example of apostasy

(Deuteronomy 4:3; Joshua 22:17, Psalm 106:28; Hosea 9:10; I Corinthians 10:8).

25:6-18. *Phinehas' Zeal.* The combination of the JE story in verses 1-5 with this P story has resulted in the mutilation of the end of the first and the beginning of the second. There is no account of the carrying out of the punishment commanded in verses 4-5. Verses 6 (Israel **weeping at . . . the tent of meeting**) and 8-9 require some account of the origin of the **plague.** 31:16 hints at a lost beginning of this story in which Balaam was responsible for the introduction of Midianite women into Israel. That resulted in disloyalty to Yahweh and was punished by a plague.

25:6-13. This story is typical of P in that it accounts for a sacral institution by narrating an incident in justification of it. Phinehas, identified as third in line in the Aaronic priesthood, by his quick action against an Israelite who has married a Midianite woman both stays the plague and obtains a **perpetual** priestly status for his family. Though connected by P with the Aaronic priesthood, Phinehas seems to represent an originally northern and very important priesthood (cf. the notice of a town belonging to the family in Joshua 24:33 and the traditions in Numbers 31:6; Joshua 22:10-34; and Judges 20:27-28). This priesthood was later subsumed in the Aaronic line.

25:14-18. The typical P genealogical interest shows in verses 14-15. The editorial addition in verses 16-18 connects the two stories of this chapter with the account in chapter 31 of the holy war against Midian in which Phinehas again leads in vengeance.

G. THE SECOND CENSUS (26:1-65)

The reason for a repetition of what was done in chapters 1-2 is that the wilderness period is now at an end. Israel is about to take possession of her land. The tribes are to be allotted territory according to their size, and so P records another census.

The total number of adult male Israelites is given here as 601,730 as compared with 603,550 in 2:32. As in chapters 1-2, the data here must come from records of some period during the monarchy, and the listing of only men capable of military service may indicate the purpose of the census. The Levites are numbered separately as before (cf. 1:47; chapters 3–4).

The section closes with the note that only **Caleb** and **Joshua** survive of those numbered in the first census. P thus ties things up according to its theories.

H. A LAW CONCERNING INHERITANCE (27:1-11)

Logically following the census preparatory to the division of Canaan among the tribes, this section makes the point that a man's property (land) may be inherited by a daughter if no son survives. As usual P backs up a law with narrative. Further legislation connected with this situation is found in chapter 36, and the execution of Moses' verdict is recorded in Joshua 17:3-4. Behind this lies the Israelite conviction that a family's land was its gift from God, from which the family should not be separated.

I. THE SELECTION OF JOSHUA (27:12-23)

Referring to the cryptic tradition in 20:2-13, P here relates how Moses, having viewed the land he is not to enter, requests Yahweh to designate his successor before he dies.

Abarim is the general term for the headlands of the plateau of Moab at the northern end of the Dead Sea. Deuteronomy 32:49 and 34:1 designate Nebo as the particular mountain associated with Moses' last days (see comment on Deuteronomy 3:23-29).

Actually the P material now in Deuteronomy 34 must have followed this section directly at one time. Supplementers added the bulk of the material now found in chapters 28–36, and the other Pentateuchal sources were later worked into P.

· The basic tradition about Joshua is preserved in Joshua 1–12. He was a hero of the northern tribes in the sacred wars in which central Palestine was won, and the phraseology of verses 17 and 21*b* preserves the memory of his military leadership.

Historically it is doubtful that his connection with Moses was as close as the Pentateuch now pictures it—if it existed at all. But already in the earliest written sources the history that led to the united Israel of the period of the judges and the monarchy is read in the light of the later unity. P carries the process to its final conclusion with a concern for orderly and valid succession (cf. 19, 23 and the role of the priesthood in verses 19, 21, 22).

The account makes clear that no successor is Moses' equal—note **some of your authority.** Whereas Moses has spoken with God directly, Joshua is to receive divine direction through priestly manipulation of the **Urim,** the sacred lot. P thus makes priestly authority final.

J. PUBLIC OFFERINGS (28:1–29:40)

This section is a supplement to P. It deals with the sacrifices to be made by the whole community, as opposed to private offerings of individuals as in chapter 15. Its subject is not treated elsewhere in the Pentateuch, but is in Ezekiel 45:18–46:15. The calendar of sacred seasons to which the regulations apply is paralleled in Leviticus 23.

Coming from the priestly school, this section must reflect the practice of the postexilic temple, though the practices it outlines go back to ancient custom. The calendar is essentially that still followed in Judaism. **Due seasons** are important to P, which holds in Genesis 1:14 that the heavenly bodies exist to mark the proper occasions for worship of Israel's God. They are not objects for superstitious worship, as among Israel's neighbors.

Definite regulations for sacrifices are provided for the following occasions:

> daily, 28:3-8;
> sabbath, 28:9-10;
> new moon, 28:11-15;

> passover and unleavened bread, 28:16-25;
> weeks (Pentecost), 28:26-31;
> new year, 29:1-6;
> day of atonement, 29:7-11 (cf. Leviticus 16);
> booths, 29:12-38.

The paradox of a new year observance **on the first day of the seventh month** reflects the fact that in the postexilic period the Jews used the Babylonian calendar, which began in the spring. The conclusion of the section makes clear that these provisions are for public, not private, offerings.

K. Vows of Women (30:1-16)

While vows made by men are binding once made, among women the same rule applies only to the widowed and divorced. The vows of unmarried women living in their father's houses are subject to the approval of their fathers, as those of married women are subject to the approval of their husbands. The regulations reflect a society in which women have little legal status. Regulations for vows are set down elsewhere (cf. 6:1-21; Leviticus 5:4-6; 27:1-33; Deuteronomy 23:1-23), but only here are women's vows treated. The section is a supplement to P.

L. Annihilation of Midian (31:1-54)

Though closely related to Israel (Genesis 25:2) and to Moses (Exodus 2:15; Numbers 10:29-32) according to JE, the Midianites are enemies of Israel in Transjordan according to P (25:6-18; cf. JE in 22:4, 7). The present chapter is a P supplement's largely fictional account of how the command of 25:16-18 was carried out before Moses' death.

The list of Midianite kings in verse 8 (cf. Joshua 13:21-22) undoubtedly goes back to authentic tradition. On **Phinehas** and **Balaam** see above on 25:6-18. Verses 19-54 betray the real purpose of the story—to show how legal provisions for the purification of warriors (verses 19-24) worked out in practice.

M. SETTLEMENT OF THE TRANSJORDAN TRIBES (32:1-42)

This chapter has defied any generally agreed analysis into sources. Certainly part of it represents the conclusion of the JE narrative in Numbers, the continuation of which is found in Deuteronomy 34. P elements are also present. It may be that an editor has recast the narrative on the basis of JE and P rather than merely combining them.

Behind the account lies the fact that the elements of later united Israel which occupied Transjordan were not really a part of the groups which won central Palestine. Yet when premonarchic Israel was established in the land, those elements were parts of the twelve-tribe league. They were obligated to go to war on behalf of their brethren and of Yahweh (note the picture of Gad in Deuteronomy 33:21).

Since the past that had led to united Israel was viewed as a common, unified history, this account came to be given of the relation of the Transjordan tribes to their Palestinian colleagues. Not sheer fiction, it may represent the entry of the Transjordan tribes into the league (see Introduction).

32:1-5. Apparently **Jazer** (see above on 21:21-25) was the city marking the eastern boundary of the territory of **Gilead,** which was famous for its **cattle.** The towns listed in verse 3 were authentic places in this area.

32:6-32. Underneath this discussion lies authentic remembrance of the duties incumbent on members of the old tribal league. Verses 6-13 recall elements in the tradition as recounted by both JE and P in chapters 13–14.

32:39-42. These verses seem to contain a separate piece of tradition from that in verses 1-38 concerning Reuben and Gad. **Machir** apparently had a complicated history. It was listed as a clan of Manasseh in 26:29 and as a full part of the tribal federation in Palestine proper in Judges 5:14. Possibly incorporating Aramean peoples, Machir came to be dominant in northeast Transjordan to the extent that Gilead could be characterized as Machir's son (e.g. 26:29; 27:1; 36:1). **Jair** is associated by tradition with Manasseh, as is Machir (cf. I Chronicles 2:23); and the fact that a place in Gilead bore the name **Nobah** indicates that this was a clan associated with Machir. These verses recall a tradition only on the fringe of Israel's history, but they indicate how complicated that history was.

N. A SUMMARY (33:1-49)

Elements of the traditions preserved both in JE and in P are present in this résumé of Israel's progress from Egypt to Canaan. The chief point of the summary is to list the forty **stages**, or stopping places, along the way (cf. the tradition of forty years). In its final form the chapter must be a supplement produced by the P school. In addition to JE and P the author probably drew on another source going back to cultic practice of premonarchic times in which Israel reenacted the tradition of her years of wandering in the wilderness. In its present form the section is dominated by P style and interest—for example, the chronological framework in verses 3 and 38-39.

The traditions in verses 2 and 4a are peculiar to this chapter. Likewise lacking in any of the other Pentateuchal sources are seventeen of the forty stations listed: **Dophkah, Alush, Rithmah, Rimmon-perez, Libnah, Rissah, Kehelathah, Mount Shepher, Haradah, Makheloth, Tahath, Terah, Mithkah, Hashmonah, Abronah, Zalmonah,** and **Punon.** Most of the places cannot be located.

O. ISRAEL'S LANDED INHERITANCE (33:50–34:29)

Israel's point of view and her theology were concrete and not abstract. What we today would call spiritual things were manifest for Israel in visible, tangible realities. Thus in all the strata of the Old Testament the land of Canaan (Palestine) is Israel's **inheritance** from Yahweh, the outward sign of his choice of Israel, of his continuing sovereignty, and of his power to work his will.

All this lies behind the present section, which is cast in the form of instruction to Israel through Moses on the eve of its entry into Canaan. This section comes from a P supplement, but ancient tradition underlies it.

33:50-53. The non-Israelite inhabitants of the land and their sanctuaries and cult objects are to be eliminated. The point of this is that no concession can be made by which Yahweh's sovereignty over the inheritance exclusively designated for his people would be compromised. Deuteronomy and Judges are dominated by this motif, and it underlies the ancient institution of the holy war.

33:54-56. The distribution of the land to tribes and families is to be by lot. Since this process involved no human decision, it meant that the land of an Israelite family was its own in a way that was rooted in Israel's theology. Even kings could not alter it (cf. I Kings 21).

34:1-15. These verses designate the boundaries of Israel's land west of the Jordan (cf. Ezekiel 47:13-20). That the picture must come from P in postexilic times is indicated by its idealistic nature and by its omission of a division of Transjordan.

The southern boundary (cf. Joshua 15:1-4; Ezekiel 47:19) corresponds to what was Judah's southern extremity, and goes some distance beyond the traditional line at Beersheba (cf. Deuteronomy 11:24).

The western boundary is naturally the Mediterranean (cf. Joshua 15:12; Ezekiel 47:20); actually Israel never substantially occupied the coast.

The northern boundary runs from some point on the Mediterranean up into Syria (cf. Ezekiel 47:15-17), and probably reflects David's conquests extending beyond Dan, the traditional northern terminus.

The eastern boundary is marked by the eastern shores of the Sea of **Chinnereth** (Galilee) and the Dead Sea and the Jordan (cf. Ezekiel 47:18).

34:13-15. To harmonize with chapter 32 it is provided that the foregoing boundaries apply only to the tribes west of the Jordan. In verse 15 the author forgets that Moses is on the eastern side of the Jordan.

34:16-29. Tribal representatives are designated to superintend the division of the land in accord with the census procedure of 1:1-15.

P. LEVITICAL CITIES AND CITIES OF REFUGE (35:1-34)

35:1-8. *Land for the Levites.* The Old Testament contains in different places provisions for support of priests and Levites. The variety in these indicates a long and changing history. This section outlines provisions quite different from those in chapter 18 (cf. 18:20, 24); 26:62; and Deuteronomy 10:9. Furthermore the lists of cities set aside are different in Joshua 21 and I Chronicles 6. The institution as described probably arose during the monarchy but is definitely idealized here. Again it arises from the theological insistence that all property is God's.

35:9-34. *Cities of Refuge.* This provision is connected with that of Levitical cities by verse 6. The names of the cities are listed in Deuteronomy 4:41-43 and Joshua 20:1-9. Their purpose is to provide for setting aside the law of blood revenge in cases where the death is not due to intentional murder. If, however, intentional murder is committed, the **avenger of blood,** i.e. the next of kin of the slain, must carry out the law of retaliation. The basis of the custom of blood revenge in the ancient taboo on shedding blood is outlined in verses 29-34 (cf. Genesis 4:1-16; 9:1-7). The institution of cities of refuge, an early form of courts of appeal, probably dates from the period of the united monarchy.

Q. SUPPLEMENT TO THE LAW OF INHERITANCE BY DAUGHTERS (36:1-13)

The purpose of this supplement to 27:1-11 is to keep property in the family to which it originally belonged (see above on 33:50–34:29). It subordinates women's rights to the Israelite theology of land as the inheritance of Yahweh. This P supplement gives an ancient law a narrative framework.

THE BOOK OF DEUTERONOMY

Norman K. Gottwald

INTRODUCTION

Deuteronomy is the fifth book of the Old Testament and the last in the division known as the Law, or Pentateuch. Tradition regards Moses as the author—except for the account of his death, often attributed to Joshua. In the book itself he is stated to have written the greater part (31:24). That this tradition cannot be defended is evident in the fact that the book presupposes the Conquest and, at points, even the Exile— events which occurred much later.

Deuteronomy is also the first in a series of books—written in the same style and vocabulary—which tells the story of Israel from the wilderness wandering to the Babylonian exile. The others are Joshua, Judges, Samuel and Kings. By subject and period Deuteronomy is joined to the books that precede it, but in style and theological outlook it is linked to those that follow. Because both the style and the theological outlook originated in Deuteronomy, the writings which exhibit them are known as "Deuteronomic" (often abbreviated as "D").

Contents

The book is set in the form of a speech of Moses delivered in Moab just before his death and the entry of Israel into Canaan led by Joshua. Its core (chapters 12–26) is a collection of "laws," which are referred to in other parts of the book as "this law" and "the statutes and the ordinances." Some of the subunits of this collection are laws in the technical sense. Many are either totally or largely moral exhortation and amount to brief admonitions or sermons based on legal texts or precedents.

The laws of chapters 12–26 are most closely related to those of the Covenant Code of Exodus 20:22–23:33. Approximately half the laws in the Covenant Code are duplicated in Deuteronomy. However, the differences are great enough to cast serious doubt on the hypothesis that Deuteronomy used the Covenant Code directly. They also seem to rule out the otherwise attractive view that Deuteronomy was intended to replace the Covenant Code. It appears rather that both codes drew on a larger body of laws.

The eleven chapters preceding the laws and the eight following are almost entirely cast in the form of an address by Moses (exceptions are 4:41-43; 31:14-23; 32:44-52; 34). The materials are of three types:

(1) Historical summaries, recalling Israel's experience from Horeb (Sinai) to Moab and the final events in the life of Moses. These include the commissioning of Joshua, the writing of the law, and Moses' death and burial.

(2) Threats and appeals for Israel to love and obey God. These are either loosely constructed sermonic admonitions or technically formed blessings and curses.

(3) Liturgical directions for writing and recitation of the laws and for rites to accompany the periodic renewal of the covenant.

Deuteronomy is very largely in prose. At times the style is crisply legal, like that of the parts of the Covenant Code which seem to have been drawn from the same source. More frequent, however, is an expansive, verbose, and sonorous style used in narration and admonition. This is the characteristic D style that pervades not only Deuteronomy but also the work of the compilers of Joshua, Judges, Samuel, and Kings. Two long poems attributed to Moses, entitled "song" (32:1-43) and "blessing" (chapter 33), have been inserted toward the end of the book.

Cultic Purity at a Central Sanctuary

To place Deuteronomy in the literary and religious history of Israel it is necessary to consider certain prominent features of the book. Of these the sharpest ideological feature is the demand for exclusive worship at a central sanctuary (see below on chapter 12). In the fierce reiteration of this point Deuteronomy and the D portions of Joshua–Kings are unique. Other parts of the Old Testament provide laws for—or simply report—practices of worship at various sanctuaries throughout the land, or else assume that centralization of worship has existed all along. Deuteronomy and its related D writings alone propagandize for centralized worship—and do so in a way that reveals the novelty of the idea and the intensity of the opposition.

Is there historical evidence of any sustained attempt to enforce worship at one site? II Kings 22–23 tells of just such an endeavor in the reign of King Josiah of Judah, beginning in 622. Of course the account itself is from the D tradition and thus is not beyond question. Yet no basis exists for denying its essential outlines: namely, that after discovery of a "book of the law" in the temple Josiah enforced centralization of worship at Jerusalem. Also enforced were celebration in the temple of the passover previously observed in homes, removal of astral worship and sacred poles and pillars, and proscription of magic and divination and the immolation of children. All these are features of the laws of chapters 12–26.

That this account is not simply an exaggeration of the king's religious accomplishments is suggested by an admission that his success was incomplete (II Kings 23:9, which reads like an apology for the failure to carry out Deuteronomy 18:6-8). He seems to have been unable to get the Jerusalem Levites to accept the Levitical priests from the countryside, who were in effect defrocked when the reform closed down their shrines.

The undoubted fact that in the period 609-586 idolatrous

practices are reported in Judah does not disprove Josiah's reforms. It only shows how much they depended on his forceful personality and how revulsion and disillusionment at the pious king's death led to repeated and widespread breach of the laws he had enforced.

It is possible that some features of Deuteronomy are reflected in reforms carried out by earlier kings. For example, Hezekiah (late eighth century), according to II Chronicles 29–31, decreed a passover at Jerusalem to which even the survivors of the fall of the northern kingdom were invited. It is difficult to be certain, however, since the reports of these early reforms tend to be conventional and lack the specific details of Josiah's activities.

The many affinities of Deuteronomy with Hosea and the E source of the Pentateuch (see the Introduction to Genesis) strongly suggest that D traditions derive at least in part from the eighth century. Furthermore allusions to worship at Shechem (see below on 11:29 and 27:1-13) argue that at least some segments of the book stem from northern Israel, probably while it was still an independent nation. Thus D traditions may have motivated Hezekiah's reforms, even though there is no direct evidence of it.

Composite Structure

Deuteronomy is a deceptive work as literature. Its style is so distinctive that the first impression is monolithic solidarity. Yet when one passes from the language to the narrative flow and the sequence of the parts one is at once confronted with proliferating cracks in its facade.

The "statutes and the ordinances" of chapters 12–26 are not consistently grouped by form or subject—as is true of all Israelite law compilations. Again and again topical or formal clusters of laws are broken by material on a different topic or in a different form or in a similar but greatly expanded form.

Though in chapters 12–20 a certain logic in the arrangement can be made out, the individual laws have obviously been drawn from various circles and treated in divergent ways. In chapters 21–26 the unity is even more precarious. 23:15–25:19 appears as a miscellaneous catch-all at the end of the laws, which are capped off by two rites in chapter 26. It is clear that the laws have had a considerable prehistory, and that in this respect Deuteronomy is like all the other bodies of law in the Old Testament.

The introduction and conclusion to the laws are marked by the same gaps and inconsistencies. Because narrative is involved, these are even more noticeable than in the laws.

It has often been noted that chapters 1–4 and 5–11 are two separate introductions. There is an obvious difference in the two sections, and both end with formal headings to the laws of chapters 12–26.

But these larger entities easily subdivide. The admonition of 4:1-40 is strikingly different in character from the historical summaries and reflections of chapters 1–3. On analysis chapters 5–11 fall into three admonitions, each begnning with "Hear, O Israel!" (5:1-33; 6:4–8:20; 9:1–11:25). In addition to the law headings in 4:44-49 and 11:26-32, another occurs in 6:1-3. It is therefore not altogether convincing to say that there are two introductions in chapters 1–11. We may need to identify at least three and possibly more.

Much the same can be said of chapters 27–34. The two poems in chapters 32–33 have obviously been inserted into literary contexts to which they are foreign. In 27:1-13 there is a natural link with 11:26-32, but the transition to chapter 28 is broken by the list of curses in 27:14-26 (see comment). Chapters 29–30 have been consciously added to the preceding (cf. 29:1, 20-21). Still more complex is the further appendix (31:1–32:47) in which the commissioning of Joshua, the writing of the law, and the writing of the Song of Moses are very awkwardly interwoven.

Thus there are abundant signs that Deuteronomy has known a complicated history. The book was not created as a whole by a single mind.

Cultic Origin

At several points in Deuteronomy cultic rites are either directly described or strongly implied. Some of these are connected with particular festivals or specific types of sacrifice. Others are rites at which the law is read and affirmed or sanctions are imposed to insure obedience to it. These sanctions are of particular interest because they give valuable clues for the origins and structure of the book.

A ceremony of blessings and curses recited from the summits (or slopes) of Mts. Ebal and Gerizim is described in 11:26-32 and 27:1-13. A text of the blessings and curses with hortatory expansion is given in chapter 28. At this same ceremony "all the words of this law" (at least chapters 12–26) are to be written on large plastered upright stones. Later, after Moses writes the law and gives it to the priests, he instructs Israel to read the law every seventh year at the feast of booths (31:9-13). How the blessings-curses ceremony and the law recitation at the feast of booths are related, if at all, is not explained.

Direct references to public reading or enforcement of the law are not all the pertinent evidence. The note of urgent decision sounds throughout many of the admonitions put in the mouth of Moses. Again and again Israel is said to stand "this day" before Yahweh, and "this day" it must decide for Yahweh as Yahweh has decided for Israel. It takes little imagination to see that speeches of this sort have their origin in the cult. The cultic foundations show through in spite of literary expansion and rearrangement which have served to disguise the original situation.

It is clear that the cultic event shaping Deuteronomy is a recitation of the law. It is also evident that this event was an entering anew into covenant with God. This constant contemporaneity of the covenant, and its cultic reenactment, is expressed in Deuteronomy by the continuity and tension between the "covenant at Horeb" and the "covenant in Moab" (see below on chapters 29–30). The two covenants are continuous in the purposes of God but they are in tension in their varying legal regulations—"new occasions teach new duties."

The shape of the covenant renewal ceremonies may be seen in the speeches of Moses (that is, the cultic figure who speaks for

Moses) in 29:10-15 and in 26:16-19, which states, "You have declared this day concerning the LORD that he is your God . . .; and the LORD has declared this day concerning you that you are a people for his own possession."

Thus it emerges that back of Deuteronomy lies a liturgy of covenant renewal in which Israel was addressed by a leader representing Moses. Elements in the ceremony included:

(1) historical retrospect of God's deeds and Israel's relation to him;

(2) recitation of the law;

(3) pronouncement of sanctions for obedience (blessings and curses);

(4) decision to enter (or reenter or reaffirm) covenant with God.

When Deuteronomy is viewed as a totality precisely this sort of structure stands out as its skeleton. Into this liturgical covenant renewal pattern, however, a vast amount of material has been inserted. The result is a literary composite which probably was never employed in its entirety in the cult. We are thus confronted with a paradox—Deuteronomy is both a highly cultic and a highly "bookish" or "scriptural" work.

Prominence of the Levitical Priests

To identify more fully the liturgical setting of Deuteronomy it is necessary to consider the official personnel of the cult in whose hands the covenant ceremony rested.

Various Israelite cult functionaries are mentioned in Deuteronomy in one of three ways:

(1) Sometimes they are associated with Moses in the narratives or speech headings.

(2) On other occasions they are alluded to in the laws.

(3) They are still more fully treated in a section that describes at least some of their duties (see below on 16:18–18:22).

Among those prominently involved are elder, judge, prophet, and king. More prominent than all the others, however, are "the Levitical priests" (literally "the priests the Levites"; sometimes simply "the priests").

A rather full profile of the Levitical priests may be drawn from the book. The Levites live "in your towns" and, being landless, must be provided for by the other tribes (12:12, 18; 14:27, 29; 16:11, 14). They are to receive designated parts of sacrificed animals and the first fruits (18:1-5) as well as triennial tithes (26:12-15). They are scattered throughout Israel, but with the centralization of worship they are to come to Jerusalem if they wish to continue functioning as priests (18:6-8). The double role of the Levite as priest at Jerusalem who receives offerings and the Levite as layman who worships is seen in the account of the first-fruits ceremony (26:3, 11).

Additional duties of the Levitical priests are:
(1) membership on and co-chairmanship of a central tribunal or court of appeals at Jerusalem (17:8-13; 19:15-21);
(2) guardianship of an authoritative copy of the D law, from which the king makes a copy (17:18);
(3) address to the military muster to assure Israel of victory (20:2-4);
(4) application of leprosy laws (24:8-9; cf. Leviticus 14:54-57).

In the narrative sections and brief headings of chapters 27–34 the Levites also appear as functionaries in the cultic renewal ceremonies. Moses and the Levitical priests declare the covenant in effect (27:9-10); Levites declaim curses over Israel (27:14-26); and the priests convene a gathering of elders and officers so that Yahweh can "witness against them" (31:28). Moses delivers the written law to the priests and directs them to read it every seventh year (31:9-13). The priests carry the text of the law beside the ark as a witness to Israel (31:25-26). In the somewhat cryptic poetry of the Blessing of Moses, Levi is portrayed as controlling the sacred lots (Urim and Thummim and as a leader in the twofold role of teacher and priest (33:8-11).

In many of these references the connection of the Levitical priests with law is unmistakable, and not merely in the general sense that they uphold it. More specifically the priests keep the standard text of the law, read it, and pronounce sanctions and admonitions concerning it. In short, public recitation of the law in solemn ceremony is their particular prerogative. It is logical, therefore, to regard Levitical priests as the earliest creators and proponents of the D traditions in their capacities as functionaries at the covenant/law renewal ceremonies.

This hypothesis of Levitical cultic reading of the law as the origin of Deuteronomy receives confirmation from the report of the reading of the law by Ezra and its reacceptance by the returning exiles. As Ezra read from the book to a public assembly, the Levites "helped the people to understand the law. . . . And they read from the book, from the law of God, clearly; and they gave the sense, so that the people understood the reading" (Nehemiah 8:7b-8).

Regrettably there are difficulties in the text. It seems probable, however, that the Levites on that occasion translated the Hebrew text of the law into Aramaic, the language of the postexilic Jews, and that they explained the meaning by paraphrase, expansion, illustration, etc. That the Levites had this role of public reading and explanation of the law around 450-400 suggests a similar role during the period 750-600.

Deuteronomy as a Book

However obvious its oral cultic origins, Deuteronomy now stands before us as a book. More than that, in its present form it stresses that "this book of the law" is so authoritative that it may not be altered by addition or subtraction and must be obeyed unequivocally (4:2; 12:32; 28:58; 30:10; 31:12). Even if we assume exaggeration—allowing, for example, that the other law codes may have been binding—the preeminence of Deuteronomy is unquestionably asserted. At all disputed points its view, notably that of centralization of worship, will have to prevail.

It is necessary, therefore, to account for the development in the D traditions from the oral-cultic setting to the written-didactic setting. It is further necessary to take account of the relation between the book itself and the several D-related books which follow it and carry the story of Israel into the Babylonian exile. All questions about authorship and date have to take into account the entire D complex, Deuteronomy through Kings, and not just the passage concerned with Josiah's reform (II Kings 22–23).

The one hard date is the year of Josiah's reform, 622. But the origins of Deuteronomy are older than the reform. Levitical reading and preaching of the law did not begin in 622. Considering the allusions to Shechem the practice must have extended back at least a century into northern Israel. The shock of the discovery of the law in 622 does not mean that such traditions were unknown in Israel previously. It means rather that the Judean monarchy had lost touch with them for as much as fifty or seventy-five years (assuming that Hezekiah knew of them and used them in his reforms).

The attempt to reconstruct the Deuteronomy found in the temple, in contrast to its later amplifications, has not yielded solid results; the criteria of separation are too uncertain. We can be sure only that the law book of II Kings 22–23 contained many of the laws of chapters 12–26 and that they were accompanied by warnings similar to the curses of chapter 28.

Was the law written specifically for the purpose of "planting" it in the temple? Perhaps—if we assume that only in this way could its claims be brought to the king convincingly and without danger to the law's advocates. Yet it is striking that even with the written law before him Josiah was unconvinced until specific supporters of the law had assured him of its validity (II Kings 22:8-20).

It is more likely that the writing and rewriting of D laws and admonitions was going on underground throughout the reign of Manasseh (around 687-642). If the Yahwistic cultic calendar was lapsing, or at least suffering from neglect, the old patterns of cultic renewal of covenant and law would be strained and even threatened with extinction. Oral materials remembered from year to year would no longer be recited. Authoritative texts of the laws inscribed at cult sites (cf. 27:2-3) would become defaced or even destroyed. Thus both oral and written records of D traditions were driven underground and fostered there until they broke to the surface in 622.

This interpretation does away with the view that the planted

Deuteronomy was a "pious fraud." No one needed to concoct a book claiming to be by Moses. All one had to do was collect materials long attributed to Moses, through the device of the cult functionary speaking on behalf of Moses, and to assert that these traditions should once again be binding in Israel.

The radically new thing in 622 was the tying of the D traditions to the single sanctuary of Jerusalem. Previously centralization had meant no more than concentration of official Yahwistic worship at the tribal center in Shechem (see below on chapter 12). It did not rule out all other types of worship at local shrines and temples. The transfer of D traditions to Judah after Samaria's fall in the eighth century, together with the shrinking of the land area in which politically independent Yahwists lived, created a situation where a total centralization policy could be realized at Jerusalem. But this new policy was merely a marriage of convenience with D materials.

It was this elevation of the single cult at Jerusalem as the sole valid cult that cut the former strong Israel-wide cultic roots of the Levitical D traditions. The various speeches, admonitions, songs, etc. that were used at various sites for the celebration of covenant renewal no longer had their original homes but were brought to Jerusalem. These old cultic materials were greatly reworked to fit the form of a narrative by Moses. They were finally given a "bookish" setting in chapters 1–11 and 27–34, with appropriate expansions in 12–26.

At the same time a concern with the post-Mosaic history of Israel, which previously had been left to JE circles, now emerged in D circles. So strongly did it emerge that a whole new history of Israel, the material in Deuteronomy–Kings, was created. Probably it drew in some measure on JE materials, but it was shaped in a wholly distinctive way. This "history" was in fact moral and cultic admonition. Its basic aim was to connect Israel's life in Canaan and her historical ups and downs with the taproot of her existence in Yahwism. Specifically it was intended as a sketch of Israel's prevailing apostasy, which was lightened only by the counterpoint of priestly and prophetic warnings, occasional favorable minority responses, and the dramatic but sporadic acts of a Hezekiah or a Josiah. But for the persistent purpose of God, his loyalty to his "word," Israel's history would have been waste and void.

Deuteronomy thereby becomes the basis not only for centralization of worship at Jerusalem but also for an extended reading of Israel's history after the time of Moses. It was the record of Israel's faithlessness balanced against Yahweh's faithfulness and the commitment of an Israelite minority.

Thus the paradox of Deuteronomy was that traditions it sought to appropriate solely for Jerusalem were, with the Exile, spread abroad in book form to all the faithful. Materials originally read and celebrated in scattered holy places and subsequently restricted to Jerusalem became available to Jewish believers wherever they were.

When we speak of the cultic character of Deuteronomy we need to recognize how profound a transition occurred in the use of the traditions. The earlier cult setting was rooted in oral recitations accompanying sacrifice. The later cult setting was rooted in the reading of a book or books from which sacrifice and other activities which could not be performed in exile had been eliminated. The abiding covenant relationship and God's communication of his will by the "word" and by the "instruction" gives the continuity.

In sum, then, Deuteronomy represents a gathering of old cultic laws, admonitions, songs, etc. developed in Levitical priestly circles from at least the eighth century. After the fall of the northern kingdom of Israel they were transferred to the southern kingdom of Judah and appropriated for Jerusalem in a reform to centralize worship. Finally they were structured as the introduction to a religious evaluation of the history of Israel from Moses to the Exile.

In a sense the writing down of the book began when the first text of laws was set up at a cult site such as Shechem (see below on 27:1-13). In the literary sense it began in the seventh century when Yahwism was driven underground. The version which came to light in 622 included laws and admonitions, but the present form is doubtless due to expansions as older D material was added to that version. This process was mainly one of supplementing a single edition from varying sources that may have been both written and oral.

We have no firm evidence of parallel or opposing editions of Deuteronomy. Rather it appears that the laws of chapters 12–26 were expanded by Levitical cultic materals in the preceding and following chapters. Probably this expanding was done by the same hand that prepared the first edition of Deuteronomy–Kings before Josiah's death in 609. The later edition carries the story down to Jehoiachin's release from prison in 561. Sections of Deuteronomy which presuppose the Exile may have been added at that time or even later.

Theological Ideas

In defining the theological point of view of Deuteronomy it is usual to stress its moral earnestness and urgency, its ringing appeals for love and obedience, and its solemn equations of piety with prosperity and impiety with adversity. These are important, but they are subordinate to the relationships among Yahweh, Israel, the land, and the nations.

According to Deuteronomy, Yahweh is the Lord of history, who determines the geopolitical position and the worship of the nations. Israel's God has also given territories to the Moabites, Ammonites, and Edomites, which they seized by destroying the previous inhabitants (2:1-23). Thus Israel must not attempt to dispossess those Transjordanian peoples, who also have a place in Yahweh's design. The Amorites led by Sihon and Og are not included in this exemption, however. God has hardened their hearts that they may be given over to Israel and exterminated in "holy war" (2:26–3:11).

Israel must have no truck with worship of the heavenly bodies, objects which Yahweh "has allotted [for worship] to all the peoples under the whole heaven" (4:19). In the Song of Moses a cryptic passage (32:8) says that in determining the territorial status of the various peoples God matched them with "the number of the sons of God"—that is, minor deities who are his servants. The idea seems to be that Yahweh has assigned each people to one of these lesser gods but has chosen Israel for himself. Israel alone knows of the historical revelation at Sinai. Thus God deals indirectly with all the nations but directly with Israel only.

As Yahweh has ordained a special cult for his special people Israel, so Yahweh grants them a special land in Canaan. From early times Yahwism was concerned with not only a cult but a land. It is the land-giving and land-keeping which occupies the D mind. The extent of the land promised to Israel varies considerably in the Old Testament traditions, and the accounts in Deuteronomy are vague. But it is assumed that Yahweh will not rest until Israel has taken the land.

Such views create an inevitable tension. How can God's guidance of all the nations be reconciled with God's particular guidance of a single nation? Specifically, what is to happen when the nations and Israel claim the same land? It is highly probable that this question pushed more and more into the forefront as Assyrian domination extended farther into Palestine. With the collapse of northern Israel and Judah's vassalage to Assyria, and with the consequent action of Manasseh to ignore or suppress Yahwism, maintenance of the land and of the cult became increasingly interlocking issues. Josiah's effort to gain Israelite independence, followed by further vassalage to Egypt and Neo-Babylonia, intensified the illogicalities and moral enigmas of Israel's position in the land. Deuteronomy offers two explanations.

The first explanation is in the nature of an unargued premise. Yahweh has by decree given Canaan to Israel because "he loved your fathers and chose their descendants after them" (4:37). This is really no explanation but the assertion of a dogmatic proposition. It is rooted in the general Near Eastern belief that a god has the right and power to will the fate of peoples. It also assumes that every people must have a land, even the people of Yahweh. In one sense Yahweh's gift of Canaan to Israel is no more inexplicable than his gift of Transjordanian territories to Ammon, Moab, and Edom. In each case earlier inhabitants had to be annihilated or expelled. Israel is merely the supreme instance of God's choosing a land for a people.

The second explanation follows from the first and introduces the uniqueness of Yahweh's cultic connection with Israel. Israel must occupy its land in such a way as to remain true to Yahweh. It cannot share it with the Canaanites because their worship of Baal will tempt Israel into apostasy and cause it to surrender its sole worship of Yahweh.

At one point Israel is warned not to assume that Yahweh's expulsion of the Canaanites is due to its own righteousness. Rather it is "because of the wickedness of these nations" (9:4). This is a curious bit of reasoning. Read in one way it would appear merely to reinforce Israel's confidence—"We are at least relatively more righteous than those Canaanites!" But if the question underlying the pasage is cultic rather than moral, then the phrasing is entirely intelligible. "The wickedness of these nations" here means their cultic practices which will entice Israel if they are allowed to remain in the land.

The sober warning against Israel's depending overly on its own righteousness has as its background Israel's notorious weakness for non-Yahwistic worship. Followed strictly, the logic of Deuteronomy says: Baal worship is in keeping with Yahweh's will to assign various forms of worship to the nations. It is not wickedness for the Canaanites. The wickedness lies rather in its appeal to Israel. Being so cultically fickle, Israel must morally and religiously sanitize its territory by centralized worship and by holy war.

It becomes evident in Deuteronomy that centralized worship and holy war are highly rationalized theological concepts as well as cult practices. They are the means appointed by God for Israel to maintain its cultic purity—that is, its identity in covenant with God. Deuteronomy has gathered snippets of information about older forms of centralized worship at Shechem and about holy war practices, but these are not presented as historical information. Rather the mass of tradition is represented as being spoken by Moses. Thus various forms of centralized worship and of holy war are elevated to the level of dogmatic principles commanded by God.

All that we know of the course of Israelite history from the occupation onward, however, shows that the Canaanites, far from being annihilated, remained in the land to mix with Israel and to form a constant cultic threat to Yahwism. All that we know of the history from Solomon on shows that Jerusalem, though a very important cultic site, was not the sole place of legitimate worship of Yahweh until Josiah's (or possibly Hezekiah's) reform.

In a sense, then, Deuteronomy is saying: This is the way history should have gone if we had really wished to remain faithful to God. If we had wiped out the Canaanites and worshiped only at Jerusalem, we would have avoided apostasy, and we would have kept our land. Deuteronomy therefore explains why the land has been partly or wholly lost. It also offers a foundation for exilic hopes that the land and the kingship will be restored. If Israel is again to possess the land it can be only through the strictest cultic purity. The essence of Deuteronomy is a total and indivisible interpenetration of morality and cult: one God for one people through one cult in one land.

I. INTRODUCTION PLACING MOSES IN THE SOUTHERN ARABAH (1:1-2)

This apparent superscription to the entire book locates Moses **in the wilderness** (i.e. desert), **in the Arabah,** the deep Jordan–Dead Sea rift and its extension to the south. **Suph** (literally "reed") may refer to the Gulf of Aqabah. **Paran** was apparently the highland south of Kadesh-barnea. These suggest an area far to the south of the Dead Sea on the western side of the Arabah. This impression is strengthened by verse 2, which speaks of the travel time between **Horeb** (Sinai) and **Kadesh-Barnea.** Such a site is far from the region **beyond the Jordan** (cf. verse 5).

II. SPEECH OF MOSES IN MOAB (1:3-4:49)

The first major subunit is presented formally, like the rest of the book, as a speech of Moses. In reality it consists of a lengthy historical summary of the trip from Horeb to Moab (1:4–3:29), an admonition to obey the law of God (4:1-40), a brief account of Moses' appointment of cities of refuge (4:41-43), and what appears to be a superscription to the laws of chapters 12–26 (4:44-49).

A. REVIEW OF THE JOURNEY FROM HOREB (1:3–3:29)

1:3-5. *Setting of the Speech.* The speech is dated in the **fortieth year** after leaving Horeb, following the defeat of **Sihon** and **Og** (cf. Numbers 21:21-35). The place is the **land of Moab.** In 3:29 this is more closely defined as the "valley opposite Beth-peor," i.e. at the edge of the Arabah a few miles northeast of the Dead Sea.

Moses is said to have begun to **explain this law,** literally "instruction" *(torah).* It is clear that the instruction, presumably chapters 12–26, is to be distinguished from the explanation, which is the speech of 1:6–4:43. It is not impossible, however, that this introduction was intended by the editor to apply to all of chapters 1–11. It may even apply to chapters 27–34, since at the end Moses is buried in the same "valley in the land of Moab opposite Beth-peor" (34:6).

1:6-8. *Command to Leave Horeb.* Israel is abruptly ordered to leave the covenant mountain of Horeb and to possess the land promised to the patriarchs. In E and D **Amorites** is the general term for the pre-Israelite inhabitants of Palestine and **Canaan-ites** is restricted to inhabitants of the northern coastal region of Phoenicia. In J and P "Canaanites" is the general term and "Amorites" are found only in the hill country of Judah and in Transjordan.

If the translation **neighbors** is correct, **hill country of the Amorites** means specifically the mountain heartland of Judah, given preeminence among the surrounding regions because it was the site of Jerusalem. Since the root meaning of the Hebrew word is simply "inhabitants," however, "hill country of the Amorites" may here refer loosely to the whole area of Palestine and Syria occupied by "Amorites." The other regions named would be subdivisions of this area.

The **Arabah** is the Jordan–Dead Sea rift, the **hill country** the central mountainous region, and the **lowland** the foothills to the west. The **Negeb** is the desert to the south, and the Phoenician **seacoast** (the **land of the Canaanites**) and **Lebanon** are on the north. The promised territory extends to the **Euphrates.**

1:9-18. *Appointment of Officials.* Moses tells how, overburdened with the people and their **strife,** he appointed men to assist him (cf. Exodus 18:13-27 and Numbers 11:16-17, 24*b*-30). This account seems to distinguish between newly appointed officials called **commanders** (literally "rulers") and **officers**— two terms used loosely in the Old Testament to refer to various types of civil and military leaders—and **judges who are being newly charged** but have been previously appointed. The functions of the officials are not discussed. The judges are said to deal with legal cases, the difficult ones being referred to Moses himself.

1:19-46. *An Attempt to Enter Canaan.* Moses relates the sending of a scouting party from Kadesh-barnea into Canaan. In general the story parallels the accounts in Numbers 13–14 and 32:8-13. It varies in that here Moses gives an explicit command to **take possession** of the land, whereupon the people temporize by suggesting the scouting party. In Numbers Moses sends out the spies, but Caleb and Joshua urge the invasion on their return and are therefore exempted from the decree that their generation must die in the wilderness. Here no reason is given for exempting these two except that Caleb **has wholly followed the LORD.** Moses himself is said to be barred from entering Canaan because **the LORD was angry with me also on your account** (cf. 3:26; 4:21). This contrasts with the view in 32:48-52 that his debarment was a punishment because he "broke faith" with Yahweh. Here he is not personally guilty. He is the representative of his people and suffers with them the consequences of their faithlessness.

2:1-23. *Passage Through Edom and Moab.* This version is only loosely related to Numbers 20:14-21 and 21:4-20 (see comment). Here the emphasis is on the order that Israel is not to **contend** with the Edomites (**sons of Esau;** cf. Genesis 36:9) or with the Moabites and Ammonites (**sons of Lot;** cf. Genesis 19:36-38) since Yahweh has awarded these nations their land.

Nothing is said about Edomite hostility to Israel. This is a different outlook from that in 23:3-8, where Edomites of the third generation may become worshipers of Yahweh but Ammonites or Moabites may not. Yahweh's explicit award of land to non-Israelites assumes importance in the total theological structure of Deuteronomy (see Introduction).

2:1. On **Red Sea** see comment on Numbers 21:4-9. **Mount Seir** was the mountain range covering most of the Edomite territory.

2:10-12. A note gives information about the previous populations of Moab, some of whom tradition viewed as giants (see comment on Numbers 13:32-33). On **Horites**, or Hurrians, see comment on Genesis 36:1-43.

2:20-23. A similar note is included on Ammon. **Caphtorim** refers to the Philistines.

2:24–3:11. *Defeat of Sihon and Og. The Amorite kings of* **Heshbon** and **Bashan,** who control Transjordan from the Arnon River north toward Damascus, refuse passage to Israel and are soundly defeated (see comment on Numbers 21:21-35). The holy war "ban" (see below on 20:10-18) is imposed on all the citizens, who are killed, but the livestock and goods are kept.

Verse 9 gives various names for **Mount Hermon.** Verse 11 describes the legendary gigantic iron **bedstead** of Og. A **cubit** was about one and a half feet.

3:12-22. *Allotment of Land in Transjordan.* The tribes of Reuben and Gad and **half-tribe of Manasseh** are given the former territories of Sihon and Og (cf. Numbers 32). **Machir** and **Jair** are specified as the two chief clans of Manasseh (cf. Numbers 32:39-42). But in Judges 5:14 Machir appears to be the name of the tribe otherwise called Manasseh.

Care is to be taken not to intrude on the neighboring territories of the Moabites (south of the **Arnon** River) or of the **Ammonites** (east of the upper **Jabbok** River) or of the **Geshurites** and **Maacathites** (north of Bashan). The Transjordanian tribes are ordered to send their warriors with the other nine and a half tribes to complete the conquest of western Canaan (cf. Joshua 1:12-18). The book holds to the concept of a united twelve-tribe conquest of all Canaan (see Introduction).

3:23-29. *Moses Told to Survey the Land.* Moses is denied entrance to western Canaan because of his identification with the sinful people (see above on 1:19-46). He may only **behold** it from the **top of Pisgah.** Three names are used of this height: Abarim, Nebo, and Pisgah. Abarim was apparently the name of the mountainous region in which Nebo was one peak (32:49; Numbers 27:12, 33:47). Pisgah was either an alternate name for the same summit or a spur or promontory of it (34:1). It is traditionally identified with a peak about twelve miles east of the outlet of the Jordan into the Dead Sea.

B. ADMONITION TO OBEY THE LAW (4:1-40)

This impassioned exhortation contains historical memories but in style and mood resembles the admonitions of chapters 5–11. It is especially close to 5:1–6:3 in its recollection of the revelation at Horeb.

4:1-8. *Call to Obedience.* The caution not to **add to or take from** the following instruction strikes a note of verbal strictness unprecedented in ancient Israel (cf. 12:32). It doubtless reflects the new stress during the Exile on the written traditions as the focus for the deported community. Temple and king might fail but not the law of God. The point is probably not so much a new concept of literal inspiration as it is practical insistence on obedience to laws that have been too frequently ignored.

Evidence that this caution should not be taken too literally may be seen in the fact that chapters 12–26 lack guidance for many areas of life—marriage practices, for example. These would have to be supplied not only from the earlier law collections (some of which may now appear in Exodus,

Leviticus, and Numbers) but also from instructions which were never included in the Hebrew Bible.

4:3. The warning against disobedience is underscored by a recollection of the Israelites who were **destroyed** by plague when they followed the **Baal of Peor** by engaging in licentious rites with Moabite women (cf. Numbers 25:1-9).

4:7-8. The section culminates with rhetorical questions about the uniqueness of Israel's God. These set the pattern for the rest of the speech.

4:9-24. *The Revelation at Horeb.* How the fearful Israelites drew near to the smoking mountain at Horeb is described in terms closest to the E account in Exodus. But if E is the source, it is freely paraphrased and expanded. The point of the reminiscence is that only Yahweh's **voice** was perceived; **no form** was seen. Therefore Israel is to make no images of Yahweh.

4:13-14. The virtual equation of the **covenant** and the **ten commandments,** which Yahweh himself **wrote . . . upon two tables of stone** particularly illustrates the D outlook. This focusing of the covenantal act and relationship on the covenantal legal instrument moves considerably beyond Exodus 24, where, though the written instrument can be called the "book of the covenant," a distinction is clearly maintained.

In another respect, however, Deuteronomy is freer than Exodus in its interpretation of the relation between the covenant event at Horeb-Sinai and the law. The "book of the covenant" of Exodus 24:7 is apparently regarded as containing not only the Ten Commandments but also the Covenant Code of Exodus 20:22–23:24. Here verse 14 treats the **statutes and ordinances** of chapters 12–26 as additional laws which Moses was to teach Israel on its way from Horeb to Moab (cf. 5:31).

4:15-24. With verses 16-18 cf. 5:8. The prohibition of worship of the astral bodies reflects the influx of Assyrian astral worship in the last of the eighth and throughout the seventh century in Judah. On the idea that worship of these objects is permitted to other peoples see Introduction. On verses 21-22 see above on 1:19-46.

4:25-31. *Consequences of Apostasy.* Continued idolatry in the land of Canaan will lead to Israel's deportation, enforced idolatry in foreign lands, the eventual repentance of the people, and their return to the land. The full description probably stems from the Babylonian exile. But the core of the passage may well come from any time after 722, when northern Israel was scattered.

The expression **in the latter days** shows how language often used to refer to the end of history (cf. e.g. Daniel 10:14) could be used about an important turning point in history. The aim of the passage is not only to warn against idolatry but to assure Israel that God is **merciful** and will not **forget the covenant.**

4:32-40. *Yahweh's Unique Revelation.* The admonition comes to a head in one of the most eloquent appeals of the book. In all known experience has a god ever saved a people or revealed his being or given such a law as Yahweh has done with and for Israel? Yahweh's goal in this tremendous historical display was to form a disciplined people who would obey. Since Yahweh has shown love for Israel and demonstrated that only Yahweh is God, Israel has every reason to keep Yahweh's commandments.

The passage closes with the conventional D promise of long life **in the land.** But the real force of the unit is in the evocation of God's numinous presence and power, with which Israel is joined in awesome intimacy.

C. CITIES OF REFUGE IN TRANSJORDAN (4:41-43)

This brief section departs from the prevailing pattern of historical retrospect. In straightforward third-person narrative Moses is said to have designated **Bezer, . . . Ramoth, . . . and Golan** in Transjordan as places of asylum for **manslayers** until their cases could be fairly tried. Joshua 20:7-9 states that these three cities were appointed by Joshua along with three in western Palestine only after the whole land was conquered. See below on 19:1-13, where the provision for such cities is outlined.

D. INTRODUCTION TO THE LAW (4:44-49)

This brief section states simply: **This is the law . . .; these are the testimonies, the statutes, and the ordinances** spoken by Moses **in the vally opposite Beth-peor**. It then summarizes 2:24–3:17.

Given other allusions in the book to "this law," it is almost certain that these verses are a heading to the laws of chapters 12–26 rather than to the Ten Commandments (5:6-21) or to any other part of the introductory speeches of chapters 1–11. If so, it is apparent that at one state in the compilation of the book, or in one version in which it circulated, these verses immediately preceded chapter 12. This introduction is similar to the one in 6:1-3.

III. THREE ADMONITIONS TO OBEY THE LAW (5:1–11:32)

A. FIRST ADMONITION (5:1–6:3)

5:1-21. *The Ten Commandments.* In its reference to the circumstances of the covenant revelation at Horeb this section is related to 4:9-14. It has its own peculiarities, especially the prominent role of Moses as mediator. Though Yahweh **spoke with you face to face**—that is, directly and commandingly—it was in fact Moses who stood **between** the people and Yahweh **to declare to you the word of the LORD.** Then follows the full text of the Ten Commandments.

5:2-3. The emphatic declaration that Moses' hearers are the same persons who accepted the covenant at Horeb contradicts the statements of 1:35-39 and 2:14 that the generation that came out of Egypt was condemned to die in the wilderness. It is unlikely that the author did not know the tradition of forty years of wandering (cf. 8:2-4; 29:5). Rather he must have chosen to ignore it in order to make his point more vivid to his own generation: **Not with our fathers** solely **but with us . . . this day** does Yahweh make his covenant as we recite the traditions and undertake the ceremonies of covenant renewal (see Introduction and below on 11:2-7).

5:6-21. This version of the Ten Commandments is substantially the same as that in Exodus 20:2-17. One difference is that the motivation for sabbath observance here is the memory of the hard labor in Egypt, which enables Israel to appreciate the value of a fixed seventh day of rest.

5:22-33. *Moses as Mediator.* Moses' function as the communicator and expounder of the law which emerges clearly in the E tradition of Exodus 19–24 is here enlarged on.

In one E tradition ambiguous sounds from Horeb are heard by Moses as "these words" (the Ten Commandments, Exodus 20:1-17) and "ordinances" (Exodus 20:22–23:33), and he writes them in the "book of the covenant" (Exodus 24:4, 7). Here the sound from the mountain is heard directly by Israel as **these words** (the Ten Commandments), which are written by God on **two tables of stone** (cf. Exodus 24:12 and 32:16, which appear to be later E attempts to harmonize the two traditions). The people are so frightened by this numinous revelation that they insist that Moses in the future be the go-between in relaying Yahweh's words to them. Moses agrees and is told to stay at hand while Yahweh tells him **all the commandment and the statutes and the ordinances which you shall teach them**—yet another reference to the laws of chapters 12–26.

6:1-3. *Another Introduction to the Laws.* This introduction to the body of laws of chapters 12–26 is similar to the one in 4:44-49. The fact that the reader may move directly from these verses to chapter 12 suggests that 5:1–6:3 existed at one time as an independent preface later inserted in its present position because it begins with the imperative "Hear, O Israel!" These chapters further develop certain topics not mentioned or only briefly referred to earlier, especially the ground and import of Yahweh's choice of Israel.

B. SECOND ADMONITION (6:4–8:20)

6:4–7:5. *Love for and Obedience to Yahweh.* The so-called Shema ("hear"), **Hear, O Israel: The LORD our God is one LORD,** is set in the context of an injunction to teach one's children love and obedience. The **words** of Yahweh are to be taught regularly through working them into the routine of daily life. This section contains two statements (verses 13 and 16) quoted by Jesus in replying to Satan's temptations (Matthew 4:7, 10; Luke 4:8, 12).

The precise meaning of the Shema is debatable. In fact it may intentionally combine two meanings:

(1) Yahweh is one, in contrast to the many Baals.

(2) Yahweh is the only one for Israel, in contrast to other peoples who are permitted, even by Yahweh, to worship other real or imagined beings (see Introduction).

The following enlargement of the Shema is structured by three "whens":

(1) What Israel must do **when the LORD your God brings you into the land**—namely, renounce all connections with pagan worship.

(2) What is to be said **when your son asks** the meaning of God's law (cf. the father-son exchange in the passover service, Exodus 12:26-27).

(3) The complete destruction of the Canaanites **when . . . the LORD your God gives them over to you** (see below on 20:1-20), for only in this way can the future generations be kept faithful to Yahweh.

7:6-26. *Israel Set Off by Yahweh's Love.* Yahweh's choice of Israel is attributed to his inexplicable love and his **oath . . . to your fathers,** the patriarchs Abraham, Isaac, and Jacob. Specifically excluded is the reasoning that Israel was chosen for its great strength, for it was in fact **the fewest** (or "least") **of all peoples.** But the continuation of God's favor depends on Israel's keeping the covenant by obeying the ordinances about to be given.

Verses 12-16 contain a brief recital of blessings Israel can expect to receive if it is obedient, a list considerably expanded in 28:2-14. Israel is not to fear the Canaanites, for Yahweh will destroy them as the Egyptians were destroyed. Yahweh will do so **little by little,** however, since too sudden a removal of the former population would return the land to wilderness and set back civilization (verse 22). The metal-adorned idols of Canaan may not be kept by Israelites, even for their ornamental value, but must be burned by fire.

8:1-20. *Israel's Probation.* These verses present a strong case for Israel's wilderness wandering as a period of **testing** rather than simply a time of punishment. The verbs **humble** ("humiliate," or "weaken") and **test** ("try," or "prove") are repeated. From verse 5 we may conclude that the author thinks also of the settlement in Canaan as a continuing probation to determine if Israel will keep God's commandments.

The two probationary periods differ strikingly. In the wilderness it was testing by privation, but in Canaan it is to be testing by abundance. The earlier bitterness and churlishness of the people may all too easily give way to self-righteousness and overconfidence. The aim of the wilderness experience is summarized eloquently: "in order to teach you that man does not live on bread alone, but that man may live on anything that the LORD decrees" (verse 3*b*, Jewish Publication Society translation). This is another word quoted by Jesus to answer Satan's temptation (Matthew 4:4; Luke 4:4).

8:19-20. The unit closes with a terse but sharp reminder that disobedience will cause Israel to **perish** like the nations they are to destroy—a point expanded greatly in the curses of 28:15-57.

This raises the question whether the author believed that these nations would not have perished had they not been idolatrous. Since he does not speak of their having any practical alternatives to idolatry it is a moot point. Yet, logically considered, how could the nations be blamed for idolatry unless they had a choice? Nor does this section face the question of the status of Edom, Moab, and Ammon. According to 2:1-23 these were given land by Yahweh in perpetuity, apparently because of their genealogical connection with Israel as sons of Esau and Lot. Yet they were certainly idolators in the biblical sense.

C. THIRD ADMONITION (9:1–11:32)

9:1–10:11. *Election by God's Promise.* The core of this unit is 9:1-5, which calls Israel to confident courage in seizing Canaan because God has **promised** it. The ground of Israel's confidence, as of the promise, is not its **righteousness** but Canaanite **wickedness** and God's wish to **confirm** his promise to the **fathers.**

The criteria for comparing the moral culpability of Israel and Canaan are problematic, since on no points of ethical or cultic conduct are comparisons drawn between the two. We are told nothing about Canaanite betrayal of moral standards (contrast the denunciations of the nations in Amos 1–2). The only reasonable explanation of the passage's rationale is that the **wickedness of these nations** refers to the lure of the Canaanite cult for Israel. The other nations are wicked, not in their own right, but in their temptation of Israel. They continually draw Israel away from its sole allegiance to Yahweh. Yahweh has given Canaan to Israel simply to plant Israel there in order to keep them cultically pure. Thus the gift of the land and the displacement of the Canaanites is an irrational and arbitrary decree. For the implications of this D view of Israel and the nations see Introduction.

9:6–10:11. The rest of this unit illustrates Israel's apostasy from earliest times, in a manner not unlike Ezekiel 16; 23. Moses reviews the story of the **tables of the covenant** and the **molten calf** (cf. Exodus 24:12-18; 31:18–32:24; 34:1-5, 28). He mentions the incidents at **Taberah** (cf. Numbers 11:1-3), **Massah** (cf. Exodus 17:1-7; Numbers 20:2-13), and **Kibroth-hattaavah** (cf. Numbers 11:31-34) and the failure to attack Canaan from **Kadesh-barnea** (cf. 1:19-40; Numbers 13–14). He sums it up by saying: **You have been rebellious against the LORD from the day that I knew you.** For the most part these traditions are either identical with or close to the E accounts of Exodus and Numbers.

10:12-11:25. *Love and Obey God and Keep the Land.* The hortatory introduction to the laws of chapters 12-26 comes to a climax with a drawing together in previous themes such as Yahweh's unique election of Israel (cf. 7:6-8) and the importance of teaching the law to one's children (cf. 6:7, 20-25).

In the Hebrew the imperative form prevails in series of verbs commanding adherence to Yahweh. Israel must **fear, . . . serve, . . . cleave to, . . . love** Yahweh, and must **keep, . . . lay up, . . . teach** his commandments.

10:17-22. A note of social justice enters for the first time in verses 17-19. It anticipates the same emphasis in several of the laws of chapters 12-26. On **seventy persons** see comment on Genesis 46:6-27.

11:2-7. The syntax of this long sentence is dubious. In an effort to make sense the Revised Standard Version supplies in verse 2 **I am . . . speaking** and the second **consider,** which are not in the Hebrew. The Jewish Publication Society translation has a preferable rendering: "Take thought this day that it was not your children, who neither experienced nor witnessed the lesson of the LORD your God, but it was you who saw with your own eyes all the marvelous deeds that the LORD performed."

The meaning of this is uncertain. It seems to envision the first generation from Egypt as still alive, contrary to the tradition that they perished during the forty years in the wilderness. Possibly here the author slips from historical guise to the contemporary ceremony of covenant renewal. He contrasts all who directly experience Yahweh's deeds (in the traditions properly recited and observed) with those **children who have not known or seen** them (because of either callousness or immaturity). See Introduction and above on 5:2-3. On **Dathan and Abiram** see comment on Numbers 16:1-2*a*.

11:8-17. The thrust of the whole passage is in the necessity of love and obedience if Israel is to possess and keep the land. A specific point is made of Palestine's dependence on the **rain from heaven.** This is in contrast to Egypt's reliance on water provided **with your feet**—that is, by irrigation from the Nile. The rains will depend on Israel's faith and conduct.

The D belief in a direct correlation between morality and prosperity, immorality and want, is one line of development that is extremely strong in the Bible. Another line, represented by Job, some psalms and prophets, and Jesus, sees all such correlations as strained or frankly broken.

11:26-32. *Blessing or Curse.* The admonition closes with a sharp statement of the moral contingencies before Israel: **if you obey . . ., if you do not obey.**

11:29. Moses gives the order for a ceremony in which **you shall set the blessing on Mount Gerizim and the curse on Mount Ebal.** Its execution is described in chapter 27. This is one of the clearest evidences that the original setting of at least some of the D traditions was Shechem, located in the saddle between these twin peaks.

11:30. This note on the location of the mountains is rather obscure. The **oak of Moreh** (or "Instructor's oak") was an ancient shrine near Shechem (Genesis 12:6). Some scholars take **over against Gilgal** to mean that there was a Gilgal close to Shechem. Others understand it as referring to the familiar Gilgal near Jericho. On the latter basis the meaning may be that from where Moses is assumed to be speaking Mts. Gerizim and Ebal can be seen by looking in a line with Gilgal, or perhaps can be reached by journeying through it.

11:31-32. This subunit is not only the summit of the admonition beginning at 9:1 but is yet another—at least the third—introduction to **the statutes and the ordinances** of chapters 12–26.

IV. THE DEUTERONOMIC LAWS (12:1–26:19)

A. CENTRALIZATION OF WORSHIP (12:1-32)

The core legislation of Deuteronomy is found here in verses 2-7 restricting worship to a central sanctuary and in verses

15-19, which permit profane slaughter of animals anywhere in the countryside. Only these verses are cast in strictly legal style. The remainder of the chapter is exhortation in a form that maintains the fiction of Moses delivering the law on the verge of the Promised Land. Most of the hortatory material either repeats or expands elements of the basic legislation.

12:5. The site of the central sanctuary is not named. It is simply **the place which the LORD your God will choose.** From II Kings 22–23 we note that this unnamed place was early understood to be Jerusalem. This seems to have been the view not only of the reforming King Josiah in 622 but also of Hezekiah a hundred years earlier (cf. II Kings 18:4 and II Chronicles 29–31). It is doubtful, however, that Jerusalem was orginally **the place.**

Mts. Gerizim and Ebal are specified as settings for recitation of the laws (11:26-32; chapter 27). This strongly suggests that before the fall of Samaria in 722 the D central sanctuary was at Shechem (see above on 11:29). On the other hand the Hebrew for **out of all your tribes** may be taken to mean "from each of your tribes," which could be understood as an original provision for twelve tribal centers of worship. It may have been to rule out just such ambiguity when the law was applied to Shechem, and later to Jerusalem, that an addition was made in verse 14 reading **in one of your tribes.**

12:6. The law gives a brief inventory of the main types of sacrifice that Israelites could offer (cf. 14:22-29; 15:19-23; 18:4; 23:21-23; 26:2).

12:15-16. The limitation of offerings to one place of worship meant the end of the close bond that had existed between sacrifice and all forms of animal slaugher. It was manifestly impossible to require that all meat be slaughtered at Shechem or at Jerusalem. Therefore permission is given for slaughter **within any of your towns** (i.e. anywhere throughout the land) of domestic animals as if they were game (**gazell,** or **hart**) being killed in a hunt. Since no cultic act is involved, one need not be ritually **clean** to eat the meat. The only restriction is that the **blood** must be drained from the carcass before it is eaten.

12:17-19. It is repeated that, in contrast to such slaughter simply for food, all religious offerings—whether of meat or of agricultural produce, whether regular or occasional (**votive** or **freewill offerings**)—must be slaughtered there and eaten there.

12:29-32. The reason for centralization of worship is the risk of becoming **ensnared to follow** Canaanite religion. With the establishment of a central place for Israelite worship all the other holy places are to be destroyed as remnants of paganism. This is to be done in order to prevent Israel's asking **How did these nations serve their gods?** and then following their practices. On verse 31*c* see below on 18:9-14.

B. WARNINGS AGAINST APOSTASY (13:1-18)

This unit is composed of three laws constructed in mixed conditional and categorical forms. The prohibition against following each type of apostate is stated conditionally—**If he says, . . . you shall not listen**—and then the death penalty for the apostate is prescribed categorically.

13:1-5. The **prophet** or **dreamer of dreams**—possibly a synonym for "prophet," but more probably a type of soothsayer—is discussed here only as one form of enticement to apostasy. But the practical religious and political problem of discerning the true from the false prophet is involved. The general criterion of successful prediction cannot be trusted too far (see comment on 18:15-22). Even though the **sign or wonder . . . comes to pass** it may be only Yahweh's way of **testing** loyalty. If the successful prophet or soothsayer advises departure from the worship of Yahweh he must be recognized as false and put to death. Presumably the person here castigated is a Canaanite prophet or a former Yahwist prophet who has transferred allegiance to a pagan god.

13:6-11. Loyalty to Yahweh must supersede even love for family.

13:12-18. Whereas the first two cases deal with individual enticements that are stopped before becoming widely influential, this third one deals with the situation where **base fellows** have already **drawn away** a whole **city** into pagan worship. The penalty is that the town is to be put under the ban of holy war and all its inhabitants and their possessions are to be destroyed (see below on 20:10-18). By their failure to **purge the evil** from their community all share in the guilt.

C. FUNERARY AND DIETARY LAWS (14:1-21)

This section consists of a series of brief categorical laws which have been amplified by a list of permitted and prohibited foods and by D exhortation.

14:1-2. That shaving the head as a sign of mourning was widely practiced is shown by many allusions in prophetic writings. Cutting gashes in the flesh is mentioned in Jeremiah 16:6; 41:5. Cf. Leviticus 19:28; 21:5.

14:3-20. The treatment of clean and unclean animals is roughly divided into mammals, marine creatures, birds, and insects. The similar list in Leviticus follows the same order and specifies most of the same mammals and birds that may not be eaten. Chief differences are that the Leviticus list permits eating certain insects and includes "swarming creatures," i.e. rodents and reptiles, whereas this list names a number of clean mammals. Probably the two lists were developed independently from a common source.

14:6-10. The only criteria offered for determining what is a clean animal are that it both **parts the hoof** and **chews the cud**, or, for marine life, has **fins and scales.**

Efforts to find a clear sanitary or cultic or moral rationale for the distinctions have not yielded convincing results. It appears that the factors contributing to Israel's sense of the unclean were highly eclectic and often so ancient that they had become uncritical custom and were thus totally lost to the view of the law compilers. Among the factors in the distant or near background may have been: fear of some animals as potential disease carriers; revulsion at the appearance or habits of certain animals;

totemic taboos; and symbolic or sacramental use of animals in pagan worship. This eclectic potpourri of dietary prohibitions was given arbitrary status as the law of God and thereby was put beyond the realm of rational inquiry or personal taste.

14:21a-c. The prohibition against eating any animal that **dies of itself** is based on the fact that the blood would not be properly drained from the carcass. A secondary motive was doubtless to prevent the eating of spoiled meat—but note that it might be given to the **alien** or sold to **foreigners.**

14:21d. This final law forbidding one to **boil a kid in its mother's milk** (cf. Exodus 23:19; 34:26) is understandable as abhorrence at a Canaanite cult practice. By extension it has become the basis for modern Jewish separation of meat and milk foods and of the dishes in which they are prepared and served.

D. TITHING LAWS (14:22-29)

14:22-27. Every year a tenth of the agricultural produce and a token offering (**firstlings**) from the flock are to be dedicated at the central sanctuary and eaten there. To allow for the **long** distance that some must travel to Jerusalem it is permitted to turn the tithe **into money** and to purchase equivalent produce in Jerusalem for the sacrificial meal. The Levites are to share in the food with the worshipers (cf. 12:12).

14:28-29. Every third year the tithe is to be kept **within your towns** instead of brought to Jerusalem, and the Levites and the poor are to be fed from it. This segment of the law envisions the Levites as still living throughout Israel, in contrast to the larger framework of D, which legislates their transfer to Jerusalem. It is yet another indication of the older origin of some of the book's contents. Whether this tithing ceremony is the same as the first-fruits ceremony of 26:1-11 is uncertain.

The P version of the tithing law (Numbers 18:21-32) conceives the entire tithe as given to the Levites, who in turn are to give a tenth of the tithe to the Aaronic priesthood. Perhaps D represents the northern practice and P that of Jerusalem. Early

Judaism harmonized the discrepancy by adding the D tithe to the P tithe. Whether the two were harmonized before the Exile, or whether D simply replaced P at Jerusalem after 622, or whether the P law did not originate until after the Exile—all are possibilities, but none can be demonstrated.

This offering of tithes and first fruits at the central sanctuary is widely thought to have been in conjunction with one of the three annual fixed feasts, especially the feast of weeks (see below on 16:9-12). This may well be true at least in the sense that the feast of weeks marked the beginning of the period, continuing on through the summer, when such offerings were made. If so, on every third feast of weeks the tithing ceremony was not observed at Jerusalem.

E. THE YEAR OF RELEASE (15:1-18)

Two laws are juxtaposed here which have in common release of contractual obligation in the seventh year.

15:1-11. *Release of Debtors.* The first law specifies that every seventh or sabbatical year there shall be a cancellation of all debts owed by fellow Israelites. **At the end of every seven years** probably means that the law covers loans outstanding at the close of the year. The sense of the passage is that the entire principal ceases to be owed, not merely the year's payment on the principal. In Exodus 23:10-11 and Leviticus 25:1-7 a sabbatical year is enjoined on the land so that it may lie fallow. But Leviticus 25:8-55 reserves cancellation of debts for the fiftieth or jubilee year.

One practical problem in such a release of debt is demonstrated in the exhortation of verses 7-11 to ignore the approach of the **year of release** and thus in effect make a gift rather than a loan. How widely this law was observed is unknown, but we can easily imagine disregard or even outright rejection of it.

15:12-18. *Release of Slaves.* The second law applies the sabbatical principle to **Hebrew** slaves. The seventh year in this case, however, is not a fixed period but refers to the seventh year of the slave's service (cf. Exodus 21:2-11). There was an intimate connection between debts and slavery in that the last resort of a debtor unable to repay was to offer himself and his physical labor to his creditor (cf. Nehemiah 5:1-13).

F. FIRSTLINGS (15:19-23)

This provision for each first-born male animal to be given to God rightly belongs with the tithing laws of 14:22-29. This is evident not only from the subject matter but also from the reference in 14:23 to the **firstlings of your herd and flock.** The intrusion of 15:1-18 may be due to an editorial desire to parallel **At the end of every three years** (14:28) with **At the end of every seven years** (15:1).

G. ANNUAL FEASTS (16:1-17)

The annual festivals of ancient Israel are here summarized. The instructions stand midway in detail between the terse law of Exodus 23:14-17 and the expanded specifications, especially of the offerings, in Leviticus 23 and Numbers 28–29. Common to all the lists of festivals is the centrality of the three agricultural feasts:

> **passover . . . unleavened bread** in the first month (March-April);
> **weeks** (harvest, New Testament Pentecost) in the third month (May-June);
> **booths . . . ingathering** in the seventh month (September-October).

The D emphasis is on the observance of these three feasts at the central sanctuary, **at the place which the LORD your God will choose,** and on the obligation of worshipers to come with suitable offerings, not to **appear before the LORD empty-handed.**

H. THE OFFICE OF JUDGE (16:18–17:13)

Administration of justice is provided for in the primary categorical law of 16:18. This is expanded by a hortatory call climaxed by **Justice, and only justice, you shall follow** and by two conditional amplifications (17:2-7, 8-13).

16:21–17:1. *Two Cultic Laws.* Intruded here are two brief laws which belong to cultic provisions such as 14:1-21 or 18:9-14. One prohibits planting a **tree**—that is, installing a wooden pole or image—dedicated to the Canaanite goddess **Asherah** or setting up a stone **pillar,** perhaps a symbol of Baal, as a part of Yahweh worship. The other prohibits sacrifice of an animal with a **blemish.** Possibly an editor thought of these two laws as illustrations of the "abominable" pagan practices referred to in the following verses.

17:2-7. *The Requirement for Witnesses.* When one is suspected of a crime—apostasy, for example (cf. chapter 13)—the judges must **inquire diligently** and secure the **evidence of two witnesses or of three.** The accused may not be executed because of one person's charge (cf. 19:15; Numbers 35:30).

17:8-13. *The "Supreme Court."* Provision is made for handling cases **too difficult** for the local judges—for example, a thorny case of **homicide,** property **right,** or **assault.** These complicated or disputed cases are to be referred to a central tribunal in Jerusalem, whose verdict is final. Death is the penalty for contempt.

The composition of the tribunal is both clerical (**Levitical priests**) and lay (**judge**). Though its organization is touched on only obscurely here, comparison with 19-15-21 and II Chronicles 19:8-11 indicates that the tribunal had two presiding officers, a priest who presided over ecclesiastical cases and a lay judge who presided over civil cases.

The D law assumes the tribunal as already in existence (**in office in those days**). The aim is not to initiate it but to insure that its supreme jurisdiction will be honored and its procedures for appeal regularly utilized.

I. The Office of the King (17:14-20)

Technically the law about kingship in Israel is framed, not as an absolute order, but as a possibility: **You may . . . set as king over you.** The warnings and appeals that follow show the monarchy as an established but embarrassing factor in Israel's life.

17:14-15. *Selection of a King.* Permission to have a king **whom the LORD your God will choose** is given. The various measures for choice and ratification of a king by the assembly of the people or their representatives are outlined. By means of these they enter a covenant with the new leader.

Though never directly described, such protocols are alluded to in the accounts of Samuel and Kings. That the present section is not a political document per se is evident in its failure to detail the method of choice and the means of formal ratification. We can only speculate as to whether the author, or editor, thought that the long-established principle of hereditary kingship could be reversed, especially in Judah.

If the older form of this provision is from northern Israel before 722, the call for extreme care in the choice of a king would be more intelligible. In that kingdom there were several dynasties and transient claimants to the throne, in contrast to the endurance of the Davidic dynasty in the south.

17:15b. The one firm requirement in the choice of a king, that he be **one from among your brethren,** seems somewhat unnecessary. There is no report that a **foreigner** ever held the throne in Israel or Judah. Some have suggested, however, that Omri (cf. I Kings 16:15-22) is a non-Israelite name and that the apparently Ammonite "son of Tabeel" (Isaiah 7:6), whom the kings of Israel and Syria intended to install in Judah in place of Ahaz, may have had Judean support. Given the theocratic character of Deuteronomy, the prohibition may rather be a dramatic way of warning against the allure of foreign worship and custom which the kingship might introduce.

17:16-20. *Rules for the King's Conduct.* The law declares that the king **must not multiply horses, . . . wives, . . . silver and**

gold. But how much is too much? This is no precise legal instrument but a solemn warning. Too many armaments (horses for cavalry), too many alliances (wives to seal political pacts), too much revenue would lead toward monarchic autonomy and absolutism and away from Israel's unique "congregational" faith. Solomon was a famous example of just such antitheocratic tendencies, but he was not alone in baleful effects on Israel.

According to II Kings 22–23, Josiah exemplifies the D ideal of a king. His political actions are modest and directly related to his cultic and religious goals of rebuilding the Israelite community of faith.

17:18. The stipulation that the king must keep and frequently study **a copy of this law** shows the vital interest in this section. The monarchy must not act in a manner that will jeopardize the D law, for that would bring about the ultimate catastrophe of alienation from Yahweh.

After a fashion we can speak of a constitutional monarchy, but only very loosely. The laws of chapters 12–26 supply a constitution, not for the monarchy, but for Israel's theocratically guided life. The king must avoid intruding into the theocratic sphere, where the priests and prophets and judges preside. These laws are not of the sort that the king would directly execute. They do not describe the authority or the functions of his office. Indeed such laws would be at cross purposes with economic, political, and military policies of monarchy as generally practiced in the ancient world.

J. The Office of Priest (18:1-8)

The Levitical priests have already been introduced as the landless clients of the other tribes and as members of the central tribunal. Here they are discussed in their own right.

It is significant to note that in Deuteronomy **all of the tribe of Levi** may be priests, though they may not all be officiating at once. This is in contrast to the view in the P writings, which regard only those of Aaron's stock as full priests. The rest of the Levites are merely assistants or cultic menials.

18:3-5. The support of the priests is the duty of the other tribes. It is to be provided regularly by giving them specified portions of each animal **sacrifice** and the **first fruits of . . . grain, . . . wine, . . . olive oil, . . . fleece.** An additional measure for the support of the Levites is that those from any of the **towns** may come to Jerusalem, **minister** at the temple, and receive equal maintenance along with the native Jerusalem Levites.

This permission for the migration of Levites into Jerusalem is doubtless an attempt to mitigate the drastic effect of closing outlying sanctuaries (12:17). Obviously if the Levites were to function as priests at all, they would have to do so at Jerusalem. It takes little imagination, however, to picture the immense difficulties in the way of realizing such an idealistic program. The practical problems stemming from interpersonal frictions and institutional jealousies are reflected in the account of Josiah's destruction of the high places in 622: "However, the priests of the high places did not come up to the altar of the LORD in Jerusalem, but they ate unleavened bread among their brethren" (II Kings 23:9).

18:8. The clause translated **besides what he receives from the sale of his patrimony** renders an obscure Hebrew text that refers to "sales according to the fathers." The most that can confidently be said is that it alludes to a limited source of private income that Levites would bring with them when they moved to Jerusalem, perhaps no more than their personal possessions.

K. CONDEMNATION OF PAGAN CULT PRACTICES (18:9-14)

The sequence of laws about offices in Israel, ending with the prophet in verses 15-22, is broken by this proscription of pagan religious **abominable practices.** There are two sorts.

The first sort (verse 10*a*) is denoted by a phrase literally meaning "makes . . . pass through the fire." This was apparently understood by the Chronicler as referring to child sacrifice (II Chronicles 28:3; cf. II Kings 16:3) and has been generally so interpreted—for example, in the translation **burns . . . as an offering.** Some scholars claim, however, that it refers rather to an ordeal by fire and that occasional failures to survive the test explain such references to it as 12:31; Jeremiah 7:31; 19:5; and Ezekiel 16:20-21; 23:37-39.

The other sort of condemned practices (verse 10*b*) includes various forms of communication with the occult, such as **divination** of the future, fixing of curses or spells, and communication with the dead. It may well have been the editor's intent to place this piece as a contrast to the description of the true prophet which follows it.

L. THE OFFICE OF PROPHET (18:15-22)

The subject is introduced under the guise of Moses announcing his prophetic successors. Though he speaks of **a prophet,** the context implies that the prophetic office is to be filled by a succession of prophets. The common messianic view that this refers to a single prophet yet to come is challenged by the criteria for distinguishing true from false prophets in verses 20-22. Obviously more than one prophet is involved, and they are currently contending for the people's credence.

18:20-22. Criteria of prophetic validity are more fully discussed here than in 13:1-5. There is agreement on the point that any prophet who prophesies **in the name of other gods** than Yahweh is disqualified. But this passage goes on to consider the knotty problem of the prophet who speaks falsely in Yahweh's name. Some interpreters take this to refer to those who deliberately claim Yahweh's inspiration when they know they do not have it. However, it is far more likely that the reference includes those who are sincere in their Yahwistic claims but who are nonetheless mistaken according to the D view.

How are the claims of prophetic inspiration to be judged? The D author answers in a somewhat heavy-handed way that the thing to do is to wait to see if what the prophet says does **come to pass.** In the long run this is probably an argument of some force. Religious claims can often best be judged by how they help us to interpret events; they have an objective social and historical reference. But it is scarcely a very helpful criterion for taking immediate action—the sort of choice that Israelites often had to make between competing prophetic claims.

At very best then this can only have been an exceedingly rough indicator of validity. Yet the very fact that Deuteronomy is the only law compilation that deals with prophecy shows how profoundly that movement had impressed the D authors—even to the extent that they regarded the prophet as Israel's equivalent of the diviner or soothsayer in surrounding religions.

M. CRIMINAL LAWS (19:1-21)

Three crimes are treated. Procedures for ascertaining guilt and administering punishment are given only for the first and third.

19:1-13. *Homicide.* The problem of protecting an innocent **manslayer** from the vengeance sanctioned by ancient custom is to be handled by establishing **cities of refuge**—places of asylum to which the accused can flee for a cooling-off period. If the homicide was committed **unintentionally** he can thus save himself from death at the hands of the victim's relatives. Cf. Exodus 21:12-14; Numbers 35:9-34; and Joshua 20.

19:7-10. This passage does not name any cities of refuge. Neither does it explicitly take account of Moses' designation of three such cities in Transjordan in 4:41-43. Two interpretations are possible:

(1) The Transjordanian cities of 4:41-43 are tacitly presupposed. The three cites of verse 7 are in western Palestine, and the three cities of verse 9 are to be in enlarged territory of Israel north from Mt. Hermon to the Euphrates. Thus there is a total of nine cities of refuge.

(2) The designation of 4:41-43 is ignored and therefore

duplicated in verse 7. The additional cities of verse 9 are those in western Palestine, making a total of six. There are difficulties in the way of either view, but the evidence tends toward the first.

19:11-13. A city of refuge will not protect one who kills with malice and premeditation. The **elders of his city** are to take him from the place to which he has fled. They will presumably judge his guilt and hand him over for execution to the **avenger of blood**—the relative of the victim who by murdering the murderer restores balance to society and the divine order.

19:14. *Removal of Boundary Markers.* An old law against stealing land by moving the stone **landmark** indicating its border (cf. 27:17) is quoted. The D author placed it in the setting of Moses' speech by adding the opening clause. Apparently he did not feel free to modify **which the men of old have set** to fit Moses' point of view.

19:15-21. *False Witness.* A provision about **malicious** perjury is added to the requirement for **two** or **three witnesses** (see above on 17:2-7). If such is suspected, the case must be taken **before the LORD**—that is, to the **priests** and **judges** of the central tribunal (see above on 17:8-13). The false witness is to suffer the penalty which he sought for his victim.

N. HOLY WAR (20:1-20)

The provisions for the conduct of holy war in this passage must be read in conjunction with similar laws in 21:10-14; 23:10-14; 24:5; and 25:17-19. They belong to a pattern of thought which underlies the entire book and permeates the accounts of the conquest and settlement of Palestine in Joshua, Judges, and Samuel. The essence of that pattern is the protection of Israel's cultic purity by extermination of the Canaanites, whose intermixture with Israel would lead inevitably to her apostasy.

20:1-9. *The Muster to Military Service.* The **priest** is to instruct the army not to fear a more powerful enemy, because God will **fight** for Israel. The conscription **officers** are to announce exemptions for those who have **built a new house, . . . planted a vineyard, . . . betrothed a wife** recently. They are even to dismiss those who are simply **fearful** so that others may not be infected. **Commanders** are to be chosen after this weeding-out process.

20:10-18. *Terms of Peace.* A besieged **city** outside Canaan is to be offered an opportunity to surrender. If it is accepted, the populace is to be enslaved. If it is rejected, captured males are to be killed and women, children, livestock, and goods are to be taken. No terms of peace are to be offered to Canaanite cities. The entire populace, livestock, and possessions are to be destroyed lest pagan religious practices infect Israel.

20:19-20. *Preservation of Fruit Trees.* The short-range military advantage of securing wood to **build siegeworks** does not overrule the long-range productivity of fruit-bearing trees.

O. EXPIATION FOR AN UNSOLVED MURDER (21:1-9)

A murder in the **open country** becomes the responsibility of the **nearest** town if the murderer cannot be identified. Its **elders** are to conduct a ceremony of expiation by killing a **heifer** over **running water.** The washing of hands over the heifer, whose blood is in turn washed away in the stream, symbolizes the removal of the **guilt of innocent blood** from the town. The regulation illustrates the Israelite notion of communal solidarity in guilt and in the expiation of guilt.

P. MISCELLANEOUS LAWS (21:10–22:12)

Ten laws, mixed in both their form and subject matter, have been arbitrarily assembled at this point. Since they are without hortatory expansion they give the impression of being from an early collection which the author or editor did not choose to redistribute topically. The motivations for these laws range from conscious efforts to achieve complete fairness in human dealings (e.g. 21:15-17) to uncritical feelings about what is appropriate or natural and vice versa (e.g. 22:9-11).

21:10-14. *Female Prisoners of War.* A captive woman (cf. 20:14) may be taken as a wife only after she is allowed to mourn a full month for her parents. If later her captor is displeased with her, she must be released rather than sold or enslaved. This law rightly belongs to the holy war regulations of chapter 20.

21:15-17. *Right of the First-born.* The oldest son's claim to a double share of the inheritance is inalienable. The father may favor one wife above another but cannot alter the status of their sons.

21:18-21. *Rebellious Sons.* The death penalty is prescribed for the son who does not obey his parents (cf. 5:16 and Exodus 21:15, 17). They must bring him for trial by the elders of his city.

21:22-23. *Burial of Executed Criminals.* Publicizing the punishment of a criminal by displaying his body is permitted only on the day of execution. The body must be buried before nightfall, for an exposed corpse is accursed by God and would defile your land.

22:1-4. *Care for Lost Property.* Duty toward a brother (a fellow Israelite) requires not merely avoiding injury to him but positive aid when his livestock or other property is lost or endangered. Cf. Exodus 23:4-5.

22:5. *Distinction of Sexes.* In addition to an obvious feeling about what is proper to the respective sexes this regulation possibly involves condemnation of pagan cultic practices (abomination).

22:6-7. *Protection of Mother Birds.* This law perhaps grows out of the same attitude toward animal reproduction as Leviticus 22:27-28.

22:8. *Parapets on Roofs.* Most Palestinian houses were built with flat roofs. Their common use made this safety regulation necessary (cf. Exodus 21:33).

22:9-11. *Prohibition of Mixtures.* The basis for these rules is historically obscure and may be merely a feeling that mixing species violates their natural purity. Cf. Leviticus 19:19.

22:12. *Tassels on Garments.* See comment on Numbers 15:37-41.

Q. SEXUAL LAWS (22:13-30)

The first of these six laws concerns chastity of a wife. The next four legislate against various types of extramarital sexual intercourse: with a married woman by consent, with a betrothed woman by consent, with a betrothed woman by rape, and with a virgin by rape. The sixth law—the only one in categorical form—appears to prohibit any sexual intercourse with one's mother or stepmother, including marriage to a stepmother following the father's death (cf. Leviticus 18:8; 20:11).

The penalties for violation of these laws range from death for both parties, through death for the man alone, to payment to the father of the violated girl (cf. Exodus 22:16-17). On close examination it is clear that the fabric of sexual values and practices in ancient Israel was fundamentally intended as a cloak for the institution of the patriarchal family. Whatever threatens the rights of the male-dominated family must be firmly rejected.

The double standard is clearly expressed in the penalties accompanying the first law. The wife shown to be unchaste stands to lose her life, whereas the most that a falsely accusing husband will suffer is a public whipping, payment of compensation to his father-in-law, and loss of the right of divorce. Such checks would prevent his making charges lightly. The woman has protection, but even this is an extension of the honor of her father—note that the compensation goes to him and not to her. It is evident that any adulterous liaison means death for the wife. But a husband who consorts with a virgin will, if caught, only pay compensation and be required to take her as his wife. This assumes that verses 28-29 include married men, since polygamy was not prohibited in Israel until post-exilic times.

R. EXCLUSIONS FROM THE RELIGIOUS COMMUNITY
(23:1-8)

A series of brief categorical regulations specifies those who are to be excluded from the **assembly of the LORD.** This means that they cannot participate in the gathering of the nation for religious purposes, not that they cannot live in the land of Israel.

23:1-2. *Sexual Bars.* The language of verse 1 evidently intends to exclude a eunuch whether emasculated accidentally or deliberately (cf. Leviticus 21:17).

Rabbinical tradition applied the word translated **bastard** to one born of marriage between persons of a prohibited degree of affinity (cf. Leviticus 18:6-20; 20:10-21). Presumably it here means any child of an illicit union.

23:3-8. *Ethnic Bars.* Anyone descended from an **Ammonite** or a **Moabite** is prohibited from entering the Israelite religious community. However, a descendant **of the third generation** from an **Edomite** or an **Egyptian** may become a member. The reasons offered are historical. Ammon and Moab did not help Israel through the wilderness but instead hired **Balaam to curse** Israel. Edom (i.e. Esau) is Israel's **brother** (cf. Genesis 25:23-26 and 36:8). Israel was a **sojourner** in Egypt, apparently implying that during part of Israel's stay the Egyptians treated the Hebrews well.

However, none of the Pentateuchal accounts agree in picturing Ammon as rebuffing Israel or involved in Moab's hiring of Balaam. The laws themselves seem very old, and it may be that the historical motivations were added later by someone whose memory lapsed or who knew of other traditions about Ammon. It is possible that the contrasting attitudes are simply based on those which predominate in Genesis. There Ammon and Moab are born of incestuous unions between Lot and his daughters (Genesis 19:30-38). Esau (Edom) is held in affection in spite of his uncouthness, and Egypt is the benefactor of Joseph and his family. No period is known in Israel's history when Ammon and Moab were her enemies while Edom and Egypt were cordial or neutral.

S. MILITARY CAMP LAWS (23:9-14)

These laws, designed to keep the Israelite soldier **from every evil thing** while in camp, belong to the rules of holy war (see above on chapter 20). They reflect profound abhorrence of uncovered semen and excrement—an abhorrence projected on the deity. If Yahweh, who **walks in the midst of your camp,** should encounter **anything indecent** (literally "naked") he would **turn away from you.** The underlying view is that Yahweh is himself powerless before such elemental magical realities and that therefore to hold on to its God Israel must be clean. Understood simply as sanitary measures the rules make sense.

T. MORE MISCELLANEOUS LAWS (23:15–25:19)

This is by far the largest block of miscellaneous laws in the book. As in 21:10–22:12 the miscellany extends to form and to subject matter. The inclusion of such D exhortations as 24:8-9 and 25:17-19 argues against the view that this section was drawn as a whole from another source. It is possible of course that one or more smaller collections were incorporated, but we cannot determine the outlines of these.

The varied items occur at the virtual close of the law code. This suggests that they were remaining materials which the D author wanted to include but did not see reason to organize topically or to combine with earlier segments of his work.

23:15-16. *Shelter of Fugitive Slaves.* A runaway slave is to be given asylum. The provision could apply equally to one who flees to Israel from another land or to one who leaves an Israelite master. Verse 16 seems to envision only the first situation.

23:17-18. *Cult Prostitution.* Among Israel's cultic function-aries there is to be no **cult prostitute** (literally "holy one")—that is, one devoted to acting out the fertility of the gods and communicating it to men and nature. Furthermore, money acquired from payment to secular prostitutes may not be offered to fulfill a religious vow.

23:19-20. *Interest.* Charging interest on a loan to a fellow Israelite is forbidden (cf. Exodus 22:25 and Leviticus 25:35-38). On a loan to a **foreigner** it is allowed. This may be simply an instance of in-group-out-group bias, but it may equally reflect the fact that loans to fellow Israelites were mainly to those in desperate straits (cf. 15:7-11). Loans to foreigners, on the other hand, were normally to tradesmen for the expansion of business. If so, behind the seeming ethnic discrimination lies an attempt to differentiate on the basis of need.

23:21-23. *Vows.* Vows to God—especially promises to make contributions to the temple in return for divine favor—are optional. Once made, however, they must be paid (cf. Leviticus 27 and Numbers 30). This "law" is illustrative of the hortatory type common in Deuteronomy, and we may well wonder how it could be enforced. It would seem to depend on individual conscience and community persuasion, especially if the vow was not heard by others or if God's favor was in doubt.

23:24-25. *Eating from a Neighbor's Crops.* A passerby may take enough food from a **vineyard** or field of **grain** to meet his immediate need, but he may not carry anything away (cf. 24:19-22).

24:1-4. *Remarriage After Divorce.* This is as near as the Old Testament comes to containing a divorce law. It is in fact a law presupposing divorce but attempting to control its abuse. A woman who is divorced and remarries may not be retaken by her first husband should the second husband die or divorce her. The apparent intent is to reduce the frequency of divorce by cautioning the husband that he may not reacquire a wife he divorces impetuously.

The **indecency** (literally "nakedness of a thing") mentioned as the cause of divorce is probably not adultery since that offense was punishable by death. It refers rather to immodesty or too open relations with other men.

24:5. *Exemption from Military Service.* The law exempting a betrothed man from military service (20:7) is here extended to include one **newly married**—that is, within **one year.**

24:6. *Pledges on Loans.* A borrower was expected to provide a

pledge, a security for repayment of the loan. The lender is here forbidden to take in pledge an object which the debtor needs in order to live, the family **millstone** used to grind grain into flour (cf. verses 10-13).

24:7. *Forced Enslavement.* Kidnapping a fellow Israelite in order to retain or sell him as a slave is strictly forbidden (cf. Exodus 21:16).

24:8-9. *Leprosy.* This is not a law at all but an exhortation to observe the leprosy laws as interpreted by the Levitical priests. Precisely that sort of guidance, "to show when it is unclean and when it is clean," is contained in Leviticus 13–14. The D author thus shows familiarity with the antecedents of these chapters of Leviticus or with a parallel tradition. On **Miriam** cf. Numbers 12:10-15.

24:10-13. *Pledges on Loans.* Another law on pledges is in the same mood as verses 6 and 17. A creditor may not enter the debtor's **house** to take any pledge he likes. If the debtor is reduced to the point of offering his **cloak** as pledge, it must be returned to him for night use as a blanket (cf. Exodus 22:26-27). In effect this means that no pledge at all is to be taken—or that it is merely to be taken ceremonially for one day or on periodic occasions as a reminder that the debt is still due.

24:14-15. *Payment of Hired Laborers.* Israelites or **sojourners** (resident aliens) who hire out are not to be taken advantage of, but are to be paid at the end of each day (cf. Leviticus 19:13). This seemingly small point probably took on importance because much hiring was for seasonal agricultural work on a day-to-day basis.

24:16. *Individual Criminal Guilt.* This categorical law specifically forbids executing a father for his children's crimes or children for their father's crimes. Joshua 7:16-26 and II Samuel 21:1-9 show that collective guilt (see above on 21:1-9) was sometimes translated into legal guilt and punishment. Even if such cases were exceptional, the very possibility would be a source of uneasiness in the community and an occasion for misuse.

II Kings 14:5-6 notes that King Amaziah of Judah executed

only the assassins of his father Joash and not their children. His leniency seems to have been sufficiently exceptional—at least for political crimes in the eighth century—to draw the special attention of the D historian.

24:17. *Justice for the Weak.* Israel is cautioned not to **pervert the justice due** the weakest elements of society (cf. Exodus 22:21-22; 23:6-9; Leviticus 19:33-34). This is illustrated by the heinous crime of taking a **widow's garment in pledge** (see above on verses 10-13). Such solicitude for the weak is to be based on the remembrance that Israel was itself once a **slave in Egypt.** As God **redeemed** Israel, so must it "redeem" its poor.

24:19-22. *Gleanings for the Poor.* When a **field** of grain, orchard of **olive trees,** or **vineyard** is harvested, enough produce is to be left that the **sojourner, the fatherless, and the widow** may gather the gleanings for food (cf. Leviticus 19:9-10; 23:22; Ruth 2:2-7). The slavery-in-Egypt motif is again the basis for this humanitarianism.

25:1-3. *Regulations for Judicial Beatings.* Beatings for crimes are to be administered only after trial and in view of the **judge.** The number of blows may not exceed **forty.** In later times it was limited to thirty-nine lest there be a miscount (cf. II Corinthians 11:24). The remark that the offender is **to lie down** suggests that the blows may have been applied to the soles of the feet.

25:4. *The Unmuzzled Ox.* This law states that the ox used for threshing must not be prevented from eating of the grain. The concern for domestic animals seems genuine in spite of Paul's argument to the contrary (I Corinthians 9:3-12).

25:5-10. *Levirate Marriage.* When a married man dies without a son, the **husband's brother** (*levir* in Latin—the word "levirate" has nothing to do with "Levite") living on the same estate is expected to marry the widow. The **first son** born of the union is to take the **name** of the deceased man. Any further offspring are presumably credited to the living brother. The surviving brother who **refuses** this obligation is to be publicly rebuked in a ceremony in which the widow will remove his **sandal** and **spit in his face.**

The aim of levirate marriage was not primarily to provide for the widow since other means were available for that purpose. Rather it was to secure the survival of the deceased's line, the only form of immortality known to ancient Israel. Secondly it was to keep in the family estate property which might otherwise be sold to pay debts. This is the only biblical stipulation on the practice, but it is presupposed in the account of Judah and Tamar (Genesis 38). The story of Ruth and Boaz is based on an extension of it to the nearest consenting relative when no brother is available (Ruth 4:1-8). Levirate marriage is also known in India, Madagascar, and Brazil.

25:11-12. *Protection of an Assailant's Genitals.* So important are offspring to a man that his genitals must be protected at all costs. For this reason even a woman protecting her husband against an assailant may not harm the aggressor's genitals. Presumably the application to women is not exclusive. It simply recognizes that, lacking the strength to fight a man by other means, a woman might be more tempted to attack the vulnerable male genitals. It is possible the passage refers to a wrestling match which a zealous wife tries to help her husband win.

25:13-16. *Honest Weights and Measures.* False weights and measures were a tempting form of commercial misconduct (cf. Amos 8:5). Israelites are warned not to have **two kinds . . ., a large and a small**. This might mean either correct ones for purchase and false ones for defrauding customers, or two false sets—a large one for fixing quantities bought and another small one for fixing quantities sold. Cf. Leviticus 19:35-36.

25:17-19. *Extermination of Amalek.* Amalekites from the desert region south of Canaan attacked Israel in the wilderness shortly after the Exodus (Exodus 17:8-16). In the time of the judges they raided Palestine alongside the Midianites (Judges 6:3, 33: 7:12). Saul and David fought several engagements with them (I Samuel 15; 27:8-9; 30; II Samuel 8:12). Though a "remnant of the Amalekites" are said to have been destroyed during Hezekiah's reign (I Chronicles 4:42-43) they seem not to have been a serious threat after David's reign. Therefore this vehement command to **blot out the remembrance of Amalek**

(cf. Exodus 17:14) is best understood as a tradition from premonarchic times that lived on as an expression of the holy war obligation (see above on 20:1-20). By the seventh century it was no more than a liturgical archaism.

U. RITES FOR FIRST FRUITS AND TITHES
(26:1-15)

The law proper in Deuteronomy is brought to a close by descriptions of how to conduct annual first-fruits offerings and triennial tithes. The heart of each ceremony is a declaration to be made by the worshiper. Each declaration has its own special character. The one for the first-fruits offering is a collective statement of Israel's faith. The other is an affirmation of individual compliance with the tithe law of 14:22-29. The "confessions" have been placed in their present position to give an appropriately resounding liturgical conclusion to the compilation.

26:1-11. *First-Fruits Ceremony.* The offering of **some of the first of all the fruit of the ground** may be one form of the tithing obligation cited in 14:22-29. Or it may be an earlier practice that developed into the tithe—that is, an original token "first fruit" which developed into a fixed tenth of the produce. An open question also is whether the ceremony was at one of the fixed public festivals.

Though our information is hazy, the feast of weeks (cf. 16:9-12) seems to have begun a period extending to the feast of booths (cf. 16:13-15) during which first fruits could be offered. The actions and affirmations described here could certainly represent a part of one of the great festivals. This may well be the meaning of **rejoice**—to "celebrate publicly and collectively." On the other hand the presentation of a **basket** of fruit before the **priest** could easily be repeated at Jerusalem as often as landowners appeared there during the summer. The fact that crops ripen at differing times in Palestine, depending on altitude, soil, and rainfall patterns, suggests flexibility in the timing of the first-fruits ceremony.

26:5-11. The liturgical affirmation begins **A wandering Aramean was my father** and is typical of a number of biblical restatements of the people's history (cf. 6:20-25). The worshiper identifies with his ancestor Jacob and the past experience of his people. He concludes on the note of responsibility for maintaining the land by loyalty to his God.

26:12-15. *Tithe Ceremony.* At the triennial tithing observance in each of the **towns,** the tithes are distributed locally to **the Levite, the sojourner, the fatherless and the widow** (see above on 14:28-29). The worshiper is then to give an oath asserting his compliance with the law and explicitly denying ritual defilement of the tithe through contact with anything **unclean.**

That the oath is to be a sign **before the LORD** suggests that it is to be offered at Jerusalem following the tithing season, possibly at the feast of booths. Since the actual transactions of this triennial tithe were carried out away from Jerusalem, this would constitute a formal report at the central sanctuary verifying that the tithe laws had in fact been properly observed.

V. HORTATORY CONCLUSION TO THE LAWS (26:16-19)

The **statutes and ordinances** of chapters 12–26 are rounded out with exhortations placed in the mouth of Moses. D's religious and moral terminology is evident. Israel's holiness is to be demonstrated in observance of the law and in its consequent position **high above all nations.**

VI. RENEWAL OF THE COVENANT AND THE DEATH OF MOSES (27:1–34:12)

As in the introductory exhortations and summaries of chapters 1–11, so in these final chapters the aim is to inculcate loyalty to Israel's God and especially obedience to the laws of chapters 12–26. The distinctive feature of the conclusion, however, is the reference to ratification of the covenant in Moab and to renewal ceremonies to be observed in Canaan after the occupation of the land.

The distinction between the covenant at Horeb and the covenant in Moab is sharply stated in 29:1. The reason for the second covenant is not that the first was annulled through faithlessness, nor that the second is to have a different content or orientation. It seems rather that the second covenant is a reaffirmation and an elaboration of the first. It is necessitated partly by the rebellion of the people and partly by the demands of the new situation they are to face in Canaan.

There is thus a certain recognition of the development of historical and legal traditions, even though the development is compressed dramatically into the lifespan of Moses. Not everything was given to Israel at one time and place. The "covenant" is in fact a series of covenants, a growing and changing relation with God. This is expressed in Deuteronomy by quoting the decalogue of 5:6-21 as the legal instrument of the first covenant in such a way as to show that it remains in effect under the second. The "statutes and ordinances" are added as instruments of the second covenant. It is in essence two phases or stages of one covenant relationship to God.

Of particular interest is the reference to renewal ceremonies to be held in Canaan. One is to be held on Mts. Gerizim and Ebal at which blessings and curses are to be recited (27:11-13) and another at every seventh feast of booths at the central sanctuary (31:10-13). On the relation between the renewal ceremonies and the growth and structure of the book see Introduction.

A. CEREMONY OF COVENANT RENEWAL (27:1–28:68)

All of chapters 5–26 in their present form appear as a long speech of Moses, introduced in 5:1 by "Moses . . . said." In contrast, chapter 27 contains three such third-person introductions (verses 1, 9, 11), each followed by a brief speech. Chapter 28 again presents at some length a speech of Moses in characteristic D hortatory style without such interruptions. These and other literary details have led many scholars to view chapter 27 as a composite of unrelated materials interpolated between chapters 26 and 28.

Such a view, however, gives too little consideration to the evidence that not only chapters 27–28 but the core of the whole book grew out of a periodic cultic celebration. During this celebration a priest in the role of Moses recited the terms of the covenant and called on the people to ratify it anew "this day" (see Introduction). In this light the third-person introductions may be recognized as "stage directions" for the person portraying Moses and for the elders (verse 1) and priests (verse 9) participating in the dramatic rite.

The climax of this ceremony was the intoning of blessings and curses by the tribes facing each other on opposite mountainsides (27:11-13). The text of their blessings and curses is to be found, not in 27:14-26, but in chapter 28, where it is much amplified by D exhortation. Chapter 28 is thus the continuation, not of 26:16-19, as often said, but of 27:1-13.

27:1-8. *The Sanctuary at Shechem.* The first instruction, by **Moses and the elders,** is to write . . . **all the words of this law** on large plaster-coated **stones** to be raised **on Mount Ebal,** near Shechem (see above on 11:29). Examples found in Egypt show that the **plaster** was used to provide a smooth light-colored surface on which letters could be painted **very plainly.** The custom of displaying public decrees, reports, or statutes on walls or on stone or metal steles (free-standing slabs or pillars) is a familiar one in the ancient world. Hammurabi's code, for example, was inscribed on a large diorite stele. The intent was to insure compliance with the laws by publicizing a standard text for recitation and instruction.

The command for an **altar . . . of unhewn stones** (cf. Exodus 20:25) to be built **there** could be explained as a temporary provision pending Yahweh's choice of Jerusalem as the exclusive center of worship. Rather, it seems to give evidence that the original central sanctuary of Deuteronomy was at Shechem.

27:9-10. *A Renewed Covenant.* The **Levitical priests** joined Moses in addressing to the people the solemn pronouncement **This day you have become the people of the LORD your God.** Since the D author does not picture the covenant in Moab as a new one, we should understand these words as typical of the renewal ceremonies. As the people relived the original covenant events, recited the laws, and promised their fidelity, the presiding religious officials would announce Yahweh's acceptance of them as happening at that moment. Each new generation and each new year or cycle of years witnesses to the people's continual "becoming" the people of God.

27:11-13. *A Ceremony of Blessing and Cursing.* When Israel reaches Shechem six of the tribes are to declaim blessings on the people from Mt. Gerizim and six are to declaim curses from Mt. Ebal (11:29). All the most important tribes are among those who **bless,** but there is no reason to believe that the tribes who must **curse** are thereby demeaned or contaminated. Manasseh and Ephraim are here treated as a single tribe, **Joseph** (their father), as in 33:13-17 (cf. Genesis 49:22-26). These verses lead on directly to chapter 28, where the blessings and curses are recorded.

27:14-26. *A List of Curses.* This has the look of an old preexilic list which has been awkwardly inserted in a context in which it does not belong. Apparently there were two reasons for this:

(1) Association of **Cursed** as the initial word of each stipulation with "curse" in verse 13.

(2) Association of **the Levites** with "Levi" in verse 12.

In actual fact the two passages clash. In verses 11-13 Levi, along with five other tribes, pronounces blessings and the remaining tribes reply with curses. Here Levi alone addresses all the other tribes with curses, to each of which they are to respond **Amen.**

The twelve curses condemn various religious, social, and criminal offenses. All are specific except the last, which curses **whoever does not confirm the words of this law by doing them.**

This suggests possibly that an original series of ten curses followed by a summarizing reinforcement was built up to twelve by adding a curse, perhaps verse 15. Or it may be that the series of twelve was formed from various older materials with chapters 12–26 in mind.

28:1-68. *The Blessings and Curses.* This chapter presents in expanded form the content of the blessings and curses which 27:11-13 instructs the tribes to intone from the two mountains overlooking Shechem.

The core blessings (verses 3-6) and curses (verses 16-19) are in parallel form, being directed specifically to human, agricultural, and pastoral fertility. The D author has amplified these by spelling out in two lists the consequences of obedience (verses 7-14) and disobedience (verses 20-46). The amplifications are replete with illustrations of types of good and evil and with vivid exhortations to obedience.

28:47-68. These verses are very likely a later addition to the original unit. They extend the curses into lurid descriptions of military and natural disaster, including threats of cannibalism during siege. **The LORD will bring a nation against you from afar** may refer to either Assyria or Babylonia, but taken altogether this section appears to come from the Babylonian exile. It is so detailed and repetitive that it has the marks of after-the-event condemnation—a kind of "I told you so" cast.

B. A COVENANT IN MOAB (29:1–30:20)

These two chapters form a unit which has marks of being one of the latest in the book. It certainly comes from sometime during or after the Exile (see below on 30:1-10). The expression **the curses of the covenant written in this book of the law** shows that the author knew Deuteronomy as a compiled work and that he composed his work as an admonition to be added to it.

The unit has as its focus the ceremony of ratification of the law in Moab. It evidently reflects the liturgy of periodic ceremonies of renewal of the covenant (see Introduction and above on 27:1–28:68).

29:1. In the Hebrew Bible this verse is numbered as the last of chapter 28. Some scholars believe it was written to be the final sentence of the book as compiled at that time. More probably, however, it is an introduction to chapters 29–30.

These are the words of the covenant may refer to the contents of this unit. More likely it is meant to join the unit to the rest of the book by summarizing what has preceded. It refers not only to the laws of chapters 12–26 but also to the blessings and curses of chapters 27–28—and probably also to portions if not all of chapters 1–11.

29:2-15. The recital of Yahweh's past favors to Israel in verses 2-9 presents at every point ideas and often phraseology found earlier in the book. On the other hand the climactic call in verses 10-15 to **enter into the sworn covenant . . . this day** does not show any direct awareness of the covenant transaction account of 27:9-10 and is presumably a parallel account. The separate units are best seen as compilations of texts drawn from, or imitative of, renewal ceremonies which have been edited only in part. No attempt has been made to create complete consistency at the expense of liturgical diversity.

29:16-27. With this warning against apostasy cf. chapter 13. **Admah and Zeboiim** were cities near **Sodom and Gomorrah** and were destroyed in the same catastrophe (cf. Genesis 10:19 and 19:24-25).

29:29. This unusual view of the law contrasts it with **secret things** God has reserved from mankind, implying that the **revealed** law is sufficient for all human need (see below on 30:11-14).

30:1-10. The late date of this unit is supported by the concern of these verses for the fate of those who have disobeyed and gone into exile. The refugees are pictured as coming to their senses, returning to God, being restored to Palestine, and being purified by God so that they will henceforth **love** and **obey** him. The curses under which Israel suffered will be transferred to her foes. This highly moralistic assessment contrasts with the presumably contemporary idea that God would restore Israel in spite of her disobedience, for his own name's sake—an idea articulated by Ezekiel and Second Isaiah.

30:11-14. A second unusual claim about the law (cf. 29:29) characterizes it as being **exceedingly close, in your mouth and in your heart** instead of enigmatic or remote. God has not left his will in doubt. It is not necessary to employ soothsayers or magicians to penetrate the future or to unlock mysteries. Everything that matters hinges on this easily accessible law, which the people carry in their very persons, and which the Levitical priests can always interpret if there is question.

C. MOSES' FINAL PREPARATIONS (31:1–32:47)

This literarily complex block of material comprises a single unit. The introduction to the closing speech, **when Moses had finished speaking all these words to all Israel** (32:45), refers back to 31:1. The section is split up by headings into subunits that some have regarded as independent additions to the book. Binding them together, however, is a concern for continuation of the work of Moses through his final acts—passing the leadership to his successor and ordering preservation of "this law," and his "song" (32:1-43) for future "witness" against the people.

Allusions to a communal liturgical setting are scattered throughout the unit:

(1) Moses gives the written law to the Levitical priests, who keep it beside the ark (31:9, 26);

(2) his successor is addressed in view of the whole assembly (31:7);

(3) Moses and Joshua present themselves in the sacred tent (31:14-15);

(4) the elders and officers of Israel are assembled to affirm their oath of allegiance to God (31:28-29).

In a kind of "play within a play," similar to the blessing-curse rite of chapter 27, the priests are advised to read the law before the people every seventh year at the feast of booths (31:10). It is not difficult to imagine that circumstantial details of the imagined congregation in Moab are actually supplied from ceremonies of covenant renewal known to the author(s). We may go so far as to say that this unit is intended to describe the origin of contemporary practice at the feast of booths—that is, to assure readers that present liturgical practice has a validly ancient foundation.

31:7-8. Cf. 1:38; 3:28. See below on verses 14-15.

31:9-13. *Sabbatical Feast of Booths.* The custom of joining a special celebration to an annual festival is familiar from the tithing procedures at the feast of weeks for two out of every three years (14:22-29). In this passage the celebration involving reading of this law at the feast of booths is only every seventh year and is to coincide with the year of release (15:1-11). Such gatherings for the purpose of Levitical reading and interpretation of the laws would stimulate the growth and elaboration of the D traditions.

31:14-15. *Commissioning of Joshua.* These verses are apparently continued in verse 23. Their position after Joshua's selection and presentation before the people as Moses' successor has been cited against the unity of 31:1–32:47. The commissioning may be understood, however, as a ritual of transferring Moses' power to his chosen successor, which occurs only when Moses is about to die. The passage has been attributed to the E source (cf. Exodus 33:7-11; also the P account in Numbers 27:15-23).

31:16-22. *Introduction to Moses' Song.* This subunit appears to interrupt the continuity of verses 15 and 23. It might more logically follow verses 24-29 and immediately precede the text of Moses' song (32:1-43; note that verse 30 largely duplicates verse 22). It provides further glimpses into the D literary circles. Moses' writing of the song and its recitation in successive generations means that it is to **confront them as a witness (for it will be unforgotten in the mouths of their descendants).** Far from being a piece of archaic poetry, it is a means of constantly reconfronting Israel with its obligation to God.

Obviously the covenant renewal ceremonies included not only reading of the law but singing of liturgical compositions that recalled the past and summoned to present commitment. The double action of Moses in writing the song and then reciting it to the people is similar to the writing of the law and the priests' reading of it in Israel's hearing. A standard text and a public reading bring the intimate relation between written and oral traditions into focus. Deuteronomy may be understood as an attempt to bring various textual versions together with a minimal loss of any of them.

31:23. See above on verses 14-15.

31:24-29. *The Law as a Witness.* See above on verses 16-22. The phrase **to the very end**, perhaps meaning "in their totality," may well be an allusion to the various forms in which the law circulated orally and literarily until finally compiled in this book.

31:30. See above on verses 16-22.

32:1-43. *The Song of Moses.* This poem is not at all exclusively or even dominantly D in phraseology and outlook. It was apparently adopted in D circles because it was recited at renewal ceremonies in conjunction with D laws. There is nothing to identify Moses as the speaker. The situation reflected in the poem is probably late preexilic, around 800-600 B.C. The conception behind use of the song and its attribution to Moses is that of Moses as liturgical leader. This lends support to the view that the chief Levitical priest functioned in the renewal ceremonies as Moses-substitute or covenant mediator who spoke on behalf of God to the people and vice versa.

The song shows a broad affinity with D thought on such points as the election of Israel, idolatrous abuse of God's gift of land, and adversity as the judgment of God. There are, however, notable differences. Negatively it lacks any reference to the law. Positively it asserts that God will vindicate Israel, not because of their repentance, but because of the urge to manifest God's strength and glory before the nations—a view shared with Ezekiel and Second Isaiah. Perhaps we are to account for the song's prominent place in the book on the basis that in D circles during the Exile the prophetic view of God's "amoral" initiative in restoring Israel for his own glory made considerable headway against the older and more moralistic view that restoration would only follow repentance.

On verse 8 see Introduction. **Jeshurun**, meaning literally "upright," is a term for Israel possibly based on similarity in the written appearance of the two words.

D. MOSES' BLESSING AND DEATH (32:48–34:12)

32:48-52. *The Order to Ascend Mt. Nebo.* These verses and their continuation in chapter 34 comprise a narrative unit. It is generally seen as containing elements of all four Pentateuchal sources. Editors displaced it from its logical place at the end of Numbers so that Moses' death might come after his farewell speech as presented in Deuteronomy.

Moses is instructed to go up to a mountaintop and **view the land of Canaan** (on **Abarim** and **Mount Nebo** see above on 3:23-29). There he is to **die** as **Aaron** did on **Mount Hor** (contrast 10:6; cf. Numbers 20:22-29 and 33:37-39). The reason given is that both of them **broke faith** in the incident of the striking of the rock at **Meribath-kadesh** (cf. Numbers 20:11-12 and 27:12-14). This reason for Moses' exclusion from Canaan follows the P tradition and is in tension with the explanation of it in 1:37; 3:26; and 4:21 (see above on 1:19-46).

33:1-29. *The Blessing of Moses.* This poem has as little of the peculiarly D style and vocabulary as the "song" of 32:1-43, but in subject it refers more explicitly to the age of Moses. It even refers explicitly to the law in the blessing on the Levites. It is evident that Moses was not its author. The Conquest is plainly in the past, and there is also a third-person reference to Moses in verse 4.

The inclusion of the blessing here may be explained as follows: One feature of the covenant renewal ceremony was a recitation of blessings on the tribes. The practice continued into monarchic times even when the tribes had lost political and social significance. The connection between the blessings pronounced on the individual tribes and the affirmation of the covenant and law is sharply stressed in the preamble (verses 1-5) and in the epilogue (verses 26-29). Both preamble and epilogue were probably already added in the liturgical celebrations. This association of the tribal blessings with Moses made it easy for a D editor to insert it as the deathbed blessing of Moses in a manner similar to the blessing of Jacob in Genesis 49.

The setting of the blessing is most likely the late period of the judges or the early monarchy. There are no identifiable historical allusions and, being liturgical poetry, it does not lend itself to confident dating.

33:2-5. The absolute distinction of Yahweh as God and Israel as **his people** is stressed in this poetic introduction to the individual blessings and in the conclusion (verses 26-29). Israel alone has such a deity and such a relation to God through the **law** that God is the **king** and the land is held in prosperity and security.

Seir was the mountain range covering most of Edom, and **Mount Paran** was evidently the highland south of Kadesh-barnea. On **Jeshurun** see above on 32:1-43.

33:6-25. Simeon is omitted from the tribal blessings, presumably because it no longer existed as a tribe. **Reuben** has become **few** and about to **die** as an independent group. **Judah** is on the defensive—perhaps the Philistines are **his adversaries**—whereas **Joseph** (i.e. **Ephraim** and **Manasseh**, verses 13-17) prospers.

Levi is already a priestly tribe discharging the double function of teacher and priest in agreement with the D description of the office (see above on 17:8-13, 18; 18:1-8). If we could be certain that verses 8-10 are as old as the eleventh or tenth century, we would be in possession of important data on the early history of the Levites. However, some interpreters suspect that the original blessing of Levi was verse 11 alone, the preceding verses having been added later.

Thummim and **Urim** were sacred lots used to ascertain Yahweh's will. The allusion to **Massah** and **Meribah** is obscure, since Levi is not mentioned in the other references to these places (6:16; 9:22; 32:51; Exodus 17:1-7; Numbers 20:2-13). **In the bush** probably alludes to the burning bush but may be a textual error for "on Sinai" (see comment on Exodus 3:2). Verse 21c-e seems to be out of place; possibly it belongs in verse 4.

33:26-29. See above on verses 2-5.

34:1-12. *The Death of Moses.* This chapter is a continuation of the narrative unit begun in 32:48-52. The extent of Canaan which **the LORD showed** Moses is of course far wider than the human eye could see from a peak in Moab (on **Mount Nebo** and **Pisgah** see above on 3:23-29). Moses looks first north across **Gilead** (Transjordan) over one hundred miles to **Dan**—as the city will be known after the tribe captures it (Judges 18:29). From Dan his gaze moves southwest to the area to be occupied by **Naphtali** west of the Sea of Galilee and by **Ephraim and Manasseh** in central Palestine. Due west he sees over the highland of northern **Judah to the Western Sea** (the Mediterranean). To the southwest he views the **Negeb** (the dry region south of Beer-sheba) and the **Plain** (the Jordan-Dead Sea rift) **as far as Zoar** near the former site of Sodom (cf. Genesis 19:22-23).

After this view of the land and renewal of the promise Moses dies. **He buried him** means almost certainly that Yahweh buried Moses. This accounts for the otherwise strange fact that **no man knows the place of his burial to this day.**

34:9-12. A concluding passage pictures Joshua's authority as deriving from Moses but maintains the preeminence of Moses over any subsequent **prophet.** On the surface verse 10 looks like a contradiction to 18:15, where "a prophet like me" is promised. The meanings of the two "like's" are quite different, however. In 18:15 the similarity is in office or function, whereas here it is in directness of revelation—that is, no prophet has known God so directly as Moses knew him.

Signs and wonders performed by Moses are cited as evidence that he is an unparalleled spokesman for God. Obviously Moses' revelation is given primacy over the accounts of prophetic calls and performance of marvels by some of the Israelite prophets. Prophecy is assimilated to Mosaic Yahwism. As a counter to

Canaanite prophetism the force of the motif is clear. But how it stands in relation to the special revelatory claims of Yahwistic prophets such as Isaiah, Jeremiah, and Ezekiel is not clear. Indeed one of the unresolved issues in the history of Israel's religion is the precise relation between the great prophets and the D movement.

FOR FURTHER STUDY

GENESIS

John Skinner, *A Critical and Exegetical Commentary on Genesis,* 1910; the basic work in English. H. E. Ryle, *The Book of Genesis,* 1914. S. H. Hooke, *In the Beginning,* 1947. C. A. Simpson in *Interpreter's Bible,* 1952. Alan Richardson, *Genesis I-XI,* 1953. S. Moscati, *The Face of the Ancient Orient,* 1959. Gerhard von Rad, *Genesis: A Commentary,* 1961. Otto Eissfeldt in *Interpreter's Dictionary of the Bible,* 1962. A. S. Herbert, *Genesis 12-50,* 1962. J. M. Holt, *The Patriarchs of Israel,* 1964. C. W. Westermann and R. Albertz in *Interpreter's Dictionary of the Bible, Supplementary Volume,* 1976.

EXODUS

S. R. Driver, *Exodus,* 1911. A. H. McNeile, *Exodus,* 1917. J. C. Rylaarsdam in *Interpreter's Bible,* 1952. Roland de Vaux, *Ancient Israel: Its Life and Institutions,* Eng. trans. 1961. Benno Rothenberg, *God's Wilderness,* 1961. Martin Noth, *Exodus,* Eng. trans., 1962. G. E. Wright in *Interpreter's Dictionary of the Bible,* 1962. R. E. Clements in *Interpreter's Dictionary of the Bible, Supplementary Volume,* 1976.

LEVITICUS

Nathaniel Micklem in *Interpreter's Bible,* 1953. J. B. Pritchard, ed., *Ancient Near Eastern Texts,* 1955; contains translations of cultic and legal texts from Israel's neighbors. Yehezkel Kaufmann, *The Religion of Israel,* abridged and trans. by Moshe Greenberg, 1960; a thorough study which argues that, contrary to the usual view, P preceded D. Roland de Vaux, *Ancient Israel: Its Life and Institutions,* 1961; Gwynne Henton Davis in *Interpreter's Dictionary of the Bible,* 1962. J. Milgrom in *Interpreter's Dictionary of the Bible, Supplementary Volume,* 1976. *The Torah,* 1962; vol. I of the new Jewish Publication Society Version (JPSV), which because of recent scholarship contains the most accurate translation of Leviticus thus far achieved. Martin Noth, *The Old Testament Library,* 1965.

NUMBERS

G. B. Gray, *Numbers*, 1903; though old, the most complete commentary in English. John Marsh in *Interpreter's Bible*, 1952. Roland de Vaux, *Ancient Israel*, 1961; a study of Israel's institutions which figure so much in Numbers. R. C. Dentan in *Interpreter's Dictionary of the Bible*, 1962. Murray Newman, *The People of the Covenant*, 1962; a suggestive study of the period. B. A. Levine in *Interpreter's Dictionary of the Bible, Supplementary Volume*, 1976.

DEUTERONOMY

G. A. Smith, *The Book of Deuteronomy*, 1918. A. C. Welch, *The Code of Deuteronomy*, 1924. R. H. Pfeiffer, *Introduction to the Old Testament*, 1941. G. E. Wright in *Interpreter's Bible*, 1955. N. K. Gottwald, *A Light to the Nations*, 1959. Gerhard von Rad in *Interpreter's Dictionary of the Bible*, 1962; *Deuteronomy: A Commentary*, 1966. N. Lohfink in *Interpreter's Dictionary of the Bible, Supplementary Volume*, 1976.

ABBREVIATIONS AND EXPLANATIONS

ABBREVIATIONS

D — Deuteronomic; Deuteronomist source

E — Elohist source
Ecclus. — Ecclesiasticus
ed. — edited by, edition, editor
e.g. — *exempli gratia* (for example)
ERV — English Revised Version
esp. — especially

H — Holiness Code

J — Yahwist source
JPSV — Jewish Publication Society Version

L — Lukan source
LXX — Septuagint, the earliest Greek translation of the Old Testament and Apocrypha (250 B.C. and after)

M — Matthean source
Macc. — Maccabees
MS — manuscript

N — north, northern
NEB — New English Bible

P — Priestly source
p. — page
Pet. — Peter
Phil. — Philippian, Philippians
Philem. — Philemon
Prov. — Proverbs
Pss. Sol. — Psalms of Solomon
pt. — part (of a literary work)

Q — "Sayings" source

rev. — revised
RSV — Revised Standard Version

S — south, southern

trans. — translated by, translation, translator

viz. — *videlicet* (namely)
Vulg. — Vulgate, the accepted Latin version, mostly translated A.D. 383-405 by Jerome

W — west, western
Wisd. Sol. — Wisdom of Solomon

QUOTATIONS AND REFERENCES

In the direct commentary words and phrases quoted from the RSV of the passage under discussion are printed in boldface type, without quotation marks, to facilitate linking the comments to the exact points of the biblical text. If a quotation from the passage under discussion is not in boldface type, it is to be recognized as an alternate translation, either that of another version if so designated (see abbreviations of versions above) or the commentator's own rendering. On the other hand, quotations from other parts of the Bible in direct commentary, as well as all biblical quotations in the introductions, are to be understood as from the RSV unless otherwise identified.

A passage of the biblical text is identified by book, chapter number, and verse number or numbers, the chapter and verse numbers being separated by a colon (cf. Genesis 1:1). Clauses within a verse may be designated by the letters *a, b, c,* etc. following the verse number (e.g. Genesis 1:2*b*). In poetical text each line as printed in the RSV—not counting runovers necessitated by narrow columns—is accorded a letter. If the book is not named, the book under discussion is to be understood; similarly the chapter number appearing in the boldface reference at the beginning of the paragraph, or in a preceding centered head, is to be understood if no chapter is specified.

A suggestion to note another part of the biblical text is usually introduced by the abbreviation "cf." and specifies the exact verses. To be distinguished from this is a suggestion to consult a comment in this volume, which is introduced by "see above on," "see below on," or "see comment on," and which identifies the boldface reference at the head of the paragraph where the comment is to be found or, in the absence of a boldface reference, the reference in a preceding centered head. The suggestion "see Introduction" refers to the introduction of the book under discussion unless another book is named.

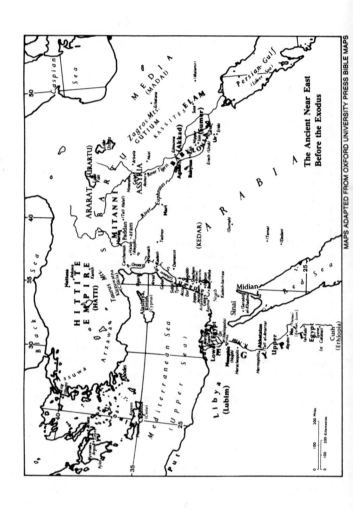

The Ancient Near East
Before the Exodus

MAPS ADAPTED FROM OXFORD UNIVERSITY PRESS BIBLE MAPS

The Land of Canaan
Abraham to Moses

GAD, etc.   Tribes of Israel
EDOM, etc   Kingdoms encountered
            by the Israelites in the
            13th century, B.C.

⊞   Cities mentioned in
           Numbers and Deuteronomy,
           but not in Genesis.

0   10   20 Miles
0   10   20 Kilometres

Grid lines mark 50 kilometre squares

100   150

— 300

— 250

T H E
G R E A T
S E A

(The Western Sea)

— 200

— 150

— 100

• Sidon

Tyre •
• Kanah

L
E
B
A
N
O
N

Mt. Lebanon

Mt Hermon
(Syrion Senir)

A R A M
(S Y R I A)

• Damascus

Achzib •

Beth-anath •
Acco •

• Achshaph

Dor •

Megiddo •

Abel • • Laish
          • Dan

Kedesh •

MAACAH

Hazor ■

Chinnereth •

Madon •

Sea
of
Chinnereth

GESHUR

BASHAN

Golan •

ARGOB

• Karnaim
• Ashtaroth

Plain of Sharon

Joppa •

• Ono
■ Beth-dagon

Japhia •

Anaharath •

• Taanach
Beth-shean •
Rehob • ■Tibleam
• Dothan

Arubboth ■

• Tirzah

Mt. Ebal
● Shechem
Mt Gerizim

Succoth ■

HAVVOTH-JAIR

• Ham

• Edrei

M
A
N
A
S
S
E
H

• Ramoth – gilead

G
I
L
E
A
D

Penuel •
Jabbok
R

Mahanaim •

H
i
l
l

C
o
u
n
t
r
y

o
f

I
s
r
a
e
l

The Jordan R

Jazer •

Beth-horon •
Gezer ■   • Ayalon
Ekron ■   Bethel •   • Ai
          (Luz)
      Gibeon ■
Beth-shemesh •
Timnah •   ● Jerusalem
              (Salem?)
Socoh •   • Bethlehem
          (Ephrath)

Rabbah ■

R
E
U
B
E
N

AMMON

PLAINS
Jericho • G   OF
    ■ Abel-shittim
        (Shittim)
    MOAB

Ashdod •

• Adullam

Ashkelon •

Gath ■

Eglon •

■ Lachish

Mt Nebo
Mt Peor ■ Heshbon ■
      ■ Medeba

■ Naboth
      R Nahaliel

A
M
O
R
I
T
E
S

• Gaza
• Beth-eglaim
  (Eglaim)

● Hebron
(Kiriath-arbai)

Mamre ●

Salt
Sea

Sea
of
the
Arabah

Ataroth ■
      ■ Kiriathaim

■ Dibon
R. Arnon ■ Aroer

City of Moab ■

Gerar •

Beer-Sheba •
Hormah ■

• Aroer

M O A B

Rehoboth •

T h e   N e g e b   Hazazon-tamar •

Zoar •

Brook Zered

E D O M

Possible location of Valley of Siddim, and
the cities of Sodom, Gomorrah, Admah,
Zeboiim, now covered by shallow waters.

MAPS ADAPTED FROM OXFORD UNIVERSITY PRESS BIBLE MAPS

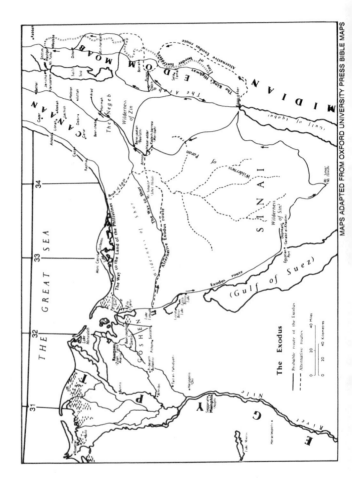

The Exodus

—— Probable route of the Exodus
- - - Alternative routes

0   20   40 Miles
0   20   40 Kilometers